EMERGING SOCIAL SCIENCE CONCERNS

About the Editor

Professor Surendra K. Gupta is Senior ICSSR Fellow working on a comparative study of Indian Diaspora. Earlier, he taught at the University of Sagar, Miles College, Birmingham (USA), and Punjabi University, Patiala. For a brief period, he was UNESCO Consultant at Bangkok. He is author of *Citizen in the Making, India in the Year AD 2000* (with Iqbal Narain), *Conflict and Communication: Mass Upsurge in Assam* (with Indira B. Gupta), and *Indians in Thailand.*

EMERGING SOCIAL SCIENCE CONCERNS

Festschrift in Honour of Professor Yogesh Atal

Editor
Surendra K. Gupta

CONCEPT PUBLISHING COMPANY, NEW DELHI-110059

ISBN 81-8069-098-9

First Published 2004

Published and Printed by
Ashok Kumar Mittal
Concept Publishing Company
A/15-16, Commercial Block, Mohan Garden
New Delhi-110059 (INDIA)

Phones : 25351460, 25351794
Fax : 091-11-25357103
Email : publishing@conceptpub.com

Preface

The Festschrift to honour Professor Yogesh Atal was conceived during an informal chit-chat with some friends and colleagues in Punjabi University, Patiala. Being his oldest student I was asked to take the initiative and approach the colleagues in the profession to contribute to the volume. I was overwhelmed by the response. T.K. Oommen was amongst the first who responded positively. While sending his article he wrote: "I am happy that you have taken the initiative to edit a book to felicitate Professor Yogesh Atal who richly deserves this honour".

There were several others who congratulated me for this initiative. For example, late Narendra K. Singhi, who sent his paper a few days before his sudden and untimely demise, had this to say: "I congratulate you for having taken this thoughtful initiative. I have known Professor Atal for more than four decades and have always admired him for his intellectual and human qualities". Similarly K.N. Sharma said "I am happy to note that you have decided to honour Professor Yogesh Atal through a festschrift, I would definitely like to join you in felicitating him. He deserves felicitation". Giri Raj Gupta thought that it was "a wonderful idea to celebrate the contributions of Professor Atal". Suguna Pathy wrote an article despite suffering from severe liver ailment. S.N. Jha, who was Atal's colleague in IIT Delhi, expressed his opinion in following words: "I am delighted to learn about your initiative for bringing out a felicitation volume in honour of Professor Atal. It will give me immense pleasure to write a piece for the proposed volume."

I was also besieged by the favourable response by Atal's former colleagues and friends in UNESCO as well as from other countries. Ali Kazancigil, Principal Director in the Sector of Social and Human Sciences in UNESCO, now Secretary General, International Social Science Council welcomed the initiative and said that "I'd like to commend you and your colleagues for the preparation of a small festschrift to honour Yogesh Atal and his great contribution to the social sciences in Asia-Pacific. Yogesh is a dear friend and I am grateful for your including me in the volume". He described Atal "as an outstanding Social Scientist and International Civil Servant". J.J. Smolicz, another friend of Atal and a professor at the University of Adelaide gave following comment on his contribution to AASSREC and I quote: "I am very much aware that since its foundation in Teheran in 1973, AASSREC owes a great debt of gratitude to Yogesh, — a tower of strength and persistence with a great talent for discourse, intellectual synthesis and decoding the essence of argument from a multitude of pronouncements in any debate."

The significant feature of this festschrift is that it includes articles from scholars of four generations and a few from international arena. Another feature of this book is that it is interdisciplinary as it includes articles from sociologists, anthropologists, economists, political scientists, educationists and experts in communication. Brij Raj Chauhan, Leela Dube and K.N Sharma represent the first generation. Those who belong to Atal's generations are N.K. Singhi, T.K. Oommen, Rajeshwar Prasad, Partha Nath Mukerji, Binod Agrawal, Giri Raj Gupta, A.K. Das Gupta, S.N. Jha, Hari Mohan Mathur, Owen M. Lynch and Jainendra Doshi. Being a student of Atal I will place myself in the third generation alongwith Vinod Mehta, J.K. Pundir, N. Jayaram and Ranvinder S. Sandhu. In the fourth generation I will include my students Suguna Pathy, D. Venkateshwarlu, Sukhdev Singh and Ruchira Mishra.

I am grateful to all the contributors for their prompt response and full cooperation and encouragement. I owe a great debt to all of them. There are many friends and well wishers who continuously enquired about the progress and prodded me to complete the volume at the earliest. Prominent among them are my wife Indira B. Gupta, Dr. Muktesh Sharma, and V. Murlidhar. In fact, V. Murlidhar also helped me during the last stages by giving the finishing touches to the manuscript and preparing a hardcopy. I am thankful to Shri Ashok Mittal of Concept Publishing Company who has been gracious enough to instantly agree to undertake the publication of this volume. This is an indication of his high regards for Professor Atal. I owe a special debt to our daughter Nayantara who not only contained her demands but also allowed me many stolen hours to complete this volume.

—**Surendra K. Gupta**

Contents

Part II: EMERGING SOCIAL SCIENCE CONCERNS: THE GLOBAL CONTEXT

Part III: EXPLORING INDIA

Profile of Contributors

Binod C. Agrawal is Director, Transnational Alternate Learning for Emancipation and Empowerment thorough Multimedia (TALEEM), Ahmedabad. Earlier he worked at Iowa State University in USA, Indian Agricultural Research Institute, New Delhi, and Indian Space Research Organization, Ahmedabad.

Mailing Address : Taleem, City Plaza, Sterling City, Bopal, Ahmedabad 380 058

Email : taleemadl@sancharnet.in

Sanket Atal, a product of Cornell and Wisconsin Universities is currently Senior Manager of a research team at Oracle Corporation with base in Portland Oregon, USA.

Mailing Address : 14010 NW Eagle Ridge Lane, Portland, Oregon 97229, USA

Email : sanket_atal@yahoo.com

Abha Chauhan is Reader in Sociology, University of Jammu. Earlier she taught at Indian Institute of Technology, New Delhi and Colleges of Delhi University. She was also associated with Centre for Women's Development Studies, New Delhi. Her area of interest includes tribal women and social change.

Mailing Address : Department of Sociology, University of Jammu, Jammu.

Brij Raj Chauhan is the Past President of Indian Sociological society. He taught at M.B College, Udaipur; Institute of Social Science, Agra, Sagar University and Meerut University. His Publications include *The Rajasthan Village* and *Towns in Tribal Setting*.

Mailing Address : 2 Darshan Pura, Udaipur, 313001 (Rajasthan).

A.K Das Gupta a distinguish economist, is Member Secretary of the Indian Association of Social Science Institutions (IASSI). Previously he headed a research unit at the Institute of Applied Manpower Research, New Delhi.

Mailing Address : IASSI Office, IIPA Hostel Building, Indraprastha Estate, New Delhi.

Email Address : stiassi@bol.net.in

Jainendra K. Doshi is currently associated with TALEEM, Ahmedabad. Earlier he taught at the Indian Institute of Mass Communication, New Delhi and G.B. Pant Agricultural University, Pant Nagar (UP).

Mailing Address : TALEEM, City Plaza, Sterling city, Bopal, Ahmedabad, 380 058.

Email : taleem@adl.vsnl.net.in

Leela Dube was a Senior Fellow of Nehru Memorial Museum and Library; and National Fellow of the Indian Council of Social Science Research. She was associated with commission on women of the International union of Anthropological and Ethnological Sciences. She was also professor Atal's teacher at Sagar University.

Mailing Address : D-504, Purvasha, Anandlok Group Housing Society, Mayur Vihar Phase-1, New Delhi-110091.

Giri Raj Gupta is Professor of Sociology since 1969 at Western Illinois University, Macomb Illinois, USA. Before leaving for USA he taught at Udaipur. He is, among others author of *Main Currents in Indian Sociology*, and a text book on sociology of mental Health.

Mailing Address : Department of Sociology and Anthropology, Western Illinois University, Macomb, Illinois, USA.

Email : grgupta@macomb.com

Surendra K. Gupta is a Senior Fellow of ICSSR, affiliated to Nehru Memorial Museum and Library. He taught at the Punjabi University, Patiala, University of Sagar and at Miles College, Birmingham, Alabama, USA.

Mailing Address : 190 D, Pocekt-C, Siddhartha Extension, New Delhi-110014.

Email : sukuguin@yahoo.co.in

N. Jayaram has recently joined as Professor Research Methodology, Tata Institute of Social Sciences, Mumbai. Before that he worked as Professor and Head, Department of Sociology, Goa University. He was a visiting fellow at the Department of Sociology, University of Surrey, England and visiting professor of Indian studies at the University of West Indies, St. Augustine, Trinidad.

Mailing Address : Department of Research Methodology, Tata Institute of Social Sciences, Post Box No. 8313, Deonar, Mumbai 400 088.

Email : njayaram2@rediffmail.com

S.N. Jha retired as Professor of Political Science, Jawahalal Nehru University, New Delhi. Earlier he taught at the Indian Institute of Technology, New Delhi. He has published extensively in many professional Journals.

Mailing Address : 145 HIG Duplex, Nitikhand III, Indirapuram, Ghaziabad 201 010.

Email : nageshJha@hotmail.com

Mandeep Kaur is a post graduate Scholar Department of Economics and Sociology, Punjab Agricultural University, Ludhiana.

Ali Kazancigil is a Political Scientist, working as Secretary-General, International Social Science Council and Executive Secretary, MOST Programme, UNESCO. He also worked as Editor of *International Social Science Journal*. He has been closely associated with Dr. Atal for the last two decades.

Mailing Address : UNESCO, 1 Rue Miollis, Paris, France.

Email : a-kazancigil@unesco.org

Satish Kedia, Assistant Professor, Department of Anthropology, University of Memphis. Earlier he taught at the University of Western Illinois, Macomb.

Mailing Address : 316 Manning Hall, Memphis, USA.

Owen M. Lynch is Charles F. Noyes Professor of Anthropology at New York University. For the last forty years he has done extensive field research in India, particularly in the city of Agra and Mathura. He is the author of *The Politics of Untouchability* and editor of *Culture and Community in Europe* and *Divine Passions.*

Mailing Address : 54, Morning Side, Dr. Apt #3, New York City, NY10025, USA.

Email : owen.lynch@nyu.edu

Hari Mohan Mathur is a retired IAS. Currently he is consultant to the World Bank working for the Economic Development and resettlement and rehabilitation programme in India. He has written extensively on development issues. He has also worked as Director, HCM Institute of Public Administration, Jaipur.

Mailing Address : C-95 Jagan Path, Sardar Patel Marg, Jaipur-302001.

Email : hmmathur@datainfosys.net
hmmsm2000@yahoo.com

Vinod Mehta is Director in the Indian Council of Social Science Research and currently heading the Research Project division. For long he looked after the AASSREC secretariat and in that capacity worked closely with professor Atal. He has specialized in Russian Studies. He has eight books and a number of research papers on Soviet Union/Russia to his credit.

Mailing Address : Director, Indian Council of Social Science Research, Aruna Asaf Ali Road, New Delhi.

Email : mehtavinod@hotmail.com

Virginia A Miralao, Executive Director, Philippine Social Science Council and Secretary General, Association of Asian Social Science Research Councils (AASSREC).

Mailing Address : Commonwealth Avenue, U.P. Diliman Quezon City, Philippines.

Email : projects@ppsc.org.ph

Ruchira Mishra (*nee* Atal) is a Ph D in Sociology from Jabalpur. Currently she is Lecturer in Sociology, Faculty of Law, Rani Durgawati University, Jabalpur (M.P.).

Partha N. Mukherji is a Senior Fellow, Nehru Memorial Museum and Library, Teen Murti Bhawan, New Delhi. Earlier he worked as Director, Tata Institute of Social Sciences, Mumbai and Director, Council for Social-Development, New Delhi.

Mailing Address : Ashraya, F2/19 Bodhi Marg, DLF Phase-1, Gurgaon (Haryana).

Email : goparani@mantraonline.com

T.K. Oommen retired as Professor of Sociology from Jawahar lal Nehru University, New Delhi. He is Past President of the International

Sociological Association (1990-94) and of Indian Sociological Society (1998-99). He is the recipient of V.K. R.V Rao prize in Sociology (1981), G.S Ghurye Prize in Sociology and Anthropology (1985) and the Swami Pramanand Award in Sociology (1997). Among his several publication are: *Citizenship, Nationality and Ethnicity: Reconciling Competing Identities* (1997) and *Nation and National Identity in South Asia* (2000).

Suguma Pathy is Professor in the Department of Sociology, South Gujarat University, Surat.

Email : sugunapathy@hotmail.com.

Rajeshwar Prasad retired as Director, Institute of Social Sciences, Agra University, Agra. He is the President of Indian Social Science Association.

Mailing Address : 48, Tota Ka Taal, Madia Katra, Agra.

Jagdish Kumar Pundir is Professor and Head, Department of Sociology at C.C.S University, Meerut, His field interest include Scheduled Caste, Dalits and Globalization

Antony Raj/is Principal, St Joseph Junior College, Cuddapah (AP).

Ranvinder S. Sandhu is Professor of Sociology at the Guru Nanak Dev University, Amritsar. He has been visiting Professor at Winona State University, Minnesota, USA, University Grants Commission's visiting fellow in Netherlands and Overseas fellow of Human Science Research Council of South Africa. He has five books to his credit.

Mailing Address : Department of Sociology G.N.D. University, Amritsar.

Email : ranvinder@yahoo.com
ranidu@yahoo.com

K.N. Sharma, retired as Professor of Sociology, Indian Institute of Technology, Kanpur. He has taught at several other institutions in India and Abroad. He has been pioneer in promoting teaching of Social Sciences though the medium of Hindi and has also authored popular Hindi Text Books.

Mailing Address : 9/76 Arya Nagar, Kanpur-208002

Nishitha Sharma is Specialist in Extension Education, and has worked on various evaluation projects in rural Rajasthan.

Mailing Address : 642 Hiran Magri, Sector 13, Udaipur (Rajasthan).

Sukhdev Singh is working as Associated Professor Rural Development, Department of Economic and Sociology, Punjab Agricultural University, Ludhiana.

Late **N.K Singhi** retired as Professor and Head, Department of Sociology, University of Rajasthan, Jaipur. He was a Fulbright Scholar at the university of North Carolina Chapel Hill, USA, Visiting Fellow at Maison Des Sciences, Paris, Wallace Foundation Fellow at Cambridge University and Visiting Professor at the University of West India, Trinidad.

J.J. Smolicz is Professor of Education and Director, Centre for Intercultural Studies and Multicultural Education, Faculty of the Professions, Adelaide University, Australia.

Mailing Address : Education Building, 24 North Terrace Adelaide University SA 5005 Australia.

Email : jerzy.smolicz@adelaide.edu.au

D. Venkateswarlu is Professor and Head, Department of Sociology, Sri Venkateswara University, Tirupati-517502, A.P.

Mailing Address : 15-54/2 Padmavathi Nagar, Tirupati-517502, A.P.

Email : drdvenkat@usa.net

Introduction

SURENDRA K. GUPTA

This book is to honour one of India's highly acclaimed social scientists—Professor Yogesh Atal—who will be completing his sixty-fifth year on 9 October 2003. He began his career in 1959 as an Assistant Professor of Anthropology, and moved on to become the Principal Director of UNESCO—the status of Deputy Assistant Director-General—towards the conclusion of his employment. For more than four decades he has assiduously worked for the growth and development of not only sociology and anthropology but also all the social sciences in the entire region of the Asia-Pacific. While working as an academic administrator he continued to pursue his research interests and led several research teams to do comparative research in Asia on themes of contemporary significance. Even now, though formally retired, he is busy completing his unfinished agenda and encouraging young social scientists in the country to do meaningful research.

It is to celebrate the achievements of such a scholar and to pay tribute to him that his friends, students, children, and admirers—including some of his teachers—have joined this project. It is a pity that his mentor, Professor S.C. Dube, is no more; his assessment of Dr Atal's work and contribution would have been most precious, as he was so close to him since 1957 when he joined the University of Sagar as a post graduate student. The association continued till Professor Dube breathed his last in 1996. I recall Professor Dube saying at the time of the release of the felicitation volume in his honour, edited by Atal, that he would be doing a piece for "Yogesh" for his felicitation volume when he turns sixty-five. Alas, that was not to be. I was also hoping to receive a note from Professor Merton, but he was ill and also unfortunately passed away early this year.

Being one of Professor Atal's oldest students, I was encouraged by friends to take the initiative in the preparation of this *festschrift*. Some fifteen months ago, I wrote to several colleagues in India and abroad about this project seeking their contributions. The response was overwhelming. Some immediately responded; others took time. In fact, some colleagues wanted more time, but it was not possible to go on extending the dates any further. I know this will frustrate those who also wished to felicitate Professor Atal but could not participate in this project. But we had to meet the deadline

Given the wide range of Yogesh Atal's academic interests and vast circle of his friends among professional social scientists, both in India and abroad, it was not easy to either select a common theme for the book, or the authors to participate in the project. In my letter of invitation I had given them ample choice in regard to the theme of their contribution. The authors were requested either to evaluate Atal's contributions, or to reminisce on their interactions with him, or to write on a topic relative to contemporary social science concerns.

A review of all the inputs received indicated that they all relate to the emerging concerns in social sciences. As much of Atal's career was devoted to the promotion of social sciences, including encouragement to scholars to explore new frontiers, these essays appear to be a fitting tribute to him. Hence the title *Emerging Social Science Concerns* for this *festschrift*.

I am also glad that the contributors represent different generations—those senior to Yogesh Atal, his own peers, his students, and those who have recently entered the profession. Such a demographic composition adds to the variety of orientations, and accounts for differing standards of the contributions but they all demonstrate a high esteem for Professor Atal.

The book is divided into three parts. The first Part is devoted to those articles that are person-specific. These include reminiscences and appraisals of Atal's contributions by some of his close associates. Part Two contains essays that take a global view of social science concerns. Part Three has essays written on researches currently carried out in India.

Professor Yogesh Atal: An Intellectual Portrait

Biographical Note

Born on 9 October 1937, Yogesh Atal holds a Ph.D. degree in social anthropology from the University of Sagar (1966), and a D.Sc. (*honoris causa*) from the Marquis Guiseppe Scicluna International University Foundation (1989). He began his career in 1959 as an Assistant Professor at the

University of Sagar and later moved to Panjab University where he taught anthropology only for a year and a half and then moved again to Agra University to teach sociology at the Institute of Social Sciences. He then shifted, in 1968, to the Indian Institute of Technology, Delhi, to teach social sciences to students graduating in engineering courses. In 1971, he was appointed the first Research Director at the Indian Council of Social Science Research. While working at the ICSSR, he was elected as the first Secretary-General of the Association of Asian Social Science Research Councils (AASSREC). In September 1974, UNESCO hired him to head the newly established Regional Social Science Office for Asia and the Pacific, based first in Jakarta, and then relocated in Bangkok. In 1993, he was called to the UNESCO headquarters at Paris to coordinate UNESCO's work related to the World Summit for Social Development. Promoted as Principal Director Dr Atal took retirement from UNESCO in October 1997 after serving it 23 years with several achievements to his credit.

Yogesh Atal was honoured by the American Biographical Institute as *Man of the Year 1990* for his contribution to the growth of social sciences in Asia. He was re-nominated for the same honour in the year 2001. In 1993, Maharana Mewar Foundation awarded him the prestigious Maharana Mewar award, and the Albert Einstein International Academy Foundation gave him a Cross of Merit. The Korean Government and the Association of Asian Social Science Research Councils (AASSREC) likewise presented him with *Plaques of Gratitude* for his services to Asian Social Science, in 1994 and 1997, respectively.

He is author of a number of books and has edited nearly 40 books and monographs for UNESCO. He has edited a trilogy on poverty, namely *Poverty and Participation in Civil Society; Perspectives on Educating the Poor;* and *Poverty in Transition and Transition in Poverty* relating to the poverty situation in Eastern Europe. His recent books are *MaNDAte for Political Transition: Re-emergence of Vajpayee; The Poverty Question: Search for Solutions;* and *Indian Sociology: From Where to Where.*

Besides being an internationally acclaimed sociologist, Atal is a poet and litterateur. Five anthologies of his poems (one of which is a translation of poems by the Spanish poet Federico Mayor, who was also Director-General of UNESCO), a biography titled *Daulat Darbar* (both in Hindi and in English) and another collection of his Hindi essays on the changing Indian Society have been published.

After retiring from UNESCO, Atal functioned in an honorary capacity as Director-General of the Indian Institute of Education, Pune, which he has recently relinquished, but he continues, as a Special Adviser to that Institute. Currently, he is Chairman of the Programmes Committee of the

Indian Association of Social Science Institutions [IASSI] and a member of the Indian Council of Social Science Research. He is also on the Governing Board of the Govind Ballabh Pant Institute of Social Sciences. He is nominee of the President to the Planning Board of Assam University. Recently he has been elected a member of the Governing Council of the International Academy of Dialogue among Cultures and Civilizations, with its headquarters in Warsaw, Poland.

My association with Yogesh Atal spans more than four decades. I came in contact with him in 1960 when I joined as a post-graduate student the department of Anthropology at the Panjab University, Chandigarh. The Department was started that very year and Atal was one of the three teachers in the department. He was the only social anthropologist; the other two had specialization in physical anthropology and prehistoric archaeology. Being in the first batch of the department, we were able to develop personal equation with all the teachers. Yogesh Atal was the youngest of the three teachers and was easily accessible. As students, we were greatly impressed by his knowledge of the subject and his teaching skills. He was lucid in his thinking and had a clear understanding of the subject. Being science graduates some of us intended to specialize in physical anthropology, and the Department as a whole was also biased in favour of that branch. But due to his influence a few of us opted for social anthropology. Though, the head of the department did his best to discourage us but we stuck to our decision. That was not easy. The odds were against us. And Atal was put to several constraints, so much so that he took the first opportunity to leave the University. We were left high and dry after his departure, but he encouraged us and offered all help even from a distance. In fact, we went by turns to him in Agra and stayed there with him for days together to get his guidance in the completion of our dissertation and preparation of our examination papers. Today, when I look back I feel that my decision was right. I have the privilege of the company of one of the great social scientists of international renown.

Atal is not only an outstanding teacher but also an excellent researcher. In the 1960s there was emphasis on empirical studies in sociology and anthropology. He saw to it that his students did not lag behind. He selected a village near the university campus and took his students there to learn the chores of fieldwork. On every Sunday, we used to visit that village on our bicycles in his company. Some of the sociology students also joined our team. He taught us how to establish rapport with the villagers, and how to conduct census surveys. In the process, we also learnt from him other finer points of interviewing and field research. This initial exposure came handy when we went to Kulu Valley for data collection to write our dissertation in lieu of one theory paper. At that time, fieldwork was compulsory for the students of anthropology. Atal went with the team, so did other teachers. However, he stayed till the last while others returned early. The training we received from him was most valuable later in our career.

Students specializing in physical anthropology also came with us to Manali for fieldwork. But they were not given any instructions by their supervisors about the basics of fieldwork. Collecting finger prints and taking anthropometric measurements these students posed as if they were medical doctors. The villagers got suspicious and somehow discovered that they were lying. They refused to cooperate with them. At this stage, Atal was dispatched to the village to negotiate with the village potentates and create favourable conditions for fieldwork. With his communication skills and humility, he was able to win the confidence of the villagers and the students could return to the village to complete their assignments.

As I said earlier, Atal's stay at Chandigarh was very brief. He took up the assignment at the Institute of Social Sciences, Agra University, in December 1961 as Assistant Professor of Sociology. His departure left us—those specializing in social anthropology—in the lurch. Pending the appointment of his replacement, we were taught a few classes by the faculty of the sociology department. We had to take recourse to correspondence with him for guidance. Thus, informally he continued to be our teacher.

His assignment at Agra offered him a new challenge, moving from social anthropology to sociology. He was asked to teach Advanced Sociological Theory and Social Statistics to begin with. Later, he taught Rural Sociology and the Indian Social System. We marvelled that without a formal training in the discipline of sociology how ably he taught these courses and how highly he was regarded even at that young age by the profession. Already, he was a nationally known scholar participating in seminars and conferences and contributing papers to scientific journals.

In 1964, he was awarded Smith-Mundt Fellowship and Fulbright travel grant to visit the United States of America for one year. He went to Columbia University in New York to work with stalwarts like Robert K. Merton, Paul F. Lazarsfeld, William J. Goode and Amitai Etzioni; the influence of these illumanaries is reflected in his writings.

Upon return from the United States he was given a project by the Planning Commission, Government of India, to carry out a study of 1967 General Elections. It may be said that a series of such studies were commissioned by the Planning Commission, most of which were undertaken by the departments of Political Science. Atal's project was the first in the area of Political Sociology in India, which used the technique of

Panel study and developed a number of indexes, including the Index for the Sense of Political Efficacy, which was used later by other Indian sociologists. It is this study that brought me once again closer to him as he hired me to work on the project that involved fieldwork in the villages of Etah District in Uttar Pradesh. Participation in this project changed my orientation. I chose to work for my Ph.D. on political socialization under his guidance.

Yogesh Atal as Research Administrator

The Government of India, set up in 1968, a central body called Indian Council of Social Science Research (ICSSR) to promote and regularize social science research. It was headed by J.P. Naik, who was then Educational Adviser to the Government. A search was immediately started to select a suitable person as the Research Director of the Council. After seeing the performance of he in a national seminar, Naik offered the post to him. Since he was not able to join the Council immediately as he was to complete his courses at the Indian Institute of Technology, New Delhi, Naik requested him to visit the Council office in the afternoons to help him transact the work of the Council until he was relieved from the IIT. Atal agreed to the proposal and, for quite some time, worked as Honorary Director of the Council. After completing his classes in the morning at the IIT, he would catch a bus in the afternoon, to reach the Council's office which was located in the hostel building of Indian Institute of Public Administration. This practice continued for some time till he was relieved by the IIT. Soon after joining the ICSSR, the Jodhpur University offered him a Professorship in the Department of Sociology, and the University of London invited him for a month as Mahatma Gandhi Memorial Lecturer. While he was visiting London, Naik succeeded in his efforts to retain him by offering the same salary as was offered by the Jodhpur University, and converting his three-year contractual assignment into a permanent position; the other two posts of Directors, however, remained contractual.

As the first director, Atal left his imprint on the working of the ICSSR. He introduced short-term research methodology courses for young scholars and teachers in various universities and research institutions. He served as the Member Secretary of the team set up for carrying out an all-India Survey of the Educational Status of Scheduled Caste and Scheduled Tribe students. Another significant contribution of Atal as a director was the survey of literature in different social science disciplines such as anthropology and sociology, political science, psychology, public administration and geography. The first survey of sociology and social anthropology covered the period from 1900 to 1970 and he was asked to vet the monographs. Since then two more survey reports have been published. He also served as Secretary to the Study Team jointly set up by ICSSR, ICMR, ICAR, and the Council for Technical Education to survey the teaching of social sciences in professional education. At the conclusion of the work of the Team an all-India Conference was organized to discuss the findings and decide about measures to promote social sciences in professional education. This exercise resulted in a very useful publication.

A UNESCO Seminar on Teaching and Research in Social Sciences in Asia was organized by the ICSSR in collaboration with the Indian Institute of Advanced Study, Shimla, sometime in 1972. The UNESCO staff participating in the Seminar, was so much impressed by the performance and the organizing capability of Atal that they decided to offer him the newly created post of Regional Adviser for Social Sciences in Asia and the Pacific with its headquarters at Jakarta, Indonesia. This was the beginning of a long innings of Atal with UNESCO, which he joined in September 1974. After working for a while from the Jakarta office, he persuaded his seniors in UNESCO to shift the headquarters from Jakarta to Bangkok in Thailand. He continued to work as Regional Adviser till 1993, when he was transferred to UNESCO's headquarters in Paris to coordinate the Organization's work related to the World Summit For Social Development.

As the first Regional Adviser for Social and Human Sciences in Asia and the Pacific (UNESCO) he played a pioneering role in the development of social sciences in the region. His Unit initiated social science surveys, which overviewed the social science situation in various countries. These were published in four booklets under the title *Social Sciences in Asia*, covering the social science situation in twenty-one countries of the region; these were later published in a book form with the same title. Though his name does not figure, he edited the entire monograph. Following this exercise, he initiated another series of country reports on growth points and trends of research in individual social science disciplines. The disciplines covered were: sociology and social anthropology, economics, political science, philosophy, international law, public administration, and psychology. His Unit also carried out surveys to know the status of teaching of social sciences in agricultural education in eight countries of the region. All these studies were published under his editorship. In addition, the Regional Unit also published a survey on *Women's studies in south East Asia* (done by Leela Dube) and a Report on *Organization of Social Science Information and Documentation* in eleven countries of the region. He was the driving force in launching the Asia-Pacific Association of Social Sciences

Research Councils (AASSREC). This Association celebrated its 30th anniversary this year. In 1986, his Unit launched an Asia-Pacific Information Network in Social Sciences (APINESS).

About his role as UNESCO Adviser in promoting AASRREC (Association of Asian Social Science Research Councils), J.J. Smolicz, Professor of Education, Adelaide University, Australia has this to say:

> "I recall the towering figure of Professor Yogesh Atal, Full of vigour and zest, in his role as Secretary- General, leading the most vital and intellectually challenging social scientific organization in the Asia Pacific region. As an Association of Social Science Research Councils, AASRREC could have been a bureaucratic and State body involved in no more than reporting the activities of its respective members. But in reality, nothing could be farther from the truth. Under Dr. Atal's leadership, the AASRREC ship steered between organizational decorum, required of an official body representing social scientific organizations in the area and the intellectually free and occasionally vigorous discussion, expected of top ranking social scientists in Asia and the Pacific."

He further writes: "Dr. Atal was always fascinated by the great diversity of cultural phenomena and he succeeded in encouraging AASSREC meeting to take up the analysis of a series of cultural issues, and dilemmas, including such themes as unity in diversity, ethnicity and nation- states and resilience in pluralistic societies".

The Regional Unit, under his guidance, also designed training seminars for young social scientists to acquaint themselves with the latest trends and developments in such areas as (i) Development theories, planning and evaluation; (ii) Human Settlements Management; (iii) Social Indicators; (iv) Social Science Research Methodology, including use of computers; and (v) Social Science Information and Documentation. The Unit took the initiative in involving women social scientists of the region in the implementation of UNESCO's Programme. The Unit evolved *Youth Related Indicators*, and came out with two monographs on India and Thailand using those indicators.

His Unit also carried out activities relating to women especially by involving women social scientists of the .region in the implementing of UNESCO's programme, and carrying out studies on women and supporting initiatives to develop social science specialization in women's studies. The Unit also published the directories of women social scientists and of institutions engaged in research on women. Under his guidance the teaching material for women's studies for India, Thailand, Philippines, Japan, Turkey and Pakistan were also published. He also edited in 1990, a monograph on *Women in Asia: Beyond the Domestic Domain* and, in 1993, on *Women in Politics* and on *Violence Against Women*. He also supervised the publication of a series of booklets on Status of Women in seven countries, namely Afghanistan, China, Laos, Maldives, Mongolia, Thailand, and Vietnam.

An other area promoted by Atal as Regional Adviser was International Law. He organized a meeting of experts to assess the status of teaching and research in International law, helped in preparation of teaching materials for children and laymen on Human Rights and supported national campaigns to disseminate knowledge on Human Rights among school children. He also published a newsletter on International Law.

Atal developed a programme for the publication of studies carried out under UNESCO auspices or through financial support from UNESCO. In all, his Unit published around 40 research monographs and papers, besides publishing 38 reports on various meetings organized by his Unit. And he personally edited all of these.

Commenting on the contributions that Atal made to UNESCO's work, his colleague, Ali Kazancigil, Director, Division of Social Sciences, Research and Policy, Executive Secretary of UNESCO's MOST[1] Programme, wrote the following in his letter to me, dated 13 August 2001:

> "I have the privilege of being a long-standing colleague and friend of Dr. Yogesh Atal. As fellow scientists, he an anthropologist and myself a political scientist, we joined our efforts, as international civil servants in UNESCO, for a quarter of a century, to serve the promotion of international cooperation in the field of social sciences.
>
> As the first head of the UNESCO's Regional Social Science office for Asia and the Pacific in Bangkok, from 1974 to 1993, Dr. Atal gave an immense impetus to social science cooperation in this region. His achievements have been internationally recognized. While serving the cause of the social science in Asia and the Pacific he continued his personal work as an eminent social anthropologist. Especially, his writings on the sociology of social sciences and development constitute important contributions to international literature. From 1993 to his retirement in 1997, as a Principal Director, Dr. Atal was called to UNESCO headquarters to coordinate the organization's work related to the World Summit for Social Development (Copenhagen, 1995), a responsibility that he fulfilled with competence and excellent results."

While going through personal files of Atal, I found the following comments by Dr. Raja Roy Singh, Assistant Director-General and Regional Co-ordinator of UNESCO in Bangkok. Singh wrote this in 1984:

"Dr. Y. Atal continues to make excellent contribution to the development of social science programmes in the region. He is held in high esteem, both by the social science community of the countries and the governmental authorities. His missions to the countries are always effective.

"Dr. Atal has quite clearly put the social science programme of the Organization on the map in the region despite the very small resources which the programme carries."

The then Director-General of UNESCO (Amadou Mahatar M'Bow) wrote the following comment about Atal's qualities of editorship:

"First of all, I should like to express my deepest gratitude and highest regards to Prof. Y. Atal, extraordinary Plenipotentiary and General Editor RUSHSAP Series, for his outstanding expertise and competence in editing.

All of us appreciate the enormous amount of substantive work involved in editing which Prof. Y. Atal has, so successfully achieved. Without his devotion, this publication would not have been possible."

Makaminan Makagiansar, Assistant Director General, wrote in 1986:

"He is held in high esteem as a most competent regional adviser for social and human sciences in Asia and the Pacific. I have known Dr Yogesh Atal for many years prior to my assuming the present functions and after having worked with him for the past three months I can only confirm my admiration for his qualities."

Makagiansar wrote again to Atal at the time of his transfer to Paris and promotion. I reproduce the same.

"While attending the recent world conference on Education for All I learned about your transfer to Paris and your promotion. I am confident that the level and the centrality of your new position will give you all possibilities for solidifying UNESCO's impact on Social and Human Science development. Globally such impact is quite minimal.

"With this letter I want you to remember always my admiration for your intellectual process and how much I appreciate working with you, your contribution in conceptualising and shaping APPEAL[2] especially in your capacity as chairman of the interdisciplinary PROAP[3] drafting group was outstandingly superb".

Francine Fournier, Assistant Director General, Sector of Social and Human Sciences, UNESCO wrote the following to the Director General:

"As a Regional Adviser for social sciences for Asia and the pacific region Mr. Atal's performance has always been rated above average, and he is professionally held in high esteem in intellectual circles and in the secretariat. He was... transferred to the headquarters in August 1993 to take charge of the co-ordination of UNESCO's work related to the World Summit for Social Development. I have great appreciation for the work Mr. Atal had done to enhance UNESCO's visibility in the Summit Preparatory process. The additional assignment given him by you to arrange the visit of the Indian Prime Minister to mark the 125th birth anniversary of Mahatma Gandhi was also carried out very efficiently. In recognition of his outstanding professional and academic achievements, his contribution to promote social and human sciences in the Asia- Pacific region through the creation and nurturing of two major regional networks—AASSREC and APINESS, and the high quality of a number of monographs edited by him as RUSHSAP[4] publications, and his *human* qualities, it will only be appropriate that he be given an end-of-career promotion to D-2 level."

In 1997, on the verge of his retirement from the UNESCO, Federico Mayor, the Director-General of the UNESCO wrote to Dr. Atal:

"I was very touched by your valedictory letter of 23 September, marking the completion of your twenty three years of loyal and dedicated service as a member of the UNESCO secretariat. Please accept my warmest thanks, not only for all you have done for the Organization, but also for honouring me personally through the gift of your translation of my poetry into Hindi. Your comments on the satisfaction you have drawn from your rich experience as a staff member of UNESCO are most gratifying. You may rest assured that the competence and efficiency as well as the human qualities of which you have unfailingly given proof have likewise been greatly appreciated by those who have had the good fortune to work with you, from the time of your initial appointment as Regional Adviser for Social Sciences for Asia and the Pacific rightup to your final assignment as Co-ordinator of the World Summit for Social Development. You will be missed by them all.

I want you to know that I shall always be happy to benefit from your wisdom and experience."

An Overview of Atal's Sociological Contributions

In 1959, when Atal joined the profession, the Indian social science scene was dominated by village studies. But very little was available on the changing aspect of the village especially the nature of caste. Atal's study published as *The Changing Frontiers of Caste* (1968) was the pioneering attempt in this direction. This was a comparative study of two villages of identical size located in Rajasthan and Madhya Pradesh. The study highlighted the regional variations in the caste system. In his Foreword to the book, S.C. Dube opined "..... book has more to offer than only careful presentation of systematically and painstakingly gathered ethnographic materials. His analytical scheme merits note. He considers individual caste as unit in a system, and studies both the units as well as the system in which they operate. His classification of attributes of caste and the consequent analysis are useful. The changing aspects of caste have been carefully analysed in this framework. Comparative treatment of two villages, located in settings that have different historical traditions, has added to the significance of the conclusion of the book" (1968:viii).

Atal is one of the leading social scientists who initiated and promoted communication research in sociology in India. Before the 1960s most of the studies of tribes and villages in India, touched upon the traditional means of communication such as oral communication, traditional media and interpersonal communication, but the modern means of communication remained completely neglected. Those specializing in agriculture extension, or working in the area of family planning conducted most of the earlier studies in communication. Of course, the Audience Research Units of the All India Radio located in Mumbai, Delhi and Kolkata also undertook some surveys. Atal emphasised the role of communication in nation building through several writings in the 1960s. When China attacked India in 1962, Atal along with V.K. Sethi (a statistician) guided a study to find out awareness among urban dwellers about the Sino-India conflict. The study was conducted in the city of Agra and was published in 1967 by the Institute of Social Sciences, Agra. Since Radio network was not so well developed at that time and television was not even introduced in India, a large number of people depended for information upon written communication in the form of newspapers and periodicals. Even the illiterates reported the use of newspapers and periodicals that were read to them by the literate members of the family or the neighbours.

Among Indian Sociologists, Atal was the first to carry out a full-length study of Indian elections. He was the first to use panel technique in India while studying the 1967 elections in a constituency in western Uttar Pradesh. It is true that Political Scientist V.M. Sirsikar claimed to have used panel technique in his municipal election study of Poona, but technically it was not a panel study, as he did not interview the same set of respondents in subsequent waves.

For his study, Atal selected three interlinked communities varying in size and in terms of communication links. He called them Small

Community (SC), Link Community (LC), and Centre-of-Centre Community (COC) respectively. A panel of respondents was selected from each of the three communities, which was interviewed thrice through carefully constructed schedules, twice before the election and once after the election. One significant feature of this study was the analysis of slips issued by the political parties and candidates to the voters to assist the polling officer in identifying and locating the name of the voter in the electoral rolls. The research team, with the cooperation of polling officers, collected these slips from the dustbins and subjected them to careful scrutiny. On the methodology of the Project CLAPP (Communication Links and Pattern of Political Participation), Atal wrote a long essay—perhaps the only one of that type—for the book *Beyond the Village: Sociological Explorations* edited by Satish Saberwal published in 1972 by the Indian Institute of Advanced Study, Shimla.[5] Atal's monograph on the 1967 elections was published as *Local Communities and National Politics* (1971). It became a landmark study. Professor Norman D. Palmer characterized this work as a "ground-breaking study of elections and political development" while paying his tributes to him in the Preface to his book, *Elections and Political Development: The South Asian Experience.*[6] Palmer has extensively quoted from Atal's study.

Atal attempted to explore, in his 1967 election study, the political links the village had with society at large and the role that these links played in breaking the isolation of the village communities. This led him to study the problem of nation building. He found the twin concepts of *apertures* and *insulators* as useful elaborations of the phenomenon of linkages. He used this conceptual framework for the analysis of caste, of foreign policy, of political behaviour, of the role of elites directly or obliquely. According to him, communication plays a pivotal role in the rise of nationalism and emergence of new nations and also in the process of modernization and political development. Communication, he further argues, "serves the dual function of meeting the demands of the government and responding to the overtures of the people". He holds the view that neglect of communication results in creating and/or reinforcing insular tendencies.

This theme was developed further in his 1972 Mahatma Gandhi Memorial Lecture, which he was invited to deliver by the School of Oriental and African Studies, University of London. In this Lecture, elaborating the concepts of *insulators* and *apertures* he argued that the creation of apertures and formation of insulators at the appropriate levels is very important for any exercise in Nation Building. According to him, " Identity of a nation is preserved through a system of insulators at the national boundary, when insulators cease to operate or become vulnerable, the system's boundaries begin to have several inlets. With manifold apertures, the system gets engulfed into another system and is reduced to the status of a sub-system, a colony. Similarly, when the many apertures of a subsystem get somehow closed, and insulators are planted on its boundary, the subsystem may become a system in its own right. It is thus, the capacity of the insular mechanisms that determines the probability of a system's independent existence"[7].

He developed the concept of *nation-set* in an article written in the late 1960s for a national seminar on foreign policy held at the University of Rajasthan. As a sociologist he proposed a paradigm to analyse the external milieu by extending the scope of the concept of "role-set" as developed by his teacher at Columbia University, Professor Robert K. Merton. Every nation-state, according to him, has its reference groups—both positive and negative—among membership and non- membership international system. Proposing the concept of *nation-set* he argued that "a nation's boundary maintenance problem are resolved through its foreign policy and through a policy of defence of its frontiers.... The way a nation relates itself with other nations is defined by the contents of its foreign policy. The nation as an actor is involved in an array of associated roles with a number of nations. Such a compliment of role relationship that a nation has is to be called a nation-set"[8].

The selection of reference nation may be influenced by various considerations. The basic requirement to identify the *nation-set* of any nation is to isolate the various fields of interactions, as there is always a distinctive *nation-set* for every field of interaction. To identify any nation-set he suggested the following procedure:

(*i*) The intensity of interaction of the nation in question (ego-nation) with the nation in the *nation-set*.
(*ii*) The pattern of mutual relationship between partners in the *nation-set*.
(*iii*) The indirect influence of the *nation-set* of a partner in the *nation-set* of the ego-nation.
(*iv*) The pattern of differing demands made by each partner in the *nation-set* on the ego-nation; and
(*v*) The size of the *nation-set* and its effect on the performance of the ego-nation" (Atal, 1981:35).

While further developing the insulators and apertures model, Atal proposed yet another concept, namely that of *Sandwich culture*. This he first used while reviewing Ravindra K. Jain's book entitled, *South Indians on the plantation Frontier in Malaya* (1979). The concept refers to the culture of immigrants settled in some alien country. According to him, a sandwich man bears two tags one representing the country of his origin and the other the country of his migration. He argues that chances of creating a sandwich culture are greater among conservative migrants as compared to those migrants ".... who come with a view to settling down", because such people "would show a more accommodative attitude towards the host culture" (Atal, 1989: 37).[9] He has listed two sets of factors that operate or hinder the process of formation of sandwich culture. He calls them as *Aperture opening* and *Insulatory mechanisms*. Some of the possible *aperture openings* listed by him include intermarriage, adoption of names of the host society, adoption of language of the host culture, religious conversion, and adoption of food habits and developing a taste for the host cuisine. His list of *Insulatory mechanisms* includes factors such as retention of mother tongue, concentration of living quarters to promote greater interaction with the members of the in-group, provision of separate educational facilities for children, practice of endogamy, concentration in certain occupations, formation of voluntary organizations, continuation of food habits and taboos associated with eating, retention of cultural diacriticals particularly in the manner of dressing and keeping apertures open to the parent culture in the form of frequent visits, affinal relations, exposure to media, and so on.

Though the model has been tested in some empirical studies, it requires more such studies to make it a part of theory. Atal has emphasized the need to develop empirical profiles of various kinds of sandwich cultures with a view to "(i) evolving a suitable typology, (ii) identifying the process of the creation and maintenance of these sub-cultures, and (iii) understanding the role they play in the dynamics of nation building and in the promotion of inter cultural understanding" (*Ibid*:38).

One of the basic pre-requisites in nation building is the problem of national integration especially in a multi- cultural society like India. It has been argued by him that national integration requires efficient handling of the three processes namely assimilation, cohesion and epigenesis. All these three processes are associated with culture, social structure and polity respectively. "The arrival of foreign elements—peoples, ideas, technology—are first accommodated and then in due course of time get assimilated in the cultural fabric of the society. The assimilation of alien elements, as also increasing structural differentiation within the society poses a problem of cohesion or solidarity. Thirdly, some new structural elements may be deliberately created, epigenetically, and hence a new entity may come into being" (1981: 265). Nation building activity, according to him requires the creation of those mechanisms and structures that allow these processes to operate and ensure continuity of the system. "On the one hand, the system should be capable of warding off all external threats to preserve its identity and, on the other, it should take care that none of its constituent parts gets disoriented. Gate keepers at the entry points and integrators, or linkages between various subunits, are necessary for the task" (*Ibid*).

In a democratic polity the citizen, who is the smallest unit, is the brick of the building blocks of the nation. "He belongs to the community, the communities make the state, and the states make the Nation. The citizen should have a feeling of 'belongingness' vis-à-vis the nation. He is invited to enter into a new 'orbit of desire' and inhale a 'secular climate of opinion'. All this essentially means his increasing dependence on wider and yet wider units of social organization. The dependence increases his degree of involvement" (*Ibid*: 267). He further argues that this dependency helps the smaller units to break their insulations and open the apertures of the small communities to develop linkages with the wider world of the society. When the local interests are articulated with regional and national interests and goals, the chances of attaining the goal of integration increase. All these processes require an effective communication system.

Atal is also internationally known for his contribution to the debate on Indigenization of Social Sciences. In 1970, a movement for the Indigenization of social sciences in the Third World was gaining momentum. As UNESCO's Regional Adviser for Social Sciences in Asia and the Pacific, he played significant role in generating debate and discussion on this issue. His ideas on this issue are articulated in his article, "The call for Indigenization", published in *International Social Science Journal* (Vol. xxxiii, No.1, 1981), and subsequently translated into a number of languages. While synthesizing the major trends of thinking he wrote: "the call for Indigenization of social sciences in Asia has not yet gone beyond the reactive phase. Since these reactions come from different sources, albeit all from the professional social scientists, they emphasize different aspects of Indigenization. Even the definitional crisis has not yet been resolved: Indigenization means different things to different people". According to him, Indigenization in Asian context has been pursued along four fronts, namely (i) teaching in the national language, and use of local material; (ii) research by insiders; (iii) determination of research priorities; and (iv) theoretical and methodological reorientation. He further argued that "a need exists to distinguish between *endogenous development* and *Indigenization*, and between universalistic and particularistic aspects of Indigenization. He underlined the fact that different countries are at different stages of social science development and this determines the extent of their readiness to accept the "Ideology of Indigenization".

Another significant area in which Atal has contributed is the problem of Poverty. As UNESCO's Coordinator for the World Summit for Social Development, held in March 1995 in Copenhagen, Denmark, he got an opportunity to focus on poverty related questions. As a follow-up to the World Summit, he commissioned a six country study on Poverty in the countries of the former Soviet block. The countries covered were Hungary, Bulgaria, Romania, Georgia, Russian Federation, and Mongolia. He not only supervised these studies but also edited them for the book, which was published in 1999 under the title *Poverty in Transition and Transition in Poverty*, as a joint publication of UNESCO and Berghahn Books, New York.[10] Two other books on Poverty edited by him are: *Perspectives on Educating the Poor* (1997) and *Poverty and Participation in Civil Society* (1997). In the Preface to his book entitled *The Poverty Question: Search for Solutions* (2002)—which is an anthology of his essays on Poverty—he wrote: "while the problem of poverty is global its solutions will have to be local. We can, of course, gain insights from the experience of others, but cannot replicate their strategies. We have to bring back local culture in our scheme of things. This is the essence of the new demand for 'think globally act locally'".

Another feather in Atal's cap was added when Professor Robert K. Merton, lauded him for innovatively linking his concepts of *insiders* and *outsiders* with the analysis of "Managing Multiplicity" in a pluricultural society of India.[11] Merton wrote: "Yours is truly a beautifully analytical application and extension of the insider-outsider concept. In the course of their application to Indian society, you not only shed new light on its distinctive character as the sole multi-religious entity in South Asia, but also manage to extend the underlying sociological concept as well. An altogether magisterial analysis".

A quick review of his contributions suggests that he has continually explored new territories. He has always responded to the challenges posed to him. Thus, when he moved from the mainstream sociology taught in the Indian universities to the Institute of Technology, he introduced sociology of science and technology in the syllabi of the IIT. Rather than reproducing the syllabus of traditional courses taught in the universities, he designed an interdisciplinary course titled "The Social Framework" for the IIT graduates, which was jointly taught by him and other colleagues specializing in Economics, and Political Science. His assignment at the ICSSR gave him the opportunity to focus on the sociology of social science—a sub specialization within the sociology of science and sociology of knowledge. This interest he carried further when he became the

UNESCO Adviser for Social and Human Sciences in Asia and the Pacific. Similarly, he encouraged research on vital social problems (which he acronymed VISOP) and for each such research project, he developed a conceptual framework, designed methodology of comparative research, and finally edited the volumes based on empirical researches carried out in different countries. His introductory essays to these volumes are not mere perfunctory administrative pieces; they are important academic contributions and are used by the new initiates. These writings cover a wide range—communication and nation building, swidden cultivation, migration to the Middle East (a phenomenon which he acronymed MIME), sociology of biogas, rural-to-urban migration, brain drain (he treated it as migration of talent), women in public life, violence against women, and finally poverty. Similarly, his conceptual contributions are important: and the range is indeed impressive. He has rigorously defined the concepts of caste, short-lived alliances, political involvement, sense of political efficacy, SES in the Indian context, *nation-set*, insulators and apertures, sandwich culture, multicultural society (in terms of insider-outsider duality), and indigenisation. In his recent speeches and writings he is busy formulating a sociological definition of the phenomenon of Globalization. And he is contemplating a theoretical book on social change and development. It would, indeed, require an entire dissertation to systematically appraise Atal's manifold contributions to the social sciences.

Let me conclude this section by mentioning yet another area in which Atal stands as a pioneer in India. He is one of the few social scientists in the country who has promoted the social sciences via the medium of Hindi. He writes and speaks with equal command in both English and Hindi. Way back in the 1960s he wrote *Adivasi Bharat,* which was published by Raj Kamal Prakashan, Delhi. The book, though in great demand, is out of print now for several years. He also translated in Hindi *Sociology: A Systematic Introduction* by Harry M. Johnson and *Indian Village* by S.C. Dube. He wrote a number of articles on social issues for prominent Hindi newspapers and magazines like *Dharamyug* and *Saptahik Hindustan* and for the All-India Radio. Many do not know that he had singly analysed all the national election results, both in Hindi and in English, for the Indian Television (*Door Darshan*) in 1972, when the only gadget that was available for quick computation was the tiny calculator!

THE BOOK

The academic profile of Atal suggests that he has not confined to only one or two areas but has worked in diverse areas including, caste, communication, nation-building, youth, women, globalization and modernization, to name a few. Keeping in mind his versatile divergent interests, it was decided that in this *Festschrift* we will not restrict to only one theme and gave free hand to contributors to select their own themes.

The book is divided into three Parts. Personal reminiscences by his teachers, former colleagues and/or students are in the First Part. The Second Part focuses on emerging social science concerns in a global context. The Third Part contains essays relative to India.

Immediately following this Introduction, are articles in Part One of this book written as personal tributes and reminiscences. These include essays written by Brij Raj Chauhan and Leela Dube—both teachers of Atal and almost as members of his family; Jainendra K. Doshi—a childhood friend who also became his student at the M.A. level; Jagdish Pundir of Meerut University—a colleague of the younger generation of Indian sociologists; like Atal, he is also a student of Brij Raj Chauhan. It is followed by an adulatory note from his son, Sanket, who heads a research team at Oracle in USA. Very aptly Sanket chose to present his own life as a "case study" of the phenomenon of "Sandwich Culture"—the concept that he has personally witnessed growing. Then there are three essays written by those who have been associated with Yogesh Atal in his work relative to the Association of Asia-Pacific Social Science Research Councils (AASSREC). Vinod Mehta, Director, Indian Council of Social Science Research recalls his association with Atal while looking after the AASSREC Secretariat that was originally located at the ICSSR. It is followed by an essay on Atal by the present Secretary-General of AASSREC, Virginia Miralao, who is the Executive Director of the Philippine Social Science Council. This section ends with a Note by J.J. Smolicz of the University of Adelaide and a long time friend and collaborator of Atal in the work related to the Association of Asia-Pacific Social Science Research Councils (AASSREC)—he drafted this tribute that was read before the assembly of the AASSREC held in Vietnam in 2001.

Part Two of the book opens with an essay by Ali Kazancigil, a friend and colleague of Yogesh Atal of long standing, and until recently the Deputy Assistant Director-General for Social and Human Sciences in UNESCO now Secretary General, International Social Science Council. In his article on "Towards a Democratic Regulation of Globalization" Kazancigil has raised the question of democratic deficit that exists within Globalization. He feels that globalization reduces the capacity of national democratic regimes to cope with the domestic effect of decisions that are made and processes that take place at the global level. He argues the need to develop democratic mechanisms beyond national borders, through which citizenship can also be exercised on the global scene and democratic politics be incorporated in global governance. Globalization has so far, according to him, focused exclusively on market related concerns but has excluded democratic accountability, transparency and justice. He emphasizes the need to introduce participatory politics into global governance with NGOs playing a significant role.

J.J. Smolicz in his paper on "Tradition and Modernity in an era of global change" has argued that in each society there are some cultural elements—the core value of the groups—whose maintenance is essential for retaining cultural identity. The abandonment of these values may threaten the disintegration of the whole cultural and social fabric of the group. These core values can be clearly discerned when the group is under threat and needs to defend its culture against external pressure. These core elements become the fundamental values of the group when it comes under threat of extinction. To counteract the homogenizing effect of globalization various local, regional and ethnic groups are demanding a place for their core values within the multiethnic nation-state. Some radical sections of the young in some Asian countries are also demanding that the 'western values' in general and science based technology and science education in particular should be indigenised and the local cultural elements should replace those imposed or imported from outside. They prefer improvements in the society within the framework of traditional values.

K.N. Sharma regards the current process of Globalization as an extension of the processes of cultural contacts which have a long history, and perceives the same ill effects of this so-called new process as those of the processes of industrialization, colonization, and modernization. He makes a plea for the return to the core Indian values of non-aggregation and non-cumulation so that the world does not get threatened by the mass production of weapons of destruction and a horrifying culture of consumption. He has aptly titled his paper by asking the question *how novel and how noble* is the process of Globalization.

Binod Agrawal in his paper "Information and Communication Technology: Challenges to Democracy in Asia" has pointed out that the electronic media have remarkable influence in the field of entertainment and recreation and have led to the disappearance of a large majority of traditional media. But the influence of information technology on politics especially in the countries of Asia is not very effective as majority of the political parties still heavily rely on traditional media, such as face-to-face communication, rallies, processions, and door-to-door canvassing, than electronic media.

Late N.K. Singhi[12], in his paper titled "Gender Construction and Media:

Presentation Representation and Repression" has argued that there is overemphasis and glorification of woman's character in media and it has been used as a weapon to denigrate her. He emphasizes the need to have media policy, regarding gender representation, presentation and reproduction. It is a part of civilizational development, and media is becoming effective in its construction, diffusion and spread.

Most of the environment and development related projects will remain incomplete and peripheral if they did not address to women's concerns, argues Suguna Pathy in her paper "Women and Environmental crisis: A Spill-over of Economic Development". She pleads in her paper that development projects need to be more supportive of women and should also encourage their greater participation not only in implementation but also while designing the projects.

Rajeshwar Prasad chose to write an extensive review article on the book on Poverty in Eastern Europe edited by Yogesh Atal. The book is titled, *Poverty in Transition and Transition in Poverty* published jointly by UNESCO and Berghahn Books, New York in 1999.

The next three articles are related to Indian Diaspora. N. Jayaram discusses the Dynamics of language in Indian Diaspora by focusing on the use of Bhojpuri and Hindi in Trinidad in the Caribbean. He has ably discussed the issue of revival of Hindi as an ethnic language by the Indian Diaspora in Trinidad. His analysis reveals that, though in the ethnic politics of Trinidad, the question of Hindi has acquired a political colour, it is rarely used in interpersonal communication in everyday life within the community. He further says that even the few who have learnt the language, remain indifferent to its use in speech. He concludes that though Hindi will certainly take deep roots as a sacral language of the Hindus, its chances of becoming the ethnic language of Indo-Trinidadians and their becoming bilingual does not appear to be bright.

Ms. Ruchira Mishra (nee Atal) and Surendra Gupta in their articles have attempted to empirically test the validity of the concept of sandwich culture proposed by Atal. Ruchira did a sample survey of Punjabis in Bangkok, whereas Gupta, adopted anthropological techniques of observation and informal interview to found the traces of sandwich culture among Punjabis and Gorakhpuris who migrated to Thailand almost at the sometime, *i.e.* about one hundred years ago. Ruchira Mishra (nee Atal) in her article on "India in Thailand" had applied Atal's concept of sandwich culture in carrying out a small pilot study on a sample of 100 Punjabis in Thailand. She tried to find out how these have adopted the Thai culture and adjusted in Thai society. While adopting to live in a different land these people have not entirely given up Indian culture, including some prominent dress diacriticals such as turban and beard—the symbols of Sikhism. They occasionally yearn for Indian things and also show a liking for Indian customs and way of life. Even they prefer to marry in India and thus maintain effective kinship links. Her study exemplifies the phenomenon of living in two cultures and of creating a distinct way of life drawn from the two sources namely the parent culture and the host culture—the very essence of the concept of Sandwich Culture as advanced by Atal. The comparison of sandwich cultures of the Punjabis and the Gorakhpuris done by Gupta shows that Punjabis have adopted more traits of Thai culture as compared to Gorakhpuris and both are sandwiched between the two cultures but the two groups represent two separate sandwich cultures.

There are thirteen articles in the Third Part that relates to India. This Part opens with an essay by A.K. Dasgupta, currently the Member-Secretary of the Indian Association of Social Science Institutions (IASSI). Both Dasgupta and Atal took their assignment at the Panjab University, Chandigarh in the same year and have maintained their relationship—professional and personal—for more than forty years. Dasgupta has written about the current concerns in Indian social science. This is followed by an article by Giri Raj Gupta (University of Western Illinois) and Satish Kedia (University of Memphis) who have explored the theoretical trends and boundaries of ethnographic writings in post-independence India. Two prominent social scientists—Partha Mukherji (a sociologist) and S.N. Jha (a Political Scientist who was Atal's colleague at the IIT, Delhi)..... have contributed on India's rural development which was the reigning theme of Indian social science in the 1960s and 70s. While Mukherji focussed on the Bhoodan Movement, Jha reviews India's experiment with decentralization in the form of Panchayati Raj. The insights provided by these two essays are indeed valuable in understanding the processes of social change in Independent India. The next essay by Ranvinder Sandhu reviews the growth and development of urban sociology in India, and highlights the achievements and lacunae in research in this branch of the discipline.

Hari Mohan Mathur chose to write on Involuntary Resettlement and Voluntary Organizations. He is working in this area for a long time, and it is interesting to note that through UNESCO, Atal had commissioned Mathur—a very dear and old friend—to work on the problem of resettlement—an area that continues to interest Mathur. The author has highlighted the role of NGOs in involuntary resettlement. But, he argues that though they are better equipped to deal with involuntary settlement rarely do they help the poor in this regard. Very often the NGOs do not operate in areas where there is need for their intervention. They are hesitant to expand their operations in places other than where they are based. Their overall effectiveness also reduces due to limited management capacity. Many NGOs lack the experience necessary to perform their job and most of them generally depend on government funding which further reduces their effectiveness.

T.K. Oommen's paper "Brain Drain or the Migration of Talent" is a revised version of his contribution to a book edited by Atal for UNESCO titled, *Migration of Talent: Causes and Consequences of Brain Drain* (UNESCO RUSHSAP Series No. 19, Bangkok, 1987). Oommen holds the view that professionals do not migrate out of sheer individual impulse, but the existing conditions in Indian society force them to take such steps. He further argues that the identification of some of these conditions would help in restricting the migration, but may also bring back those who had already left. This, according to him, will require drastic changes in the official policy towards scientific personnel. It would also require analysis of two sets of factors –socio-economic and Psychological attributes of the migrants and structural properties of the situation both at the point of departure and the destination—to find out the causes responsible for migration and to prescribe remedies to prevent further exodus.

In his paper "Contesting and Contested Self-identities: Mathura's Chaubes", Owen M. Lynch has discussed the self-identities of the people of the Chaube caste on the basis of scripture, history, contesting and contested identities. Professor Lynch is an old India hand. He met Atal in 1962 when he was doing his fieldwork on the Jatavs of Agra that resulted in a famous book titled *The Politics of Untouchability*. Later he shifted his interest to Mathura and did intensive study of the Chaubes of Mathura through the time-tested technique of participant observation. This paper is based on that intensive fieldwork that involved a number of sessions with the knowledgeables, reading of vernacular literature relative to the Chaubes and participation in a number of social and religious ceremonies including a month long barefoot circumambulation of the *Brijbhumi*. His study concluded that the Chaubes trace their self-identity through a variety of sources depending on the narratives. One narrative traces their origin in Afghanistan! "The 'authentic'..... narrative of scriptural discourse is not coherent, essential and univocal. Rather, it is contingent, semiotically constituted, and equivocal; it is historically and situationally refracted into the multiple, contesting narratives of Karua and Mitha, Panda and Kulin". According to him, self-identities cannot be reduced to material or political factors without depriving them of what is most humanly significant about them.

While discussing the customs, religion, and social change among the Meos of Mewat, Abha Chauhan says that despite the Meos being the followers of Islam some of their customs hint to their Rajput origin. For example, the Meos follow the customary practice of the Rajputs regarding inheritance and adoption but observe Muslim personal law in regard to divorce and remarriage. Islam continues to play a catalyst role in their lives but education and new employment opportunities have brought changes in their kinship structure. This had led to the emergence of religious consciousness and identity leading to the realignment of groups and creation of situation of conflict.

Jagdish Pundir has attempted to trace the identity of Dalits. Though the Dalits are referred to by different terms, their common substantive image signifies their perception of oppression, suffering from traditional socio-cultural disabilities, under privileged status, and cumulative deprivation. Some changes have been noticed in their over-all conditions in the last few decades.

Venkateshwarlu and Anthony Raj evaluate the impact of proselytization on the social status and educational mobility among the Christian converts from scheduled castes as compared to those of the scheduled caste Hindus. They found some change in the social status of Christian converts, but the impact was more visible on educational mobility. The educational achievement of Christian converts led them to gain better employment, which in turn made them more respectable.

Why the adversities for Punjab farmers are increasing in the last one decade and what are its implications especially on smaller farmers is the subject matter of the paper of Sukhdev Singh and Mandeep Kaur. They found that the small farmers are spending much more on machinery as well as on other costly times such as car, scooter, refrigerator etc. disproportionate to their land holding and income level. To meet the demand they take loans from the lending agencies, and in the event of their inability to pay back they either sell their land or migrate to other region in search of employment, or worse, they commit suicide.

Nishitha Sharma (nee Atal) in her paper "Kitchen to Kitchen Via the Market" has presented a case study of a cottage industry cell established by Udaipur's Mahila Mandal. This NGO project is carried out by a small team of dedicated workers and provides employment to about 160 women and indirectly to several others. The commodities produced by them are not seasonal but are in continuous use as consumable item in the kitchen.

Let me conclude by wishing Yogesh Atal many more years of creative life contributing to the growth of social sciences in India, and also to Indian literature.

NOTES

1. MOST stands for Management of Social Transformation. Incidentally, this acronym is also Dr. Atal's coinage as are AASSREC, APINESS, and APPEAL—all part of UNESCO vocabulary.
2. Asia Pacific Programme of Education for All.
3. Principal Regional Office for Asia and the Pacific.
4. Regional Unit for Social and Human Sciences in Asia and Pacific.
5. This essay is reproduced in Yogesh Atal's book *Social Sciences: The Indian Scene*, New Delhi, Abhinav Publications, 1976.
6. Norman D. Palmer, *Elections & Political Development : The South Asian Experience*. New Delhi, Vikas Publishing House. 1976. p. viii.
7. See Yogesh Atal, *Building a Nation: Essays on India*, New Delhi, Abhinav Publications. 1981, pp. 8-9.
8. *Ibid*. p. 9.
9. Yogesh Atal "Outsiders as Insiders: The phenomenon of Sandwich Culture" in *Sociological Bulletin*, Vol. 38, No. 1.
10. This book is now prescribed text in a post-graduate course at the University of North Carolina.
11. Published in *Economic and Political Weekly*, No. 36 in 2001.
12. Within few days of the receipt of his paper I got the sad news of his sudden demise.

Part I

Personal Reminiscences

1

Yogesh Atal: The Making of A Social Scientist

BRIJ RAJ CHAUHAN

Yogesh Atal caught my attention as a debator when he joined Maharana Bhopal College, Udaipur, after his matriculation. As a faculty member I relished my role as one of the judges at debate competitions in which he invariably participated. The ranking was not difficult; for language and expression, he would score 6 to 7.5 marks out of 10 each, and for subject matter, between 5 and 6.5. Normally he stood first. When he represented the college in elocution contests held elsewhere in the country, my question to him after his return used to be: "who stood the second?" If that was not his name, the inference was obvious: he could not have scored a lower rank than that, and must have stood first. A smile on his face was the confirmation of my anticipation. As a student of intermediate class (then known as FA), he participated and won in debates of a Degree (with a few post-graduate departments) College. We would discuss a few points prior to, or after, such contests.

"Atal" at the end of his name has a history. When he was still at school he happened to speak at a railway rally organized to celebrate the first Republic Day. The Manager of the Rajasthan Railway—in which his father was a Station Master—was greatly pleased by his performance and awarded him a silver medal. Soon after his father took him to Chittorgarh where he was posted. There he went to the Gurukul to meet the Principal. His father told the Principal about Yogesh's speech. On asking, Yogesh summarized his speech for the Principal and highlighted his criticism of the caste system. The Gurukul Principal then queried him about the surname "Sharma" that he used. Embarrassed by the question, Yogesh showed his helplessness. On this, the Principal wrote four words on different slips, folded them and asked Yogesh's brother accompanying him to draw a slip. That slip bore the word "Atal". And that became his pen name. Yogesh replaced *Sharma* by *Atal* as his last name. This inspired some other young students of the College who wrote poetry and short stories to follow suit. They also decided to have pen names. A few names were written on chits and the lots were drawn, and each adopted the name that figured in the slip of the draw. That is how Shankar Lal became Shankar "Krandan". Yogesh's surname "Atal" sticks till now. That was his first victory over caste.

From where did he get the taste for creative writing in literature? I once asked him. Then the lines of the English poet came to memory: "Our sweetest songs are those that tell of saddest thought". One could recall the buff of Tulsidas' wife as well in castigating the husband to show equal love to the Almighty as was being shown to a woman! The moment that made Yogesh turn to the pen came when he felt the pain at seeing his younger brother being somewhat ill-treated by his stepmother! The requisite sensitivity having been generated, the grip over the linguistic expression made him a popular member of the city's literary group. His short story, *Asman to bahut phata*—'the clouds have lots of holes' and cannot be patched, became very popular. It was printed in the College magazine, and also broadcast from All India Radio, Jaipur. A non-believer in taking medicines then, he felt indisposed and was made to take tablets. On getting well through a semi-critical period he exclaimed in a small poem *Goli Khakar Main Zinda Hoon*[1] at a party held on his recovery. It looked as if Yogesh Atal was on his way to becoming a creative writer and that Hindi literature could be the channel for the same for graduation and post-graduation. But this was not to be. At his B.A., he chose Sociology as one of his options along with Hindi and Economics.

The all important question is how do the aspirations of the youth get shaped or their direction get decided when they have alternative role models before them. The student could opt from any of the three optional subjects offered at the B.A. level to pursue his Masters programme. In making such a selection, a student's own perception of the life-chances mattered. His own inclinations or self-perception for the suitability and liking were significant, particularly in case of brilliant students. Resources of the family were a constraint. Amidst all these it also became crucial as to which type of teachers and their style of teaching had an appeal. And then the results of the examinations too could shift the balance. As a student in Lucknow University, I distinctly remember the teachers from different subjects influencing us; yet the greatest attraction was D.P. Mukerji who took classes in B.A. Part I and convinced us of the limited extent to which a subject like Economics could provide understanding even of economic forces at work. He could say 'Price of a shoe in Hazratganj—a posh market in Lucknow, is Rs. x; in Aminabad—a medium status market in Lucknow—the price of the same is Rs. x_2; in Chowk, Rs. x_4' and so on. He could use apt illustrations from every day life to clarify a point, and draw upon references from literary figures to present a near holistic picture. Some of us were certainly attracted to him, as also by the galaxy of teachers like D.N. Majumdar and Radha Kamal Mukerjee. Then on one occasion, Majumdar told us that the choice of a subject or place of study at the Master's level could depend on the quality of the teacher, and one could go anywhere for the purpose. I used this advice on my own selection of the university where I could go to avail of a Population Council Fellowship to the USA. "Where would you like to work?" was the question at the Interview Board and I said, "Wherever Kingsley Davis is." "That is University of California," I was told. And that became my option. I went to the University of California to be the student of Kingsley Davis. In the case of Yogesh Atal, his performance at the B.A. level in various tests and presentations distinguished himself from the rest; he participated in field trips, wrote small papers, and presented one to the first Rajasthan Sociological Conference, we had organized in Maharana Bhopal College, Udaipur in 1955. The late Professors K.M. Kapadia (who presided over it) and I.P. Desai lent grace to the Conference. Their encouragement further instilled in us sociological insights. Yogesh Atal's interests and inclinations for the subject began by going through the reading of *Society* by MacIver and Page and then recently released *Indian Village* of S.C. Dube. With performance in the examinations at the top level, he was sure to get admission in the newly opened M.A. classes in sociology at the College. But I advised him to go to Sagar and study with S.C. Dube. That was a difficult decision. I had to convince his grandfather of the difference it would make. When he asked as to why am I advising him to go to Sagar when Sociology was now being offered in Udaipur itself. I told him in reply: "Here he will be running after a job, from there jobs will flow towards him". "Why Sagar?" was still the query, as it was distant. Making a pun on Sagar (sea) I replied: "if I had my way, I would send him across the sea". That settled the matter and Yogesh went to study Anthropology under Professor S.C. Dube at the residential university of Sagar.

Dube exercised great influence on the younger talented minds of India at that time, and encouraged them to feel confident. As an excellent teacher with competence in the latest trends in the subject, and an avid reader of books till 2 a.m. at home, he cast a spell over his students. His lectures were interspersed with what he called 'absurd illustrations'—that is down-to-earth examples. His diction, both spoken and written, had its own authenticity. Though Fowler's *Usage of English* was always at hand, he hardly needed opening it. His expression was clear and simple and his capacities as an able teacher were superb. All these had an influence on the young minds. Additionally, Sagar was a place where a small group of teachers—hardly half a dozen—frequently met to discuss the complex philosophical issues, which used to be neatly summarized by Daya Krishna of the Philosophy Department. University library was respectable with the availability of all prominent journals. For example, Srinivas' article on "Dominant Caste" published in the *American Anthropologist* was available soon after its publication. Besides this, Dube enjoyed drawing room conversations where he had stories to tell about most of the sociologists of the country, including their styles of life. I myself joined that University for a year and found myself taking care of some teaching and dissertations at the Master's level. Dube had a unique sense of feeling the pulse of emerging questions in sociology in the world at large and their relevance for India. He guided the students along those channels thereby encouraging and equipping them to work in the advanced fields. Some of them could seize the opportunity and acquire self-confidence. Yogesh Atal was one of them; others—and there were quite a few of them—interpreted the ease and cordiality with which Dube mixed with them as if nearness could also extend to the academic domain, and got disappointed for various reasons. Dube wanted the students in the late 1950s to work on the Changing Frontiers of Caste, Unity and Extensions of the Village, and such related themes which had put him in the limelight through his work at Cornell. *The Indian Village* (1955) was followed by *India's Changing Villages* (1958) and the field work tradition linked to changing societal concerns. Dube used his opportunities as Director of the National Institute of Community Development (first at Mussorie and then at Hyderabad), and later of the Indian Institute of Advanced Study, Shimla to bring together intellectuals of the country, spot growing talents, and to organize seminars and conferences to initiate debate and discussion among the academics across disciplines on matters of social concerns. Dube continued his fascination for neatness of production both of personalities and the works that made him the centerpiece of social pursuits in the country for decades. One of the American anthropologists told me about Dube that "he writes like one of us", and no doubt the *Indian Village* had tremendous readership outside India. Then Dube showed his brilliance in Hindi literature and this brought young Yogesh Atal into still more empathic touch with him, a relationship that continued all through Dube's life and even after. Yogesh

Atal's interactions with S.C. Dube were marked by a process of learning and thinking and getting accustomed to academic and executive functions. The youngster became an effective teacher in Chandigarh and Agra.

The visit to the United States in 1964 on a Smith-Mundt Fellowship and a Fulbright Travel Grant in 1964-65 added to Atal's capacity for undertaking exercises in collating and interpreting secondary data and planning for researches "beyond the village". His association with Paul Lazarsfeld and Robert K. Merton made him an interesting learner in the process of research in which an empirical expert joined issues with a theoretician. This made it possible for Atal to plan for an inquiry into the local communities and national politics, which in point of time marked a systematic effort in the growing area of political sociology as well as election studies in India. It also marked the stage whereby a trained social anthropologist acquired sociological sophistication in the choice of the theme, linking the local with the state and the national scene, and introducing panel studies as technique of social research at the operational level in India. From Merton, more specifically, Yogesh drew a new source of inspiration as a teacher who would take a newspaper cutting for the day, and go on explaining the nuances of sociological formulations through it, the manner in which history of ideas and science could be traced to seventeenth and eighteenth century sources, and the ever continuing interest in classics, with Merton feeling the need to have one more look into Durkheim's works, besides the concepts like functions and dysfunctions—manifest and latent—that effortlessly became a part of the vocabulary. Yogesh Atal's recent article on "Managing Multiplicity" (published in the *Economic and Political Weekly* of 9 September 2001) received personal notice of Merton who complimented Atal for making a significant step in the extension of his formulations on Insiders and Outsiders to a situation like the one in India.

Beyond the academic arena, Yogesh Atal conducted himself with dignity as a Director at the Indian Council of Social Science Research (ICSSR) from where he graduated to become UNESCO's Regional Director for Social Sciences in Asia and the Pacific and then working at the headquarters in Paris as Principal Director of Social Sciences till his retirement in 1997. He was actively engaged in macro-level studies in India on the (i) perception of national threat during the Chinese invasion, (ii) a series of election studies covering various states of the country, and (iii) study of educational problems of the children of Scheduled Castes and Scheduled Tribes. The tenure with the ICSSR brought him under the guidance of an able administrator of the quality of J.P. Naik, who was well known for his dexterity in dealing with the files, his grip over details, particularly in the educational field, and his acceptability by the greats in social sciences and administration. At short notice, he could produce documented texts for important addresses to be delivered by the cabinet minister. Yogesh Atal imbibed quite a few of these qualities, yet assiduously kept himself away from the simple Gandhian style of life that had become a hallmark of J.P. Naik's personality. What mattered, however, was the work culture. The placement also meant increased meaningful relations with the prominent social scientists, philosophers, and historians of the country. A seminar organized at the Indian Institute of Advanced Study, Shimla, brought scholars from Asian region together, creating the climate for an initiative for Asia. The word reached UNESCO headquarters in Paris where the idea of the Asian Regional Office was mooted and the young Atal who had delivered the goods in practice was picked up for the position of its director, of course after due advertisement and recruitment process. A stint of training in the French language, and then training in UNESCO culture of work made Yogesh an effective administrator. Success at an early age made Yogesh Atal a talking point in drawing room conversations amongst professionals. As UNESCO Adviser for Asia and the Pacific, Yogesh Atal helped social science organizations of different countries of the region, establishing relations with such social scientists as mattered cutting across disciplines. He could pick up a political scientist from the Philippines where he had a significant role to assume in the country's polity, could observe the recycling process of irrigation and electricity generation in North Korea, besides getting entry into China and Pakistan through his diplomatic passport, thereby informing himself of the areas hitherto not familiar to the Indian social scientists. I was happy to learn from the Vice-Chancellor of the New England University in Australia of his appreciation of a UNESCO official in the person of Yogesh Atal, a relationship he mentioned to clinch support for a proposal mooted at a seminar in Sydney. And this was in the absence of Atal. While doing a stock taking of Asian Social Science, Yogesh Atal hit the nail on the head when he said, "Asian social scientists are geographically proximate and culturally close, but they are academically remote from each other". Even the limited access was through the Western scholarship both in ideas and methods. This made him rethink on the need for *Indigenization* of social sciences, a theme on which the Asian social scientists concentrated their attention, his Paper providing the impetus. At the international fora, now the stress on national sociologies is being discussed, and we are asked to provide a sort of justification for being 'Indians' in terms of our concerns and approaches that could be our trade-mark. It is one of the ironies of circumstances that the initial sustained work put into this debate by a social scientist working through an international agency has yet to be noticed in this country, leave aside recognized.

Beyond the Asia-Pacific region, Yogesh Atal conducted seminars on rural-urban articulations at the inter-continental level in New Delhi and Nairobi, with contributions being published first through the *International Social Science Journal* (Paris), and reproduced in several languages.

Atal retired from UNESCO after playing a major role as UNESCO's co-coordinator for the World Summit for Social Development held in Copenhagen in March 1995. As follow-up to the Summit, he encouraged a series of studies on Poverty in the former Socialist block, and came out with the very first publication under the title *Poverty in Transition and Transition in Poverty.*

On retirement he has begun to serialize his experiences for various publications. He returned to his pet theme in Political Sociology and researched the 1999 elections in India that brought back Vajpayee to power. That book, titled as *Mandate for Political Transition,* compares the manifestoes of contending political parties, essays the success of the BJP and its alliances and cautions them on dangers of over-enthusiasm in certain directions. This is once again a work on macro dimension in India with newspapers providing data, but the author insists, during my conversations with him, that anthropological insights pervade his interpretations, a claim that I would not accede to with the felicity with which it is offered. With a computer at hand, Yogesh Atal sets and re-sets his contributions to provide timely pieces for publication in areas where he thinks social scientists have the capacity to work, but are somehow shying away from making timely interventions.

I may now specify a few of the areas where his hard serious work could have received greater recognition. His analysis of group alliances cutting across castes in a village, and the application of a theoretical construct of 'basic or pivotal', 'sufficiently relevant', and 'peripheral' attributes to the nature of caste as a unit and a system, that figures in his work on *The Changing Frontiers of Caste,* comes in that category. The link between the rural, town, and urban centre to see the impact of communication on election choices, and his use of the panel technique for the first time in Indian sociology for election studies are significant in his second work titled *Local Communities and National Politics*. His paper on "The Call for Indigenization" deserves to be noted. Expanding the frontiers of sociology to nations as units and the relevance of the Asia-Pacific region, as also the exercises to research issues relative to development and poverty are other contributions of Atal that deserve to be acknowledged. Beyond the academic areas, there lies the effort on the part of an Indian social scientist (Yogesh Atal) working and surviving in a highly surcharged atmosphere of power games in an international organization by taking initiatives wherever he could and advance to an extent even national interests there, rubbing shoulders with academic politicians of sister countries.

Yogesh Atal's journey through life has been initially marked by an aspiring young student accustomed to lead in matters academic, literary, and oratorical skills that kept him going amidst a lower middle class family. His brilliance was recognized by his teachers and fellow students which earned for him praise as well as envy. The early impressions continue to dominate their assessment even to this day and quite a few people in his own time remember the days when he was their equal or even economically less comfortable than themselves. The theory of cognitive dissonance, of recognizing the person at his lowest points and discarding all positive gains, is quite visibly operative in his case. For his own family and kins he became a role model, to be emulated in a case or two, or to be used as a ladder for their own growth. Others in the kingroup enjoy being just sharers of the advantages arising from his position, or emanating from his prosperity. To his credit, it must be said that there are only a few families in which a rising star has taken care of the sensitivities and life chances of one's kin—consanguineal and affinal, or shared prosperity as he has done, despite all talk of the breakdown of the joint family and kin obligations. The little portion of life he spent as a teacher carried the goodwill of students in ample measure, and he took pains to improve their life chances. At times, the recipients of the good offices overstated their claims, made him improve their performance as well as returns with such a persuasion that the generous teacher could not refuse to respond. He edited the scripts meticulously, would at times insert a few things that in his own estimate made things more presentable or impressive. Yet he would not grant the editors of his own script that liberty.

Atal reached the high point in educational administration in UNESCO, remembers his time with the Directors-General—A.M. M'Bow and Federico Mayor, a few Prime Ministers or heads of governments whom he met at UN meets, and a galaxy of academicians from different continents. He fondly recalls his conversations and classroom contacts with Robert Merton, Paul Lazarsfeld, Amitai Etzioni, William J. Goode, Bernard Barber, academicians of the caliber of Rudolfo Stavenhagen and Roger Batra of Mexico. He played hosts to several dignitaries visiting Bangkok or Paris. He recalls the personal care with which M.N. Srinivas extended courtesies in both academic and personal relations.

Atal is today comfortably placed as a retired UNESCO civil servant that makes him unfit to hold any position where the honorarium is calculated as emoluments less than the pension, for that would come to a negative amount. He has a decent house in Gurgaon where he continues reading, writing, drafting things for various Addresses for which he is sought—his oratorical skills both in Hindi and English and seminar interventions being sought for. Yet amidst all these measures of success an undercurrent of dissatisfaction is visible, of not being recognized duly either by the establishment of Indian Sociology professionally or academically. Considered as a man of success, or a 'great man' by the youngsters in the profession, tolerable by the peer group, and 'also there' by the elderly as a sum total of their own visions—academic and personal—Yogesh Atal continues to lead an active life with its pleasures and tiffs, in a manner he has defined for himself.

NOTE

1. I am alive after taking—which could also mean-bullets, a euphemism in Hindi.

2

A Personal Note

LEELA DUBE

This is a small note to celebrate the happy occasion of Yogesh Atal's felicitation by his students, professional colleagues, workmates and friends. His beloved teacher, who initiated him into sociology and has had a special place in his life, is also collaborating in the venture.

How should I look at myself here? A teacher? Wife of someone whom Yogesh considered his mentor? A mother figure? A professional colleague? A part of a common kinship network? Or a mix of all these capacities and many more that emerged as occasions demanded?

I first met Yogesh when, on the advice of Dr. B.R. Chauhan, he ventured to come to Sagar in Madhya Pradesh to join the Department of Anthropology at the University of Sagar. This was the year 1957, and Yogesh' was the first batch of masters students in the freshly constituted Department headed by Professor S.C. Dube. In fact, it was S.C. Dube's *Indian Village*, first published in 1955, that had goaded Dr. Chauhan to almost push Yogesh, his most promising pupil, to leave Udaipur to come to Sagar, a small, out of the way place, reached through a loop line of the railway network.

On the very day he entered the Department, Yogesh was brought home by Professor Dube. Fair, lean and thin, Yogesh had a boyish, glowing face and an eager countenance. We spent some time at the dining table and then in the living room, where Yogesh recited a few poems of his. One could easily gather that he had come to Sagar with great expectations and yet with many apprehensions.

The Department was understaffed, the content of some courses had been changed, and I was fully qualified to teach and to guide students in research. So I had started teaching, though in an honorary capacity. Professor Dube was not inclined to have me on his faculty on a regular basis, for he did not want to be charged with nepotism (then a feature of the U.S. academic culture). I taught Yogesh only in M.A. Previous. Some of his batchmates who did their masters dissertations under my guidance in the M.A. Final year and interacted with me closely, looked upon me as their teacher.

I wonder, therefore, if there is any justification in my looking upon Yogesh as my student. At the same time, association with him during the two years of his M.A. was continuous, though in a way indirect. I was closely linked to the process of building up the Department and would participate in its multifarious activities—academic, non-academic, mundane, infrastructural. And since our home tended to become an extension of the Department, communication with students was perceived as a significant aspect of the familial rhythm.

Whenever Yogesh came home, he received attention and care from me, perhaps more so because I had gathered from Professor Dube that he had lost his mother while yet a child. I did nothing special which might appear discriminatory to his batchmates, but Yogesh happened to present many more occasions for receiving care and affection from me. His multiple interests, enthusiasm and eagerness to learn, and his capabilities and willingness to render assistance to Professor Dube made his visits regular and long. For instance, he participated in the literary activities that went on at our residence, also accessing recent publications in Hindi literature. He looked for offprints and not easily available books in our personal library, came forward to systematize scattered papers from conferences and seminars, and rendered competent assistance to Professor Dube in his on-going work in Hindi. He was ever eager to discuss with Professor Dube not only issues that came up in course work, but more importantly the exciting and vexing points in the current debates in the twin disciplines.

My close interaction with Yogesh began when, immediately after his M.A. Final exams, he joined as a Research Assistant in the research project on Leadership, Communication and Decision-Making financed by the Research Programmes Committee of the Planning Commission. As its Deputy Director, I worked closely with the Supervisor, T.R. Singh, and Yogesh (other Research Assistants joined a little later).

Keeping in mind the themes and related issues to be explored, we prepared our plan of action and proceeded to the already chosen area, a Tehsil in Sagar District. Fortified by discussions with officials in the Community Development Programme in the Tehsil town, we proceeded on a whirlwind tour of the villages that appeared to have the potential for final inclusion in the project. With carefully prepared points for interrogation and exploration through other means, we undertook a quick survey of a number of villages before arriving at the final selection of four villages.

This phase had needed a quick comprehension of the features of different villages and their evaluation, in reference to our objectives, along with a consideration of their accessibility and practical conveniences, including the willingness of the local people to cooperate with our project. This was a complicated activity, demanding a workable feel of both the field and the conceptual issues involved.

In the hectic activity, both in the field and in the project office in the University, I could see Yogesh' perceptiveness, initiative and limitless capacity for hard work. He enjoyed hard work, was remarkably quick on the uptake and had an ability to negotiate with the local people and to seize the clues that vaguely emerged, both during fieldwork and during analysis.

Besides doing fieldwork in the village assigned to him, Yogesh participated in the collective activities of the project even after he began teaching in the Department. For one and a half years he was closely associated with the work of the project and made a very substantial contribution. Indeed, the conjunction of fieldwork as a total activity and conceptual and theoretical inputs gave a clear indication of his multi-dimensional potentialities in the academic field and also as a person. I missed his presence when he left for Chandigarh.

This narration about our research project might appear *trite ad pedestrian* to some high-brow intellectuals; but its purpose is to assert that the potentials assessed at that point of time more than proved themselves within a fairly short period and perhaps also that the ground was being prepared for Yogesh' future achievements.

In continuation of the above assertion it would be appropriate to refer to Yogesh' ambitious and imaginative research endeavour around 1967, pursued while he was in Agra. Conceived and executed by him, the research project "Communication Links and Patterns of Political Participation" constituted a study of the 1967 elections in Etah district of Uttar Pradesh. It demonstrated his daring in entering an entirely new field and his initiative in devising or modifying efficacious techniques of investigation and analysis. He came up with unprecedented results that challenged earlier assumptions about caste and politics. The book based on this study (Atal, 1971) was the first work of psephology by an Indian sociologist, and the first in which the technique of panel study had been employed and a series of indexes constructed on political awareness, participation and opinion. The book received much appreciation and was used by researchers and teachers (S.N. Jha, personal communication). Norman D. Palmer (1975) referred to Atal's work in glowing terms. To quote just one sentence, "My debt to Dr. Atal's ground-breaking study of elections and political development in three communities in a district of Uttar Pradesh is obvious in the following pages" (p. viii).

After leaving Sagar, Yogesh moved from one place to another, occupying different positions in a variety of institutions and organizations, national and international. This is not an inventory of his publications or of the positions he has held. However, from the viewpoint of someone who has seen him at different times, in different circumstances, functioning in different situations, I would like to make a few observations.

Yogesh accepted the challenges that posed themselves and turned them into opportunities. He adapted himself to different kinds of work, positions and institutions and to their varied ethos. At the same time, through imagination, the use of wide perspectives and incessant effort, he brought in innovations, thus expanding the content and scope of the positions he held and of the work associated with them. This is apparent in what he did at the IIT, in the ICSSR, and during the UNESCO period. Many innovations aimed at improvement and enrichment may not look harmless or workable, and so capacious initiative and imagination in formulating one's ideas, skilful presentation and negotiation and persuasive follow-up are required to make others agreeable to them. Wherever he was, Yogesh succeeded in somewhat altering the character of positions and the content of jobs and of the on-the-ground programmes.

When based in Southeast Asia, Yogesh expanded the activities of the UNESCO Centre for Social Sciences in Asia and the Pacific and initiated and executed a number of projects and programmes involving collaboration of scholars, activists and other professionals from different countries. This is clearly reflected in the list of his publications. After moving to Paris, Yogesh' field of operations changed, and so did his concerns and related programmes. But there also he made his mark.

All along, while working for different organizations, Yogesh did not leave his own academic pursuits. After his return to India he has become more active in the twin disciplines. I shall be happier if he begins thinking seriously about enriching social science literature in Hindi, a language in which he has great facility.

In passing I may make an observation that is very personal. Yogesh is very affectionate towards the members of his extended kinship network. He does not differentiate between those who have done very well in life and those who have not done well or who are confined to their small towns and middle class situations. Perhaps, I suspect, he is more concerned about those who are needy.

Yogesh has his weaknesses but he himself is affected by them the most. Why play them up here? Let him express some of them in his poems.

During all these years, my ties with Yogesh have sustained themselves. I do not wish to analyse how and why they were sustained. Surely the relation began through a powerful link, but then gradually acquired a dyadic character, and continue to be so, although often expressed through some kind of mediation. One cannot measure the depth or assess the quality of such relations. They are there for good.

I convey my blessings to Yogesh for many more active years and good health.

REFERENCES

Atal, Yogesh. *Local Communities and National Politics*. Delhi: National Publishing House, 1971.

Palmer, Norman D. *Elections and Political Development: The South Asian Experience*. Delhi: Vikas Publishing House, 1975.

3

Yogesh Atal: Through A Friend's Eye

JAINENDRA K. DOSHI

I have known Professor Yogesh Atal since school days. He was of course one year ahead of me. We both joined Maharana Bhopal College in Udaipur, in the mid-fifties. Dr. Yogesh Atal made his mark in college days as a debater and a poet. Not only he won several prizes in various debate and poetry competitions at the college level, he brought laurels to the college by winning prizes at the state and national levels too. At the Sagar University, where he moved for his post-graduation he was instantly recognized as an outstanding public speaker. In the literary circles, first in Rajasthan and later in Madhya Pradesh, he was admired as a promising poet and an essayist. As a founder member of Jagrat Sahitya Samiti in Udaipur, he encouraged young talented youth to contribute to Hindi literature. Many among them earned name as poets and writers.

Though poetry continued as a passion for Atal, his interest in sociological writing in later years overtook and he carved out a career for himself as a sociologist of international renown. Beginning as a teaching assistant at Sagar University he soon became a full time faculty member. Soon he was appointed at the Panjab University. From there he went to teach at Agra University and at IIT Delhi. He left IIT to become, Director of Sociology at the Indian Council of Social Science Research (ICSSR). Finally, he was hired by UNESCO to become its first Regional Adviser for Social and Human Sciences in Asia and the Pacific.

I am, however less inclined to talk about his accolades in the academe, as I am sure there are more competent persons who can better described his journeys and landmarks in the territory of social sciences.

In his formative years Dr. Atal had major influence on his personality of three individuals—his faher Daulat Ram, Professor B.R. Chauhan and Professor S.C. Dube. He was very fond and proud of his father who retired as a station master in the Western Railway. Dr. Atal paid his tributes to his father by writing a book 'Daulat Darbar—the story of a Station Master'. That book reveals Atal, both as a son and a sociologist.

Professor Chauhan groomed him as a sociologist and instilled in him a strong orientation for fieldwork. Late Professor Dube became his mentor and a role model. Some of his close friends would not hesitate in describing him as Professor Dube's spiritual and academic heir. I regard both Dube and Atal as great teachers and scholars. Like Professor Dube, Dr. Atal is also very articulate and writes with equal facility in English and Hindi. Professor Dube was sophisticated and highly cultivated individual and connoisseur of art and literature, so is Yogesh Atal.

In my M.A. final year (1960) Atal joined the Department faculty to teach us Advanced Social Anthropology. He was also my thesis supervisor. Those were the pre-computer days. After finishing a forty-days stint of field work in tribal Rajasthan, when I returned to the University with my bagful of notes, it was Dr. Atal who guided me in the analysis and reporting. When the manuscript was nearly ready, he helped me even when it was being typed. We both would go from the hostel to the Department soon after supper where a clerk would be waiting for us to type the manuscript. The whole process of writing thesis went like this. I would first write a chapter in long hand, pass it on to Dr. Atal, who after scrutinizing for sentence construction, analysis and style of writing would suggest changes to finalize the script. On many days Atalji, the typist, and I worked past midnight. Not even once Dr. Atal made me feel that he was doing any favour to me by devoting so much of his time to my work. I have also not kept record of the number of cups of tea and coffee I drank in his hostel room during that period.

In 1982 when I was teaching at the Indian Institute of Mass Communication, he visited us at my residence in South Extension in Delhi. Till then I had no opportunity to travel abroad. Some how this came up in our conversation. Only a few days later, an offer. came to me from Asia-Pacific Institute for Broadcasting Development (AIBD) in Malaysia to come as a resource person for a seminar on development communication. I knew that this was arranged by him. But never in our personal conversation did he make any mention of this favour. In his vocabulary 'obligation' was not the word among friends. My participation in AIBD opened the doors for international interaction. AIBD hired me as a consultant for their training programme in Audience Research that took me even to Pakistan.

Though I don't remember the dates precisely, I was the organizing secretary of a session on Culture, Communication and Development in the World Anthropological Conference in Delhi. I had requested Dr. Atal to deliver the Key-note Address in that session. He took the pain to come all the way from Bangkok to deliver the Address. When I met him just before the session, he humorously told me, "Jainendra I have got this suit stitched only for this occasion". He would go any distance to make his friends happy. Friendship is a most cherished value for Dr. Atal.

During a maiden foreign tour to Kuala Lumpur for participation in AIBD Seminar, in 1979 or 1980 I made a stopover in Bangkok. I wanted to spend a couple of days with Dr. Atal's family there. He saw to it that I was properly received at the airport. During my stay with him he did everything to make me feel at home and overcome all anxiety of a maiden foreign assignment. He and his family took me around for shopping and sight-seeing. Despite my insistence to pay him back for shopping, he refused to accept. On another occasion, while returning from Kuala Lumpur perforce I had to break journey at Bangkok. Though none of his members of the family, was in Bangkok, I stayed in his house and his neighbour, a UNESCO employee and his colleague, completely took charge of my stay and food and dropped me at the airport on the day of my departure.

One remarkable quality of Dr. Atal is his cool headedness and not being vindictive or revengeful even to his opponents and adversaries. Even his opponents and critics will vouch for his generosity, magnanimity, and lack of ill-feelings for others. He is certainly a large hearted person. That is the reason that he has such a wide circle of admirers in various walks of life. One likeable thing about Dr. Atal has been that success has not gone into his head. Despite touching phenomenal heights in his career, his friends feel completely at home in his company. He cuts jokes, tells anecdotes, and pampers his friends. I don't think he has cultivated these qualities. He is a genuinely sincere, well-meaning, and warm hearted person. He is at home with young and old. No doubt he is such a good conversationalist.

Though he continued interacting with scholars and leaders in academics even after joining UNESCO, I personally feel that it was a great loss to the Indian academic world. Had he continued to teach in India, he would have had a whole generation of students following him as a role model. Of course it could be said to his credit that during his tenure with UNESCO he always encouraged young scholars and enjoyed their respect and love.

Dr. Atal's qualities of a good human being—a good son, protective but a democratic father, an extremely understanding and an exemplary husband, a warm hearted friend, a good student, and equally a good teacher make him a special person, different altogether from a common specie. In this world of cut-throat competition, rat race, a genuine person like Dr. Atal is indeed a rare specie. All his friends and admirers are proud of him. We also wish him a long and active long life to inspire the younger generation for years to come.

Besides being an intellectual, Dr. Atal has also broadcast several talks and participated in discussions on radio and T.V. Having a rich baritone voice of a broadcaster, he easily became the darling of broadcast houses. In my opinion, if he had not taken to anthropology, he would have made an excellent carrier in broadcasting. He would still be remembered for his analysis of election results' on T.V. in the 1970's much before stalwarts like Pranoy Roy and Vinod Dua made their appearance.

On a concluding not I would like to quote a few lines of one of his poems he had penned in his adolescence. गगन से टपका नहीं मिट्टी से बना है, इसका हर पल मिट्टी से सना है।

(loosely translated, it would mean that no one is so high and mighty. In reality human beings are product of this earth and hence should always be aware of this). Recently, sitting in his study room in a posh locality of Delhi I had the privilege of listening to some of his recent poems. These poems reflect different moods of the man—sometimes shattered, sometimes broken, other times looking straight into the eyes of death and mocking it.

Looking at the man one can't escape the feeling of being face-to-face with colossus and humble Yogesh Atal.

4

Rendezvous in Paris

JAGDISH KUMAR PUNDIR

It was my first visit to Paris for a brief sojourn to do comparative research that I had the opportunity of meeting Professor Yogesh Atal. When I was preparing for the trip, I was advised by many friends and colleagues to have a rendezvous with him. My teacher, Professor Brij Raj Chauhan, who was incidentally also teacher of Professor Atal, has instructed me to the effect that my stay in Paris will be incomplete if I did not meet him. Knowing of his high position in UNESCO, I was also a bit apprehensive about the prospects of our meeting. Soon after my landing in Paris and reaching at the Maison de l'lnde (India House), I told my hosts about my eagerness to contact him. Unfortunately, when I phoned him he was not home. Next day, I tried to reach him in his office once again from the Maison des Sciences de I'Homme. I was lucky to get him on the other side. Surprisingly he immediately invited me to visit him at his office at my convenience. Knowing that I was a stranger and not conversant with the French language, Dr. Atal took the trouble giving me elaborate directions to reach his office.

When I arrived his office on the appointed day and time, I was received by his Secretary in his absence. He had been called for an urgent meeting by the Director-General of UNESCO, but he took care to instruct his Secretary to receive me and even offered a cup of coffee. When he arrived he apologised for the absence and then shot the first question in a humorous manner: "Am I a good guide"? I hope you were not lost". Professor Atal was unexpectedly humble and nice and put me at ease. I was already mesmerized by the setting of his chamber in the elegant UNESCO building. His hospitality and warm reception diluted all my hesitation of the first real encounter. Because of our common bond through Professor Chauhan it was natural for him to enquire about the latter's health and welfare. In fact, he immediately dialled Professor Chauhan in Udaipur to inform him of my arrival. That also gave me the opportunity to speak to our common teacher.

Leaving aside his work, Dr. Atal took me to UNESCO campus spread into seven buildings. I was keen to see the auditorium from where Shri Narsimha Rao the Prime Minister of India had delivered the Mahatma Gandhi Memorial lecture that was compared by Professor Atal and seen live on Indian television.

Professor Atal must have thought that I was missing my Indian meal. He therefore took me to a restaurant, run by a Pakistani in the vicinity of UNESCO. We had to walk nearly a kilometre to reach our destination. I was surprised to find that the owner greeted Professor Atal as "uncle" and conversed with him in urdu. We had a sumptuous Indian vegetarian meal with complement of French wine, Professor Atal told me that in France no meal is regarded complete without a glass of wine. He also remarked that while the owner is Muslim from Pakistan, he cannot run the restaurant without serving liquor? In business religious considerations are conveniently over looked. When self interests are involved religion recedes into the background.

A busy man that he was, occupying the position of Principal Director, Dr. Atal found time to receive and entertain me. While extending hospitality and showing me the UNESCO buildings Dr. Atal did not forget to enquire about my academic interests. He made my Paris visit very memorable indeed, for which I will remain grateful for ever.

5

Sandwich Culture: A Case for Study

SANKET ATAL

I had a unique upbringing. There are not many people in this world who have had the privilege of growing up in many countries, surrounded by intellectuals, attending the best schools, and having a world class Social Anthropologist as a father and a friend. It has been an interesting journey…

Since as far back as I can remember, I have always taken great pleasure in explaining the meaning of my name. *Sanket* means an indication or a hint and *Atal* means adamant — a perfect name for the fifth and final progeny. This also leads into the discussion of how the family name became Atal. After denying any relationship to politicians with Atal in their name, I go into the story of how Uday Nand Sharma became Yogesh Atal – Professor Chauhan discusses this in his contribution to this *festschrift*. Briefly Atal is the pen name adopted by my father at the age of 14 to replace the caste name used as a suffix; at that time he did not know that he had a talent for poetry. Strangely, it has now become a family name. Even my grandfather used it once while making a gift to Professor Dube on his first visit to Udaipur. "From Atal Parivar" he inscribed on the gift-wrap; this prompted Professor Dube to remark: "this is perhaps the first instance where the father is adopting the surname of his son!!" This is how a personal name adopted as a revolt against caste has become a family name that may turn into a lineage. One of my sisters has decided to use this surname even after her marriage. This individual instance has been particularly helpful in my discussions with non-Indians who had been curious about the state of the caste system in India. Ours is a family that has not only shunned the caste name but also taken lead in arranging inter-caste marriages. My father is an authority on Caste, having worked for his Ph.D. on this subject, but he has also worked toward its dissolution. How aptly did he title his monograph as *The Changing Frontiers of Caste*. He is indeed a Frontiers Man — as he always explored new frontiers even in his academic pursuits.

One of my earliest memories of spending time with one of Bapu's intellectual friends is that of debating with Professor S. C. Dube. He was almost a member of the family, treating my father not only as his student but also as a son. During one of his visits to our house in New Delhi, he saw that I was carrying around a bottle of nail polish. To ensure that I wouldn't actually put on nail polish, he said, "*Nail polish lagaaney sey moochhey nahin aati*" (if one applies nail polish, one doesn't develop a moustache). I tried to convince him otherwise but was to no avail. He would also tutor me to say "*Buddhey Pipe Pee*" (old man, smoke your pipe). I still have fond memories of sitting in uncle's lap while he engaged in discussions with Bapu. Years later, when I designed the cover page for one of his books edited by my father, I chose to draw a portrait of him *without* a pipe — which was his prominent distinguishing mark. That is how I wanted to see him; and I was happy that he approved of the cover design. I always knew that he did not treat me as a parrot; for, he always encouraged everyone to think for himself. When I was getting married, and Professor Dube came on a wheel chair to bless us, I showed him my nails to remind that I have followed his instructions about the use of nail polish, although I was clean-shaven.

That was the climate I grew up — free to interact and even cut jokes with elders.

Words are not simply words to me. Having discussed the beauty of language and the subtlety of words with *Bapu* — that is how we children address him, and now even his brothers and other students address him the same way — throughout my life, I have developed a keen appreciation for the power of the pen. Whether it was the discussion of his "Quotable Quotes" (he called them QQs) or the search for the perfect word for a collection like this, he always made it a point to involve me.[1] He used to review poetry I wrote in seventh standard and made me feel like a master poet while pointing out ways I could improve. Along with his social science books, we had a wonderful collection of books for our generation. Reading and research became not just an activity for formal education; it became a way of life. With him, the Home became a surrogate School.

Bapu's vegetarianism is quite famous. Being a diplomat, he travelled to numerous countries and must have attended countless luncheons and dinners Whether it was a lavish gala in Beijing, or a fancy restaurant in Paris, he always looked for and ate only vegetarian fare. He stresses that his vegetarian diet is a cultural influence rather than a religious one and to prove his point he has tasted a morsel of chicken occasionally — I still don't understand how a Hindu can differentiate between religion and culture.

To immerse me in an Indian setting and to ensure my vegetarianism, he sent me to a boarding school, Sawan Public School, located on the out skirts of New Delhi. His friend, Anil Bordia, then Secretary of Education in the Government of India, had recommended the institution. It was a very interesting experience for me. I learned about various Indian religions, strict discipline (it was run by ex- NDA[2] people), homesickness, and the benefits and importance of a vegetarian diet. It was not long after I enrolled that I had my first taste of chicken, in a strictly vegetarian school where even teachers were not allowed to boil an egg in their homes. It is there that I had also taken a crash course in rebellion!

It was, again, in Sawan Public School that I realized for the first time that I was rather different, culturally, from the rest of the students. I could speak four languages — Hindi, English, Indonesian, and Thai. My personality was not as aggressive as the rest of the children — perhaps, a Thai influence. I had a father who was more of a friend than the fathers of most of my schoolmates. I never did quite fit in and couldn't figure out where I would fit in.

After three years of boarding school, I made the decision, all by myself, to move back to Bangkok. I wanted to spend the rest of the school days under Bapu's guidance because I knew that I wanted to go to the United States for college. My friends were shocked that I had been able to take this unilateral decision and that my father easily endorsed it. While communicating my decision to Bapu I cited the reasons that prompted me to leave India and join him again, and I also allayed his fears about how I would manage my stay, as he would be travelling on official mission half the time, with my mother staying in India with my sisters. Somehow he found the arguments convincing and honoured my decision. The International School I enrolled in Bangkok was heavily influenced and dominated by Americans. Thus began the next phase of Sandwich creation in my personality.

Being back in Bangkok was spectacular. I got to be with my family and also to enjoy the benefits of being Dr. Atal's son. We frequently had scholars stay with us when they came to Bangkok to attend seminars. I had the pleasure of spending a great deal of time with them. By far, the most memorable guest we had was Professor Moonis Raza who once stayed with us for one full month. That was the time when my mother was away in India and I was staying with my father along with one of my sisters —

Shuchi—who unfortunately died soon after. Each evening, after I fixed him his Cognac[3] with an ice-cube in it, we would sit and discuss anything that came to mind. The discussions ranged from music to politics to literature to Chinese culture. He was deferential to my opinions as was I to his. I am indebted to him for the profound affect he had in shaping my intellectual self. When he was returning to India I chose to go to the airport to see him off. In him, I saw the image of my grandfather.

Among the several issues that I discussed with Moonis uncle was the issue of Bapu's concept of Sandwich Culture, on which he was then doing a paper By then, I had heard numerous examples of how I was shaping up to be the poster-child for this Sandwich Culture concept. Putting the same concepts to use to analyze how Bapu had changed over the years, we realized that his culture had also evolved since he had moved abroad. Perhaps the affect of sandwiching on adults is a bit different than that on children but it definitely is there. It would be quite interesting to compare Dr. Atal circa 1975 (when he left India) with Dr. Atal circa 1997 (when he returned to India after retirement).

I left for my undergraduate studies at Cornell University in August of 1985. I made friends from my countries and also with people who had never left the United States. During my first month, I often got strange looks from people when I first met them. This perplexed me and I began to wonder whether there was something wrong with me, or perhaps that I was encountering some form of racism. It was a good friend of mine who finally opened my eyes. In Thailand, people are very gentle and soft spoken. It is common to touch your friend's arm, or shoulder, in a conversation and it is considered rude to shake hands too firmly. My American friends took my touchy-feely demeanor and my relatively limp handshake as a sign of effeminacy. I was very surprised at this reaction and made up my mind to adjust to the host culture right away.

I have always had to adapt to different environments and this was just another case of the same. Over time, I have become a Chameleon of sorts. My mannerisms, expressions and even my accent changes with the setting I am in. Once during a meeting in my Oracle office, I got an important phone call from India. All those attending the meeting heard me talking in English but with an Indian accent. After the call, I switched back to my Americanized accent and everyone found it quite remarkable. I had no idea I had just done this till they told me about it. Living in so many cultures has made me develop this ability to have a "different Sanket" for each culture. Some might view it as a sign of identity-confusion; I see it as a way of showing respect for the people I am dealing with.

There is a great deal of discrimination that I dealt with in the US. This discrimination, contrary to what one might imagine, was from other Indians. Being an Indian, who had grown up in many different cultures, my Indianness did not conform to expectations. The Indians who had come to the US directly from India found me to be quite different from them; for instance, I didn't know the first thing about Cricket. The Indians who had been born in the US also found me to be different — I could speak fluent Hindi, which they could not. As a result, it was very difficult for me, initially, to make Indian friends. It was only after I got married that I made Indian friends. My Indian bride gave me some semblance of validity and acceptability in the Indian community.

Everyone had expected that I would marry a non-Indian. I had gone to an American school in Thailand and then moved to the US for college. My friends were mostly non-Indians. I also had friends who were girls. In the eyes of most of my relatives, I was too Americanized to opt for the traditional method of getting hitched. Nobody realized the sense of emptiness I felt. Even my father was surprised when I asked him to find a bride for me. He selected this wonderful lass named Rachita and she became my *ardhangini* and his *bahu*. Despite his claims that he was very open minded and would accept anybody that I independently chose to marry, I know that Bapu was quite happy that I had him make this important decision in my life. His Americanized and rebellious son had behaved according to the norms of a traditional Hindu family.

Having grown up in the Atal household, I feel that I have a very different way of looking at life. My Sandwich Culture greatly helps me understand what my children are coping with, growing up in the States, and as American citizens. A number of my friends with children are going through the same set of issues that we went through when I was growing up. My prescription to them is to read a few of Bapu's papers on the topic.

As a person shaped by several variants of Indian Sandwich Cultures— the parent culture confronting different host cultures — I offer a good material for a case study to illustrate the powerful concept of Sandwich Culture authored by my father. Is that not a fitting tribute to Bapu and a social scientist of that distinction?

NOTES

1. His magic touch can be seen even in the title of this essay. I called it a *Case Study;* but he suggested the insertion of "*for*" between case and study making all the difference so subtly.
2. NDA stands for National Defence Academy.
3. That was his favourite sip, and he never crossed the limits. I realized how wrong the rumours were regarding his being "a drunkard"!!

6

Demonstration Effect

VINOD MEHTA

I met Dr. Yogesh Atal for the first time in 1969 when the Sociology Department of the University of Bombay was celebrating golden jubilee of its existence. Dr. Atal at that time was teaching at the Indian Institute of Technology, New Delhi while I was a Ph.D student in the Department.

Later on, he joined as a Director in the Indian Council of Social Science Research. Thereafter he joined UNESCO as Regional Advisor in the Regional Unit for Social and Human Sciences in Asia and the Pacific (RUSHSAP) Bangkok.

I joined ICSSR in 1981 long after Dr. Atal had left it. In December 1981, ICSSR was elected Secretary-General of the Association of Asian Social Science Research Councils (AASSREC) in Seoul. Dr. Atal had been associated with it since its inception and in fact AASSREC was his brainchild which was founded in India during a UNESCO sponsored Conference of Asian and Pacific Social Scientists organized by the ICSSR. The then Member-Secretary asked me to set-up and look after AASSREC secretariat. It was a new kind of experience for me. I was designated as Executive Secretary of AASSREC by the ICSSR. This gave me an opportunity to interact with him for a number of years and through this association, I quietly imbibed many ideas and approaches to work culture. It brought me in touch with the work culture of other countries. This was also the beginning of introduction to new technology in the ICSSR of which unwittingly I became an agent of change.

In the 1980s all the work in the ICSSR was being done on a manual typewriter; leave aside electronic typewriter, even electric typewriter was unknown. Photocopy was unheard off; cyclostyling was the watchword.

When the AASSREC secretariat was transferred to ICSSR from Korea the Member-Secretary asked me to get the minutes of the AASSREC meeting typed and circulate among all the member councils. I called my typist and asked him to cut the stencils and get them cyclostyled. Only the cover page was got printed from a press. I complimented myself for doing a good job; it was a shade better than the Council minutes.

After two months when Dr. Atal came to India on an official visit he chided me for the shoddy work I had done. Peeved, I said that this is what we have been doing in the ICSSR all along. He smiled and said that I was conveying a bad impression to the foreign member councils. Well I became defensive saying that with the available infrastructure in the office this is the best I could do. He asked me why don't I use electronic typewriter for official correspondence with the AASSREC members. Suddenly I blurted out, if he would give me funds to buy the new gadgets for AASSREC work? He asked me how much? I said just enough to buy an electronic typewriter and a photocopy machine. I made a proposal for the same and sent through the Member-Secretary to him in Bangkok. Within weeks I got the funds but it is another story that it took almost eight months to cross the bureaucratic hurdle to buy these two gadgets.

There was resistance from my steno on working on electronic machine. He would not leave the manual typewriter. I was left with no option but to do my own typing. My colleagues sneered at me that being an officer I was doing the work of a typist. But the work was so neat that the Member-Secretary also wanted his secretaries to use only electronic typewriters. Thereafter the member-Secretary's secretariat bought two electronic typewriters. The "demonstration effect" was so powerful that within one year almost every division had one electronic typewriter. This was followed by computer and other gadgets. Today almost every officer has a computer and a photocopier and other modern facilities in their rooms.

Apart from the introduction of new gadgets I had the occasion to learn many things about the organization of international conferences, office meetings and so on. During the meetings of the executive councils of AASSREC and biennial conferences it was my duty as executive secretary to prepare the resume of meeting and conferences. Here again Dr. Atal asked me to shed the bureaucratic approach to writing the minutes days after the event was over and write the resume every day and be ready with the full draft for adoption at the last day of the meeting. In the ICSSR we used to write the minutes of meetings days or weeks after the meeting was over. Here I learnt the art of making minutes during the meeting itself. This practice was then introduced by me in the ICSSR as far as the preparation of IC Committee minutes or doctoral fellowships selections were concerned. The minutes would be ready within half an hour after the meeting was over.

The biennial conference of AASSREC used to be 5 to 6 days affair. Even during these conferences I was asked by Dr. Atal to prepare a resume of each day's discussion, get hold of the reports from repporteurs and be ready with the final draft report on the conference on the last day of the conference. This appeared to me an Herculean task to begin with but with prodding from Dr. Atal I was able to imbibe this type of work culture and was always ready with the draft report on the last day of the AASSREC conference. At a personal level my approach to work also changed.

Though I was junior to him by several years but he always treated me as a friend. He never let me once feel that I was junior to him in hierarchy. Once or twice he came to receive me at the airport at Bangkok and during free time he would drive me around the city in Bangkok.

His contribution to AASSREC is well known. But through AASSREC's associations with ICSSR he indirectly brought about some changes in the technological level and work culture of ICSSR.

7

AASSREC and Dr. Yogesh Atal

VIRGINIA A. MIRALAO

I do not recall exactly how Dr. Yogesh Atal and I met. After returning to Manila from graduate school in the US in the late 1970s, I kept hearing of his name from my friends that I felt I also already knew him. But our actual meeting probably took place in 1979 or 1980 when I and colleagues from the Ateneo de Manila University's Institute of Philippine Culture and Department of Sociology and Anthropology were assisting the Philippine Social Science Council (PSSC) in its efforts to develop social science research centres in different regions of the country. We conducted short-term training programmes in research methods and techniques which faculty members from universities in the provinces took in the summer months; and we helped formulate comparative research undertakings which they could pursue in their own areas and come to share with one another at another time. Dr. Atal was a big supporter of endeavours like these.

At that time, Dr. Atal was working from his office in Bangkok as UNESCO Regional Adviser for Social and Human Sciences in Asia and the Pacific, a post that he used fully to advance the social sciences in the countries of the region. PSSC benefited much from the support that Dr. Atal lent the Council and its activities. Dr. Pilar Jimenez, now Professor and Research Fellow at the Behavioural Sciences Department of De La Salle University, who was then PSSC"s Programme Coordinator recalls that Dr. Atal did not only come and visit and discuss matters and programmes at PSSC. He stayed and attended several fora, lectures and meetings held by the Council. According to Dr. Jimenez, Dr. Atal listened closely and followed up on developments and was very observant[1] and thus, he provided valuable inputs in the assessment of PSSC's programmes. Dr. Jimenez further remembers that Dr. Atal's comments during these assessments were full of substance and insights, and that he had a way of delivering his comments (that included criticisms) which was liked by everyone. Dr. Jimenez also says that he had this knack of seeing the bigger "meta" picture quickly—recognizing the issues and problems at hand, anticipating future needs, and acting on what could be done at present.

Dr. Atal is also known widely for his excellent organizational skills. Dr. Loretta Makasiar Sicat, PSSC's first Executive Director, describes Dr. Atal as "an indefatigable organization man and institution-builder always brimful of ideas on things to be done." Though a relatively new or young organization at that time, Dr. Atal recognized PSSC's potential for developing local social science capability and managing various programmes as holding conferences, undertaking research and publications work, and participating in international collaborative work and exchanges. He helped PSSC accomplish the latter by getting it into the orbit of the Association of Asian Social Science Research Councils (AASSREC) which he helped found and establish in the early 1970s while he was still Director of Sociology at the Indian Council of Social Science Research (ICSSR) in New Delhi.

PSSC hosted AASSREC's Third Biennial General Conference in Manila in 1979, which gave PSSC its first experience in handling an international gathering. The event dwelt on those "felt needs" of the day—that of indigenizing the social sciences and revisiting the uses and applications of social science research in Asian countries. The conference was very well attended not only by AASSREC's member-councils from other countries but by the representatives of various international and regional donor agencies and of course, by the Philippines' own social scientists and ranking government officials. Since then, PSSC has remained actively involved and connected with AASSREC, convening its own national forum or roundtable discussion to prepare for upcoming AASSREC Biennial General Conferences, and identifying the scholar who would be requested to prepare the Philippines' country paper and represent PSSC at these conferences. Through the 1980s, Dr. Atal came to Manila quite regularly from neighbouring Bangkok that he befriended many Filipinos within and outside PSSC.

After my involvement with PSSC's research training programmes in the early 1980s, my next working contact with Dr. Atal came several years later in 1994 when he had already moved to the UNESCO Headquarters in Paris to assume the post of Director of the Coordinating Unit for the World Summit for Social Development (WSSD) and the International Year for the Eradication of Poverty. I was tasked by PSSC for AASSREC to write the Asian regional background paper for the WSSD scheduled in Copenhagen in March 1995. For this regional paper, I was expected to draw from some six country papers (China, Indonesia, the Philippines, Sri Lanka, Thailand and Vietnam) presented at a special regional symposium on New Strategies for Social Development in Asia and the Pacific convened by AASSREC in Manila in November 1994. It was not an easy job trying to pull together the country papers' descriptions and analyses of their governments' responses to the social development "deficits" of their countries considering the diversity of the participating countries, and the writers' varying outlooks and perspectives in approaching the subject matter, not to mention other differences in the styles and quality of their writing. I did what I could and sent the paper to Dr. Atal not feeling too good about my own output. But thanks to Dr. Atal's expert editing—where, after changing phrases here and there and supplying some sub/side headings, the paper, which formed part of the UNESCO-WSSD publication released in 1996, emerged far more coherent than I thought it could ever become.

Without realizing it then, this brief UNESCO-WSSD assignment kind of prepared me for the listening and blending that I soon had to do as AASSREC Secretary General, a post I assumed in 1995 shortly after I was chosen to head PSSC and its secretariat. Although I was familiar with AASSREC's Biennial General Conferences and the publications that came out from these, I knew little else of AASSREC's operations as an organization. So in my initial years as AASSREC Secretary-General, I relied heavily on Ms. Lorna P. Makil, then Chief of PSSC's Technical Services and Information Section who also served as Secretary of AASSREC ever since PSSC assumed the AASSREC Secretariat functions from ICSSR in 1993. Also a dear friend of Dr. Atal, Ms. Makil has now retired from PSSC and returned to Silliman University in her home city of Dumaguete in Central Philippines which is among the regional universities that benefited from PSSC's local capability building programmes in the social sciences in the 1980s, then encouraged and supported by persons like Dr. Atal. Mrs. Makil then briefed me about how AASSREC conducts it affairs—how it chooses its officebearers, conducts its Executive Council and business meetings and prepares for its Biennial General Conferences, and the schedule of all these activities. Even then, it struck me that AASSREC had actually regularized many of its rules, procedures and activities and attained a level of institutionalization that augured well for the Association's future viability. Much of this institutional base of course was laid down by Dr. Atal and I felt it my civic duty to keep AASSREC well and alive as its new Secretary-General. Thus, Ms. Makil and I began attending to some housekeeping tasks, maintaining records, collecting membership dues and writing to member-Councils to sustain their ties and connections with AASSREC. We were fortunate that during our first term as AASSREC Secretariat, ICSSR was hosting AASSREC's 11th Biennial General Conference (then 1995), and Dr. Vinod Mehta and the ICSSR staff took care of much of the arrangements for this, while we at PSSC were learning a little bit more about our role as AASSREC Secretariat.

In the next few years, I came to appreciate even more AASSREC's organizational features which gave it momentum though it did not have substantial funding support from external sources. After Dr. Atal moved to Paris in 1993, there was anxiety that AASSREC would no longer enjoy the same funding support from UNESCO-Bangkok in part because of Dr. Atal's departure and also because of certain other changes in UNESCO's budgetary policies. I did not fully comprehend the latter but our experience was that Dr. Tae Ho Yoo who succeeded Dr. Atal in Bangkok remained rather supportive of AASSREC, advising us on the types of funding requests we could avail of from his office.

Though the question of funding was worrisome, this was not at all insurmountable given the support, cooperation and goodwill that Dr. Atal had generated among AASSREC's member-Councils. I remember for example that after AASSREC's 11th Biennial General Conference in New Delhi in 1995, the question of funding AASSREC's next Executive Council meeting to plan the 12th Biennial General Conference and conduct this itself, remained a major concern as AASSREC really did not have much operating money on its own. Sensing the predicament, LIPI (Lembaga Ilmu Pengetauhan Indonesia) through its representative then, Dr. Brojonegoro, offered to host the Executive Council meeting in Jogyakarta and assume part of the organizing expenses for the event. Too, the AASSREC Committee of the Science Council of Japan (JSC) represented by Dr. Joji Watanuki offered to host the dinners of the Executive Council meeting; while the Chinese Academy of Social Sciences (CASS) through Professor Teng Teng, then its Vice-President, assumed the responsibility of raising the necessary funds for hosting and holding AASSREC's 12th Biennial General Conference in Beijing in 1997. And prior to the Beijing Conference, Professor Watanuki and then JSC Vice-President Nobuyoshi Toshitani invited Professor Teng Teng and myself to Tokyo to take part of the Convention of the International Studies Association and to finalize the preparations for AASSREC's Beijing Conference. These kind offers and gestures came from AASSREC member-Council representatives who knew Dr. Atal or who had heard of him and his dedicated efforts in establishing AASSREC as the defining organization for Asian social scientists and who similarly felt committed to continuing this legacy.

AASSREC's 12th Biennial General Conference opened in Beijing on 13 October 1997 with an equally impressive ceremony as that prepared by ICSSR in New Delhi in 1995. (Each AASSREC Conference opens with a touch of solemnity and the host country's local colour and ritual which lends importance to the conference and to the guests and foreign delegates who come to attend the affair.) Dr. Atal came to the Beijing Conference as representative of Madame Francine Fournier, UNESCO Assistant Directors General for the Social and Human Sciences, and his presence was most welcomed by his many friends at AASSREC including Dr. George Smolicz, Executive Director of the Centre for Inter-cultural Studies and Multi-cultural Studies (CISME) at the University of Adelaide, a long-time associate of Dr. Atal from AASSREC's early years in the 1970s and who has remained a most loyal supporter of AASSREC. Towards the close of the Beijing Conference, CASS further offered to shoulder the cost of printing the papers and proceedings of the conference, setting a precedent that has helped conserve AASSREC's resources. Member-Councils that hosted AASSREC's subsequent conferences have since assumed the costs of publishing the conference papers and outputs.

I must mention that the task of keeping AASSREC organizationally well has been lightened as well by the willingness (eagerness even) of member-Councils to assume the Association's leadership posts of President and Vice-President when they are chosen to do so, and with this the responsibility of hosting and organizing and raising the funds necessary for carrying out the next Biennial General Conferences of AASSREC.[2] Though the challenge of raising enough money to fly member-delegates and accommodate them in the host country for the duration of the conference is always daunting, I have learned no longer to be overly concerned with this. After Beijing, both the Korean Social Science Research Council (KOSSREC) which hosted AASSREC's 13th Biennial General Conference in Seoul in 1999 and the National Centre for Social Sciences and Humanities of Vietnam (NCSSH-V) which hosted the 14th in Hanoi in 2002 managed these events most successfully. Member-delegates who attended the Seoul and/or the Hanoi conferences will attest not only to the hospitality and friendship of our hosts but also to the excellent preparations and smooth conduct of these conferences. The Academy of Social Sciences in Australia (ASSA) is now in the midst of preparing for AASSREC's 15th Biennial General Conference which we will be holding in Canberra a few months from now (in November 2003) and again, despite some anxiety over funding and how to raise enough of this, I am confident that like previous AASSREC conferences, this too will be just as successful and noteworthy.

My account of AASSREC's current state of affairs will not be complete without some reference to the way that members themselves have maintained their affiliation with AASSREC. Most of the member-Councils that joined AASSREC over the years regularly pay their membership dues and send delegates to the association's biennial conferences.[3] The few exceptions include the North Korea's Korean Association of Social Scientists (KASS) and the Academy of Sciences of the Republic of Tajikistan which have been constrained by the political and/or economic developments in their countries to more actively participate in AASSREC. At the same time however, two new members—Iran and Malaysia—have joined AASSREC, thanks to the efforts of Dr. Smolicz and Dr. Malama S. Meleisea (the current UNESCO Regional Adviser for Social and Human Sciences in Asia and the Pacific) in encouraging the Social Sciences and Humanities Research Commission of Iran's Ministry of Science, Research and Technology and the Malaysian Social Science Association (MSSA) respectively, to become AASSREC regular members. Through Dr. Meleisea too, the UNESCO Regional Office in Bangkok continues to be most supportive of AASSREC. Dr. Meleisea has been generous in extending the services of his office, assisting with AASSREC's Executive Council meetings and attending these too, meeting with AASSREC members in the region and keeping them in-the-loop with UNESCO's concerns and programmes.[4]

But if AASSREC today remains a relatively intact and functioning organization, this owes as much to Dr. Atal's well-known ability as an organization person, institution-builder and international bureaucrat (who knew how to "network" and move "social capital" across countries long before the common use of these terms in social discourse) as it does to Dr. Atal being himself an accomplished, and quintessentially Asian, social scientist. Throughout, he remained ever-sensitive to the region's (and its countries') local contexts and specificities, while being keenly aware of global developments and the importance of international exchange and engagements in the social sciences. His views on the growth of the social sciences in the Asia-Pacific and contained in the summary chapters/sections that he wrote for earlier AASSREC conferences read like a good historiography and sociology of the beginnings, concerns and trajectories of Asian social sciences. Many of his friends and colleagues will remember this distinct contribution of Dr. Atal which informed many of the debates and discussions on the pursuit of the social science disciplines in post-colonial Asia. Professor Ponciano Bennagen of UGAT (the Philippine Anthropological Association) who represented PSSC at the AASSREC meetings and conferences on the indigenization of the social sciences has but praises for how Dr. Atal evolved his construction of an "Asian perspective" in the social sciences, which expressed his own reservations and critique of Western social science theories and methodologies without being in the least defensive or offensive, while stressing too, the limits of indigenization (which can lead to isolation/insularity and parochiality) and the importance of being open to international, including Western, social science developments.

Personally too, I have found Dr. Atal's views a most useful guide in negotiating the paradigm shifts in the social sciences overtime. In the latter 1980s following the aftermath of martial rule in the Philippines and the termination of the US-bases agreement in the country, there was much discussion and debate on the "relevance" of social sciences in the Philippines. On many occasions, the debate would turn more ideological and political rather than scholarly and during these times I would remind myself (and some colleagues as well) of Dr. Atal's wise words that social science theories and paradigms—be they of the positivist structural-functional mold or the interpretive ethnomethodological ones or the more Marxist critical ones—are at bottom, no more than "heuristic devices" for understanding social phenomena in a changing world. Following this outlook (of theories as heuristic tools), I have not been affected as much by the subsequent "passing" of theories of dependency, Marxist perspectives and even development theory, whereas colleagues who were somewhat too "wedded" to these paradigms either had to painfully bid these farewell or isolated themselves by continuing to espouse views that have now lost relevance and currency. It is also to Dr. Atal's credit that today, I can look at post-modernism as a diagnostic aid for understanding better the features of contemporary life and culture. I must admit to even enjoying and learning from some of the good "narratives" and self-reflexive accounts of post-modernists. This is saying much I think, considering that not a few of my generation of social scientists trained in the positivist, empirical and quantitative approaches of the 1960s and 1970 would have nothing to do with post-structuralists and post-modernists.

Finally, a word must be said about how Dr. Atal committed his work and ideas into writing which is likely to leave a lasting impact on future generations of social science scholars and researchers in the region. This is shown by the long list of publications that he has authored on many different topics and issues. These include the overview-introduction chapters or the concluding-synthesis chapters that Dr. Atal wrote to go with the printed copies of AASSREC's conference papers and proceeding and research outputs, and several other articles and books that he has written over the course of his career. I myself have benefited from many of his writings which I consult for my own research and lecture assignments. I have used extensively *The Changing Family in Asia*, a collection of country papers which he compiled and edited in the early 1990s and *Poverty and Participation in Civil Society* which he and Else Ôyen produced in 1996 for the International Year for the Eradication of Poverty. On his part, Professor Bennagen mentions that Dr. Atal's work on *Swidden Cultivation in Asia* which appeared in three volumes in the 1980s remains a useful reference in the research and community work that he does among the Philippines' upland communities and indigenous peoples.

If Professor Bennagen and I and other colleagues keep using and referring to Dr. Atal's work, I think this is because his writings seem to provide the kind of knowledge that has both breadth and depth, and history and context than then makes us understand a given phenomenon more holistically. This ability no doubt draws from Dr. Atal's much-admired knack for synthesis, which allows him to view matters from some special vantage point and draw all these to some unity. In a tribute that he had prepared for Dr. Atal to go with the publication of the papers of AASSREC's 14th Biennial Conference in Hanoi in 2001, Dr. Smolicz writes that whenever Dr. Atal produced a synthesis of AASSREC conference discussions and meetings "...disparate themes miraculously fell into place to produce a radiant mosaic, that held together, yet contained all...seemingly irreconcilable points of view." I could not have said it better. I just want to add that what Dr. Atal has is the kind of gift that keeps us, as individuals, organizations or societies, from falling apart.

NOTES

1. Years later, while attending an Inter-governmental Committee meeting of the UNESCO Management of Social Transformation Programme in Paris, Dr. Atal invited me to dinner and on the way to the restaurant, he asked me casually if I still smoked. Noting that the question took me aback, he added that he remembered me smoking the time when I was lecturing in PSSC's training programmes.
2. The member-Council elected as AASSREC President is expected to host the conference following its election. After the conference, the President steps down to become 2nd Vice-President while the 1st Vice-President-elect assumes the Presidency and hosts the next conference and so on. This system allows for a rotation of leadership among AASSREC's member countries and a sharing of the major task of keeping both AASREC and its conferences alive.
3. AASSREC has now adopted a multi-tiered membership fees system with members from better-off Councils and countries paying higher rates than those less well off. Also member-Councils are increasingly sending more than one delegate to the biennial conferences. The delegates thus include the member-Council's paper presenter and an officer or a member of its staff.

4. Ever since assuming the post of Regional Adviser for Social and Human Sciences in Asia and the Pacific, Dr. Meleisea has attended all AASSREC Executive Council meetings and biennial conferences except the Hanoi Conference when he sent a representative. Also, his office assumed the cost of publishing the final report of AASSREC's four-country study on *"Poverty, Environment and Development"* released in 2001.

8

Professor Yogesh Atal: A Moving Force behind AASSREC*

J.J. SMOLICZ

I recall the towering figure of Professor Yogesh Atal, full of vigour and zest, in his role as Secretary-General, leading the most vital and intellectually challenging social scientific organization in the Asia-Pacific region. As an Association of Social Science Research Councils, AASRREC could have been a bureaucratic and stale body involved in no more than reporting the activities of its respective members. But in reality, nothing could be further from the truth. Under Dr. Atal's ledership, the AASSREC ship steered between organizational decorum, required of an official body representing social scientific organizations in the area, and the intellectually free and occasionally vigorous discussion, expected of top ranking social scientists in Asia and the Pacific.

Without Dr. Atal's leadership skills and bureaucratic know-how, the ship would have sunk, bereft of necessary funds and lost in the political storms that raged in the region in the past quarter century. Skilful at getting the necessary UNESCO support, but also mindful of the need to preserve the intellectual independence of the AASSREC, Dr. Atal provided the kind of leadership that was unique in the international academic scene. The perfect synthesis of a high powered academic and skilled UNESCO organizational man, he was always able to guide AASSREC towards a choice of themes that were intellectually challenging and socially relevant,

* A Special Tribute paid at the 14th AASSREC Biennial Conference held at Hanoi, Vietnam, November 2001.

while bridging the gap between social scientific organizations in nations which were often politically poles apart.

Dr. Atal's goal was to make AASSREC as inclusive of all nations of the region as possible. Soundly supported by such long time members as India, Sri Lanka, Indonesia, Republic of Korea and the Philippines, he succeeded in bringing both China and Japan into the AASSREC fold. The pacific nations of Australia and New Zealand always had a steady friend in him, as did the smaller countries which he strive to support and whose social scientists he sought to nourish and integrate into the global educational scene. It was a great joy to him to bring Fiji into one of the conference and he invited observers from countries such as Laos. While membership of North Korea was precarious but achievable, it was bringing Vietnam into AASSREC that was particularly pleasing to him, as well as maintaining firm ties with Bangladesh and Pakistan.

Dr. Atal was always fascinated by the great diversity of cultural phenomena and he succeeded in encouraging AASSREC meetings to take up the analysis of a series of cultural issues and dilemmas, including such themes as unity in diversity, ethnicity and nation-states and resilience in pluralistic societies. Dr. Atal's own studies of "sandwich cultures" and migration phenomena were well known and appreciated by scholars. He had a particular flair for summing up conference themes and hence was almost invariably selected to act as rapporteur-general at all the AASSREC conference which he attended. I was always amazed at the way he could extract the kernel of any symposium theme out of a plethora of the most complex and controversial debate. When he produced his synthesis, the disparate themes miraculously fell into place to produce a radiant mosaic, that held together, yet contained all the seemingly irreconcilable points of view. In this way, Dr. Atal turned AASSREC into a great forum for unity and amity in the Asia-Pacific region, a forum which linked the powerful and nourished the smaller members of our family of nations.

While engaged in all these activities he has always remained a warm and loyal friend of all the participants who could hardly imagine a conference without his active participation. I was first privileged to see Yogesh in action in Sydney in 1983 and subsequently in Den Pasar, Seoul, Christchurch, Manila, Kawasaki and Beijing, as well as having the pleasure of being his guest at his headquarters in UNESCO's Regional Unit for Social & Human Sciences in Asia and the Pacific (RUSHSAP) in Bangkok.

Dr. Atal succeeded in laying such solid foundations for AASSREC that it survived his departure from the Regional Office to UNESCO headquarters in Paris, from where he remained an ever watchful and faithful friend. He was never quite been able to detach himself from

AASSREC, as the body that meant so much to him, while, for their part, its members have always felt a high admirations for his services to social science in the region. This mutual regard was manifest when Dr. Atal flew from Paris to attend the AASSREC Conference in Beijing in 1997, and will no doubt show itself again on his return visit to Australia in 2003.

Part II

Emerging Social Science Concerns: The Global Context

9

Towards a Democratic Regulation of Globalizaton

ALI KAZANCIGIL

I shall present below some thoughts on the governance of globalization, the conditions of which are the object of an international debate. There are frequent assertions that globalization is ungoverned. I would say that this is correct, as far as its social regulation and democratic governance are concerned, but not as regards global trade and financial issues. The latter are steered through regulatory regimes, evolved in leading global fora, such as the G-7, IMF, WTO, the World Bank, the European Union and OECD, dominated by the USA, the UK, Germany, France and Japan. Let me quote in this respect Samuel Huntington, taking however the citation out of its ideological and strategic context, *i.e.*, the empirically unsustainable thesis of the clash of civilisations and the author's main concern, which is the preservation of Western hegemonic interests.

The West, writes Huntington "...dominates international political and security institutions and with Japan international economic institutions. Global political and security issues are effectively settled by a directorate of the United States, Britain and France, world economic issues by a directorate of the United States, Germany and Japan, all of which maintain extraordinary close relations with each other to the exclusion of lesser and largely non-Western countries. ...." (1993; 26)

Such economic and financial regulatory regimes I mentioned aim at fostering neo-liberal globalization. The global governance to which I refer may include these areas, but basically it is a different kettle of fish, as I shall try to explain in the rest of my paper.

To the proponents of neo-liberalism, the only surviving this—wordly ideological system, or "grand narrative", as the post-modern speak would have it, the very notion of a relationship between capitalist markets, globalized or otherwise, and governance is either anathema or an oxymoron. The problem is that their position is not supported by historical evidence. Indeed, as Karl Polanyi (1957) showed in markets in various cultural contexts, including in the West, have always been embedded in society and "...man's economy, as a role, is submerged in his social relationships" (46). He continued, referring to the European experience of the late 19th century and the 20th century up to World War II, that civilized life is not compatible with..."the utopian experiment of a self-regulating market .." (249-50).

Such views have been acknowledged in certain periods, and neglected in others. For example, from mid-1940s to mid-1970s, a period which the French economist Jean Fourastie dubbed "the thirty glorious years" (*"les trente glorieuses "*), illustrated Polanyi's call for "...a development under which the economic system ceases to lay down the law to society and the primacy of society over that system is secured". This was achieved through the relative balance established between capitalism and redistributive justice, thanks to the Welfare State. The latter explains why, amongst the three political systems of the 1930s, only democracy survived, while fascism and communism have disappeared. As of the early 1980s, however, under the impact of the neo-liberal wave, and the unleashing of globalization of the same persuasion in the 1990s, this historical experience and the Keynesian paradigm which inspired it were discredited for two decades. The mood is now changing again, even amongst some of the leading actors of globalization: if a beginning date is to be identified for this slow change of perception, it must be December 1999, in Seattle, where the global village discovered that it has a public opinion, and a vocal one at that.

At this point, let me formulate a personal definition of the current globalization, ironically inspired by Lenin's well-known formula: "Socialism is the Soviets plus electrification": "Globalization is unfettered global capitalism plus the new information and communication technologies". In fact, such a parallel between communism and neo-liberalism is not that irrelevant, since both creeds maintain that economical and technological factors drive humankind, each one neglecting in its own logic the fact that the global transformation are also based on political, social, cultural and environmental factors.

So, the current globalization is characterized mainly by deregulated capitalist markets (please note that there are historical forms of markets other than capitalist) as Fernand Braudel (1981-84) analyzed as well as by

Internet, global networks, shrinking time and space, a trend towards de-territorialization, the transformation (rather than the progressive extinction) of the sovereign state, the rise of powerful new economic actors and transnational NGOs. Globalization generates economic efficiency, but also "public bads", such as growing inequalities, drug trafficking, crime, pandemics, as well as environmental and climatic problems. Although the globalization that we witness displays a new configuration, it is not without antecedents, which were more limited in scope.

As anthropologist Eric Wolf (1997) has discussed very early in history, human groups travelled, exchanged and mixed with each other. International and inter-continental trade routes were established long before the modern era. Phenicians and Greeks developed an international trade area, with market pricing and trade centres such as Carthago and Alexandria. Similar developments took place in the Chinese and Indian civilizational areas. Buddhism, Christianity and Islam spread as world religions. Also, products of the mind based on reason, shared by practically all human beings, *i.e.* philosophy, science and technology (compass, telescope, gunpowder, printing press) spread across the world. Later, world-wide inter-conexions and expansion took place, from the end of the 15th century onwards, through the era of discoveries, colonisation and the age of enlightenment. The 19th century industrial revolution gave such developments a new impetus. For example, at the time of the monetary gold standard (around 1887-1914) the volume of trade between developed countries was similar to the current level. This process was interrupted by World War I, the financial crisis of the 1930s and World War II. Today, of course, the economic and technological globalization and its positive and negative impact on the daily lives of individuals and societies are much stronger and more pervasive. But a historical perspective is always useful, to relativise and not to be carried away by the exuberance of enthousiastic propagandists of globalization, such as Kenichi Ohmae (1990) or Peter Schwartz and Peter Layden (1997), who announce nothing less than the emergence, thanks to neo-liberal globalization, of a "civilization of civilizations".

The expansion of deregulated global financial markets, supported by the new ICTs, pushed up global financial flows to over US$1500 billion per day, in the late 1990s. At that level, it is obvious that the power of global markets is way beyond the jurisdiction of sovereign states and the coping capacity of national political authorities. Such a development was met with unmitigated satisfaction by the globalised elites, until a succession of financial crises hit the world economy, as of the summer of 1997 in Asia, then in Russia, Brazil and more recently in two other emerging economies—

Argentina and Turkey, raising fears that such crises may ultimately reach the developed economies, putting in jeopardy the neo-liberal globalization. Consequently, the necessity of mitigating the latter's worst excesses through certain global governance arrangements started to make its way. This is now accompanied by an acknowledgement that there are in the game a minority of winners and a majority of loosers and that, while the globalization of markets increase aggregate wealth in the world, it generates increasing inequalities within and between nations, as well as growing political contestation and resentment. In particular, there is a growing perception gap and political tensions between the Northern and the Southern countries, not so much about the globalization itself, but about its current conditions and direction, and the fact that the international organizations which steer globalization almost exclusively reflect the interests and agendas of the political and economic powers situated at the centre of the world system, at the expense of those in the periphery. From the early 1990s, the development strategies under the condition of globalization were steered by a Western Agenda, known as the "Washington Consensus", focusing on socio-economic orthodoxy, structural adjustment, opening up of the economy, financial deregulation, a shrinking state, reduced basic social services, privatization of public services, lower labour costs. In the second half of the 1990s, there were attempts to reform such policy prescriptions, in the guise of the "Post-Washington Consensus". But this reform, which introduced a concern with poverty reduction, social equity and transparency, to mitigate the negative impact of neo-liberalism and global markets, still reflects a "top-down" Northern Agenda, with the same "rule makers" and the same "rule takers". Thus, the possibility of generating new global public goods suitable for the South as well as the North is limited, while the probability of growing North-South conflicts remains high.

Deregulated markets and unrestricted capital mobility, especially short-term capital flows, facilitated by the ICTs, weakened and destabilized welfare states, which cannot tax capital to provide compensation to the loosers of globalization and thus secure social cohesion. This situation undermines the political legitimacy of national governments, as well as their capacity to deliver basic public goods. Yet, to the extent that the market economy is a social construction and its functioning depends on the support from the society at large, the continued existence of globalization and open economies depend on the welfare states, *i.e.* governments which can associate economic efficiency and redistributive policies. Otherwise, the unregulated globalization, pursued as an end in itself, may become self-destructive.

It is in this context that the triomphalistic outlook of neo-liberal globalization which prevailed in the first part of the 1990s met with growing contestation of market dominated globalization, originating:

- Firstly from developing countries, which blocked the negotiations at the Seattle WTO meeting, for they refused to be marginalised in the on-going global trade arrangements and constantly subjected to Northern Agendas relating to environment, social norms, competitivity and investment, while the Southern Agenda, requesting the removal of the obstacles to their exports to industrial countries has been constantly postponed by the latter. As a matter of fact, since Seattle, no progress was made on this score.
- Secondly from the growing constellation of non-State actors—NGOs and Global Social Movements, mainly from the North, which also effectively contributed to paralyzing the WTO in Seattle. These movements, using the ICTs for networking and organizing protest, as effectively as the actors of the "new economy" do use them for their business, were able to modify the terms of the political debate on globalization and its governance.

There is a controversy about the nature and long-term implications of such transnational anti-liberal globalization movements, that have been demonstrating in the streets of Seattle, Davos, Washington D.C., Prague, Millau in Correze, at the heart of "la France profonde", and Nice, or getting together in more orderly fashion, like the "First World Social Forum" (25-30 January 2001), in Porto Alegre (Brazil). That this Forum takes place at the same time as the Davos World Economic Forum is obviously not a coincidence.

Conservative analysts contemptuously consider these movements merely as an urban law and order problem, to be handled by the police. They are of course pathetically missing the point. Indeed, the more foresighted actors of globalization, such as James Wolfensohn, the President of the World Bank or Alan Greenspan, the President of the US Federal Reserve Bank (International Herald Tribune, 2 February 2000), made public statements that such street demonstrators were expressing important concerns, which should be taken into account. The title of an article by Joseph S. Nye in the *International Herald Tribune* (25 November 2000) sums it up perfectly: "Take Globalization Protests Seriously".

Given such developments, global governance has now become a central issue of globalization. What is at stake here is global governance with a democratic content and objectives, and not governance as institutional and policy arrangements to continue to expand the "Market Imperium" (see on this Kuttner, 1996), involving the marketization of most spheres of human activity, social relations and public goods, such as education, culture, knowledge and health. Concerning the latter areas, I refer to the current WTO negotiations which aim at subjecting them to the general rules of free trade, thus changing such public goods to market goods, and transforming public services which treat equally all citizens, whether rich or poor, into privately supplied services, catering to customers, according to their purchasing power.

There is now an increasing awareness that a globalization which tends to the marketization/commodification of the world is not sustainable. To quote once again Karl Polanyi, whose following assessment of the 19th century society and economy written in 1944 is not irrelevant for the current globalization: " Nineteenth century civilisation was not destroyed by the external or internal attacks of barbarians. [It was] the conflict between the market and the elementary requirements of an organized social life [that] provided the century with its dynamics and produced the typical strains and stresses which ultimately destroyed that society ..." (249)

About the features of governance, I should like to draw attention to an issue of the *International Social Science Journal,* edited at UNESCO, on "Governance" (No. 155, March 1998), which explores this concept and its uses. In this issue, Gerry Stoker defines governance as "governing styles in which boundaries between and within public and private sectors are blurred" (17). I would add that governance is characterized by the involvement in the policy-making process, of the state and local authorities, as well as the business sector, labour unions and the civil society agents, such as the NGOs and citizen movements. All these stake-holders participate in this negotiation-like, relatively horizontal decision-making process, in opposition to the more hierarchical style of traditional government.

The governance mode fits very well the conditions of the transnational scene, where there is no central authority and where the stake-holders, *i.e.* sovereign states, transnational corporations, international organizations and more recently and restrictively NGOs generate issue-specific policies and regulatory regimes, through negotiations.

Governance has so far been based on the principles of effectiveness and efficiency. No doubt, it is participatory, but because it involves only those stake-holders concerned by the issue under consideration, it does not replace democratic institutions, which represent the totality of the citizens and look after trans-sectoral common interests of the society as a whole. Only representative democratic politics can look after the common good. The gist of the matter is that governance as it has been practised is a mode of policy-making without politics. At the domestic level, such an issue-specific way of managing public affairs may not create a real problem, as long as there are representative institutions which take care of overall political choices, the governance mode being complementary to it; and a useful one at that, particularly for policy-making at the sectoral and sub-national levels (*e.g.* urban governance).

On the global scene, however, there are no representative institutions. Democracy is territorially based and citizens express their political choices only within the national boundaries. Yet, as long as some form of democratic representation and/or participation are not projected beyond the territorial state, global policy-making and regulatory regime setting within international institutions will remain technocratic, exclusively concerned with specific sectoral issues and with efficiency, but not with democracy, citizen's representation and justice. The latter are not technical, but political issues.

A central question, then, is how to instaure global governance that incorporates democratic politics? This is a *conditio sine qua non* for making globalization operate to the benefit of the world citizens and not only of those who can harness the resources of the capitalist markets. That amounts to transforming globalization in such a way that it serves *homo politicus,* as well as *homo economicus,* the citizen as well as the consumer.

The dominant economistic paradigm bears responsibility as regards the inadequate understanding of the centrality of politics in the social regulation of globalization. This paradigm does not integrate insights from historical sociology and fails to borrow concepts such as conflict of interest, power relations and cultural specificities from political science, sociology and anthropology. It claims that the determinants of individual and collective behaviour, as well as of institutions are susceptible to analysis by the tools of economic theory, standing in splendid isolation.

To be fair, there are economists such as Joseph Stiglitz who understand that the complexities of a phenomenon such as globalization cannot be understood by their discipline alone. But then he is a neo-keynesian and not an adept of the neo-liberal. Supply-side economics, and the fact that he had to leave his position as Chief Economist of the World Bank is an additional evidence of the still on-going, even if contested, predominance of the neo-liberal paradigm.

Another evidence in this regard is the Tobin Tax. Its adversaries claim that its introduction is technically impossible and more importantly, that it would not serve the purposes, on the one hand, of curbing down global financial speculation, and on the other combatting fiscal paradises. They are right on these two scores. However, there is a third purpose, which is very rarely mentioned in the debate and in the international media, aiming at funding development strategies, poverty reduction policies, access to education, clean water, health and decent habitat. In these areas the Tobin Tax makes sense. Indeed, provided that the G-7 members and other major economies accept the idea, and fiscal paradises are put under control, which can be achieved with some political will, the rest of the world-on the beneficiary side of such a tax-would follow, and the mechanism could function. Technically, the matter would amount to introducing appropriate softwares in the PCs of world markets. A very small percentage tax could thus be levied from currency transfers between markets, generating several hundred billion dollars per year for development, to be managed by a multilateral body. But this is unlikely to happen, unless the dominant neo-liberal ideology of globalization and the enormous power concentrated in the hands of its major actors are seriously challenged and replaced by a global governance that displays democratic features.

The fact is that the currently dominant ideology is not concerned with equity, justice and reducing inequalities. It reflects an instrumental rationality, justifying unfettered markets, competitive efficiency and labour market flexibility, wage-earners being the safety valve of the system, and creation of additional wealth an end in itself, and not a means in the service of higher order, humanistic goals, situated in the realm of what Jurgen Habermas calls emancipatory rationality.

Introducing such concerns in the conduct of globalization is the object of global democratic governance. The question is how to overcome the democratic deficit that exists within globalization. This is not only a problem of political theory, but a practical necessity: globalization reduces the capacity of national democratic regimes to cope with the domestic effects of decisions that are made and processes that take place at the global level. Hence the necessity of establishing democratic mechanisms beyond national borders, through which citizenship can also be exercised on the global scene, and democratic politics be incorporated in global governance, which has so far excluded concerns with democratic accountability, transparency and justice, to focus exclusively on market related concerns.

The role of the NGOs and global social movements is important in this respect. Such civil society actors are to be incorporated in global governance, and more specifically in the negotiation processes and decision-making in the international organizations. So far, the Bretton Woods institutions resisted such developments, even if things tend to change. Market actors, and transnational corporations, even more reluctant than the IGOs, will also have to accept this. So far, the current technocratic global governance does not incorporate civil society. It is too top down, and not accountable.

Important as it is, the participation of civil society and its organizations in global governance is not without raising questions. Firstly, NGO participation towards the democratization of global governance is necessary, but not sufficient from a democratic perspective. The representative nature and legitimacy of NGOs are not easy to establish. Their democratic accountability is not clear. Civil society is a basic element of democratic regimes, but it is not to be equated with the latter. Still, the NGO pressures are having an important impact on the IGOs. Their actions tend towards the instauration of a global public opinion, and a global public space. These are bound to be important foundational elements of a future global democratic governance. Secondly, civil society participation is mainly a Northern development. It will not solve the problem of the under presentation of the developing countries in global decision-making. The latter express concern that the NGO participation at the global level may take place at the expense of the South. To obtain proper representation, developing nations request a reform of the global institutional structures, such as enlarging the membership of G-7 and changing the decision-making procedures in other organizations, to make room for Southern participation. This is a crucial issue, for without such an improved representation, an equitable global governance and the production of mutually acceptable global public goods will not be achieved. Developing countries as a whole are not against globalization as such, but often have views different from the North as to what constitutes a global public good and a global public bad. For example, totally deregulated short-term capital flows may be a public good for market actors, they are a public bad for developing nations. The same can be said of WTO driven trade negotiation, competitive policies or labour standards.

In short, to make progress on an adequate regulation of globalization there is a need to introduce participatory politics into global governance, which currently is utilized as a neutral mechanism (on such aspects of the concept of governance, see Ali Kazancigil 1998; 69-79).

Generally, the key players of globalization, such as the market actors and Bretton Wood institutions reserve the term governance to national and sub-national levels: at the global level, they refer to global public policy, a term which allows by-passing confrontational and political dimensions. This vocabulary reflects the rational choice theory, which has been dominating the UN thinking and speak as of mid-1980s. Rational choice has its strong analytical points, but it is unable to understand issues of power, social conflict and contestation. An a-historical and a-political approach, it is not an appropriate theoretical framework to think about the social regulation and democratic governance of globalization and critically analyze the ideas underlying globalization, which display an "End of History" sort of outlook and the view that the world has entered in a "post-history" and "post-politics" era. Such intellectually dubious constructions of the current *Zeitgeist* should be laid to rest. Of course, this will not be easily done, for they are promoted and disseminated by some of the most powerful globalized interests and actors.

The requirement here would be to introduce in the thinking and operations of the international organizations and other global actors, a concern with the welfare of all. The IGOs, such as IMF and WTO involved in globalization matters need to be given mandates in social issues, beyond the promotion of unfettered capitalism. There are signs of this happening more actively in the World Bank, and cautiously in the IMF, which recently started to get involved in poverty reduction programmes in developing countries [the Poverty Reduction Strategy Papers (PRSPs)]. At long last there seems to be a timid awareness, within the I.F.I.'s, that the only purpose of the globalized economy and its governance is not to serve the needs of the market but also certain requirements of society and citizens.

But there is a necessity to go much further, in order to subject unfettered capitalism to the requirements of a more equitable world order and social life. This can only be achieved through a systemic balance between three equally important dimensions: democratic politics, civil society and the capitalist economy, at the national as well as global levels. An initial condition for this is to accept that the market economy is embedded in society and culture, and while it should be allowed to operate with optimal efficiency, it should not be an end in itself, but a tool in the service of higher-order requirements.

To sum up, the gradual construction of a global governance that displays democratic features should be founded on the principle of the non-dissociation of the economy and politics, the taking into account of factors such as redistributive justice, welfare, social cohesion, equality, cultural identities. Such concerns, familiar in national democratic politics, have so far been ignored or by-passed by global governance. If globalization is to acquire wider legitimacy and thus become sustainable, its key actors have no alternative but to accept dealing with such concerns.

REFERENCES

Huntington, S. (1993). "The clash of civilizations" in *Foreign Affairs*, 72, Summer.
Polanyi, Karl, (1957). *The Great Transformation*, Beacon Press, Boston.

Brandel, Fernand 1981-84, *Civilization and Capitalism, 15-18th century,* 3 Vol. Harper and Row, New York.

Wolf, Eric (1997). *Europe and the People without History,* University of California Press, Berkeley (reprint),

Ohmae, Kenichi (1990). *The Borderless World: Power and Strategy in the Interlinked Economy,* Harper, New York.

Schwartz, Peter (1997). "The Long Boom: A History of the Future, 1980-2020" in Peter Layden *Wired* (July).

Kuttner, R. (1996). *Everything for Sale: The Virtues and Limits of Markets,* Alfred Knopf, New York.

Kazancigil, Ali (1998). "Governance and Science: Market-like Modes of Managing Society and Producing Knowledge" in *International Social Science Journal* No. 155 (69-79).

10

Tradition and Modernity in an Era of Global Change

J.J. SMOLICZ

Two decades of lively discourse among social scientists grouped together in the Asian Social Science Research Councils (AASSREC) (1988, 1989, 1997, 1999) have demonstrated beyond reasonable doubt the falseness of the dichotomy which has been frequently drawn between the concepts of modernity and tradition. Modernity is in fact a value-laden term which for long has carried an implication of positive evaluation for virtually any innovation, as opposed to tradition, which, within this context, has acquired a negative connotation of backwardness and unthinking conservatism. Western derived social sciences have been prime purveyors of such notions, with progress identified as a 'de-traditionalisation' of society. Modernity was then perceived as a solely western achievement, while the rest of the world was regarded as still shackled by the bonds of tradition.

In consequence of academic debates stimulated by AASSREC over the years, such a position is now rejected as a form of Eurocentric universalism, to the extent that even the very concept of modernity has become suspect. The view which has finally achieved much support is that tradition does not invariably hinder social change since, in a society with a long established civilization, resilience depends on new development being incorporated into traditional values (Szacki, 1969, 1997). It is acknowledged, however, that tradition can only survive the vicissitudes of time if it accommodates itself to the present. This contention can be sustained with the proviso that not only are there many different tradition, but there are also *different modernities* (Eisenstadt, 2000). In this sense, Islamic, Hindu and Confucian civilizations are no less modern than European, and each has succeeded through its own political and cultural dynamics, in turning its traditions into modern ideologies (Huntington, 1996).

This account differs from the 'instrumental' perspective which argues that a "living" tradition is simply an "invention" of manipulative elites rather than the re-interpretation elaboration or extension of pre-existing cultural elements (Hobsbawm & Ranger, 1983; Gellner, 1983). From the standpoint adopted in this paper, the "invention" hypothesis confuses our understanding of cultural change and undermines the contunity of a society's cultural heritage and misrepresents its core values as transient symbols and myths (Smolicz, 1998).

While acknowledging the need to adapt to current needs and contemporary challenges, there is accumulating evidence of the negative influence of Euro-centric models, such as those generated on the basis of the European concept of the "nation-state", when imposed on developing countries in the name of western style "modernization" or "progress" (Tombaih, 1986; Oommen, 1997). Writing on the subject of the culture development interface, the theme of the AASSREC symposium held in Christchurch New Zealand in 1989, Atal (1991:10) concluded,

The development path followed by the newly independent societies was meant to lead these countries towards economic progress, modernization and democratic polity. In their desire to achieve these goals, developing countries adopted alien models of development and rushed headlong to welcome money, men, and machines from abroad to accelerate the process of modernization. But things did not seem to have happened as expected; proponents of the earlier paradigm of development attributed the failure to the indigenous cultures, regarding them as obstacles to development. The discussion at the Symposium questioned this diagnosis.

The disenchantment with the prevailing paradigm of development seems to be shared by all countries-developed and developing, resulting in an exercise in rethinking development. The developing countries consider that development has been externally induced and has disregarded their indigenous cultures; therefore, it should be replaced by some sort of endogenous development. The developed countries feel peeved at the "ungrateful" as response to their "aid", and yet regard "development" as essential to usher the world into the era of new technology. Both of them acknowledge that Asia-Pacific region is rich in human resources, and the focus should, therefore, be on Human Resources Development.

Culture Development Interface in Education

Subsequently debate has supported the view that, in the current climate of "global" change, a system of higher education can only fulfill its human resources developmental function if it is based upon the resilient foundation of the country's own cultural heritage and modulate by its people to meet their changing needs (Smolicz, 1999). From this perspective, the education system can be seen as concerned to transmit the cultural heritage of the group, in a way that is responsive to the following processes:

1. *Conservation and Re-interpretation of* Heritage to meet the current needs and aspirations of members of society;
2. *Innovation through Cultural Creativity*: cultural growth and creativity (spiritual, scientific, artistic and technological) that originated from within a given society ('internal innovation');
3. *Innovation through Cultural Diffusion*: the diffusion of culture from other and groups in conformity with given civilisation's core values ('external innovation'); and
4. *Crystallisation of Tradition*: culture modified in the light of 1, 2 and 3.

All these processes need to be considered concurrently if we have to understand how cultural change can contribute to the resilience and development of a society through its education system. Furthermore, it cannot be assumed that the processes listed above proceed at a uniform pace, or that development (be it social, scientific or technical) invariably leads to an increase in societal resilience. Examples could be found in Asia where measure, deemed as progressive and 'modernising', but introduced with disregard for, or even in defiance of traditional values and structures, ultimately stunted society's stability and development, thus underlining the fact that technological progress is not invariably synonymous with cultural growth (Toynbee, 1978).

An examination of the processes of cultural growth, diffusion and heritage modification, requires a rejection of the idea that tradition is 'the heavy hand of the past', that weighs upon the present. From this perspective, the whole concept of unilinear evolution of society, with its abandonment of the 'past' as a pre-condition for the acceptance of the present, is seen as one-sided and even irrelevant. Instead, the role of higher education is to encourage the crystallization of tradition. This involves the transmission of heritage in a flexible way which provides the opportunity for each generation to modify it by responding to new inputs and current needs. The society concerned may then undergo a transformation, while retaining its integrity and preserving its links with the past through the maintenance of certain core elements of its culture. This approach is diametrically opposed to the insertion of the 'forces of modernity' into an established society, as if their introduction was occurring in some kind of cultural vacuum. Education based on such premises must therefore be regarded as no more than the intrusion of outside cultural elements that, if unchecked, could lead ultimately to the disintegration of society.

The other side of the coin is represented by the refusal to adapt society's culture. Such ossification through the isolation or rejection of any innovation can usually be viewed as the prelude to more rapid and violent changes in the future, as witnessed, for example, in Russia and subsequently in the USSR. (Obolensky, 1974). Cultural growth without social disruption requires the integration of internal and external innovation and the consequent modification of heritage. Hence the need to regulate the overall course of education that facilitates the crystallization of living tradition in harmony with the integral pivots (core values) of the civilization concerned.

The study of such processes is of importance for social scientists in all societies, and especially those upon which a number of different forces impinge, as in the case of parts of Asia and the pacific, where the nature of the group's heritage has been clouded by so many inputs, as to create a confusion about what constitutes 'indigenous', as opposed to 'alien' elements.

The phenomena of cultural modification, and crystallization of tradition will vary in different societies, depending on their particular 'native genius' or original cultural substratum, their core values, as well as on the nature of the later infusion, the tempo of innovation and the extent to which there has been time for an internal process of creative regeneration (Association of Asian Social Sciences Research Council, 1988, 1989, 1997, 1999). An interesting example of these processes at work is provided by countries in South East Asia, such as the Philippines, which have probably been subjected to more extensive and far-reaching external cultural inputs than most modern societies (Andres, 1981; Smolicz, Nical and Secombe, 2000). Furthermore, in the past at least, these inputs were generally far from voluntary, but forcibly thrust upon the people through colonial imposition. It is not the richness and the variety of these influences that are perplexing modern Filipinos, so much as their inability to accept all these inputs as an integral and genuine part of their own past

(Constantino, 1982). Indeed, no one single layer of this Filipino heritage would be acceptable as an adequate basis for modern Filipino development. The consequence of this multiplicity of outside influences has made for the well-known Filipino flexibility and adaptability, and the ease with which Filipino appear to 'fit in' as migrants in other countries, or take up foreign innovation at home. This "flexibility" or "tolerance" may, however, conceal a lack of certainty as to what constitutes the "real" core values of Filipino heritage-a stage of mind which breeds insecurity and many actually hinder the crystallization of tradition at the most fundamental level. The current Filipino generation can now take advantage of their country's independence to activate those aspects of its complex heritage which fit its current needs and to give them new significance (Gorospe, 1988). Important moves have been made in this direction by the importance assigned to universities in achieving this goal through the placing of "values education" at the centre of the curriculum (Quisumbing, 1987; Licuanan *et al.*, 1989).

Core Values and Education

The higher education system plays a vital role in the emergence of a viable tradition, by balancing its dual functions of cultural transmission and cultural innovation. Both the university professors and their students, as members of society, must therefore safeguard their culture by singling out some of its aspects as a living tradition, while at the same time modifying it to meet their care in the face of rapid change, and on whose maintenance and modification the resilience of society largely depends, will bereffered to in this paper as the *core values* of the group (Smolicz, 1988; Smolicz, Secombe and Hudson, 2001). The name emphasizes their connection with the survival of a given people as a distinct collectively, possessing its own identity which is transmittable from generation to generation. Like other aspects of culture, core values may also be affected by new valuations and external or internal influences, but their excessively rapid or forced abandonment threatens the disintegration of the whole cultural and social fabric of the group.

In a period of social calm the process of innovation operates fairly smoothly, so that cultural change may seem virtually imperceptible. At other times, when violent fluctuations occur as a result of external or internal upheavals, tensions arise when conquerors or even some elements of the indigenous population want to rapidly 'modernise' the country in the name of progress and change, often with a disregard for the core vales of the group.

The identification of certain aspects of culture as its core, and appreciation of their significance for group survival, can be most clearly discerned when the group concerned is under threat and needs to defend its culture against external pressures. If the identity of a people is seriously undermined or even threatened with extinction, be it under the pressure of colonial power, post-colonial cultural or economic dominance, or internal colonialist policies of the dominate entity, cultural life grows correspondingly more important and vital, until culture itself, and especially its core elements, become the fundamental value around which people rally (Kundera, 1984). This has been shown in the history of Asian civilization under colonialism, as in the case of Korea subjected to Japanese rule and subsequent Western influences (Byong-Je, 1988). In Europe itself, a determination to safeguard their culture was shown by the Greeks under the Ottoman rule, by the poles following their country's partitions by Austria, Russia and Germany, by the Irish under British dominion, and by the Baltic peoples in the Russian Empire and several other peoples of Asia either colonized or subjected to imperialist pressures by the "West" (Davies, 1996). This increase in cultural vitality and search for inspiration from the past can be observed at present in independent Asian nations in the fact of more subtle Western influences, as illustrated by the way Thai youth has turned towards spiritual renewal through attendance at monastic retreats for meditation practices (Banphot, 1988).

The same phenomenon can be observed among ethnic groups in societies where the dominant majority is bent on a policy of cultural assimilation, as has been the case in the United States and Australia. From this perspective the concept of the interdependence of 'tradition' and 'modernity' applies both to cultural diffusion of innovation across national boundaries, and to transmission of cultural knowledge among a variety of groups within the same society. The latter type of internal cultural interaction is of significance in ethnically plural societies in the Asia and Pacific region. It is applicable not only to societies that exhibit long established ethnic pluralism (such as India, Malaysia and the Philippines), but also to those where ethnic diversity has been greatly augmented by the post-war migration from overseas (as in the case of Australia). Within Australia for example, attempts by the Aborigines to return to their indigenous origins, point to the importance of core values both for the maintenance of identity and for the cultural and social continuity of the group (Fesl, 1988; Bourke, Bourke & Edwards, 1994; Gale *et al.*, 1987, Jupp, 2001).

Under the impact of economic, political and cultural globalization, there has been an expectation that the whole world would tend to become more and more culturally homogeneous until a convergence of cultures eventuated. As homogenizing forces have impinged upon all countries, both East and West, nation-states have been losing some of their traditional omnipotence and charisma (Eisenstadt, 2000). Such weakening authority of the state has paradoxically generated forces that counteract the homogenizing effects of globalization. As control slips out of its grasp, the state faces the rising demands of local, regional and various other ethnic groups which are gaining confidence and demanding a place for their core values within the multi-ethnic nation-state.

The emphasis placed upon these cores as elements essential for cultural survival may appear to introduce a certain rigidity into the life of a group and its ability to adapt to change. Indeed, core values themselves, be they linguistic, religious, social or territorial, may appear changeless and immutable, rather in the way a medieval scholastic might have regarded his limited and static Aristotelian world. This, of course, is not the case since even core values may undergo a change in their nature, as well as in the interpretation given to them by each succeeding generation (Smolicz, Secombe and Hudson, 2001). There is also little doubt that the evaluation of , for example, the functioning of religion, in terms of its significance for everyday life, has shown fluctuations, and that for some groups it has a greater unifying ethno-specific significance, as in the case of Iran, Brunei or Nepal . than for others (say, Singapore or Korea).

Such modifications in the meaning of a particular core does not alter its overall significance. Thus the Malay language and the Islamic religion retain their position as hallmarks of Malay ethnicity. Indeed, can people be regarded as members ('authentic' and ' non-residual') of the Malay ethnic group, if they are unable to communicate in their ethno-specific language? (*cf.* Asmah Haji Omar, 1982, 1983). And what of someone who has formally and actively embraced a religion other than Orthodoxy in the case of the Greeks, or Islam in the case of Malays—what is their status in their respective communities?

The question which is open to debate is how stable or fragile such cultural values may be in the present situation, and how persistently they are activated as a living tradition, when confronted with challenge or competition from the core values of some other groups, especially these which may currently enjoy either world or national dominance. In his synthesis of the AASSREC Symposium on the role of culture in development, Atal (1991:15) concluded;

> that a living culture has its own ways of screening the new entrants either brought from the outside or invented within. No culture has been so rigid

as not to change; and yet no culture has been so docile to allow itself to be fully submerged in the deluge of outside influence. It is remarkable to notice that the advent of new technology and exposure to the outside world has resulted in reinforcement of cultural identities and even in the revival of old and forgotten traditions and values... Paradoxically enough, outside modernisers began their attack through the criticism of primitive or traditional (non-western) religions while not only continuing practising their own but also proselytizing others. With growth of literacy and exposure to the wider world, native scholars have begun to detect the logical fallacies in the modernization-development paradigms and have taken steps to return to their own cultural roots.

Asia and the Cultural Diffusion from the West

Over the years, AASSREC symposia have provided evidence of a growing counter-reaction among more radical sections of the young, who looked upon many aspects of scientific and technological change as a new form of 'colonialism'. This view finds its reflection in the demand that 'Western values' in general, and science-based technology and science education, in particular, should be indigenized and that local cultural elements should replace those imposed or imported from outside. The general phenomenon of restlessness among youth was directed towards ensuring that improvements in their society took place within the framework of traditional values, with the latter acting as a spring-board, rather than hindrance, to social and economic advance.

In his review of youth and society in Indonesia, Prijono Tjiptoheriyanto (1988) provided evidence of a new interest in, and allegiance to, a cultural heritage that predated the colonial past. He argued that the energy and enthusiasm of young people should be harnessed to positive ends, by making them innovators in a development process which would help to modernise Indonesia without the loss of national identity. He considered education to be of vital importance in this process, since it could provide knowledge of scientific and technological development, on the one hand, and the linguistic and cultural heritage of the Indonesian people, on the other. He noted that "greater attention should be paid to the role of indigenous educational institutions, (so that) the modernisation process was not based completely on western development paradigm". But while there was a need for educational institutions to safeguard indigenous culture, these same traditional places of learning "should also adjust themselves as the place for proper socialisation for the roles of innovation and modernisation demanded of these institutions". It is therefore imperative that education establishments should (increase their currently limited absorptive capacity and that they should) foster innovation, but that such activities should be carried out within the framework provided by the specifically Indonesian heritage, "in order that the national goals can be achieved without the loss of national identity."

In some countries of the region this reaction against Western cultural supremacy and its association with science and technology, has involved a variety of revivalist or revolutionary movements, searching for strictly local, national or regional roots, involving the repudiation of foreign influences as evil and corrupt, and as utterly incompatible with the cores of the cultures concerned. The predominantly Western character of modern scientific and technological enterprise, previously so much praised for its openness and international outlook, has become suspect, not only as a source of social disruption, but also as a cloak for domination by foreign cultures and world powers.

A pessimistic scenario of future events, which could result from the neglect of indigenous cultures and their cores in the current educational and societal frameworks of some of the Asian nations, was drawn-up as long ago as 1980 by professionals forming the ASEAN Scholars Group (1980). Members of this group were social scientists who had been working for their respective national governments. They had "all earned advanced degrees in the West in some education-related field...and lived long enough, during a momentous period of South East Asian history, to have experienced sweeping changes in the culture of their respective nations". They stated:

> Pessimistically, there will be further breakdown of traditional value systems and religious beliefs as a result of rapid modernisation, industrialisation and urbanisation, increased impact of impersonal bureaucratic organisation and a strong tendency to succumb to consumerism. Crime will become rampant. Intellectuals will come to regard education in the indigenous traditions as a useless hindrance to progress. Education for secular utilitarian ends will continue to be heavily stressed, thus further contributing to the general deterioration of religious faith and religiously guided behaviour. Traditional community ties and spirit will deteriorate. Life will become impersonal and encapsulated. Considerable cultural stagnation and distortion will result.

While accepting the dangers that may result from an indiscriminate "culture transfer", it is also important to note that such criticisms may be regarded as a not unexpected reaction in a period when local tradition is changing faster than it can be absorbed and assimilated by some group members. At the same time, appeals to the earlier version of heritage, which involve careful selection of just one aspect of the past as a model to be followed and rejection of others, may result in the repudiation of some of the most valuable developments in the group's own 'indigenous' tradition. Hence excessive zeal to "purify" the tradition from outside influences, which may have long become absorbed and "indigenised" over time, creates its own danger.

The essential process which should accompany or, preferably, precede 'modernization' is the crystallization of a coherent body of tradition that in-corporates the cultural inputs that the country has experienced in the past. In this regard, Thailand could be taken as an example of a country which has been subjected to a variety of outside inputs, and which showed probably its most conspicuous success in the integration of a large number of citizens of Chinese ancestry. The Thai language and Buddhist religion have been gradually accepted by the Chinese-and overwhelmingly so in the third generation-while both the Thais and the Chinese have also relied upon their long-standing historical and racial links to foster inter-group marriage. This generation has allowed the Thais of Chinese ancestry to play a vital role in the economy of the country, while their acceptance of the Thai overarching values has brought them within the country's cultural 'umbrella'.

From this theoretical perspective, Filipinos, too, would need to consolidate their cultural heritage and embrace it as their own, before embarking upon its major reconstruction to serve the needs of the present. The Filipinos themselves view the situation as critical, requiring urgent action to ensure the stability of the country. The essential role of the educational system in the shaping of Filipino values and in the enculturation of the young has been most clearly articulated by the former Filipino Secretary (or minister) of the Department of Education, Culture and Sport, Dr. Lourdes Quisumbing (1987:7-12). She wondered why, even though the country had produced so many professionals and intellectuals, it had "not been able to bring about any real change in society". This was caused, she claimed, not by any lack of exposure to new ideas, but because traditional values had "not undergone sufficient study and qualitative change". Indeed, the minister was convinced that what the Filipino system had neglected was this kind of 'values education'. Through her sponsorship, compulsory courses on values were given additional stress, as part of the curriculum, and core programme in colleges and universities. The aim of this education endeavour has been to uncover the solid bedrock of Filipino values and consolidate them, before embarking upon changes that affected the country's core values, including its spirituality and family virtues.

Asian Culture and Scientific Evelopment

The example of the Philippines shows that while it is obvious that modem nations, whether in Asia or elsewhere, cannot return to "village technology", it must be recognised that the societal and cultural 'envelope' of technology and science should be more closely related to national cultures of Asia and their local needs, *i.e.* that it should be decolonised.

The previous cultural colonialism of the West was buttressed by a belief in the purely European origin of science and technology (Hall & Hall, 1964). This was deemed to justify the denigration of Asian cultures as 'inferior', 'old fashioned' or 'non-scientific', and hence unsuitable to catalyse economic development without the assistance of some European *lingua franca* and cultural know how. Since the imported values and structures were regarded as the only way to ensure progress and development, local cultures needed to be trimmed to provide an appropriate cultural matrix for the development of the 'scientific state of mind'.The danger has been that it was the core values that were being trimmed, in a way that endangered the culture's integrity, its creative powers, and its ability to sustain intellectual effort and the interest of youth.

Such dangers were ignored when it was deemed necessary to foster a Western-based "scientific climate" of values for the "proper education of scientists". It was assumed that the developed world had managed to perfect such an education and that the application of this model was the *sine qua non* for economic development. As Claude Ake notes, this development came to be observed as a "celebration of the achievement of the West (with) Western society regarded as ideal and the development process as a matter becoming more like the West (...) When it encounters cultural resistance, it proclaims the need for modernisation of attitudes. (1988 : 485). 'It was only later that it was discovered that such "trimming" of cultures did not invariably create an improved climate for science. Instead, by impoverishing the cultures concerned, such modifications seemed to exert some important dysfunctional effects upon society as a whole.

Gradually it became recognised that the "indigenous" cultures had their own internal dynamic based upon their cores. It was through these cultural cores that societies could adapt most successfully to scientific innovation and technological development. Hence, the supposed antithesis between 'local' cultures and 'western' science was shown to be vastly exaggerated and often simply false (Smolicz, 1981b; Dube, 1988). Science and technology could flourish within the local cultures, which need not be either static or inimical to scientific discovery.

This realisation received additional support from the recognition that science could not be regarded as some kind of private property of the West and that it was the product of centuries of interpenetration of the cultures of East and West, Babylon and Persia, Egypt and Greece, China and India, Byzantium and the Islamic world, Catholic and Protestant Europe.

Science and technology are indeed international enterprises; and scholars such as Joseph Needham (1963) and Lynn White (1962; 1968) have shown that their origin should not be sought in Western cultures alone, but in the cultures of the East as well This has involved an appreciation of the contribution of Asian tradition to science and technology, of identifying Asian cultures with modernity and innovation, and of seeking ways in which the still untapped resources of Asian civilizations and technological knowledge can be brought to bear upon the development of their own societies. There is also a need to demonstrate the linkages between traditional cultures, so that they not only continue to thrive during the technological development of their societies, but also contribute towards the process. Such a need places great demands upon the Asian countries' higher educational system and upon research undertaken by scholars and scientists.

Asian Cultural Context for Education and Development

In practical terms educational curricula and the foci of research initiatives may best be directed towards the following goals:

1. Recognition of Asian co-authorship in scientific and technological development.
2. Rejection of those aspects of technological progress that act as mere channels of foreign influences and domination, while welcoming participation in scientific development in co-operation with other nations.
3. Search for new ways in which the still untapped resources of local and regional traditions can contribute to innovation, and in this way strengthening these traditions, while aiding progress and social and economic development.

Research in this field would have to be based on those latent forces which were previously locked within a society's heritage, but which must be released as a living tradition, if innovation is to take place in harmony with the culture of the people whom it is intended to serve.

It would seem that the most important problem is concerned with the question of culture-fit and continued disbelief in some countries and among some elites concerning the viability of local Asian cultures to sustain scientific development and technological growth. Study and research in the various branches of the social sciences (be they the sociology of science and technology, sociology of culture, economics and education) may help to illuminate this culture-science connection within different national settings. The search for indigenous cultural roots can then be viewed in a perspective which accepts that the process of cultural and educational development can be advanced, without subscribing to the activities of those who would dismiss some of the contributions of science and technology to their societies merely on the ground that they were based on Western origins, and hence smacked of 'cultural neo-colonialism'. Europe, too, must play its role, in collaborating with scholars within a framework that emphasises the socially relevant applications of research findings, and stipulates that "social science needs to be related to the circumstances of the countries where it is practised". Such studies require the examination of what constitutes the essential integrity of each national group and its *core values*, and which cultural aspects may be altered in the course of scientific and technological development without rupturing the whole socio-cultural entity.

It may also be sometimes overlooked that certain Asian values, that were 'borrowed' by the West in the past, may be returning to Asia in a new Western guise. This underlines the essential dynamism of living cultures, and the significance that should be attached to the process of interaction through the cross-national diffusion of values, leading either to the co-existence or synthesis of cultures.

One further point which should be noted is that the previously unquestioned Western model of scientific education, has, in at least some respects, been found wanting, even in countries where it was first developed. Over the past decades we have witnessed an increasing criticism of modern science initiated by people such as Kuhn (1969) and Feyerabend (1970). They have succeeded in generating scepticism about such previously entrenched dogmas as those of rationalism, individualism, positivism and belief in the perpetual progress of mankind that was virtually guaranteed by rationally-based Western science. The emphasis of these sceptics is away from what they label as the "myth of rationalism" and towards "tradition and community". These criticisms are generally related to some of modern science's "Western-bound" cultural characteristics. It would be ironical if some of those alleged defects of modern science, which have emerged from Western cultural contexts, were to be introduced into Asia, in violation of Asian cultural traditions which, on the contrary, should have been developed and even transplanted to the West.

Rejection of Euro-centrism with its assumption of the superiority and even universal validity of Western standards and norms does not in itself provide an answer to the fundamental question: posed by Wallerstein (1997), namely the relationship of the universal to the particular in the study of cultural values. He notes that while all knowledge activity is a search for universals, "there is another sense in which all knowledge activity is particularistic. The difficulty resides in the fact that while no universalising knowledge activity can ever achieve a universalistic stance...no particularising activity can ever escape making claims that take the form of at least mini-grand narratives". Since there is no escape into either the universal or the particular, Wallerstein conclude that the only alternative is to construct a "pluralistic universalism". However attractive such a concept may appear, it cannot be allowed to lead to a moral vacuum of indecision, or be employed as a convenient subterfuge for the inculcation of the values of the dominant group or civilisation—be it language, culture or social values-in the guise of their supposed universality.

REFERENCES

Andres, T. D., (1981). *Understanding Filipino Values.* Quezon City, Metro Manila: New Day Publishers.

Atal, Yogesh (ed.) (1991). *Culture-Development Interface,* Association of Asian Social Science Research Councils (AASSREC), New Delhi: Vikas Publishing.

ASEAN Scholars Group (1980). Alternative futures for ASEAN: An educational perspective (Minneapolis, Alternative Educational Social Futures Program, University of Minnesota), Reprinted from *Journal of Cultural and Educational Futures* 2, (1).

Asmah Haji Omar (1982). *Language and Society in Malaysia.* Kuala Lumpur: Dawan Bahasa Dan Pustaka".

Asmah Haji Omar (1983). *The Malay Peoples of Malaysia and their Languages,* Kuala Lumpur: Dawan Bahasa Dan Pustaka. Association of Asian Social Science Research Councils.

AASSREC (1988). *Youth in Asia: Viewpoints for the Future,* New Delhi, New Statesman Publishing Co. Association of Asian Social Science Research Councils.

AASSREC (1989). *The Development Culture Interface: Cultural Perspectives on Economic Progress,* Eighth Biennial Conference, Christchurch, New Zealand, Association of Asian Social Science Research Councils.

AASSREC (1997). *The Papers of the XIIth AASSREC Biennial General Conference,* Beijing: Chinese Academy of Social Science, Association of Asian Social Science Research Councils.

AASSREC (1999). *The 13th Biennial Coniference of Association of Asian Social Science Research Councils*, Seoul: Korean Social Science Research Council.

Banphot (1988). "Youth and society": Thailand, Proceedings of the Symposium of the Association of Asian Social Science Research Councils (AASSREC) *Youth in Asia: Viewpoints* for the *Future* (pp. 115-25). New Delhi: New Statesman Publishing Co.

Bourke, C., Bourke E. and Edwards B. (eds.) (1994). *Aboriginal Australia*, St. Lucia: University of Old Press.

Byong-Je, J. (1988). "Youth and society: Republic of Korea", Proceedings of the Symposium of the Association of Asian Social Science Research Councils (AASSREC) *Youth in Asia: View Points for the Future* (pp. 126-58), New Delhi: New Statesman Publishing Co.

Constantino, R. (1982). *The Miseducation of the Filippino*, Manila, Philippines: Foundation for Nationalist Studies.

Davies, N. (1996). *Europe: A History*, Oxford and New York: Oxford University Press.

Dube, S.C. (1988). Cultural dimensions of development. *International Social Science Journal*, pp. 118, 485-97.

Eisenstadt, S.N. "The Vision of Modern and Contemporary Society" in E. Ben-Rafael and Y. Sternberg (eds), *Identity, Culture and Globalisation*, The Annals of the International Institute of Sociology, New Series, Vol. 8, pp. 25-48, Leiden, Boston, Koln: Brill.

FesI, E.D. (1988). "Language loss in Australian languages", Paper presented to the Conference on Maintenance and Loss of Minority Languages, Institute of Applied Linguistics, University of Nijmegen, The Netherlands.

Feyerabend, P. K. (1970). "Consolation for the specialist", In I. Lakatos and A. Musgrave (eds.) *Criticism and the Growth of Knowledge*, Cambridge: Cambridge University Press.

Gale, F., Jordan, D., McGill, G., McNamara, N. and Scott, C. (1987). "Aboriginal education", In J.P.Keeves (ed.) *Australian Education: A Review of Recent Research*, Sydney: George Allen and Unwin.

Gellner, E. A. (1983). *Nations and Nationalism*, Oxford: Basil Blackwell.

Gorospe, V. R. (1988). *Filipino Values Revisited*. Manila: National Book Store.

Hall, A.R. and Hall, M.B. (1964). *The European Scientific Tradition*. New York: Princeton University Press.

Hobsbawn, E. J. and Ranger T. (1983). *The Invention of Tradition*, Cambridge: Cambridge University Press.

Jupp, J. (2001). *The Australian People: Encycolpedia of the Nation, Its People and Their Origins*, Cambridge: Cambridge University Press.

Kuhn, T.S. (1969). *The Structure of Scientific Revolutions*, Chicago: University of Chicago Press.

Kundera, M. (1984). "A kidnapped west or culture bows out". In B. Burford (ed.) *Granta*. Cambridge.

Lansang, T.A. (1988). "Retelling Philippine History". *Trends: Journal of Ideas of the Polytechnic University of the Philippines*, pp. 2, 15-32.

Licuanan, P. *et al.* (1989) "A moral recovery program: Building a people—building a nation". In R. L. Schwenk (ed.) *Moral Recovery and the Democratic Vision* (pp. 10-33). Manila: Seed Centre, Philippine National University.

Needham, J. (1963). "Poverties and triumphs of the Chinese scientific tradition", in A.C. Crombie (*ed.*) *Scientific Change*. London: Heinemann.

Obolensky, D. (1974). *The Byzantine Commonwealth: Eastern Europe* 500-1453 London: Cardinal Edition, Sphere Books.

Oommen, T.K. (1997). *Citizenship, Nationality and Ethnicity: Reconciling Competing Identities,* Cambridge: Polity Press.

Quisumbing, L. (1987). "Values", *Philippine Value Digest* 2 (1), pp. 7-12.

Smolicz, J.J. (1988). Tradition, core values and intercultural development, *Ethnic and Racial Studies,* 11 (4), 387-410. (London).

Smolicz, J. J. (1999). "Privatization in Higher Education: Emerging Commonalities and Diverse Educational Perspectives", *Development and Society,* 28 (2), 205-228.

Smolicz, J.J., Nical, I. and Secombe, M.J (2000). "Educational Policies and Language Maintenance in Multilingual Settings—Australia and the Philippines", *International Journal of Bilingual Education and Bilingualism,* 3 (4), 242-264.

Smolicz, J.J., Secombe, M.J. and Hudson, D. (2001). "Family Collectivism and Minority Languages as Core Values of Culture among Ethnic Groups in Australia", *Journal of Multilingual and Multicultural Development,* 22 (2), 152-172.

Szacki, J. (1969). "Three concepts of tradition", *The Polish Sociological Bulletin,* 2, 144-50.

Szacki, J. (1997). O Narodzie i Nacjonalizmie (On Nation and Nationalism), *Znak* (Krakow, Poland) 49 (502), pp. 4-31.

Tijpoheriyanto, P. (1988). "Youth and society: Viewpoints for the future: An Indonesian experience". Paper presented at the Sixth General Conference of the Association of Asian Social Science Research Councils (AASSREC), Bali. Published in *Youth and Society: Viewpoints for the Future* (pp. 96-114). New Delhi: New Statesman Publishing Co.

Tombiah, S. J. (1986). "The Nation-State in Crisis and the Rise of Ethnonationalism". In E. N. Wilmsen and P. McAllister (eds.) *The Politics of Difference* (pp. 124-143). Chicago and London: The University of Chicago Press.

Toynbee, A.J. (1978). *A Study of History* Vol. 1, New York, Laurel Edition, Dell Publishing.

Wallerstein, I. (1997). "The West and the Rest", Presidential Letter No. 6, International Sociological Association, ISA (16/4/97). White, L. (1962) *Medieval Technology and Social Change,* Oxford: Oxford University Press.

White, L. (1968). *Machina ex Deo.* M.I.T. Press, Massachusetts Institute of Technology, Cambridge, Massachusetts and London.

11

Globalization: How Novel? How Noble?

K.N. SHARMA

Yogesh Atal belongs to the third generation of Indian sociologists/social anthropologists. During the last forty years or so I have seen him grow from a poet bridegroom to the status of an eminent sociologist grandfather. By now his presence is widely felt in the international academic firmament. In addition he has been an effective communicator of sociological analysis of national affairs in standard popular Hindi magazines. These qualities of his head have not ebbed out the poet sitting in his heart. Three collections of his Hindi poems have just been published, adding to two others published earlier. I am confident he will soon acquire a national stature in this realm as well. Atal represents a rare blend of expression of solid social scientific analysis with sensitive literary flourish that strikes a chord or two in the hearts of readers. Whether his strong local roots have given him amazing sustenance for flowering on the global plane or not but the fact remains that neither one has choked the other.

Recently both of us participated in a Conference (February 28 through March 2, 2003) in Lucknow on Globalization, organized as part of D.N. Majumdar Centenary Celebrations. Most of this paper is based on my oral presentation at the aforesaid Conference. Globalization is the new academic fad. While surfing the Internet I discovered that in 1998 alone as many as 2822 academic papers and 589 new books on globalization appeared. Expectedly, they have differed on the meaning as well as consequences of globalization. And the literature is mounting up over the years, although confusion continues to persist as regards its definition and desirability.

No wonder then that Atal and I also differed at the Conference in our perception of Globalization.[1]

I hold the view that the process of Globalization is not a new phenomenon. It did not emerge suddenly with the establishment and operation of the World Trade Organization (WTO) or the break-up of the USSR. Interactions between different societies is an age-old feature. The movement of peoples, inter-cultural economic transactions, and dialogue between philosophies, religions, and civilizations can be traced back to the pre-historic and ancient times. Of course, the character and consequences of these transactions have changed overtime.

For the sake of convenience I propose to divide the brief history of such movements into four phases: the Pre-historic, Pre-colonial, European colonial, and Post-colonial—which is now named Globalization.

A. Movements During Pre-historic and Ancient Times

India offers a good example of movement of peoples, goods and ideas. It has both received and dispatched men, materials and messages. These processes did not add elements of other cultures to Indian culture in India—thereby 'globalizing it'—but also spread Indian culture world-wide.

In terms of ethnic plurality India offers an excellent example. Nobody knows for sure how many tribal groups are fully indigenous and how many had immigrated through the porous borders. There are enough proofs to state that even Aryans came from North-West, although it is not clearly established as to whether they came from Afghanistan, or Ukraine, or other parts of Eastern Europe.

Even within the country migrations from one part to the other had been taking place for long. For example, Kumaon region of the current state of Uttaranchal contains ethnic groups that immigrated from other regions of the country. Most of the Brahmans came to Kumaon in the wake of Shankaracharya's visit for establishing his PEETH (centre) for propagating non-dualistic *(Advait)* philosophy and *Sannyasa*. Vaishya caste, known as Shah, immigrated from Nepal when the region was occupied by the Nepalese rulers in the nineteenth century.

Not only goods and peoples were exported from India to other lands but also philosophies and religions have travelled to far off places both within and outside of Asia—for example, China, Indonesia, Thailand, Greece, and the Middle East. We are told that Chinese students used to go to Indonesia for studying Sanskrit.

Briefly speaking this phase of Indian history is characterized by the following:

1. To begin with, there were no fixed boundaries of States. Therefore movements of people and goods encountered only geographical, and not political, obstacles.
2. The immigrant groups, by and large, came to the new habitat and accepted it as their home and delinked themselves from the areas of their origin.
3. Those who settled in the new area, found enough space for pursuing their life style without any interference from others. For example, we find migrant tribal groups in the Kumaon region. In some cases, geographical proximity of two tribal areas paved the way for exchange and borrowing of cultural items—material as well as non-material.
4. The process of integration of isolated migrant groups within a single socio-political entity had been long drawn. Its success depended on a large number of factors, including geographical contiguity, emergence of political authority and interdependence of economic activities of different ethnic groups. The living together for generations had resulted into a shared common culture. In Kumaon, this process started from the 4th century A.D., when political regimes of Katyuris and Chand kings emerged. Their contacts with the Northern kingdoms of India, probably, provided the caste-occupation framework for structuration. The arrival of Brahmanas with Shankaracharya, and their settling down in the region, ultimately helped in the emergence of a Hindu social structure, similar to the rest of India. Tribal groups continued to be absorbed in the emergent social framework. This social fluidity, however, could not absorb all the tribal groups. There still exist tribal groups in the same geographical area that are outside the pale of Hinduism.
5. Greek philosophers appreciated Indian philosophies. Likewise, India also borrowed the set of nine planets and their astrological significance from the Greek thought.
6. Conversion to Hinduism or Buddhism in the Eastern Asia was not associated with any political compulsions. While remaining separate political entities people of these countries espoused Hinduism and Buddhism.
7. Both land and sea routes were used for 'international' trades.
8. By and large, these movements were non-violent and non-political.

B. Pre-Colonial Phase

The establishment of Ottoman Empire in the Middle East changed the character of movements of peoples, goods, religions, etc. Arabs spread both in Europe right up to Spain in South and eastwards in Asia, particularly towards India. Their movement combined economic, political and religious objectives. In a series of violent responses Christian Crusades started and halted the movement of Arabs towards Europe. The Ottoman Empire finally collapsed during the First World War. But the Arab or Muslim invasions of India had already started and continued for about five centuries. The purpose of these invasions was primarily political, but spread of Islam, both through violent and non-violent means, remained associated with it. In any case most of the invading groups settled in India and accepted it as their home. In contrast to the migrating Parsees, Jews and converted Christians, the Indian Muslims do maintain religious links with their holy centres, especially in the form of Haj pilgrimage. Gradually economic, political, social and cultural exchanges with Hindus paved the way for some degree of reciprocity between Muslims and Hindus. Yet the fact remains that the widely differing identities continued to promote occasional hostilities. The emerging social structure was only a large edition of the pre-historic structuration in which some groups remained on the periphery.

C. European Colonialism

European capitalist mode of production replaced the family as a unit of production by the corporation and factory. New technology replaced animate power by inanimate energy for production, whether it was electricity or oil or gas. This shift to new technology based on inanimate energy required more capital and additional labour for expansion of production. It also necessitated expansion of markets for the sale of products produced on a large scale. All these economic and technological factors had various and wide ranging effects on the economy, polity, and society. Marxism, as a critique of capitalism, also emerged as an ideology.

Colonialism was an offshoot of European Capitalism. It got a boost by the first circumnavigation of the earth between 1519 and 1521. Trading contacts were established with countries in Asia. Adventurist and expansionist Europeans who succeeded in colonizing them discovered new geographical areas like North and South America, Africa, and Australia. These colonies became suppliers of raw materials for the industries of the West and new markets for the finished products of the European industry.

One of the most important contributions of scientists and technologists of the West was the identification and exploration of petrol and gas as the most efficient source of energy. It led to a big expansion in world trade and investment in the late nineteenth century.

Appearance of trading companies and colonies led to the establishment of imperial hegemony. The case of India can be cited as a good example of how an innocuous looking East India Company paved the way for the foundation of British Raj. The Raj created a new system of administration and introduced Western (English) system of education.

Spread of colonialism in the countries of Asia, Africa, and Latin America resulted in the emergence of patterns of behaviour that can be called "Western" or "modern". Acceptance of English as the main language of international communication, adoption of the International Date Line, and universal use of the Gregorian calendar brought the countries of the world closer. These developments had far-reaching impact on values, life style, and even on religion. Colonialism was accompanied by mass scale conversion of indigenes into Christianity. All these changed the character of the cultures of the colonies.

Industrial revolution in the West resulted not only in the spread of colonialism and imperialism, it also equipped the world with lethal and dangerous weapons of mass destruction. Imperial powers competing for markets and colonies became involved in hostilities and plunged the world into the theatrics of War. The post-Industrial Revolution Era witnesses to devastating World Wars.

The First World War had both negative and positive effects on the nascent processes of globalization. To avert the possibilities of a future war there came into being the League of Nations, but it met its nemesis in its infancy. Countries of the North pursued the policy of protectionism, which obstructed free international trade. Within three decades, the world witnessed the Second World War that was much more brutal than the first. The end of the Second World War gave enormous impetus to the expansion of capitalism round the globe, on the one hand, and on the other, the rise of the Second World in Eastern Europe dominated by Marxist/Stalinist Soviet Union. The collapse of Soviet Union is the most important landmark in the unrestrained march of current globalization.

Post-Colonial Globalization

I regard globalization as neo-capitalism propelled by modern technologies of mass production of weapons of mass destruction and of goods for mindless conspicuous consumption as well as their free international trade under the 'benign' regime of W.T.O.

In his own characteristic way, Yogesh Atal characterized the periods of colonial rule, the early years of post-colonial self-rule, and the recently ushered era of Globalization as "periods of *dependence, independence,* and *interdependence* respectively". His argument was that the countries under the colonial rule were heavily dependent on the colonizer country, which was, for them, the only 'aperture' to the outside world. Attainment of independence meant opening of more apertures although the former colonies still remained recipients of outside traits and complexes. It is, according to him, the process of globalization that has created situations of interdependence where each country has become both giver and receiver. To an extent, Atal's formulation is right. But I am of the view that all the three periods have seen the dominance of the countries of the North in cultural, economic, political, and even technological spheres. And this pattern of domination continues in this era of globalization as well.

Role of Modern Science and Technology

The interesting feature of modern technology is that it becomes obsolete in increasingly shorter time spans. Armaments and consumer goods become obsolete in less than five years. But with faster means of transportation they reach different corners of the world almost instantaneously. Thus, obsolescence of the prevailing technology is felt the world over simultaneously. However, their replacement may not arrive at the same time everywhere. In such circumstances, the agenda of research and development in science and technology is guided by self-interest and ego-satisfaction, and not by holistic and cosmological perspective. Such research can never remain *Sattwika*—"Enlightening". According to the Gita (XVIII-23) *Sattwika* action is that which is obligatory, which is performed without attachment, without love or hate, and unconcerned about the outcome (*ma faleshu kadachana*—never desirous of fruit). Modern research does not qualify as *Sattwika* in terms of this definition.

The preceding verse of the Gita holds that "The knowledge which clings to one single effect, as if it were the whole without concern for the cause, without grasping the real and narrow is declared to be of the nature of "dullness" (*i.e.* taamasa; it also means ignorance).[2]

In fact, it has the potentiality of total annihilation in the long run because ignorance (*Tamas*) can never be enlightening (*Sattwika*). Magic-like wonders of science and technology conceal the embedded ignorance. In this context it is worthwhile to draw the attention of readers to two questions raised by T. S. Eliott; where is wisdom in the pursuit of knowledge? Where is knowledge in the pursuit of information? The emerging unintended consequences of globalization propelled by the flowering of modern science and technology, present the preview of the future scenario.

Consequences of Globalization

There is a very large number of actual and potential consequences of Globalization on economy, polity and society. Some of these are highlighted here.

Economic Consequences

1. The most significant economic consequence of Globalization is the social malady that I would like to call *'moneyitis'* for want of a better term. It is like uncontrollable obesity caused by unabsorbable supply of money. A steep fall in interest rates all over the world is due to this phenomenon. Aggressive promotion of mindless, wasteful conspicuous consumption facilitated by the supply of money, and the investment of profits in production has produced more money, creating greater social inequalities, and rising income disparities.
2. The targetted consumers belong to upper reaches of the society. It leaves a large section of human population deprived. The deprived groups are then motivated to indulge in crime and in corrupt practices. Poverty and deprivation are likely to generate unrest and protest, and even instigate people to revolt. Terrorism may also be abetted by the oversupply of money and consequent deprivation of large segments of population.
3. Modern technology requires huge capital and therefore it promotes MNC's. Their success and survival in a competitive world and the consequent saturation of the market is always problematic. And the failure of MNCs renders their workers jobless. The growth of unemployment in the developed economies is a major problem, and a source of disorganization.
4. The website on globalization offers conflicting reports and opinions on increase/decrease of inequalities and poverty globally. World Bank and W.T.O. now claim that inequalities between developed and developing societies are narrowing down and that there is reduction in the rates of poverty. Contrary to such assertions, the UNDP 1999 *Development Report* notes that the gap between the rich and poor nations of the world is increasing.

Political Consequences

1. In the changing milieu the MNCs, large industrial corporations,

and international funding agencies within the UN System considerably influence policies of states, especially in developing societies. Such policies completely disregard local cultural context and severely affect their social and political structures. This was evidenced by the policies of structural adjustment initiated at the instance of the International Monetary Fund and the World Bank.

2. There are several regional organizations of States in addition to the United Nations. Besides Security Council itself has five permanent members with Veto power. These bodies have to check the emergence of USA as a super-power and its tendency to unilateralism. Though USA possesses both economic power and military might, yet it failed to get an endorsement from the Security Council for its proposed Resolution in regard to Iraq. Ignoring the world-wide protests against attack on Iraq, it commenced War on March 20, 2003. In doing so, USA undermined the authority of United Nations and disregarded public opinion of its own citizenry. Under the circumstances, one can ask questions about the role of American armament as well as consumer goods industry, which may be pushing Bush to ambush Saddam. American attack on Iraq raises a fundamental question: Can economic globalization survive with the weakening of the global political order and unipolarization by the super-power? It is impossible to gauge all the dangerous unintended consequences of the currently waged war in the Gulf.

D. Cultural, Social and Environmental Consequences

1. Increasing popularity of consumption of imported food and drink items to luxury cars are a clear evidence of outside cultural invasion. Aggressive advertisements and availability of easy bank loans are responsible for promoting conspicuous consumption. This has changed the life style of the people and also their worldview. It reminds me of a Sanskrit verse of philosopher Charvak which means so long you are alive enjoy life. Borrow money and drink ghee (now scotch). Once you die, who the hell can get the money back? Politicians and industrialists-cum-businessmen, in collusion with the Bank officials, have identified workable holes in the lending policy that facilitate delay—in some cases, even non-payment—in the repayment of borrowed money.
2. Individualism as a guiding philosophy of life became quite prominent during the capitalist-colonial phase. Now in this age of

neo-capitalism or globalization, the separation of individual from society and family has become a contagious societal disease. It has already eroded the foundation of marriage and family as the core institutions of society, not only in the USA and Europe but also in the societies of the East. Individualism produces egoism and hubris, that is, selfishness and insolent pride—the values that are contrary to Indian culture. These psychological developments are bound to tear the fragile fabric of our society.

3. The processes of Globalization have accelerated migration of talent from the developing countries to USA and other developed societies. The existing and emerging modern technologies require skilled workers and managers of corporations, finances, markets, banks etc. The developing societies like India, which have established internationally recognized institutions for training in science, technology and management, have become major suppliers of the required skilled workers. Apart from IT specialists, medical doctors are also drawn into this net. Lure of money and the fascination of leading Western life style have taken the talents of the developing societies to these new pastures causing serious shortages in their parent cultures.

   In the developing societies, the cost of education in technical and professional institutions has become so prohibitive that only the rich (who do not send their children for higher education abroad) can afford to send their wards for studies. The rest of the educational system is in shambles. The hiatus between the two streams of education may have serious social, political, and economic consequences.

4. The NRIs now suffer from a certain identity crisis. They differ from the breed of migrants of the pre-historical and colonial era who accepted the land of immigration as their own. In the USA, temples are being constructed; priests trained in India are recruited in these temples. They are being invited to help maintain their identity. Many priests go on lecture tours also. For these services, Vishwa Hindu Parishad is collecting huge donations, which are being used to assert Hindu identity. This fight is not against globalizing culture but against the recorded historical past. It may not be out of place to mention that the second generation of NRIs is revolting against rigid Hindu codes, and life style, despite all the efforts of the first generation migrants.

5. Pollution, exploitation and degradation of environment and space in addition to the problem of disposal of waste material are

unintended consequences of mindless mass production. The environmentalists have been trying in vain to attract the attention of the powers-that-be.

FINAL COMMENT

One may ask the unhappy question: Does globalization make us happier? To quote Robert Wright: "Globalization makes us richer, but also does it make happier? For the already rich wealth seems to bring little gain in happiness; in poor countries, money really can buy happiness, but only if the poor can cope with the fierce pace of change". [3]

It is half-hearted and unbaked question, especially in the light of enormous Sanskrit literature dealing with happiness. Let me quote one verse from the Mahabharat (Adi Parva 75.49) and one verse from the Gita (XVIII-38) in order to underline the value of philosophical perspective on the meaning of happiness and its nature.

Na Jatu Kamah Kamanam Upbhogen Shamyati
Havisha krishnavartmev bhooy evabhivardhate
(Mahabharat: Adi Parva 75.49)

It broadly means that consuming the articles that are supposed to bring happiness can satisfy nobody. The longing for these articles goes on increasing in the same degree in which they are consumed, as is the case with fire which burns more with throwing of more burning material in it.

Vishayendriya Samyogadi Yat Tadagreamritopamam
Pariname vishmiv, tad sukham rajas am smratam
The Gita (Chapter 18, Verse 38)

To freely translate: that happiness which arises from the contact of the senses and their objects and that is like nectar at first but like poison at the end—such happiness is to be regarded as passionate (*raajasa).*

According to the Indian philosophical perspective, all the materials for the pleasure of the body and senses fall in the category of *taamasa*. False fear of insecurity is also *taamasa* in nature.

Globalization is fuelled by the modern technology of mass production of weapons and consumer goods. In terms of Indian traditional vision these activities are rooted in blind self-interest, which promote only *raajas* and *taamasa actions.* The absence of a holistic/cosmological vision guarantees enormously dangerous exploitation, pollution and degradation of environment on the one hand, and unmindful pleasure-hunting by egoistic selfish individuals, on the other. They may create fissures, if not divisions, between haves and have-nots. But the greatest danger is to fragile fabric of the society. Egoism and hubris are its greatest enemies.

The only antedote to these unintended and undesirable consequences of globalization is wisdom. Collection of information, and generation of knowledge without the enlightening wisdom have the potentiality of not only wars but, most importantly, of irreparable damage to environment and the human society.

NOTES

1. In passing I may raise a question. How far has this enormous literature on globalization contributed to the welfare of the masses and succeeded in preventing pollution and degradation of environment? Similar questions can be asked on our debates on the concepts and consequences of westernization, modernization, post-modernization *et al.*
2. See S. Radhakrishnan, *The Bhagwadgita,* Blackie & Son Publishers, 1982, p. 349.
3. See 'Will globalization Make you Happy? http://www.foreign policy.com/issue/Sept. 2000/essay.html.

12

Information and Communication Technology: Challenges to Democracy in Asia

BINOD C. AGRAWAL

My association with Professor Yogesh Atal spans to over three decades. It was in 1971 that I met him in New Delhi upon my return from United States to join Indian Agricultural Research Institute, New Delhi. Since then we have been off and on in touch. As a young, inexperienced but enthusiastic professional, I went to Professor Atal for advice and consultation from time-to-time. Professor Atal being optimist, encouraged and supported me. Though brief, the intense interaction with Professor Atal made an imprint on my future course of life. When I came to Ahmedabad in 1973, Professor Atal helped me in planning and implementation of the social evaluation of Satellite Instructional Television Experiment (SITE) at Space Applications Centre, Ahmedabad. He made valuable suggestions during the preparatory meeting held in Ahmedabad. At this juncture Professor Atal moved from ICSSR, New Delhi to Bangkok and I continued working at Ahmedabad. Since Professor Atal had shaped my life and helped achieve the task of SITE social evaluation, it is appropriate to discuss communication implications pertaining to political sociology, it being earlier interest of Professor Atal.

In this paper a synoptic view as to how social scientists have postulated communication and information technology influence on democracy and the likely challenges it can pose to human freedom, of expression and human rights. Further, attempts have been to portray the likely scenario and the challenges that communication and information technology can pose to the world's largest democracy of a billion people in India.

Discourse or debate on the technological challenges of information and communication to political paradigms requires an appropriate analysis of socio-cultural context and historical experiences of the people and country. Unprecedented technological revolution seen in the field of communication and space technology stretches over a very small span of Asian history and the collective memory of ancient civilisations of India and China. The techno-political events in the modern political paradigms, of parliamentary democracy in India and communism in China, are just about half century old. In such a situation, any expectation that information and communication technology would alter or influence recently adopted political systems and worldview needs an in-depth analysis of the social structure and capabilities of information and communication technology.

Earlier analysis was to examine the likely challenges that information and communication technology can pose to the parliamentary democracy in India. Three forms of challenges that information and communication technology can bring to bear on the political paradigms were proposed. These were "techno-positivism", "techno-neutralism" and "techno-negativism". The 'techno-positivism' "...view refers to the opinion of those engineers, scientists, and political leaders who believe that satellite-based broadcasting helps political and emotional integration, thereby strengthening democracy. The 'techno-negativism' endorses the views of those who think that satellite-based broadcasting in plural civilisations having multiple languages and 'worldview', imposes the views of a politically dominant minority over the majority. In the process, this kind of broadcasting tends to create emotional dissonance, increases control over information by few, and thereby weakens the democracy. The third view of 'techno-neutralism' represents views of those who believe that technology by itself does not create any condition for weakening the democracy; rather the aims and goals of the communicators are directly responsible for strengthening or weakening the democracy. (Agrawal, 1993:222) (see also Hamelink, 1986).

The situation has not substantially changed in the last decade and so have the views and arguments on the issues under debate, except the emergence of information technology in a big way in large part of Asia and few more shades of opinion and viewpoints. A large number of social scientists working in the interrelated fields of information and communication technology have cast futuristic views on the basis of experiential knowledge about the repercussions on individual freedom of speech and expression, and human insights as a result of the all pervasive technological penetration in human society. The fundamental assumption being that information and communication technology willy-nilly will influence the existing political paradigms since information and communication is an essential ingredient in maintenance and perpetuation of clearly held values like democracy.

History and Democracy

Over last two hundred years of world history, major political revolutions whether American declaration of independence in 1776 or French Revolution in 1789 have given rise to "freedom of opinion", "freedom of expression" and "freedom of the press". Inherent in these paradigms are individual freedom, human rights and equality among all humans. "Socialist revolution" whether in Europe, Asia or Latin/South America in the wake of political upheavals "...ushered in the second generation of human rights". It aimed at the fundamental restructuring of society on the basis of people's power (Traber, 1993 : 29).

Post World War II brought forth the emancipation of the suppressed in several Asian and African countries for freedom, political self-determination and equality among people and nations. During this period of human history, there is little evidence that information and communication technology in any major way entered as a key component in the debate of freedom of speech, freedom of expression and human rights.

It is only recently that a serious question is being raised as to how information and communication technology may or can challenge the political paradigms within the boundaries of democracy and democratic forms of governance in Asia.

Communication and Democracy

In the book *Communication and Democracy* (Splichal and Wasko, eds., 1993), several communication scholars tried to examine the relationships between communication and democracy, while focusing on similar themes. Lately identical questions have been raised by a number of Asian scholars (Tankha, ed., 1995). In the year 2000, a compilation was brought out by Asian Media, Information and Communication Centre entitled *Media and Democracy in Asia* (2000). One of the main questions raised in the book is "whether free media are a pre-condition for the development of democracy or whether the development of democracy will see the emergence of free media". Given the historical and colonial experiences of many Asian countries, it may appear that the issue in this compilation has somewhat focussed only on free media. However, the issue needs to be examined in the broader perspective.

It must be mentioned in passing that these issues have been discussed in international forums, seminars and conferences in last two decades, especially after the publication of *Many Voices One World* (Mac Bride, *et al.* 1980). The Mac Bride report states "The principle of freedom of expression is one that admits of no exceptions, and that is applicable to the people all over the world by virtue of their human dignity" (1980:10).

What is the core issue behind all these debates and discussions? As can be seen, the world's dominant leaders and political philosophers especially those who profess and are committed to democracy believe that only free information and communication opens the path for freedom, free expression and human rights. Today, several forms of democratic governments are in existence in Asia, though whispers can be heard in the corridors of power to conform to single democratic form of governance.

Information Technology and Democracy

In the wake of information technology revolution in the last decade of the 20th century a view had been advanced that "totalitarianism is latent in [information] technology" which gained currency among some scholars. However for others, "information and communication technologies, for instance, both contain and signify the cultural and political values of particular human society. Accordingly, these technologies are always expressions of socio-economic, geographical and political interests, partialities, alignments and commitments. In brief the will to technical knowledge is the will to technical power" (Armitage, 2001:2). To a large extent, another view is that information and communication technologies in more than one way reflect socio-cultural and political values of the society in which they were invented and nurtured. Personal telephone, if invented in Asia, would have taken "family" rather than "individual" as focus of two-way exchange of views and information. It is a common occurrence in many Asian homes where family members take turns and talk to a caller. If it were invented here the receiver would have been omni-directional instead of multi-directional to facilitate group talk on the phone. One can think of several such technologies which would have gone through cultural transformation if designed in Asia.

Neoliberal discourse on information and communication technology as a political philosophy is associated with the idea of liberal fascism, free enterprise and economic globalization. The concern is "...legitimating the political and cultural control of individuals, groups and new social movements through the material and ideological production, promotion, distribution and consumption of self-styled virtual 'technologies like virtual reality and cyber-space" (Armitage, 2001:2). This line of thinking has conceived a new social 'virtual class', trying to manufacture "virtual distractions" like movies, interactive video games and other kinds of technology based entertainment products. In the process a whole host of other issues are camouflaged and pushed aside due to overpowering technology. In real life situation to what extent information and communication technology challenges the existing political ideology or precisely how it infringes or influences the political governance, the individual and community is yet to be deciphered. There is an article of faith that technology will, can and should promote and preserve the democratic process. The democratic process in terms of freedom of speech and expression is seen as an end in itself. It is considered an ultimate achievement of human societies without a critical examination.

There are unique historical and political experiences in countries of South Asia, China, South East Asia and Western Asia. In each of these countries there is a longstanding tradition of developing political philosophy shaped by religious beliefs. This to a large extent determines the process of democratization and in creating unique features of democracy whereby value loaded words like individual freedom, freedom of speech, freedom of expression and human rights including participation in political decision-making are redefined.

Some of the recent publications, especially in the field of information technology, have presented a picture of high level of individual control over world in which he/she lives. Shapiro (1999) thinks "Computers are Control Technology". More than a decade ago, James Beniger had an another view (as cited by Stalder, 1999). These authors seem to have drawn two opposing conclusions. Shapiro has argued that the control revolution would lead to decentralisation of control thereby higher level of freedom of expression and speech. On the contrary, Beniger argued that it would lead to centralisation of control of more power in few hands. I am not certain whether such simplistic conclusions would be fruitful from a limited database and without studying long-term trends.

At present, consensus is that "radically new social and political paradigms are fading away and a more nuanced and complex discussion of social and political issues is beginning" (Stalder, 1999: 1). He believes that the entire argument advanced by Shapiro "rests upon the premise that technologies are political, rather than neutral, and change is characterised by a lack of pre-ordained outcome" (*Ibid*: 2). In sum, control revolution throws a great deal of light on complexities in understanding democracy, freedom, public policy and related issues.

Expansion of information technology in Asia is phenomenal just short of wildfire. Internet connections in Asia has multiplied manifold in less than three years. Pare and Desbret (eds. 1998) had asked the question: Does information technology represents a threat to freedom of expression and to individual and human rights? Or does it represent a too far freeing speech and democratising behaviour? While there is no clear answer, it leaves no doubt that information technology cannot be neutral. Drucker and Gumpert (1999) while examining the regulatory aspects of information technology confronted with the challenges posed by the information technology. Legislators, service providers and courts are grappling with the liability and free expression implications of information technology developments in the Euro-American countries. The Asian countries have also beginning to face country specific problems and few of them have started responding through regulatory mechanism though still in an infancy stage. Will these legislative efforts and controls bring freedom of speech, expression, human rights, and individual participation in decision making is yet to be demonstrated and experienced in Asia.

Reflection from World's Largest Democracy

The Asian continent consists of several pluralistic and ancient civilisations. It is the birthplace of the world's major religions and linguistic groups. Above all Asia has passed through truly remarkable and varied experiences of governance, political systems and philosophers over several millennia dating back to pre-Christian era. Throughout Asian history, social elites controlled power, hogged resources and enjoyed social position. They remained dominant over large majority. Recent changes in the political system of governance have brought about some changes in the civilisation patterns. In the long journey of Asian civilisations was "colonialism" which began in the 18th century when commercial ventures of European powers especially Britain ended up in a conquest of large part of Asia. India was no exception. Political freedom and democratic governance is only about half a century old. Hence, the historical experiences of democracy at present are very brief and yet it has emerged from the shackles of the past. But then the information and communication technology experiences are also recent in origin. So, it would not be possible to establish, if there are any, relationships between information and communication technology and democracy.

The world's largest democracy of over a billion people defies any prediction during parliamentary elections in the country. Social scientists, opinion polls and communication experts are put into quandary each time there is an election in India. Apart from cultural factors, research methods used for data collection may be responsible for such recurrent errors. There seems to be a serious cynicism on the part of people about information and communication technology, which they believe, cannot touch the core of their belief. Further people believe that there is no substitute to inter-personal and face-to-face communication in influencing the electoral behaviour in a highly "familial society" where kin, caste and community affiliations, associations and affinities overrides all other political and ideological considerations.

In spite of over exposure of many leaders, both national and regional, whose voices are often heard, who appear regularly on television, whose pictures are published on the front pages of newspapers and magazines, an average voter expects that at least he/she should have a real glimpse of their leader and if possible, chance to touch and feel. It seems that technological breakthrough in information and communication technology has touched very little of the lives of large majority or it has touched only the surface.

In the field of entertainment and recreation, one observes remarkable electronic media influence and disappearance of a large majority of traditional media. Whether theatre, drama, dance, music or folk entertainment, all have been gradually engulfed by electronic media and cinema. These forms of entertainment can be found in archives and museums for research scholars to study, and as far as possible has been somehow kept quite consciously away from political communication in India. Use of theatre for political ends known in ancient India and even today, to some extent, are used for ridiculing people in power, making fun of political leaders, exposing their misdeeds and their exploits. Probably, it may be for this reason that all pervasive communication technologies have limited role to play in the Indian democracy.

Review of literature on "political sociology" in India made no reference whatsoever on the information and communication technology challenges on democratic process in India. While carrying out the review on this topic Gupta (2000) made no mention of the term information or communication or media anywhere relating or interfering in democratic functioning. Sociologists, social anthropologists, political scientists and communication researchers though involved in election study, 'polling behaviour', 'poll prediction' have little to contribute in analysing and understanding the relationships between information, communication and media and their influences on democratic development in many Asian countries.

In the context of India, communication technology is used extensively for reaching to people, listening to people's queries as means of two way communication between people, administration, politicians and political movements. However, the information and communication technology remains on the periphery of the "real" political activities except its recent use in exposing corrupt politicians.

Historical experiences, borne out the fact that extensive information and communication technology, have played little or limited role in the mobilisation of public opinion. Political parties continue to rely heavily on face-to-face communication, rallies, processions, door-to-door canvassing more than electronic media, as they are considered essential for reaching and influencing the voter. Election after election "poll predictions" have gone terribly wrong. In the recent five state election in India poll predictions were no exception.

In India's general elections of 1999, it was reported that a large number of Indian voters participated in live internet chats with the candidates and other political leaders of major political parties which had hosted their websites. While no systematic analysis was published, it is reported by Singh (1999) that voters were able to grill candidates on issues ranging from sanitation to the fiscal deficit. In the existing plethora of traditional election campaign methods "internet chats" took a place of pride with the hope that the English speaking urban youth would be attracted to it and in turn would play a vital role in forming public opinion.

It is estimated that the ruling political party—Bhartiya Janta Party website got five million hits during the campaign in which about one-third were from non-Indian residents living abroad. Claims and counter claims have been made about internet technology contributions in opening new opportunities to have an informed electoral decision. An interesting feature is that the Bhartiya Janta Party (BJP) still failed to improve its 182 seat mark from the earlier election held a year back in 1998.

On the other hand, the Chief Minister Chandrababu Naidu of a Southern State in India known as Andhra Pradesh, baffled political analysts, when he returned to power in spite of several unpopular decisions taken against the poor and farmers. Commentators were unanimous that Naidu returned to power because of his high-tech information and communication technology image and his achievements in introducing information technology in State administration. On the other hand it is widely believed that his political achievements and personal charisma easily overshadowed the information technology interventions in voting Naidu to power.

It must be mentioned that another national party Congress (I) switched off and stopped internet chat with the electorate in middle of general elections. The party spokesman Jairam Ramesh reported that "There is a lot of pizzazz in this medium but you certainly don't reach voters through net campagins." (as quoted by Singh, 1999: 2) How far did it hurt the political fortune of the party is unknown.

The brief impressionistic analysis of the Indian elections has left too many unanswered questions. For example, it would be difficult to say whether information technology interventions lead to techno-positivism or techno-negativism. The precise contribution and role of internet cannot be assessed and no changes in the existing political paradigm can be predicated. It seems there is a need to go beyond polemics to understand and throw some light on the possible relationships and connections between information and communication technology and democratic process in some of the Asian countries as it cannot be panacea for freedom of speech, expression and human rights.

Looking Ahead

The limited observations and database both are at best in the realm of speculation and creative imagination. This is a high degree of theorisation about positive contribution of information and communication technology in charging the political paradigms. The other view tends towards techno-negativism, which argues that technology being totalitarian may undermine individual freedom, free expression and human rights. Earlier, I have argued that information and communication technology will weaken the democracy and would lead to the centralisation of power among few hands (Agrawal,1993:231). Today I am not certain about my earlier conclusion. Since, I see little or no shift in basic human instinct and behaviour, the chances are that technology cannot push political paradigms in any direction, the historical and structural changes might. I am inclined to postulate that the relationship between democracy and information and communication technology that one assumes is quite tenuous and thin, especially of information technology. Hence, there is serious need to look at these issues afresh before we venture further in this area of debate.

REFERENCES

Agrawal, Binod C. (1993). "Communication Technology and Democracies of South Asia: The Danger of Curbing Freedom" In S. Splichal and J. Wasko (eds.),

Communication and Democracy, Norwood, New Jersey: Ablex Publishing Corporation.

Anonymous (2000). *Media and Democracy in Asia*, Singapore, AMIC.

Armitage, John (2001). "Resisting the Neoliberal Discourse of Technology: The Politics of Cyberculture in the Age of the Virtual Class". From *Internet.*

Drucker S.J. and Gumpert, G. (eds.) (1999). *Real Law @ Virtual Space: Regulation Cyberspace* New Jersey, Hampton Press.

Gupta, Dipanker (2000). "Political Sociology and Political Anthropology in India" in M.S. Gore ed., *Third Survey of Research in Sociology and Social Anthropology* Vol. 1, pp. 326-370. New Delhi: Indian Council of Social Science Research and Manak Publications.

Hemlink C.J. (1986). "Is Information-Technology Neutral?" In J.Becker, G. Hedebro and L. Paldan, eds. *Communication and Domination: Essays in the Honour of Herbert I. Schiller*, pp. 16-24. Norwood, N.J: Ablex Publishing Corporation.

Mac Bride, *et. al* (1980). *Many Voices One World*. London, New York: Kogen Page, Unipub., UNESCO.

Pare, Michele and Peter Desbret (eds.) (1998). *Freedom of Expression and New Communication Technologies*, Quebec, Orbicom.

Shapiro, Andrew (1999). The Control Revolution: How the Internet is putting Individuals in Change and Changing the World: New York: Public Affairs.

Singh, Ajay (1999). "Politics. Com: The Indian elections", Asiaweek.com December 3, Vol. 25, No. 48, pp. 1-3.

Splichal S. and Wasko, J. (1993). *Communication and Democracy*, Norwood, New Jersey. Ablex Publishing Corporation.

Stalder, Felix (1999). "The Control Revolution (Review)" In *Computers and Society*, Vol. 29, No. 4 (December 1999), pp. 1-3.

Tanka, Brij (ed.) (1995). *Communications and Democracy: Ensuring Pluralisam*, Penang, Southbound.

Traber, Michael (1993). "Changes of Communication Needs and Rights in Social Revolutions." in S. Splichal and J. Wasko (eds.), *Communication and Democracy*, Norwood, New Jersey: Ablex Publishing Corporation.

13

Gender Construction and Media: Presentation, Representation and Repression

N.K. SINGHI

Conceptual Articulation

The relationship between gender and media necessitates understanding of certain conceptual distinction for clarity and effective discourse. Generally three basic terms require clarity in relation to their differentiated meanings. The terms are Femaleness, Feminity and the Feminism. The term Femaleness focuses on physical and biological differentiation between man and woman, which provides variation necessary for reproduction and continuity of humanity. The term Feminity refers to social and cultural construction of women, wherein they are shaped differently not only in terms of representation of body but also in relation to institutionalized role performances, internalization of specific values and conformity to certain cultural practices. Feminism is an ideological position which emphasises the equality of gender and advocates maximisation of potential of both men and women so that culturally created constrains do not hinder the process and pattern of individual development.

All societies have created differential norms and practices, structures and institutions, images and perceptions for social placement of woman in the society. In this process, women have been subordinated to men through denial of dominant areas of expression, creativity and acquisition of power. Generally, the domestic role has been assigned to women while the public domain has been given to men. The power relationship between men and women has become asymmetrical in this process. Apart from institutionalization of specific of men and women, there have been several social and cultural practices which further empower man and create inequality between sexes. The stigma associated with widowhood in Indian society, practice of sati, notion of virginity, barrenness, purity, pollution, devadasi system, prostitution, reveal the subordinated position of women which lower her status in society. Dominance of sexualization objectification of women, whereby her body has been converted into a commodity.

Media: The Broad Framework

The media has played pluralistic role in the image construction of women at one level, the women's body has been constructed for entertainment and for marketing and on the other hand women have been presented in a traditional role model in which there is a great emphasis on control and conformity. Woman has entered the media into several ways through (a) advertisements, (b) serials, (c) articles, (d) fiction, (e) news reporting. The contemporary media reveals not merely projection of what is going on in the society but has created role models for the emerging women.

By and large, there are no emancipatory intervention through media and even when woman's issues are taken up by it, the contents generate surplus meanings. The surplus meaning relates to the news items and the visuals which subverts the very purpose regarding the main issue and instead creates pervert person in issues. In such a situation, one does not really feel concerned after reading the rape news but reads the news about rape or molestation for perverse delight. There is a greater depiction of woman's body and greater sensuousness in representation of situation involving men and women in magazines, television and cinema.

The media is an instrumentality of the transmission of information, values, norms, images, ideas, ideologies, linguistic and paralinguistic symbols of communication, aspiration, fantasies, style of life, belief system, which have cognitive, cathetic, aesthetic, physical, spiritual dimensions. These dimensions are transmitted visually, orally both or in linguistic written forms.

The dominant modes of media popular culture are T.V., Radio, newspaper, magazines, book and journals.

The classical construction of woman was through textual, artistic-aesthetic carvings of stone, paintings and other material. The textual form was presented in prose and poetry. The portrayal of women in the texts provide ideal normative construct in abstracted form, wherein she has been both positively and negatively represented. The presentation of women in folk culture has been done through tales, songs, proverbs, dance, drawings and paintings. These representations depict the existential reality of constructed women. The regional cultural variations are reflected in these constructions.

The historicity and contemporaneity of women's construction through approach of epochs, texts, literature, mythology, oral traditions, folk lore has not been part of serious cognitive concerns of social scientists. However, Feminist scholars have done significant serious work through pre-figuring of the field—which implies that this has been done through linguistic protocol in this field and its elements are constructed in their terms and not from the documents. The act of pre-figuration is a poetic act, it suggests use of terms, concepts and mode of establishing relationship between them. There are four modalities of such poetic linguistic presentation. These are: metaphor, metonymy, synecdoche and irony. In metaphor, phenomena are characterized in terms of similarity or difference with one another. These appears to be an elective affinity between the formist mode of historical narrative with its vivid representation of individual facts and the trope of metaphor, *e.g.*, 'Razia—The Great'. In metonymy, the name of the part or aspect of a thing is substituted for the whole for example, 'Shakti', 'Motherhood'. The trope of synecdoche, conveys an intrinsic, integrative relationship between the elements of a whole. Expressions like, 'women's liberation'; 'empowerment'; 'personal is political', illustrate this. Irony shows discrepancy between words and their meanings. The intention of an ironic statement is to affirm tacitly the negative of what is stated positively. The question thus is, do historical documents, texts, oral traditions represent the mentalities of that particular period as entities in themselves or as communication to influence the future. To constitute a past by constructing an image of it, is not 'seeing' but a 'seeing us'. The representation can be shown to be the product of a particular system of meaning. It may be outside the text. The language of the text, the object oriented aesthetic presentation, are signifier, a set of signs the meaning signified, but not a neat set of correspondence. No meaning is wholly present in writing (Banthia, 1994). The present is more immediate to us and has facts, as it is not construct where gaps are filled with logic and imagination.

It is in this context that, despite certain gaps, due to non-accessibility or non-presence, the gender presentation becomes significant in terms of its implication on women's status, role, image, empowerment, perception, attitude, values and relationships.

The textual discourse of women is a construction while pictorial and

T. V. create representational discourse. However, even in these cases the Derridarian notion of 'difference' becomes relevant. 'Difference' is the gap between objects of perception and the meanings these have as symbols or representations, and its theoretical importance in deconstructionism reveals the essentialist elements at its foundation, for it proposes that there are 'real' social objects outside or beneath the social construction of these (Stanley and Wise, 1993).

Essentialism is defined in opposition to 'difference', around the rejection of any claims for the existence of relatively stable set of properties which differentiate between people-such as gender, class, race (*Ibid*: 220). There are competing meanings of the same phenomenon. *Vis-a-vis* history, the 'contemporary' evokes larger number of competing meanings. One of such reason lies in the fact that past is inaccessible, hence the limitation, while the contemporary is immediate and visible, hence pluralistic perceptions and interests define the reality in its own framework.

Media and Construction of Women

The mass media-construction of women takes place in several ways:

(*a*) The cultural construction of women's body: *The Constructed Body*.
(*b*) The cultural construction of status, role and relationship: *The Constructed Role*.
(*c*) The cultural construction of women's nature-emotions, attitudes, temperament: *The Constructed Emotions*.
(*d*) The cultural construction of oppression, violence, discrimination and inequality: *The Representation of Oppression*.
(*e*) The institutional representation of women—within marriage, family, polity, economy, work: *The Institutional Presentation*.
(*f*) The problematic institutional representation of women-dowry, purdah, prostitution, child marriage: *The Representation of Problematics*.

(A) The 'body' can be conceptualized in abstract, universal and essentialist terms as a biologically constituted organism which is differentiated as man and woman. In feminist ontology, the body is seen in terms of embodiment, a social and cultural process by which the physical body becomes a site of culturally ascribed and disputed meanings, experiences and feelings. The body is positioned within culture and social structure—wherein there are competing meaning, authority and control. The body has closure and fixity in physical change—but there are processes of bodily growth, change, ageing, illness and death. The 'body' is the construct, an elaborate system of production through the process of socialization-toilet manners, table manners, appropriate dress, posture, responses, giving and losing of face.

The media at one level, is generating sexual meaning of woman's body—through cinema, wheres in selective reproduction, sensuous scenes, which combined with songs, create erotic meaning of woman's body. The meaning gets further heightened by focus on certain body parts and body movements. The impact is instant and its depth and continuity varies from person to person, depending upon age, background, personality and shifts to other pre-occupations. There is repetition, reproduction and imitation of the theme through ancillary programmes like singing competitions, dance competitions and in-home wedding ceremonies. Such a presentation becomes part of one layer of cultural representation in a society—both in classes and masses exposed to mass media. This process makes commodification of women through cultural circulation. Women are signified through institutional signifier of media. This view of body as erotically beautiful, leads to increased demand for it. The hunger for this increases with every satiation. The impressions on mind set of such viewing leads to formation of structuration of mind which demands this gratification. It creates a style of life where body of women becomes dominant expressive mode. It creates market forces which generate and supply demands of people for articles which make body expose in the image of media presentation. The body becomes *what one has*, rather than *what one is*.

(B) The status-role-relationship refers to typically and specificity of women's roles and norms which govern their relationship with outer world. The role of daughter, wife and mother as depicted in media has changed compared to its earlier version. However, the change is not substantive and fundamental. The public sphere of woman has increased, yet she is susceptible and vulnerable outside the home. She is supposed to perform both the domestic work and non-domestic work. She is more free with men—but still not accepted as a person or suspiciously so. There is a great deal of diversity and conflicting messages generated through serials, episodes, programmes and advertisements. The serials present life-course events in women's lives, consisting of pre-marital sex, pre-marital pregnancy, rape, divorce, familial-maladjustment, extra-marital relations, physical liberties, leud jokes and presents both an essentialist and deconstructionist meaning of women.

The deviation from the main-stream ideal normative expectation is characteristic of woman as a social category as well as woman in sub-categories of race, class, caste and woman as a person. Although these presentations make her sit in board rooms, corporate offices, administrative positions, yet her sexual construction tends to be the dominant one. The global T. V. channels have brought all these saleable stuff in developing countries. Instead of projecting democratic norms, notion of justice and equality and other values, which are imitable dimensions of western society, marketing of ignoble things have led to a new and culturally alienated image of women in India. On the one hand, outdated cultural practices continue as part of social structure, while on the other hand the sexual presentation of women, reinforces the negative aspects of women's role, status and relationship. The 'appropriate' is missing in the media discourse. Globalization and liberalization have lowered the image and status of woman in terms of her body-meaning, although it has opened new opportunities for role mobility and in certain ways role reversal. It has changed gender-based role hierarchies.

(C) The emotive-attituditional fixity of women has been reinforced by media. The woman cries, fears, gives in, needs protection, is loving, caring and tender. The 'mascho' is man, woman is delicate-slim, with standards of measurement which prescribes her sizes. The advertisements give messages which set her standards of behaviour, emotive expressions, gait, speech modulation and the cat walk. Body itself express her nature—as it ought to be.

Emotions are culturally induced, created and structurally reproduced. There is nothing like natural nature of women, women are taught to be like women. It takes place through the process of socialization. They are taught to be shy, polite, submissive, obedient and crossing the boundaries is considered deviance. Emotions are thus culturally created, induced and maintained. Not all emotions are part of encounters of individual woman. The media exposes the women for anticipatory socialization, through creating live situations, which depicts media presented women in meeting different situations. The emotive expressions of woman disempowers her—she needs support, help and care. The ever present two women—the good and the bad, create polar dichotomies and do not provide space for being a normal human woman. Woman express tenderness in ads, of rubbing the balm, she is competing with her neighbours in whitening of clothes through particular detergent soaps, and she waits for children and husband on dinning table as she has cooked the food in a particular brand of oil.

These representations reveal meanings couched in activities. It conceals the inner experience of drudgery, routinization of life and suppression of potentials.

(D) The oppression of the women in varying degrees is part of everyday experience. The discrimination begins from conception—once it is known through sonography. The unwanted girl child is aborted. This is extreme violence to her essence of body, arising out of cultural meaning and denial of right to be born, despite having the life. The socialization process is discriminatory often in the name of differentiation. The inequality of opportunity is part of growing up for girls. The gender discrimination, inequality and oppression cuts across race, caste, class and nations. There is certain degree of universality in these processes although their forms vary.

(E) The institutional representation of women within marriage reveal greater freedom along with subordination. The patriarchy has redefined itself, where there is depiction of freedom but lack of control over choices and segmental division of decision-making power. Women continues to perform domestic chores and also earn. The ideal continues to be commitment to family—husband and children. Mother-in-law might be subdued but she is a woman. Patriarchy helps in creating tensions between woman and woman. It creates conditions of rivalries amongst them. Dowry is decried, condemned in verbalized idealism but accepted and demanded in subterrean forms. Media projects women in polities but those in polities are required to keep public face of decency—Indianness, as a vote catching device. Her work space has expanded but invariably media brings out sexual harassment of women or man's duality and duplicity of keeping 'office wife' and 'wife at home'. The theme of "husband, wife and she" fits into being progressive through deviance.

(F) The problematic representation of women-prostitution, child marriage, rape, purdah gets into media as seductive sensuality rather than concerned issue. It communicates pervert delight while sanctimonious verbalized sympathy and concerns are meant for consumption of other. There is more of objective spectacle rather than subject pain. The propoganist mode helps the cause of those who want to come in lime-light. The issue gets marginalized as some quarrel on the issues of who should be interviewed for which channel. In Satihood a woman embraces pain, not only death, although she is constituted to deny pain and commit herself to co-death with husband. That there has been social-cultural recognition of this, through religious deification is indigenous innovation and not textual treatise.

The Dominant Theme of Media: Commodification and Marketing

The media has neglected the real, basic and deeper issues of women's empowerment, equality, justice and has consequentially reinforced the continued image of women albeit in different discourse, symbol and mode of representation. Media thrives on salebility not substance, on consumeristic values not common cause, on sensuality not significance, on market forces not morals. There is a shift in presentation, representation and signification which is geared to commodification and not centrality of concerns.

The media construction, even though art films and prescriptive documentaries are the forms of agitprop representation which are closer to the reality than the liberal discourse denouncing 'certain' problems like Sati, Devdasi, child marriage, widowhood or the religious or sectional discourse glorifying these. The media in a recent rape case has devastedly confused the issue. Female willingness and involuntary desire have been raised as part of hypocritical and mediated confusion by saying, "what she did was in her nature".

The institutional aspects of sexual intercourse, the customary rules, the body relationships in sexual encounters—as depicted in media, articles and advice produced through magazines, consistently keep men in dominance and women in subordination. There is need to understand its consequences on male-female relationship in general. The cultural manipulation of sex and reproduction in fact is at the root of subordinated and oppressed social position of women. Genderism has developed out of this. According to Kate Millet, when one gender rules another, the relationship between the two is that of power asymmetry hence political. When such an arrangement is carried over a long period of time it develops into an ideology (feudalism, racism, genderism) (quoted from Grant, 1993:34). According to Atkinson, sexual intercourse, is a political institution when institution is defined as any form of activity, activities shared by all, many, or a group, which are governed by a system of rules. These define roles, moves, penalties, defenses and which gives the activity its structure (*Ibid*: 34).

Cinema and serial purposefully do not use symbolism for acts of rape, instead they prefer replication of the act in the movements of narratives. The viewers are taken to the actual occurrence of scene. The viewer does not revolt. he enjoys the enactment and identified himself with the raper. All men become rapists—if they sensually, sub-consciously take delight into this. The classical mythologies illustrate the need for trials to be absolved of the doubt. Both Ahalya and Sita underwent trials to prove their innocence. The voyeuristic aspect of viewing women in oppressive distress is media made. Woman becomes a subject through rape rather than one who has been subjected to.

There is a general framework of rape rooted in genderism. Rape is made to appear as accidental and specific to a person. Rape supports the male gender by projecting its power and aggressiveness on the world. It is seen as a prerogative of his category and consequently influences the sexuality of women. All men are perceived as potential rapers.

The structuring of post-rape narratives instead of tracing strategies of her survival focuses on rape-centered narratives that privileged chastity. She is not located in the structure of oppression but heterosexual romantic relationships. Rape is the feared and fantasized possibility amidst multiple struggles (Rajan,1993). Specifically it is an arbitrary act of violence located into structure of oppression—political and cultural. Non-pluralistic theory of knowledge conceptualise 'women' as the basic category of oppression from which all other follow. It is rooted in systematic theory of structure and phenomenological theory of experience. What would be society like, if there were no social and cultural differentiations, differences, inequalities, discrimination, oppression directed against and towards women? Supposing there were no class differences but only gender hierarchies? Comparing the two hypothetical world-orders, can it lead to significant anticipatory formulations?

The issue should be seen within potential rape situations like harassment of women in the workplace, the phenomenon of independent single women, the fact of widespread child molestation, child incest, eve's teasing, secret video filming and black mailing of adolescent innocent girls. The rape of lower caste/class woman is expression of social power, rather than of sexual desire. It is rooted in the structure of hierarchies in Indian society, find expression in new economic and political spaces where man is the boss and has power to sack, transfer and promote. Several unknown suffered rapes take places which are not known, concealed and not reported. The price of making it known or reporting are far serious, and reporting does not help in any way—so think many a victim.

Pornography is a part of climate of violence against women. There are special magazines of pornography, which have wide circulation. Blue films are part of secret selling and shady dealing. It leads to nexus of law, police, administration and mafia. Such nexus becomes support system for illegal activities. Pornography has been termed as "cultural sadism". It is the male sexuality that defines all that a woman is—whose sexuality exists for someone else who is socially male. Woman is measured by a male standard for woman, a standard that is not her. Women value care because men have valued them according to the care they have been made to give them (Grant, 1993). Sexuality is a form of power. Women's experience take place within gender hierarchy in which women exist as subordinates (Mackinnon, 1987). Women have been part of "mothering theory-values women have learnt as part of cultural practices attached to motherhood"(Grant, 1993:59). Texts have glorified the motherhood, enlarging to the notion of motherland, country and media reinforce it through selective reproduction. Both have valorized moral sensibilities of women.

The overemphasis and glorification of woman's character is being used as a weapon to denigrade her. Elected women panchayat members are gossiped about in relation to concocted sexual deviances. This is used as an instrumentality to weaken her and make her withdraw from participation and decision-making from public related issue.

The media can be educative and not merely informative, sensitive and not only sensational, responsible and not sheer recreational. There is need to have media policy regarding gender representation, presentation and reproduction. It is a part of civilizational development, and media is becoming effective instrumentality in its construction, diffusion and spread.

REFERENCES

Banthia, Ruchi (1994). *From Historicity to Post Modernity*, Jaipur, Rawat, pp. 100-02.

Grant, Judith (1993). *Fundamental Feminism*, New York, Routledge.

Mackinnon, (1987). *Feminism Unmodified:Discourse in Life and Law*, Cambridge, Harvard University pros, pp. 242-44.

Rajan, S. (1993). *Real and Imagined Women*, London, Routledge, pp. 66-87.

Stanley, Liz Sue, Wise (1993). *Breaking out Again*, New York, Routledge, p. 34.

14

Women and Environmental Crisis: A Spill-Over of Economic Development

SUGUNA PATHY

Notwithstanding constitutional guarantees discrimination against women is deep rooted in cultural beliefs and practices. International and national agencies, and a large number of NGOs undertake women's concerns. While one cannot deny the overall impact with regard to women, frankly speaking the effect is negligible as millions of poor women in general and third world women in particular continue to reel under grim poverty struggling to meet the survival needs like food, fodder, fuel and water. Unfortunately innumerous academic gatherings on "women's related issues" mean nothing to an ordinary woman although she is "represented" in the scholarly debates. However this does not deny some related works at grass-root level. Mega international conferences on environment and development cover crucial areas intrinsically linked with women and any discussion on environment without women's concerns can only remain incomplete and peripheral. However, the gender related issues in environmental need to be analyzed from a wider perspective as we can neither attach nor detach the term gender conveniently. There is a close connection between environment, economic development and women which is very complex and thus definite answers are not possible. Besides, environmental issues demand a larger and holistic perspective devoid of conventional atomistic and reductionistic notions. Accordingly the present paper attempts to raise some concerned issues with regard to environment and the related issues in general.

The problem of environment has come to the fore only during the recent years. People have been living in harmony with nature through ages. Scriptures as well as folklore of different faiths also mention and stress the need for harmony with the universe comprising humans, animals and plants. The support of all living things is crucial for a balanced social existence. Besides, all philosophies also mention of the unique relationship of humans with the environment in its totality. However. the onset of technological revolution has turned this harmonious relationship into exploitative relationship following the dawn of industrial revolution. The past century experienced, the worst technological disaster like the tragedy of Hiroshima, Nagasaki, Bhopal and Chernobyl are the warning to set our planet in order.

The rise of modem environment movement dates back to the turbulent decade of the nineteen-sixties. For the decade witnessed an upsurge of movements for social transformation which included capitalist and socialist alterations and decolonisation. The socio-political mutations and combinations gave rise to a New World. Repressive colonial period left three fourths of humankind in abject poverty and these countries were expected to seek rapid economic development. Accordingly, the new nation-states began experiencing the resource crunch as the industrialised countries consumed the resources on an unprecedented scale. The point is that the consumption has been unequal both on ethical and logical grounds as the largest number of marginalised people are concentrated in the third world with limited access to resources. On the other side, the industrialised countries began experiencing social fragmentation with increase in crime rates, drug abuse, alcoholism and the like. Incidently this social crisis is accentuated by the type of consumer culture of capitalism not only in the affluent states but also chaos in third world countries as well. This raised the question of very line of direction generated by the industrial capitalism which became one of the causes of environmental movement in the west. In tandem with the socio-political factors the atomistic pattern of scientific and technological advancements brought environmental degradation in turn forming the basis for environmental awareness. In addition destructive nuclear power generated radiation clouds causing irrevocable damage to the biosphere that nature painstakingly constructed over millions of years (Balasubramanium, 1984).

There is no dearth to the plethora of existing literature, seminars and conferences at national and international levels on violence against women. More often than not the deliberations in these fora analyse violence, isolating from wider political economy. The extent and nature of violence broadly comprises (i) structural violence emanating from the unequal social order resulting in the marginalisation of people both men and women; and (ii) the specific violence against women, children, minorities, weaker sections etc. The latter operates in the former matrix and is historically specific corresponding to various socio-economic formations. It seems today that increasing violence both, general and specific, are the result of politico-economic crisis at national and international levels.

In this context, patriarchal coercion along with various forms of capital, caste, community, religion, region, etc. controls women's freedom and sexuality to maintain the *status-quo* and the corresponding relations of production. This lethal combination culminates in wife-battering, rape, murder (for inter caste/community marriages), dowry deaths, female infanticide, and various forms of physical and mental abuse of women. Further victimology of women sans age besides other variables like class, caste and education particularly among married women. On the contrary, the forms of violence increases in this category as women begin to assert with age, experience and social awareness. In brief the more the women assert the more victimisation (physical and mental) and the lesser the assertion the more "domestic harmony" and the *vice-versa*.

This is so due to the nature of unequal relations between men and women which in turn are embedded in the wider unequal social order. Ergo violence against women is the result of crumbling social values and dehumanisation. Subsequent flow of trans-national capital reflecting in unfettered market economy, unabated consumerism, widening inequalities, individualism, increasing abuse of drugs and alcohol, etc. cumulatively accentuate violence in general and on women in the *sanctum sanctorum,* the family in particular. This primordial violence culminates into spiral violence where each act of violence begets further violence.

Meanwhile existing social relations are shaped by unequal relations between men and women which are constantly reproduced resulting in the subordination of women in society. In this connection violence against women is the worst manifestation of extreme inequality resulting in the oppression of women which inturn serves the system in different ways. For, in the family woman is a "possession" (not companion/friend) of her husband with the male hierarchy and the very social fabric of male domination denies woman her right as a human being, a few exceptions notwithstanding. Under this scenario woman is viewed as sexual object wherein sometimes only *sexual relations* determine the overall relations in the family as a whole: any imbalance invariably will generate a chain of conflicts. The institution of marriage and the relations of reproduction further ensures women's subordination as men exercise right over their women to keep them "in order by any means" is yet another dimension of sexual relations. Thus, *a prima vista* female-male relations are the prototype relations of domination and subordination. Unarguably violence against women originates in the family as several Nidhis, Roop Kanwars...are eliminated to keep family's honour (sic). Whether it is child abuse or wife beating or other assaults conveniently take place with in the four walls of the family *i.e.* private. It seems then home represents one of the "underworld crimes" that goes unnoticed. Further, family is a vital organising principal of social relations as specific combination of gender and economic relations entrench gender division in the fabric of social relations. Under this structuration the family reproduces both the workers, capitalists and other classes, sustains them and inculcates children and adults alike to maintain the legitimacy as well as the existing arrangements. In the interim consumerism overtakes rest of the contradictions, polarising women subsequently.

Through both its patriarchal structure and patriarchal ideology, the family and the need for reproduction also structure society. This is very relationship between family and society *i.e.*, production and reproduction defines the position of women. Mention may be made that patriarchy neither originated with capitalism nor it will disappear with it. Besides overthrow of capitalism will not necessarily destroy patriarchy. Ergo patriarchy is pan-cultural and pan-national reflecting differently in different societies, as subordination or women cannot be generalised due to its varying nature according to specific historical conjectures. The patriarchal socialization controls women in various ways *i.e.*, (i) it defines women; (ii) defines the external world and defines women's position within it; and (iii) provides women's definition of others and their relationship with them. The women belief in the precepts of sexist ideology reflects the enormous power of coercion and control. By the way, gender relations are so pervasive that most of us are not even aware of its manifestations. Together patriarchal family, class, caste, community, religion and state control women in various ways by depriving their basic rights; particularly women from the lower strata of the society face the worst forms of violence from the upper caste men and also by their own castemen including. Accordingly structural violence gets organised institutionally in kinship, economic, cultural and political structures to victimise the marginalised people in general and more so women in particular owing to their very position in the patriarchal world.

Under the existing conditions the available alternative to combat violence against women is the conscientisation of both men and women besides evolving suitable strategies. Therefore, it is essential for various concerned women's organisations to come together on a common platform to forge the struggle against various forms of violence on women. This can be done by prioritising issues that are common to the oppressed. It is equally essential for women's organizations to join with other democratic movements to achieve just social order where everyone can live with dignity and freedom, not with coercion and fear.

It is necessary to understand environmentalism in a broader historical perspective. However, the scope of the present paper does not allow us to delve into this aspect. In the recent past economic assumptions were reviewed and global perspective was evolved to understand environmental issues. Accordingly the "Club of Rome" concluded in 1968 that ecological, environmental and economic catastrophe could be averted by limiting population and industrial development. The Club of Rome envisaged world development model based on population, food, natural resources, industrial output and pollution by limiting population and a state of global equilibrium (Club of Rome, 1972)" The model however ignores the impact of market forces on resource allocation and technology.

Secondly, this also implies that the third world countries would be forced to remain in poverty and have to depend for development on the charity of west (Ward and Dubos, 1972). At the very outset this is an unacceptable proposition to the third world. This brings us to examine the issue of environmentalism more closely than ever *i.e.*, can there be a model called eco-development? The link between environment and economic development, is very complex and definite solutions are thus difficult to evolve; Secondly, at times environmentalism can become a tool of exploitation by the developed countries. Third world just cannot stop economic growth because it causes ecological degradation as warned by the developed countries. For, they have now realised after plundering the resources and are cautioning the poor countries to limit economic growth. Is it ethical in its first place? As of today the confronting, issues in the poor countries are food, water, health, shelter and education and it is unfair to deal with the peripheral ecological issues at the cost of more urgent demands. However, this is not to deny the impact of economic development on environment and *vice-versa*. Ignoring the environmental implication would result in retarded economic growth, as both the issues are interdependent. The point is that we need to identify growth with ecological sensitivity by leaving atomistic notion of environment. As we know there is a reaction to every action and the nature of reaction depends on the relativity of action. Environmental sensitivity demands an interdisciplinary approach based on environmental philosophy. This in turn requires change in modern technology covering ecological and gender friendly values. Put simply the environmental issues are not of merely concerned with environment but raise major political and policy questions related to the power, matrix. Therefore, it is necessary to cognize environmental related issues from the wider political economy.

It may be mentioned in this context that continued commercialisation of agriculture and forestry is leading to genetic erosion. This erosion has devasting effect on ecology. Meanwhile bio-diversity is not global resource, as it is not uniformly distributed across the world. Rather heavily concentrated in the third world by and large. The threat to bio-diversity is not caused by the countries from South. It may be noted that technological as well as political factors contributed to the genetic erosion. For instance, agricultural programmes like Green Revolution destroyed the genetic diversity, while international agencies harm the biodiversity than conserving through its biodiversity action plan. World Bank finances the programmes like Green Revolution to cultivate monocultures in third world since 1970s. Genetic diversities of maize in Mexico and rice in Asia are the examples of Green Revolution (Shiva, 1990). As a matter of fact World Bank repeatedly projects genetic uniformity as a means of biodiversity conservation in its programmes. World Banks social 'forestry schemes in India are a case in point where genetically diverse agro-forestry was replaced by monocultures of eucalyptus plants. It may be noted that International Bureau for Plant Genetic Resources (IBPGR) which is governed by Consultative Group of International Agricultural Research (CGIAR) was specially created to collect and conserve genetic resources. Eventually it has become an instrument of transferring resources from South to North (*Ibid.*).

Not surprisingly biotech industry is one of the main causes of environmental problems. Because more often biodiversity is commercialized through biotech industry as genes are made as the object of value through patenting which in turn ends up in devaluation of life forms. In fact, it questions the very philosophy of life forms as well as the centuries old peoples knowledge. The gene patenting violates the "integrity of life forms and common property rights of the third world people (*Ibid*, 375). The present world trade and technology work against the ethics of ecology and sustainability. Unfortunately, the call for sustainability is more often given scant regard for equity while improving the poor countries to cut further their minimum consumption patterns so that rich sustain their luxury life styles. Sometimes unsustainable patterns are projected in the name of sustainable development like forcing people to conserve the forests without providing alternatives. By the way, the term sustainable development is a buzz world of 1990s, denotes a pattern of development which is sustainable within the context of planets ecosystem and human society. This concept emerged out of a series of conferences and reports in the United Nations. However the term sustainable development is being exploited by marketing and media hype. The commercial houses have jumped on to the green bandwagon, combining advertising its product and its impact on environment. If women cutting wood for fuel is unsustainablde affluence is more unsustainable. It seems we lost the track, the essence of conservation that invariably denotes sustainability for the future generations to come and therefore conservation is not an end in itself.

There is a mutual relationship between the land, water and atmosphere and the snowballing impact the human society has on their unique system. Global environment change is complex and interwoven with socio-economic, political and scientific factors. Politically speaking the geo-political changes besides people's movements especially from the South has forced the analysts to reconsider the assumptions and the future possibilities. Thus, the current principal world political agenda is global environment comprising diversity of species. The diversity of species constitutes the world's available gene pool as "one of our planet's most important and irreplaceable resources" containing from one million to 10 billion bits of information on its genetic code, the product of thousands or millions of years of evolution" (Wilson,1988: cited in Silver and Detries, 1991:115).

As it stands, on the whole the present economic development under Globalization fundamentally unsustainable, for the approaches cannot reduce inequalities, as growth patterns are accompanied by degradation of natural resources. The loss in the quality of natural resources is not reflected in prices as the sale of resource-based products in domestic or in foreign market (Dasgupta and Maler, 1990). The diversion to sustainable development demands shift in property relations. Consumption patterns, production, technologies, institutions and so on with gender sensitivity approaches. In this connection the nature of structural relationships in third world countries suggest that the inequalities between rich and poor, urban and rural, male and female, powerholders and powerless have been endangered by the process of their development in subordination to capitalism (Oxall, *et.al.*, 1975). Because imperialism did not discover the underdeveloped countries but created them (Griffin, 1968). It is not out of context to observe that colonialism left profound implications on environmental imbalance in the third world and presently we are continuing the legacy in newer forms. For instance, many large-scale development projects financed by multi-lateral and bilateral donors more often not only undermine but also underestimate the ecological balance and complex social arrangements of resource management and survival mechanisms. The reason being that the Environment Policy is more often dominated by external forces like World Bank, World Trade Organisation. International treaties like Convention of Biological Diversity (CBD), International Convention to Combat Desertification (ICCD) and so on.

None the less sustainable development can only succeed by placing livelihood patterns of the marginalised people in general and women in particular in the centre stage through access to resources, control and management. In other words, this denotes empowering the people politically and economically—a formidable task. There are neither ready-made solutions nor quick fixes to environmental concerns. However there is a tremendous potential for transforming the economies conserving biodiversity and associated knowledge systems along gender oriented strategies. Development projects need to be more supportive of women and should encourage their greater participation in the design and implementation of environmental schemes. For human activity is always embodied and is an expression of a given conception of the world, its historical validity determined in terms of its impact on human society.

REFERENCES

Balasubramaniam, A. (1984). *Ecodevelopment: Towards a Philosophv of Environmental Education*. Singapore: RIHED.

Club of Rome (1972). Meadows, D.L. and Meadowos, D.H., Randers, T. Behrens II, W.W. *The Limits to Growth.* New York: Universe Books.

Das Gupta, P. and Karl-Goran Maler (1990). "The Environment and Emerging Development Issues", *Proceeding of the World Bank's Annual Conference on Development Economics*, World Bank: Washington.

Griffin, K. (1968). *Underdevelopment in Spanish America: An Interpretation*. London: Allen and Unwin.

Oxall, I. *et. al.* (ed.) (1975). *Beyond the Sociology of Development*, London: Routledge and Kegan Paul.

Shiva, Vandana, (1990). "Biodiversity Convention: Ecological *vs.* Commercial Approaches" in *Return to the Good Earth*, A Third World Network Dossier, Penang: CAD.

Silver, C.S. and De. Fries, R.S. (1991). *One Earth, One Future*. New Delhi: East-West Press.

Ward, B. and Dubos, R. (1972). *Only One Earth: The Care and Maintenance of a Small Planet*, New York.

15

Poverty in Transition and Transition in Poverty: Poverty, Poverty and Poverty

RAJESHWAR PRASAD

Dr. Yogesh Atal was in the service of UNESCO and at the fag-end of his career he was actually involved in preparations for the International meet on Social Development held at Copenhagen, Denmark. Issues of development make one to seriously ponder our the problems of poverty, exploitation, under development, development as related to the economic system(s) and political structure(s). In the process Atal has shown interest in the issues of poverty by bringing out two volumes on poverty in the last five years. The Review-Article that follows is concerned with his edited volume *Poverty in Transition and Transition in Poverty—Recent Developments in Hungary, Bulgaria, Romania, Georgia, Russia, Mongolia* (1999).

I may however, mention here that approximately five decades back social science-sociology, anthropology, political science—was marginally concerned with poverty. In our student days the text books in sociology dealt with the problem of poverty in a perfunctory manner. Anthropology studied tribes but did not focus on poverty *per-se*. Anthropologists were romantically concerned with cultures. The economist craftly avoided the ideological issues related to poverty and for quite a long time harped on welfare economics. However, the defeat of socialist of ideology, rise of unipolar world and the thrust of the new economics agenda through LPG (liberalization, privatization and globalization) has brought to fore the question of poverty, pauperization and pelf world over.

It may not be out of place to record here that increasing interest of social science in poverty issues is perhaps, due to an increasing interest of the Bretten Wood institutions, particularly the World Bank in gauging poverty conditions in different societies. There are both funds and dotted lines available for poverty studies which may be utilized by selected social scientists. Hence, a plethora of studies on poverty.

> Apart from the Introduction by Yogesh Atal, the book under review is organized in six chapters: Chapter 1 'Recent Trends in Poverty in Hungary' by Julia Szalai'; Chapter 2 'Emerging Poverty in Bulgaria' by Sasha Todorova; Chapter 3 'Poverty in Romania' by Traian Rotariu and Livia Popeseu; Chapter 4 'Toward Poverty Eradication in Georgia' by Avtandil Sulaberidze; Chapter 5 'The Russia Case: Social Policy Concerns' by G. Pirogov and S. Pronin; and Chapter 6 'Mongolia: In the Grip of Poverty' by Tsogt Nyamsuren. All these papers are related with poverty conditions in six selected countries, describe the contemporary situation in these countries, belonging to the former Soviet Block; all these countries are in transition from socialism to capitalism—the modern 'globalised capitalism', that is engulfing all societies and capturing all economies through LPG. In the era of socialist governance, it is argued by almost all the authors, there was either no prevalence of poverty or it was not so pronounced, but with the break-down of the socialist order and the opening up of economies to LPG, poverty had progressed in geometrical progression. This is described as the 'problem of transitory period' and hence, the title of the book—*Poverty in Transition and Transition in Poverty*. Almost all the chapters are written on a common pattern discussing the Measurement and Definitions of Poverty; the Economic Dimensions of Poverty; the Social Dimensions of Poverty; Political Dimensions of Poverty, apart from the Introductory remarks and Conclusions.

Social scientists and particularly the economists are very fond of devising measures to gauge poverty, delineate social, economic and cultural indicators for such measurement and finally, attempt at 'indexing' poverty in a society. In the discourse on poverty there may be found umpteen definitions of poverty with bewildering explanations of the poverty-phenomenon, leading to an amazing effort on its classification. But, when it comes to the alleviation and eradication of the dreaded problem of poverty, most prescriptions given by the social scientists, may economists, are either impractical or mere sops. In the majority of cases social scientists for the official line, legitimize the political prescriptions and ignore the interests of the masses. It is evident from the dilemma reflected in the arguments given by the authors of the six chapters. All the authors are *nostalgic* about the social security of the socialist regime but *eulogize* the market economy inspite of the fact that the data for all countries under review speak of a staggering decline of employment and a steep rise in poverty.

Extent of Poverty

Yogesh Atal in his Introduction to the book has made certain assertions and observations which may be relevant in the above context:

(*i*) Survey of European Union Countries, March 1997 revealed that 57 million households from the 'market economy oriented countries' of Europe (*i.e.* approximately 17%) are poor (p. 25). These countries, it may be seen are under the spell of capitalistic economic order for decades and are certainly not socialist.
(*ii*) Except Poland and Hungary all other countries of Eastern Europe recorded a steep increase in poverty *e.g.* between 1989-94, 75 million people fell into the poverty trap (p. 24).
(*iii*) It is estimated that in the countries of the former Soviet Block approximately 120 million people live below the income of US $ 4 a day (p. 6).

Atal's observations that 'Countries in Transition' from a state controlled economy to a free market economy may have been poorer in GDP in the socialist regime but there was virtual absence of income inequality (p. 26), is very crucial and important to explain the post-communist quagmire. The so called economic reforms in these countries has created a big gap not only in the incomes of different groups and classes but has virtually marginalized the masses, thus, pushing them to the category of 'abject poor'. It may be evident from the following data given by Atal and the authors:

(*i*) In Romania 17.7 per cent people live below US $ 1 a day (p.18). Unemployment increased from 180,000 to 800,000 in 1991-96 periods (p.131).
(*ii*) In Georgia 71.5 per cent urban and 42.7 per cent rural population identified itself as poor (p.19).
(*iii*) In Hungary the proportion of poor within the population has steadily increased during the 1990s (p. 45). The suspension of 'Compulsory Employment' (1989) has completely changed the employment scenario in the country (p. 49), and there has been a closure of 36 per cent mining work places, 29 per cent

manufacturing units, 11 per cent electricity, gas, steam, water supply centres, 36 per cent agriculture operations, and 1.4 million workplaces have been downsized (p. 51) thus, creating huge unemployment. This is certainly responsible for spreading poverty conditions in Hungary of post-socialist regime.

(*iv*) As far as the situation obtaining in Bulgaria is concerned even after 7 years of transition from a socialist, centrally planned economy to a democratic regime and marketization, things have not improved. Bulgaria is in a deep economic crisis (p. 78). Consequently, progressive impoverishment of large groups of the population (pp. 91-92) has occurred.

(*v*) While describing the situation in the Russian Federation, Atal has remarked that in the communist period only 10 per cent lived below the poverty line but now the percentage of the poor is estimated at 24.7 per cent. From yet another estimate it is revealed that in 1989, the subsistence level was 140 rubles per month for an adult; with inflation, if the same subsistence level is maintained today, it would be as high as 14,00,000 rubles. In present-day Russia, only 10 per cent of the people receive more than a million rubles per month, thereby implying a poverty rate of 90 per cent (p. 21). While analyzing the poverty situation in Russia, G. Pirogov and S. Pronin rightly say that the sudden switch from a state-controlled economy to the market-oriented economy has been traumatic for the people (p. 177). In the socialist system there was indeed, no poverty. However, contemporary Russian society is characterized by the phenomenon of the *new poor.* These new poor include the most valuable labour force, other vulnerable groups, and their pauperization is an evidence of a dramatic depreciation of human capital in Russia (pp.184-185). In fact, the new economic order has created joblessness, and in certain regions of Russia, unemployment is as high as 75 per cent (p.188).

(*vi*) The case of Mongolia is a solitary case taken from the Asian region. The erstwhile Soviet Union had many other Asian nationalities as its constituents now independent of USSR, but the case of Mongolia is quite unique. Mongolia is a land locked country located in the centre of Asia sandwiched between the Russian Federation and the People's Republic of China. Commenting on the poverty situation in Mongolia, Tsogt Nyamsuren perhaps nostalgically, writes that "People received free education and medical care (before 1989, in the communist regime). The government sent people abroad to study for free, and when they came back a job

> was there for them and the salary was not bad either... the lifestyle was guaranteed; all children went to school and received education; the word 'unemployed' was unheard of. Everyone lived a similar life so nobody lacked anything, that is, no one was deprived in comparison with others.... No one was poor, and no one was rich; 'Poverty' did not exist" (p. 227).

In the post-liberalization period Atal, in his 'Introduction' gave the percentage of poor in Mongolia at 36.3 per cent (p. 23). Whereas, Nyamsuren mentioned that in 1996, hardly seven years after the collapse of the socialist State in Mongolia, around 100,000 household were categorized as poor (p. 229). Poverty is reflected not only in low income of people and a deterioration of the population's living standards, but also in several other negative consequences, such as the deterioration of people's health due to malnutrition, a decline in morals, the disintegration of family structures and a rising crime rate. More particularly, there has been a decline in education and cultural achievements (p. 235).

Socialistic Nostalgia, Free-Market Euphoria: Brinkmanship of Social Science

A nostalgia for socialist-social security system and an euphoria for free marketization is an usual tone of almost all the write-ups in the book. Not only Tsogt Nyamsuren, as quoted above, eulogized the socialist support structure for the people in Mongolia but others too although quite sub-consciously, extolled the socialist order and blamed the new free-market economy-liberalized, privatized and globalized as it is, for the poverty explosion, yet euphemized the New Economic Policy (NEP) for the sake of 'democracy, freedom and human rights'. However, not only the authors but the people too craved for the socialist social security umbrella, which may be evident from the statement given below. However, before giving the relevant material in support of my assertions, that mostly the contributors to this volume waver between the two systems—socialism and free-market, I would like to give an instance of Germany after unification. After unification of Germany a team of software experts happened to visit India and one of its members belonged to Agra. He had migrated to Germany in his adolescence. I had a chance to interact with him. And naturally, my inquisitiveness made me to ask about the conditions of people in the two parts of Germany—East and West. It may be noted that in the 'East Germany', which was governed by the communist leadership, every one had a job, a house, free education for children, free health services, subsidized food, transport etc. In the Western part however, not only that everything was priced and charged for but the costs were quite high. For example, in the Eastern part one could eat dinner with beer and dessert, at a price by which he could buy a piece of loaf sandwich and a cup of coffee only in West Germany. Under the new arrangement after unification, the wages of the workers in the Eastern part were fixed much lower than their counterparts in the West. The dismantling of the Wall between East and West Germany facilitated free movement and interaction between the two populations and I was told by the visitors, that the population of the East Germany demanded wages equal to their Western counterparts whereas, the West Germans craved and agitated for the facilities and subsidies available in the Eastern part. It seems true also of the experts, professionals and working populations of the 'Countries in Transition' so rightly described by Atal. This ambivalence may be evident from the following:

(*i*) Economic growth alone is not enough to ensure social development. Economic growth should be so planned that it serves the cause of social development rather than creating crises in the social sphere, asserts, Yogesh Atal (p. 2). However, there is no exposition done in Atals write up to whether the exponential economic growth propelled by the LPG economy is, or is not serving the cause of social development. It is to some extent, however, explained by some crucial statements made by the different authors. Atal boldly captions 'Countries in Transition: From No Poverty to Poverty' but hastens to mention that during the socialist period these countries officially denied the existence of poverty (*Ibid*) This statement too needs carefully and critical analysis in the light of the bulldozing effect of contemporary marketization on livelihood, need fulfilment, quality of life and social existence of people the world over. The statement made by other authors given below may be examined objectively.

(*ii*) Sasha Todorova in the context of 'Emerging Poverty in Bulgaria candidly says that *poverty* began to be discussed after 1989. In 1970s and 1980s there was an attempt made to estimate the living and social minima in the country but the phrases used in totalitarian regimes for the needy people were "populations with low incomes"; "the needy' groups. But, even these populations and groups received social and economic benefits from the state. *Social Security* was high in the socialist policy. The basic necessities of life were guaranteed to each and everyone. Health, education, maternity privileges to women workers and a house for every family were guaranteed. Gypsies comprised a small deprivated group but the Ministry of Welfare adequately looked after them (p. 77).

In the changed scenario however, only those people who managed to participate in the re-distribution of the state property were able to improve their *status-nomenklatura* (high ranking state employees); party *nomenklatura* (ex-communist party officials ruling party officials); participants in the parallel economy; those whose capital, property was restituted by the 'new state'; some of those who were engaged in their own business and commerce (p. 85). It has altered the societal picture completely.

More and more people are getting deprivated and fewer people are becoming rich, and Sasha in this context perhaps, asserts that 60 per cent people still feel that it is the responsibility of the State and the Municipalities to take care of the poor (p. 98). In the contemporary context the poor are thoroughly neglected.

(*iii*) In the context of the Romanian poverty situation, Traian Rotariu and Livia Popescue state that Poverty had little political visibility until 1994 (p. 103). The majority of the conditions inducing poverty seem to be concentrated in the ethnic Romany (Gypsy) (p. 112). But they were taken care of by the State in the communist regime. However, now the poverty is spreading fast.

The present government is aware, and has publicly accepted that economic restructuring will bring about an important decline in the living standards of the population (p. 102). The post-communist distributive policies had effects that contradicted the official pro-egalitarian discourse. Those who accumulated wealth, legally or illegally, during the communist or post-communist regimes, were provided favourable conditions (p. 115).

The authors' avered that although the country's social security system has not changed radically since 1989 and its basic components (public health fund; pension insurance, child care allowance) have not only been maintained but new provisions such as unemployment benefits, social benefits etc., have been added yet, the actual social security infrastructure is far from satisfactory/ adequate (p. 119). No doubt, there is an universal entitlement to free medical service but it is available only to fully employed people, students, pensioners etc. (*Ibid.*). Social Welfare, it seems doesn't constitute the first priority of the Romanian government

(p. 116). No positive measures have been taken to empower the disadvantaged groups of society, such as women, youngsters, disabled people, and the Gypsy minority (*Ibid.*).

The authors have come out with a very significant observation that the "Social safety nets" which were critical under the communist regime, became totally inadequate during the transition to the market economy (p. 123). And, at present, the social aid provisions in actual administration represent a mere "Survival income"; it does not aim at enabling the users to have an independent life (p. 124). The Social Aid Law, 1995 provides a mere *last resort income* to the poorest people, (p.104) rather than extending comprehensive social security of the communist pattern.

The new economic process has exploded the social, economic and political situations and it is in this context that the present ruling party and important sections of the working class favoured state protectionism to ensure proper income distribution and to preserve the privileges inherited from the previous system of the non-market economy (p. 104).

(*iv*) The Georgian case is not much different. Avtandil Sulabridze confirms that Georgia is also experiencing disillusionment with regard to a quick transition to a rapidly developing economy (p. 130). It is affirmed in the case of Georgia that the complexity of the process of socio-economic transformation resulted in a drastic fall in the standard of living of the people (p. 131).

Praising the communist regime Avtandil asserted that historically the developed countries have been characterised by social inequality, and even today, a large part of their population lives below the poverty line. In contrast, Georgia, like other post-communist countries, enjoyed a certain social well being under the communist regime, and the manifest social differentiation in living standards used to be less visible. Of course, the quality of life was below the modern standards of developed countries but whatever living standard was maintained, all people had the same standard. That is why during the previous regime, under the conditions of guaranteed employment and with free state social services, the concept of unemployment and poverty were unknown (p. 132). This assertion certainly controverts the formulation of Atal that in the communist countries 'poverty was officially hidden'.

It may be interesting to note that the changes in market relations caused changes in social relations: (a) new social layers and groups are created; (b) there is formation of a Pyramid in society—the conical top consists of an oligarchic elite and the base consisting of numerically preponderant poor. It is an alarming fact that Georgian intelligentsia has been considerably impoverished (p. 162). Yet another disturbing development being that the active redistribution of national wealth among elites and the oligarchic groups is in progress, and representatives of foreign countries take part in it secretly. In this situation, few think about the eradication of poverty, the creation of jobs and the resolution of other social problems (p. 170). It is because of poverty that a significant proportion of the population is excluded from full participation in development and nation building (p. 155).

It is in this context that the approaches of the *Union of Citizens* (established by Edward Shevernadze) and the *Socialists* are at logger heads, yet very interesting. The former more or less, leans on the on-going *Reforms,* on the readymade prescriptions of the Bretten Wood Institutions—International Monetary Fund (IMF) and the World Bank, while the latter firmly believe that these 'readymade prescriptions' contributed to the growth of poverty and are likely to cause a social explosion (p. 170).

(*v*) The case of Russia is very special. It was the centre of communist operations. It was also responsible for dismantling of the Socialist infrastructure that was the only hope, succour and strength in an era of the capitalist onslaught. G. Pirogov and S. Pronin aptly observe that the switch over to the new economic system has been traumatic to the Russians. While it has been responsible for the emergence of new labour relations the majority of the population still sub-consciously feels inclined to act in accordance with the behaviour pattern of the previous system. It has been too difficult and rather, painful to adjust to the new system. However, an adjustment to the new conditions is accompanied by the loss of previous social norms, creating a state of *anomie* (p. 177).

The Russian economy has virtually been shattered. Not only that in certain regions of Russia unemployment is as high as 75 per cent (p. 188) but in 1995 the aggregate level of industrial production was only 51 per cent of the 1989 level (p. 193). It may also be true that all the unemployed may not be poor as some of them are engaged in secondary jobs which are mostly illegal and some of these jobs may even be criminal. It is reported that a very large number of people are engaged in the illicit *Shuttle Trade,* wherein, people go abroad, buy cheap goods in Third-world countries, push these in the Russian retail market illegally to earn money (p. 189). Through this and many other racketeering operations the *Shadow Economy* is increasing in volume and is both aggravating and alleviating poverty (p. 201). Alleviation of poverty as done by employing people in illegal and criminal trade/activities!

In a society where income inequalities were negligible and class differentiation despised, there is now a wide gap between the haves and have-nots. The capitalistic system has taken over the administrative structures. It is common knowledge that the salaries of the government officials start at a point where the salaries of the "intellectuals" for example, end (p.185). Thus it must be acknowledged that privatization in Russia has primarily been an illicit redistribution of wealth to the super rich which, on the one hand, has caused further impoverishment of the already poor and on the other, has resulted in the *criminalization* of society (p. 205).

The authors have rightly concluded that the so called creative market forces coupled with Western assistance can hardly raise Russia and other former USSR Republics to the level of the well-being characteristic of the most developed market economies of the West. Poverty has become the genetic label of the so-called transitional economy (p. 214).

(*vi*) Mongolia a 'poor' country of a 'poor region' did not face *poverty* in the communist regime and while discussing the poverty situation in the erstwhile communist countries under discussion elsewhere, we have given the statement made by the author Tsogt Nyamsuren (p. 227) that the country (Mongolia) which was not accustomed to "poverty" (in the communist regime) has thus, become a country of the poor (after the collapse of the communist regime). But, like other scholars who have contributed to this volume, Nyamsuren too is ambivalent, rather contradictory in his analysis, which may be reflected from the following statements. He says, "It is now acknowledged that socialism, once practiced by the countries of the Eastern Bloc, was not able to solve cultural, social, economic, political, and ecological problems. Moreover, it will take several decades to repair the damages caused by *totalitarian socialism*" (p. 223). In the next breath however, Tsogt Nyamsuren accepts that the process of economic reform and structural adjustment operates in the face of rising unemployment, growing poverty, and an emerging disparity in the living standards of the population. These changes in the national economy have had a strong impact on the status of women and children (p.226). Not only the women and children but the other *viz.* elderly, disabled, ethnic minorities etc., in most *societies intransition* have been extremely deprivated.

Two more statements made by Nyamsuren are important to depict the deteriorating socio-economic conditions of people in Mongolia due to the deterimental effects of global capitalism. With the continuous decline in domestic industry many are underpaid and rendered unemployed. In addition, the policies pursued by the government were totally counter to the welfare of the people (p. 253). The second observation is more significant sociologically. Sadly enough, poverty is not the worst part of the unfair system, what is worst is the loss of social and ethical values. Mongolia is a nation rich with historic traditions, where "the truth triumphs". However, in recent years, it has become a society in which "money and power triumphs" (p. 253).

An *Alibi* for Rampant Poverty: Tacit Support to Societal Destruction

Needless to mention that the corrupt politicians, cunning bureaucrats, inept professionals, de-ideologised intellectuals and 'national (anti-national) bourgeoisie' have all, by and large, played an anti-people role in embracing the 'global capitalism', under the influence, pressure, threats and corrupt afflictions of World Trade Organization (WTO), Multi-national/Trans-national Corporations/Companies, Super-Developed Economies especially USA. Inspite of the fact that all the authors speak of the humane qualities of the socialist system, the rising incidence of poverty in the societies-in-transition is attributed to either inefficient or slow pace of structural reforms! Yogesh Atal while echoing the arguments given by the analysts of poverty in six countries *viz.* Hungary, Bulgaria, Romania, Georgia, Russia and Mongolia says that post-communist poverty is caused by inefficient structural reforms, foreign debt servicing; high rate of inflation; ineffective tax policy; harsh fall of GDP and lack of political consensus (p.16). The uneven socio-economic impact of the economic crisis, negative consequences of the systemic changes on employment and disastrous repercussions of prevailing property dealings are attributed to be the main causes of increasing poverty (p.15). The issue of poverty, it is argued, is closely bound to essential aspects of post-communist transformation (Szalai), communist transformation'? One may find contradictory statements on crucial questions like these, which shows ambivalence of the authors. Such ambivalence may be seen from the following statements:

(*i*) All the authors accept that in the communist system there was no unemployment and basic needs-food, shelter, clothing, education and health services were available to all but there has been 'a rise in unemployment.... continuing impoverishment, limitations in free medical aid due to the extremely high price of medicine, heating, electricity, and so on (it might) once again, aggravate social tension, (Todorova, p. 100).

(*ii*) There was *Food Security* which is lost. Gypsies are in deep poverty. Prejudices against minority groups have increased and it is now asserted that 'they cannot perform a powerful role due to prejudices' (Szalai). Social security expenditure is questioned; with the growth of new needs due to marketization both relative and absolute poverty have increased (*Ibid*, 59). 'The Social Welfare Act, 1993 has eroded all universal regulations and the situation of the poor has become dependent on the arbitrary judgments of the decision-making bodies of their respective communities' (*ibid*, pp. 60-61). It is accepted that poverty has increased due to marketization, inequalities in income and due also to the negative effects of the withdrawal of the State and drastic cuts in spending on social benefits and services (*Ibid*, 33). It was further recognized that poverty and especially social and economic inequalities, have heightened due to the fact that property is being released by the state injudiciously and some people, particularly officers, politicians, neo-rich acquire it and become rich (p. 74). The state officials, managerial staff get fat salaries and the benefits to these groups follow the Western pattern; the higher-ups are highly benefited whereas, the lower cadres languish (p. 55). Szalai harshly comments that in the new system there is *recognition of basic human rights but not the fulfillment of basic human needs* (p. 34). With these pronouncements the ambivalence may further be identified from the following observations.

(iii) Yogesh Atal observed that transition from capitalism to socialism nourished the hope of completely terminating all oppression and all forms of social inequality to fulfill the Marxist dream. Feeling frustrated, these countries are now experiencing a reverse transition, from socialism to capitalism. Just as the entry into the era of socialism raised hopes amongst the masses of an emerging egalitarian society, the collapse of communism has caused a similar euphoria; people are hoping that all the troubles of the past will dissipate and sudden riches will appear (p. 5). Firstly, it may be understood that the first stage of transition was not from capitalism to socialism; it was from feudalism to socialism as in the case of Russia and other countries of the Federation and Mongolia, and from commercialism and primitive capitalist system to communism as in the case of other eastern European countries under discussion. Another observation that transition from socialism and central planning to a market economy and democratic from of government has been a 'mixed blessing' (p. 23) need closer examination. The 'blessing' is not exemplified except for an assertion that people got freedom, democratic from of government and 'human rights'. They got these (if at all they got it), at the cost of employment, food security, healthcare, education and human values. The joblessness, hunger, disease, criminalization of society is attributed by most authors to 'the slower pace of privatization and marketization as also a substantial decline on the expenditure on social welfare' (p. 18). Atal also refers to Washington Consensus—a mix of liberal capitalism, democratic polity, and good governance that has gained international currency pushing aside socialism. As it is presented, it also seems to be a single recipe for all situations. Atal is correct in asserting that like other models—development, modernization, etc., it is also likely to fail (p. 29).

(*iv*) Let us now examine some contradictory statements made by Julia Szalai and Sasha Todorova while analyzing poverty in Hungary and Bulgaria respectively. Julia in the tone and tenor of Laissez-faire economy maintains that '...amid certain conditions and in certain sub-groups of the poor, poverty is inherited from one generation to the other, and the culture of poverty becomes a strong factor in itself in blocking actions for poverty alleviation' (p. 74). Even after accepting the disastrous consequences of lost food security to the people and its negative effects on minority group-Gypsies in Hungary, Julia tries to convey to the readers that expansion of poverty cannot be attributed to marketization (p. 69); instead, she declares that 'poverty is a fated phenomenon, a price which should be paid by some people for the advancement of society as a whole' (p. 71); the bourgoise's aspirations for autonomy embodied in the informal economy urge a reduction in the political power of the state and its capability to intervene, embittered struggles are being waged to preserve the state resources and institutional channels that provide economic backing for the private sphere (p. 62). And, the crux of the issue lies in the fulfillment of aspirations of the new elite—the oligarchic elite of the capitalist system in capturing both economic and political power.

(*v*) The blame for rapid increase in poverty conditions so far, is put on '*slow pace of structural reforms*' but other analysts put an altogether different argument. For example, Avtandil Sulaberidze (p. 150) while analyzing the poverty phenomenon in Georgia agreed with the findings of Papava that the official economic policy heavily leaned on the Gerogian version of "shock therapy", having a great deal in common with the Polish and Russian "therapy-models". At that time, given its socio-economic situation, Georgia was not at all ready for "shock therapy treatment". The eye-wash stage of economic reform led to suffering, causing major difficulties for the country's economy and society (Papava, 1995 quoted by Avtandil). 'Shock therapy' in psychiatric domain is referred to electric shocks given to the patient to control 'super/hyper activities'; it gives tremors to the patient and puts him in an unconscious state. In economic domain, shock therapy refers to speedy transformation of an economy into the capitalist, market-oriented economy. This also includes 'tremors' and makes the society unconscious—unconscious of distributive justice, morals, values and humane social relations.

(*vi*) The arguments put by Traian Rotariu and Livia Popescu in explaining the Romanian quagmire are not straight; these are at times, at a tangent to each other. The authors do blame squarely the new economic order for the depressing economic condition in the country but also hasten to mention that the poverty risk of the household depends very much upon the occupational status, the educational level, and the number of children in the family' (p. 111). On the health front it is accepted that poverty has a sagging effect on health of the population and the 'process of insinuative marketization and privatization may be seen in health care', where doctors, though officially paid to care for people's health, are 'paid by the clients in terms of gifts and gratitude money' (p. 120).

If carefully examined, these statements are indicative of ambivalence of the authors; on the one hand they speak of social and economic ills, particularly the poverty and pauperization, caused by adventurous liberalization, privatization and globalization, on the other hand however, they lament that the market and private sectors have not developed due to strong state involvement.... no significant move had been made towards the market economy, there is still a profitless industrial sector and low level of free economic competition with an outcome of 'lame hybrid' between a command economy and a market economy (p. 112). This was the situation after seven years of "economic reforms", but even today after more than a decade, the situation has not improved, it has rather worsened on employment and poverty fronts. Social inequalities and economic disparities have not only increased but destroyed the very social fabric of most societies, especially developing societies the world over. East European societies are no exception.

Poverty, Poverty and Poverty

The phenomenon of poverty was absent from the 'primitive societies' by our standards and the whole group might have been poor but there were no poor in the group as such. The accumulation of wealth by a few, more so in the feudal system, created the class of the poor. The phenomenon of mass poverty however, is seen as a result of economic circumstances and cultural environment of man. Religion as a cultural category treated poverty as a glorious stage of man's social existence. Most religions considered poverty to be 'golden' and the 'poor being dearest and nearest to God'. Poverty was not regarded as an outcome of economic injustice or systemic failure in religious discourse on poverty. However, from the purely economic view point, poverty came to be discussed and analyzed only in the period of Enlightenment in Europe. Poverty was associated with 'guilt', 'outcome of immorality', excessive fertility of the poor'; incapacity of some people to earn'; 'fate', 'past deeds' (outcome of Karma in the previous birth), 'exploitation by the powerful, the rich and especially employers in the commercial and industrial systems'; ideology of the state *e.g.* Laissez-faire, and capitalism'. And today, mass poverty is associated with the contemporary LPG economy, a weird version of capitalism. As for capitalism is concerned German economist, Karl Georg Winkleblech (1810-1865) writing under the pen name Karl Marlo, attributed mass poverty and the pauperization of the proletariat to an intrinsic principle of the capitalist system. The economists have largely avoided facing odd and inconvenient facts and did not help much in alleviating/eradication of poverty. The economists got 'elevated in the professional ladder by devising measure of poverty: Gini Index; Deciles Coefficient; Engel

Coefficient; Poverty Gap; Head Count Index; PPP estimates of GNP per capita, survival minimum, living minimum; the subsistence minimum; social minimum; decent minimum, etc. etc.' Some of these measures relate to the Food Basket Model is largely used wherein, the social minimum defines the upper limit of poverty, and the living minimum defines the lower line of poverty. Without going into the details of measures of poverty, I may hasten to mention that apart from definition, the classification of poverty and the poor has confused the very course of positive action to eradicate it. The classification of poverty into absolute poverty, relative poverty, abject poverty, normal poverty, pseudo poverty, ideological poverty, fatal poverty etc. etc. and the classification of poor *e.g.* indigent, poor, destitute, miserable, needy, impoverished, marginalized etc. may be an academic finesse but cannot either describe poverty or define the poor; can anyone else except the hungry gauge hunger? Only his pangs can explain his anguish. One may partly agree with Sasha Todoorova that the range of indicators expressing subjective definitions of poverty shows that it is strongly connected with 'the individuals' ability to meet elementary physiological needs' (p. 79). I am inclined to note with dismay that the social scientists squabble on the definition of poverty, engage in fruitless attempts to classify the poor, burn the midnight lamp to devise indicators of poverty and compete with each other in drawing measures of poverty but the poor endlessly suffer poverty and they brave the onslaught of neglect and exploitation by the handful of rich and powerful.

Yogesh Atal has given three distinct approaches for treatment of poverty as enunciated by UNDP. These are: Income Perspective; Capability Perspective; and Human Development Perspective (which includes capability perspective also) is preferred by UNDP and is also supported by Yogesh Atal for remedial action. The real difficulty in accepting it however is that it does not elucidate modalities of social/economic structural changes which would, in really, eliminate poverty. It is widely recognized that "poverty is structural", but social scientists are shy of elaborating strategies of significant structural changes in society that would alter the existing Pyramid. I would rather opt to advise Dr. Yogesh Atal not to get involved into the polemics of real, pseudo, hidden and/or apparent poverty or to stress the assertions that poverty is a multi-dimensional phenomenon and is caused by a variety of factors. That it is but the problem lies in its banishments. Its manifestations also differ from context to context. There is no linear chain of cause and effect: an interrelated web of economic, social, psychological, cultural, and political factors influence the occurrence and persistence of poverty. Real poverty may not be apparent poverty may not be real. Thus, there cannot be a single strategy to eradicate it in different societal contexts. In order to develop realistic national strategies for poverty eradication, it is of utmost importance that these be based on an objective appraisal of the etiology of poverty, its spread, and its pathology. (p. 4.). It is certainly true in the classical social science idiom but when it comes to real action-orientation, the whole scientific method of finding out multi-causality and final a etiology may involve such a protracted process an take such a long time that the whole context may change itself. Hence, the need for social sciences today being to act as a proactive instrument rather than a mere analytical tool; and social scientists, at least in areas like poverty, must be agents of change and activists rather than mere 'scientists' and fence-sitters. For, it must be recognized now, before it is too late, that poverty is a consequence of exploitation. Karl Marx (1818-1883) had rightly held that a lasting improvement of the position of the workers was impossible within the frame of the existing economic order based on the private ownership of the means of production. Any analyst of the contemporary situation must recognize that it is not the individual or company ownership that was once responsible for bashful exploitation of workers; rather it is now the unseen, cross national-boundary corporate ownership which is interested in controlling the world economies without qualms. The example of six analyzed in this book societies/economies speak volumes of this loot and plunder.

Atal says that the structure of poverty in Eastern Europe is radically different from that of the developing countries. In the latter, while the actual number of poor is still on the rise, their percentage compared to the total population is declining. As a result, the poverty gap is also being somewhat reduced. The situation in Eastern Europe is quite the opposite: an increase is registered on all three indicators of poverty (Number of poor, Head Count Index and Poverty gap). But this interplay of figures does not alter the situation of 75 per cent unemployment in Russia and mass hunger in some African countries. What is needed is the security of job, a guarantee of meals, provision of shelter, opportunities of un-hindered education and care for the health of people.

Tsogt Nyamsuren accepting the inevitability of transition asserted that the transition process requires not only a change in the structure of the economy but also in the system of polity. Social transformation involves the creation of a democratic polity and a system of social justice for all. The democratic order can become stable only when the economic, social and legal systems are just and fair. It cannot survive without the rule of law....The process of transformation is made difficult by the phenomenon of poverty (p. 223). It is possible through social policy. But social policy entails choice, change and conflict. It is in these three stages of social policy formulation and implementation that the intentions of the power elite may be understood. Traian Rotariu and Livia Popescu rightly observe that 'the reform of social policy must be based on decentralization'. Transparency in bureaucratic procedures is essential to transform decision-making into a democratic and efficient process (p. 127). But a critical analysis of the six societies under review shows that there is a big claim for ushering in democracy, freedom and human rights but there is neither decentralization, nor transparency and not even human concern in the post-communist transition of these societies. Hence, only poverty, poverty and poverty all over.

However, the present work is very important and useful. Atal has done a yeoman's job in not only motivating experts in writing exciting pieces but also in putting all these in a coherent manner. This work certainly helps in understanding the processes of transition in the erstwhile communist Russian satellites. He deserves our congratulations for this informative and critical work.

REFRENCE

Atal, Yogesh (*ed.*) (1995). *Poverty in Transition and Transition in poverty—Recent Developments in Hungary, Bulgaria, Romania, Georgia Russia, Mongolia,* UNESCO Publishing Paris/Berghahn Books, New York, Oxford.

16

The Dynamics of Language in Indian Diaspora: The Case of Bhojpuri/Hindi in Trinidad*

N. JAYARAM

Indian diaspora is a complex and heterogeneous phenomenon: In terms of the history of their emigration; their regional, religious, social, economic and educational backgrounds; the politico-economic context in which they have developed over time; and the socio-cultural experiences they have undergone, the Indian communities in diaspora vary considerably. Expectedly then, the status of the languages which the different diasporic communities carried as part of their socio-cultural baggage is highly variable. They have experienced attrition and disappeared altogether, or they have survived in extremely limited spheres of life, or they have been modified and retained, or they continue to exist and are in contact with their ancestral roots, or they have been sought to be revived and revitalised with varying degrees of success.

Thus, the Estate Tamils in Sri Lanka, the Sikh Punjabis in England, and the Hindu Gujaratis in the United States of America have retained their ancestral language, whereas the Indians in Jamaica have lost all their ancestral languages. In Mauritius, Fiji and Surinam, Indic languages are still spoken. A local dialect of Bhojpuri is used in all informal spheres, and

* This paper was originally published in *Sociological Bulletin*, 49 (1), March 2001: 41-62. Considering his abiding interest in the study of Indian diaspora, it is reproduced here with the kind permission of the Managing Editor, *Sociological Bulletin*, as a tribute to Professor Yogesh Atal.

Standard Hindi in religious and cultural domains. In Fiji and Mauritius, Standard Hindi is even officially recognised. In Guyana and Trinidad, Bhojpuri is used in folk songs and Standard Hindi in religious services and ceremonies. In all these countries, the lingua franca is the dominant local language(s)—Sinhalese in Sri Lanka, English in England and the United States of America, Creole French or Creole English in Mauritius, Fijian or English in Fiji, Creole Dutch in Surinam, and Creole English in Guyana and Trinidad.

What accounts for the differential dynamics of language in Indian diaspora? In the literature on Indian diaspora, there is neither an empirically cogent sociological answer to this question nor a theoretically sound socio-linguistic formulation about it. Such an answer or formulation, no doubt, can only come out of extant comparative studies of the history and status of Indian languages among different diasporic communities. Before such comparative studies can be embarked upon, however, we need benchmark socio-historical surveys of the dynamics of language among the different diasporic communities.

Surprisingly enough, the dynamics of language has hardly attracted the attention of anthropologists and sociologists working on Indian diaspora.[1] The focus of a few socio-linguists who have dealt with this subject is understandably circumscribed by the concerns of their discipline: The effect of Creole and to a lesser extent of Standard Hindi on Mauritian Bhojpuri (Domingue, 1971), the formal changes in Trinidad Hindi as a result of language adaptation (Durbin, 1973), the koine formation in the Indian speech community in Guyana (Gambhir, 1981), the socio-linguistic structure and process in Mauritian Bhojpuri (Gambhir, 1986) and Fiji Hindustani (Siegel, 1975), the linguistic adaptations of Fiji Indians (Moag, 1979), the Sarnami as a living language in Surinam (Damsteegt, 1988), the morphology of Trinidad Bhojpuri (Mohan, 1978) and the death of that language (Mohan and Zador, 1986), and the relationship between language and socio-economic and cultural factors in a Trinidad village (Sperl, 1980).

This paper analyses the dynamics of language among diasporic Indians in Trinidad. It traces the linguistic element in the socio-cultural baggage brought by their ancestors during the indenture era; it examines the metamorphosis and attrition that this element experienced in the course of over 150 years of their presence in this country; and it documents the efforts at reviving and rejuvenating the linguistic element of their cultural heritage and reflects on the prospects thereof.

Diglossia and the Evolution of Trinidad Bhojpuri

Between 1845 and 1917, 143,939 Indians were brought into Trinidad under the scheme of indentured labour, of which only 33,294 (or 23.13 per cent) eventually returned to India (Laurence 1971: 26 and 57). There is no official record of the languages and dialects which they brought with them. It is now difficult to determine the numerical strength of emigrants from each district and the language and dialect spoken by them. Nevertheless, considering the region from which an overwhelming majority of the Indians were recruited, namely, the western part of Bihar, the eastern part of the then United Provinces and the southern (or Ranchi) plateau of Chota Nagpur—it is justifiably presumed by linguists that most of these immigrants 'must have been native speakers of the various dialects of Bhojpuri'[2] (Mohan, 1978:8). This is further confirmed by 'the striking similarities between the Bhojpuri widely spoken in Trinidad (in comparison with other Indic languages) and the different varieties of Bhojpuri spoken in India' (*Ibid.*:11).

Besides the dialects of Bhojpuri, the emigrants brought other languages and dialects. The small groups of recruits from outside the Bhojpuri-speaking areas brought with them Avadhi, Magahi and Maithili. Mohan claims that 'there is anecdotal evidence that these languages were once spoken in Trinidad, as well as languages from further afield, such as Bengali, Nepali, and Telugu' (*Ibid.*:11). The immigrants hailing from the Madras Presidency (forming about 10 per cent) brought with them south Indian languages, most notably, Tamil.

The linguistic confusion resulting from a multiplicity of languages and dialects among the immigrant Indians was often remarked by observers.[3] For instance, Reverend W.H. Gamble (1866:33), a British missionary, noted:

> The Bengalis speak Hindustani and Bengali, while the inhabitants of the Madras Presidency speak Tamil, a totally different language. When these people meet in Trinidad, it strikes me as somewhat strange that they have to point to water and rice, and ask each other what they call it in their language. So totally different are the languages, the Hindustani and the Tamil, that English has to become the medium of communication.

How Reverend Gamble's forecast eventually became true we will see later. Initially, however, the languages brought by the Indians were preserved. According to Tinker (1993:211), this was due to the persistence of the Indians in speaking their mother tongue among themselves. This was also assisted by the lack of educational facilities for their children, which would have forced them to learn an alien language in school. Even when educational facilities first became available, most Indian parents kept their children away from school for various reasons, not excluding the fear of conversion to Christianity (Singh, 1985:48-49).

At the outset, the exigencies of plantation life made two linguistic demands on the Indian immigrants: First, they were required to develop a language for communication among themselves, a lingua franca as it were. And second, they had to develop the ability to communicate with the authorities and in the market, which meant acquiring a more or less intelligible English patois and adopting Creole English as their link-language. About the latter, Tinker (1993:211-12) observes that 'the plantation Indian learned to regard language as a means of protecting himself—making himself understood, when this was needed, and making himself hard to understand when that would serve him'.

The development of a lingua franca for internal communication was not easy, despite the fact that those hailing from the Bhojpuri-speaking areas of north India formed the numerical core of the Indian community. Even the Bhojpuri brought to Trinidad was not homogeneous, and it reflected the dialectal variations of the parts from which the speakers came.[4] In due course, however, through a process of koineisation (that is, levelling) of different dialects, a new variant of Bhojpuri was evolved as a reasonably homogeneous lingua franca on the sugar plantations.[5] This variant is called by linguists as 'Trinidad Bhojpuri' (see Mohan, 1978; Mohan and Zador, 1986) and by historians, following plantation and colonial officials, as 'Plantation Hindustani' (see Tinker, 1993:208).[6]

According to Gambhir (1986: 193), the process of dialect-levelling was almost automatic as the various dialects and languages of the immigrants more or less represented 'a linguistic continuum of the western to the eastern dialects in India in such a way that there were minimal differences between any two geographically adjacent dialects'. This process was boosted by the 'psychological and emotional unity' provided by the perception of the speakers of the various north Indian linguistic systems as forms of Hindi or Hindustani.

In the opinion of socio-linguists, Trinidad Bhojpuri is a linguistic system by itself (see Mohan, 1978; Gambhir, 1986). It is governed by linguistic rules like any other natural language. That it is a compromise between different speakers, or that it is a simplified version of Indian Bhojpuri, does not make it linguistically less different. Some of 'the competing linguistic alterants from the second stage' may, no doubt, persist in the speech of some people. These are only redolent of the multi-dialectal origin of Trinidad Bhojpuri (Gambhir, 1986).

The evolution of Trinidad Bhojpuri as a distinct language has not been documented, and 'it is extremely difficult to reconstruct' (Mohan, 1978:12). It may be surmised, that with every succeeding generation, the relatively greater impact of peer groups as compared to that of parents in the matter of language use must have contributed to the increasing homogenisation of Trinidad Bhojpuri. That is, there must have developed 'a single system [of language] incorporating residual dialectal variation rather than persisting as a series of distinct dialects' (Mohan, 1978:13). By the time the Indians had settled down as an agricultural community in the last decades of the 19th century, Trinidad Bhojpuri had become their ethnic language. Thus, in his 1914 Report on Trinidad, J. McNeill could observe that 'soon after arrival all immigrants learn Plantation Hindustani' (quoted in Tinker, 1993:211).

Although Trinidad Bhojpuri evolved as a language different from the ancestral languages, it never became a 'native language'. This was due to the fact that with the expansion of education, the younger generation, especially those in urban areas, gradually adopted Creole English and/or Standard English as the native language. According to a socio-linguistic profile prepared by Sealey (1983: Intro-2) on the basis of 1970 Census data, currently the Indo-Trinidadians 'share with the rest of the population...varieties of Trinidadian Creole English as the major L1 and language of daily communication'. This community-wide language shift over the decades has meant that Trinidad Bhojpuri is a dying language (see Durbin, 1973; Mahabir and Mahabir, 1990:3; Mohan and Zador, 1986).

Using Roger Bell's socio-linguistics formula, Sealey (1983: TB-1-2) arrives at the following profile of Trinidad Bhojpuri: 'A dialect of "mainland" Bhojpuri', 'a Tolerated Language', 'spoken as an L1 by less than 3 per cent of the population' and 'used as a language of restricted internal communication', Trinidad Bhojpuri monolinguals are generally over 75 years of age, and Trinidad Bhojpuri and Trinidad English bilinguals (including semi-speakers) are generally in the age group of 55-75 years. The fluent speakers of that language are Hindus who have remained fairly isolated in rural areas.

The few native speakers of Trinidad Bhojpuri use it among their restricted friends or kin circle. It is reportedly used by the elders in the presence of strangers or children when they discuss something confidential or when they wish to exclude them from conversation. The same is said to be true of the very few elderly persons in the 'Madrassi' settlements in rural areas who still speak Tamil, and the elderly Muslims who speak Urdu.

Missionaries and the Introduction of Standard Hindi

The process of dialect-levelling and the emergence of Trinidad Bhojpuri was spontaneous and unconscious, and it was determined by the exigencies of plantation life. Not surprisingly, the speakers of this language did not even give a name to it and observers called it 'Plantation Hindustani'. Parallel to this was the conscious effort of the Canadian Presbyterian Mission at introducing Standard Hindi in Trinidad. The credit for this goes primarily to the doyen of that Mission in Trinidad, namely, Reverend John Morton of Bridgewater, Nova Scotia in Canada.

Reverend Morton came to Trinidad in 1868 and established a Mission to work almost exclusively among what were then called the 'East Indians'. He at once appreciated the need to use the native language of Indians for propagating Christianity among them.[7] The native language which he found best suited for his work was 'the Hindi dialect'.[8] By the end of 1870, he notes in his diary: I have now familiarised myself with the Hindi and use it or the Urdu, according as the person to whom I speak may be a Hindu or a Mussalman'. In December 1871, he was granted a Government License 'to practice as a sworn Interpreter of the English and Hindustani languages in this colony' (Morton, 1916:66 and 67).

In the early days of the Mission, its members had to learn Hindi so that they could communicate with the newly arriving immigrants from India. The first regular church of the Canadian Presbyterian Mission was the 'Susamachar Church' in San Fernando. In this Church religious service was given in Hindi. As of August 1871, there was only one complete copy of 'the Hindi Scriptures' in Trinidad, and that was Reverend Morton's own. In January 1872, there arrived from Calcutta boxes of books containing Bibles, and tracts and catechisms in Hindi. In 1872, Reverend Morton began translating and preparing hymns, assisted by Reverend Andrew Gayadeen. A little book containing 30 hymns thus produced was printed (in Halifax, Canada) in 'the Hindustani language, employing Roman character' (Morton, 1916:110 and 111).

Considerations of economy of time and money soon made the Mission think of starting a Hindi printing press of its own. First, Morton purchased 'all the East Indian's type' and got press-work done in Port of Spain. Then he bought a hand-press and moved the plant to Tunapuna and started his own press. At this first Hindi press in Trinidad were printed, in 1903, thousands of copies of *Prarthna Mala* (The Garland of Prayers), the Hindi hymn book, which came to be used at all Hindi services not only in Trinidad but in far away Jamaica too. Also brought out from this press were copies of 'a simple catechism' adapted to 'the Hindi using the Nagari character'. At this press Morton also translated, printed and published 'for the Government all their Hindustani notices and circulars' (Morton, 1916:425, 432 and 433).

In March 1905, Morton began printing four pages of Hindi in those copies of *The Trinidad Presbyterian* which circulated among the 'East Indians'. Morton also brought out the International Sabbath School Lessons' in Hindi with a simple commentary in English. This publication went a long way in systematising the teaching of Hindi in the Sunday School, allying it closely to the religious instruction in the day schools (Morton, 1916:432).

Thus, under the stewardship of Reverend John Morton, the Canadian Presbyterian Mission played a pioneering role in introducing and propagating Standard Hindi in Trinidad. Though the Mission continued to use Hindi for its activities right through the first half of 20th century, gradually the initiative was lost and Standard Hindi experienced attrition even among the Presbyterians. According to Niehoff and Niehoff (1960:149 and 151), who observed the situation in the late 1950's, the Mission gave up the emphasis on Hindi as its administrators found that 'the young Indians no longer have any interest in it'. In fact, their field work revealed that 'except for the very old, they [the Presbyterians] show very little interest in maintaining Hindi as a spoken language and it is very rarely heard in Christian homes' (*Ibid.*:151).

At a thanks giving ceremony in a Presbyterian household in LaRomaine in south Trinidad in December 1995, the author heard an octogenarian lady recite what she called a *bhajan* in Hindi, and freely translate it into English for the benefit of those (*i.e.*, nearly the entire audience?) who did *not* understand the original. She lamented on the loss of Hindi among her Presbyterian brethren. The religious service that evening was carried out exclusively in English, and the hymn book (*Hymns and choruses*, published by the Presbyterian Church in Trinidad) circulated among the members of the audience, consisted of five *bhajans* in Hindi printed in Roman characters.

Attrition of Trinidad Bhojpuri and Standard Hindi

By all accounts then, the spontaneously evolved Trinidad Bhojpuri and the deliberately developed Standard Hindi did not survive for more than a century in Trinidad. If at all they are still spoken fluently, it is almost exclusively by the very elderly in rural areas, and as such there is no speech community of these ethnic languages left among the Indo-Trinidadians anymore.[9] Whatever has survived is mostly in their folksongs and in their lexicon of kitchen and food, and to some extent in their kinship terminology. The only systematic ethnic use of Hindi in contemporary Trinidad is to be found in the religious realm among the Hindus.

The attrition[10] of native languages among diasporic Indians in Trinidad, and the attrition of the lingua franca which was spontaneously evolved (Trinidad Bhojpuri) and deliberately developed (Standard Hindi) by them are intriguing to scholars engaged in the study of Indian diaspora. This is particularly so considering that the diasporic Indians are the single largest ethnic community in Trinidad (forming 40.3 per cent of the population, according to 1990 Census), and considering that other elements of culture (*e.g.*, religion and food habits) and social organisation (*e.g.*, marriage and family) have been reconstituted relatively successfully (see Klass, 1961; Vertovec, 1992). What explains this linguistic attrition among diasporic Indians in Trinidad?

To begin with, throughout the period of indenture, and later too, the life of the immigrant Indians was witnessed by the patterns of their ancestral culture being ignored, ridiculed or suppressed by the carriers of the dominant culture of the colony. Their economic exploitation was matched by cultural subjection, and there was continuous pressure on them to Creolise. That the Indians did not allow the total obliteration of their 'Indianness' under these conditions is indeed surprising. Though with some loss (including their language), the Indians still retain more of their own cultural identity than their African counterparts (see Tinker, 1993:208).

Although through a process of koineisation the Indians evolved Trinidad Bhojpuri or Plantation Hindustani as a lingua franca, 'few recognise it as a language distinct from rather than derivative of Standard Hindi'. The lexical similarity (notwithstanding the morphological and grammatical differences) between the two languages resulted in this language being viewed as a 'corrupted' variety of Standard Hindi (Mohan, 1978:2). The speakers of Trinidad Bhojpuri themselves referred to it as 'broken Hindi' or 'bad-Hindi' (Sealey, 1983: TB-2). Some even refer to it disparagingly as '*chamar* Hindi (low-caste Hindi) or *gaoo bolee* (village speech)' (Mahabir and Mahabir, 1990:3).

The Trinidad Bhojpuri speakers used Standard Hindi as their index of comparison. Standard Hindi was viewed as 'Good Hindi' or 'Proper Hindi' (Mahabir and Mahabir, 1990:3). They heard this Hindi spoken in Hindi films, which have a wide audience in Trinidad, and by the few expatriate residents (*i.e.*, Indian nationals) there (Sealey, 1983: TB-2). In other words, the native speakers of Trinidad Bhojpuri themselves had feelings of inferiority about that language. This, according to Mohan (1978:2), is 'partly responsible for the failure of its speakers to transmit this language to younger generations of Trinidad Indians'.

Significantly, right from the beginning, the Canadian Presbyterian Mission adopted Standard Hindi, and not Trinidad Bhojpuri, as its language of religious propagation. Whether the Mission too had a poor image of Trinidad Bhojpuri ('the language of the heathens') *vis-à-vis* Standard Hindi ('the language of the civilised'), is difficult to say. Be that as it may, the Mission's efforts did not ensure the survival of Standard Hindi. As noted earlier, even before a century after its establishment, the Mission almost entirely switched over to English.

From the point of view of the larger community of Indians, the identification of Standard Hindi with the Canadian Presbyterian Mission was perhaps what subdued its chances of developing as a second language in the country. The use of Standard Hindi by the Mission was suspected by many a Hindu and Muslim alike as a stratagem for their conversion to Christianity. In Seepersad Naipaul's (father of V.S. Naipaul) perceptive work of fiction, *The adventures of Gurudeva and other stories*, depicting the life of Indians in rural Trinidad in the 1940's, Sohun (the school teacher) tells Gurudeva (the protagonist): 'In school you never were keen on Hindi. Your father felt that teaching you Hindi was only a ruse on my part to teach you the Bible. He preferred his sons to grow up as ignorant Hindus rather than as intelligent Christians....'. (1976:91-92).

There is no gainsaying the fact that when educational advancement was unthinkable for the indentured immigrants, the doors of English education were opened for the children of those Indians who got converted to Christianity, more so to Presbyterianism. Along with this came the prospects of employment in the emerging modern sector, including the cherished professions of medicine and law. Such an education also meant exposure to Christianity and to a new outlook on life. One element of their culture which English-educated Indians sacrificed as part of the process of modernisation was their ethnic language.

English, and literacy in English, carried high prestige in the colonial period.[11] As a language of education, English became a *sine qua non* of upward mobility in the colonial social order. Sperl (1980), who studied the language shift towards Trinidad Creole English in an Indian village in Trinidad, concluded that this shift reflects the acculturation to wider society and the decreasing meaningfulness of 'guiding principles' which are rooted in tradition and religion. The later part of her conclusion is, however, certainly contestable (see Vertovec, 1992).

Not only has there been a shift towards Trinidad Creole English as the first language, and even as the mother tongue, among the diasporic Indians, but also there has been a pronounced strain towards monolingualism in that language. This is explained by the fact that their native language has no use whatsoever in commerce and administration. Trinidad Creole English is the first language of most Trinidadians and Standard English is the official language of the country.[12] Trinidad Creole English (at primary level) and Standard English (at secondary level and beyond) are used in education. From the utilitarian point of view, those who study an additional language, invariably choose Spanish or French.

Retention and Survival of Linguistic Heritage

According to Berko-Gleason (1982:21), 'the traditional linguistic sub-systems (phonology, morphology, syntax, and vocabulary) may suffer differential loss in attrition, since they are learned separately'. It is important to note that both Trinidad Bhojpuri and Standard Hindi were predominantly a part of the oral culture, and the script was basically confined to the religious literati—the pandits among the Hindus and the ministers among the Presbyterians. This accounts for both the general attrition of these two languages among the Indians and the survival and retention of some elements of their native languages.

Thus, Hindi is still used in liturgy and Bhojpuri has been retained in folk songs. The survival of Bhojpuri or Hindi (and even Tamil) words in the spheres of food, domestic worship, and kinship relations, is also to be understood in this light (Winford, 1972:13-14).[13] The polite routines and routinised sequences, which are taught/learnt explicitly, have been similarly retained'.[14] These expressions have little intellectual or referential content, but serve socio-cultural purposes. Similarly, numbers, songs, and emotionally laden words like curses or swearwords have survived.[15]

Language retention is also an age-related phenomenon. It was mentioned earlier that Trinidad Bhojpuri monolinguals are generally over 75 years of age, and Trinidad Bhojpuri and Trinidad Creole English bilinguals (including semi-speakers) are mostly in the age group of 55-75 years. The same could be said about the retention of Standard Hindi. The elders retained their first language mainly because they did not know English.[16] They did not develop as a bilingual community. With the younger and newer generations becoming increasingly proficient in English, their incipient bilingualism gave way to monolingualism in English. If language survival is noticeable at all among the young Indo-Trinidadians today, it is only at the lexical and idiomatic levels (Mahabir and Mahabir, 1990:3).

There is a gender dimension in language retention. The social organisation which the Indian settlers reconstituted in Trinidad was pronouncedly patriarchal, resembling that of their ancestral land. In the post-indenture period, men had the major share of interactions in the outside world where English (Creole or Standard) was the ruling language.

While the role of woman was not entirely confined to the family, the responsibility for running the household and the socialisation of children was primarily hers. Not surprisingly, it is in the spheres of kitchen and food, and household and kinship that the survival of the lexical and idiomatic elements of Trinidad Bhojpuri and Hindi are most pronounced.

Ethnicity and Linguistic Revival

In Seepersad Naipaul's fiction referred to earlier, there are perceptive observations about the linguistic situation among Indians in rural Trinidad in the 1940's. A few characters in this novel speak Hindi: 'In nearly half a century's residence in the island Boodhoo still spoke nothing but Hindi,...he being India-born'. Some characters speak 'mongrel Hindi'—'a sort of patois Hindi which, spoken elsewhere but in Trinidad, would be unmeaning gibberish'. Though he himself is a pretender speaking Standard Hindi, Gurudeva, the protagonist of the novel, bemoans the fact 'that not two in a hundred knew their mother tongue' and he exhorts the village youth to regard it as 'their duty to learn Hindi' (1976:64, 38 and 106).

Seepersad Naipaul's portrayal of the Indian community in rural Trinidad reveals the realisation among some Indians as early as the 1940's that with their community shifting to English their linguistic heritage was facing extinction. The celebration, in 1945, of the centenary of their arrival in Trinidad, and the introduction of adult suffrage in 1946, gave the ethnic self-perception of Indo-Trinidadians a boost. This combined with increasing contact with visiting religious personages from India triggered off a concerted effort at cultural revival and rejuvenation among them. As part of this general movement, Standard Hindi, not Trinidad Bhojpuri, was sought to be revived.

It is true that an ethnic group is not necessarily coterminous with a linguistic or speech community. But, there is no gainsaying that in a multi-ethnic polity characterised by cultural contentions, language could become an important element of ethnic identity. Thus, the efforts at revival of Hindi and its propagation, which began in the 1950's, could be viewed as a conscious reaction by sections of the Indo-Trinidadians against the loss of their distinctive cultural heritage through linguistic attrition. Several organisations and individuals, religious and/or cultural in orientation, played a role in this.

The Sanatan Dharma Maha Sabha (established in 1952), the major religious body representing the Hindu population, the Arya Pratinidhi Sabha (incorporated in 1943) and other Hindu religious bodies took an interest in Hindi[17] as a liturgical language of the Hindus.[18] Pandits went to

India to study Hindi and learn scriptures like *Bhagwad Gita, Ramayana, Srimad Bhagavta, Shiva Purana, Vishnu Purana*, etc. Hindi has now become a religious requisite of the pandit class. Many leading pandits of Trinidad, both in the Sanatan Dharma Maha Sabha and the Arya Pratinidhi Sabha are Hindi graduates. Hindi is taught in *mandirs* (temples) under the jurisdiction of the Sanatan Dharma Maha Sabha, and as part of the radio programme '*Dharm Shiksha*' (Religious Education) for school children sponsored by it.

Although the cultural aspect is not ignored, the Hindi orientation of the Hindu organisations is primarily religious in nature. However, Hindi, unlike Sanskrit which has become essentially a sacral language, has far wider socio-cultural potential. The recognition of this fact was behind the establishment, in 1952, of the Hindi Education Board under the sponsorship of the then High Commissioner of India, Anand Mohan Sahay. The Board had as its objective the teaching of Hindi and elements of Indian culture in villages. It offered Hindi courses at three levels—*Prarambhik* (Beginner), Junior and Senior (equivalent to India's lower secondary). Books published by the Dakshin Bharath Hindi Prachar Sabha, Madras (now Chennai), were used as approved textbooks.

Till 1957 the Board functioned under the able directorship of Edward Joseph Pillai.[19] He was replaced by Induthai Kelar, who was deputed by the Government of India. Under her directorship about 650 students passed the Board examination. After her departure from Trinidad, the Board slackened in its activities, and the number of students began dwindling steadily. The propagation of Hindi was resumed after the arrival, in 1966, of Hari Shankar Adesh as a Secretary at the High Commission of India in Port of Spain. Because of his efforts several classes were restarted, seminars were held, and a cultural camp was organised. In the last Board examination, held in 1970, 251 Hindi students were successful.

Though the propagation of Hindi was resumed under the leadership of Adesh, the Board continued to be embroiled with internal differences about the scope of its activities. Some wanted the Board to confine itself exclusively to teaching Hindi and conducting examinations. Others wanted the scope of the Board to be extended to include fine arts too. The infighting within the Board aggravated to such an extent that it even became difficult to convene a General Body meeting. Eventually, the Board became defunct.

As if in anticipation of the void about to be created by the collapse of the Hindi Education Board, Adesh had founded the Bharatiya Vidya Sansthaan in November 1966. This organisation sought the all round development of Indian culture, including the teaching of Indian languages (Hindi, Sanskrit and Urdu), music (both vocal and instrumental), and performing arts (like dance and drama). The Sansthaan has made considerable contribution to the revival and propagation of Hindi in Trinidad. Starting with a few students, the Sansthaan has established more than 30 schools spread all over the country. It prepares students for the Hindi examinations conducted by the University of London, the Rashtra Bhasha Prachar Samithi (Wardha) and the Bharatiya Vidya Bhavan (Mumbai). Starting from March 1968, the Sansthaan has been publishing a monthly magazine called *Jyothi*. One of the former pupils and a notable activist of the Sansthaan, Kamla Ramlakhan, has written two Hindi language textbooks-*Hindi Prabhaat* (Dawn of Hindi)—keeping in mind the socio-cultural background of the Trinidad learners.[20] Incidentally, it is the Sansthaan which has sought to popularise *Namaste* as a form of greeting among Hindus, whose culturally rooted mode of greeting has been *Sitaram* (Panday, 1993).

The Hindu bias in the propagation of Hindi by the Sanatan Dharma Maha Sabha and the Bharatiya Vidya Sansthaan hardly needs to be emphasised. Contrasted with this is the pronouncedly less religious orientation of the Hindi Nidhi (Hindi Foundation of Trinidad and Tobago), established in 1986 to propagate Hindi in Trinidad. The Nidhi has brought out a few Hindi textbooks for beginners, and it sponsors the teaching of Hindi in schools and the *Hindi Sikhen* (Let us learn Hindi) programme on the radio. It had organised an International Hindi Conference at Couva in central Trinidad in April 1992, and in collaboration with The University of the West Indies, St. Augustine, it organised the Fifth World Hindi Conference in April, 1996.

It is appropriate here to mention the keen interest that the Government of India has evinced in the revival and propagation of Hindi in Trinidad, as also in some other countries with a substantial proportion of population of Indian origin. The initiative taken by the High Commission of India in the establishment and working of the now defunct Hindi Education Board has been referred to earlier. The Commission had started free evening classes in Hindi in 1985 which, after being suspended for some years, were restarted in 1992. It also observes Hindi Divas on January 14 every year.

The Government of India has been providing scholarships to Trinidadians for studying Hindi in India. The Indian Council for Cultural Relations has been offering the services of two Hindi Professors—one at the St. Augustine campus of The University of the West Indies (since 1989), and the other at the National Institute of Higher Education and Research in Science and Technology in Port of Spain (since 1987).

Also important to note here is the sudden spurt in the use of Hindi in the audio-visual media in the recent years. Before 1993, Indian cultural programmes hardly got a few hours of broadcast time on the radio. Now there are three radio stations broadcasting Indo-Trinidadian and Hindi programmes, and two exclusively so. They also carry a few advertisements in Hindi. In 1995, two of them offered Hindi lessons—*Hindi Sikhen* (Let us learn Hindi) anchored by V.R. Jagannathan on WABC's FM 103, and *Hindi Mein Bath Chith* (Conversation in Hindi) anchored by Sumita Broomes on Radio ICN. Hindi films and film-based programmes, and cultural programmes using Hindi in varying degrees are regularly telecast by the local television stations. Cinema halls regularly screen Hindi movies, whose audience has reportedly grown over the years. Also, the innumerable cultural organisations and associations often use Hindi in varying doses.

Prospects of Hindi as an Ethnic Language

It is more than 40 years now that concerted efforts have been on at reviving Hindi in Trinidad and propagating that language among Indo-Trinidadians. What has been the outcome of these efforts? What are the prospects of Hindi becoming an ethnic language of Indo-Trinidadians, and of Indo-Trinidadians becoming a distinct speech community and bilingual (in English and Hindi)? The growth of interest in Hindi in the recent past and the increasing observability of Hindi in the audio-visual media may suggest that the prospects are bright. However, a sociological review of the historical experience of language attrition and revival among Indo-Trinidadians does not allow one to be sanguine. The development of a speech community is a complex and long drawn socio-linguistic process, and more so in an ethnic group in diaspora which has experienced language attrition.

First is the problem of the interface between Hindi and Hinduism. Certainly, there is no intrinsic linkage between language and religion. When conscious efforts are made to introduce a language or revive it, however, language can hardly be religiously neutral. One may recall here that the Canadian Presbyterian Mission carefully chose Standard Hindi, and not Trinidad Bhojpuri, as its liturgical language. This move kept many a Hindu away from Standard Hindi in the colonial era. It was in a way ironical that when the Christian Missionaries were getting their scriptural materials translated into Hindi, the Hindu religious leaders were using English translations of their scriptures.

Successful efforts at propagating Hindi today are associated with Hindu religious bodies or organisations leaning towards Hinduism in one form or another. Whereas for the Hindu pandits Hindi is a sacral language, for the Presbyterian ministers it has long since been replaced by English, and for the Muslim mullahs Arabic rather than Hindi or Urdu is the sacral language.[21] Any effort at propagating Hindi is expected to be articulated by groups which have an element of religious agenda, with its own consequences. The excessive emphasis on the sacral nature of Hindi and its identification with Hinduism is, therefore, likely to alienate non-Hindus from learning it, let alone adopting it as an ethnic language.

The emphasis on *Shudh* (Pure or Standard) variety on the part of most propagators of Hindi, including the Indian and India-trained teachers, is an impediment to the revival of Hindi in diaspora. As Sperl (1980:9) has observed, 'language loyalty movements among Indians in Trinidad attempt to counter the language shift towards Creole/English by promoting not Trinidad Hindi, the ordinary local vernacular, but Standard Hindi as spoken in India'. For Indo-Trinidadians learning Standard Hindi is as good as learning an alien language. In fact, most of those who have learnt Standard Hindi become diffident, and even apologetic, when they have to use that language in interacting with Indian nationals.[22]

How to interpret the burst of Hindi in the audio-visual media over the last few years? One must remember that Hindi movies and Hindi film music have always been popular among Indo-Trinidadians. Hindi movies portray what Indo-Trinidadians perceive as the society and culture of their ancestral land. They even seem to sub-consciously identify themselves with the dynamics of family and folk culture depicted in the Hindi movies. The impact of Hindi film music, both songs and dance, on what Indo-Trinidadians call 'the Indian culture' in Trinidad is pronounced, as witnessed in such extremely popular programmes as *Mastana Bahar* and 'Indian Cultural Pageant'.[23]

What the average Indo-Trinidadian is interested in Hindi *movies*, and not Hindi *per se*. Hindi movies screened in Trinidad invariably carry English subtitles, and a few popular Hindi movies have even been dubbed into English. In their Sunday magazine section, the two prominent dailies often include supplements—*Tamasha* (*Sunday Express*) and *Savera* (*The Sunday Guardian*)—containing news and articles in English from Bollywood, the Indian equivalent of Hollywood. The average Hindi moviegoer's familiarity hardly exceeds a few routine phrases or popular expressions and a few lines of film lyrics.

Similarly, most Indo-Trinidadians listen to Hindi songs without understanding them.[24] These songs may be characterised by soothing melodies, lilting tunes, or fast beats. Their appeal may be in the emotions or sentiments they seem to convey or in their easy adaptability to dance. Reviewing Mani Ratnam's film 'Bombay', Joannah Bharose wrote in *Trinidad Guardian* (7 September 1995): I could not understand a word of

Hindi or Arabic but the music sounded great'. Similarly, columnist Omatie Lyder declared in *Daily Express* (6 May 1995):

> For years I have listened to Indian singers and sung along with them. It never mattered to me that I couldn't translate a verse of Kishore Kumar's or Lata Mangeshkar's songs. Not understanding them didn't take away the joy of listening. The same can be said of my fascination with Latin music.

The interest in Hindi songs sans their meaning can result in piquant situations with songs being sung in wrong situations. The author has heard a funeral song sung at a farewell function and a love song with sexual innuendoes sung at a Thanksgiving party.

Considering the nature of Trinidadian ethnic politics in general and the politics of culture in particular, the increasing observability of Hindi in the audio-visual media appears to be an attempt by sections of Indo-Trinidadians to occupy the keenly contested cultural space in the country. In ethnic terms this 'culturalisation of politics' (see Jain, 1997:351) is significant considering the Indo-Trinidadian perception that 'national culture' in Trinidad is almost exclusively identified with the Creole culture of Afro-Trinidadians. Substantively too, the Hindi programmes (mostly film-based) offer ready-made material to fill the available broadcast/ telecast time. Shrewd entrepreneurs are always alert to exploit the situation to their advantage.

In the ethnic politics of Trinidad, the Hindi question has often acquired a political colour. According to John La Guerre, in the post-colonial suffrage situation, 'Hindi and the institutions associated with Hindi...were seen as centres of resistance against the newly independent government and also as centres for opposition resistance'. Viewed in this light, the first International Hindi Conference held in Trinidad in April 1992 appeared to him to be a celebration, of 'not really a language, but the presence of the Indians on the social and political stage of Trinidad and Tobago' (*Daily Express*, 20 April 1992).

In view of the ethnic tag attached to Hindi, anybody explicitly advocating its introduction in schools during the early decades of independence would have been accused of advancing an ethnic cause. Campbell's (1992:84) following commentary is indicative of this:

> ...the biggest surprise in terms of Indian demands for something which would benefit Indians alone came from Hans Hanooman Singh in December 1970, when he called for a full debate on the teaching of Hindi and Urdu in Indian schools. Nothing had been heard in Parliament about

> this since the PNM[25] first came to power. Hanooman Singh never got his debate; and there is no indication that the majority of the Indian parliamentarians would have supported him.

Even today nobody dares to raise the cause of Hindi without being apologetic about it. In his speech at the flag raising ceremony to officially signal the launching of the Fifth World Hindi Conference, Foreign Affairs Minister Ralph Maraj was constrained to assure that there was nothing to fear from sections of the national community seeking to re-discover their roots, since Trinidad and Tobago is a cosmopolitan country. He even expressed a desire to see the Afro-Trinidadians teach their ancestral languages (*Daily Express*, 17 February 1996).

Conclusion

The revival of Hindi in Trinidad and the prospect of it becoming an ethnic language of Indo-Trinidadians is thus apparently enigmatic. The basic material requirements for the revival and development of Hindi are there: The Indo-Trinidadians form 40.3 per cent (1990 Census) of the population; organisations such as Bharatiya Vidya Sansthaan (established in 1966) and Hindi Nidhi (Hindi Foundation of Trinidad and Tobago, established in 1986) provide the institutional base and direction; the Indian Council for Cultural Relations and the High Commission of India extend academic support and guidance; Hinduism, the religion of the majority of Indo-Trinidadians, uses Hindi in liturgy as well as in popular religion; and the audio-visual media give exposure to the language in high density.

However, what is lacking is functionality. Hindi is seldom sought to be used in interpersonal communication in everyday life within the community. Even the few who have learnt the language, feel diffident to use it in speech. The possibility of Hindi being used in economic transactions or in administration is extremely remote as these involve inter-ethnic group interactions. Moreover, since ethnicity has evolved even without language providing the emotional glue, and in view of the likely identification of Hindi with Hinduism, there is not much use of Hindi as an ethnic binder either.

Thus, in the light of the general domination of Trinidad Creole English and Standard English in the wider society, and in the absence of economic motivation or the administrative necessity for learning Hindi, the prospect of Hindi becoming the ethnic language of Indo-Trinidadians and their becoming bilingual does not appear to be bright. Hindi will certainly take deep roots as a sacral language of the Hindus and it will be widely tapped and used in the cultural domain. Motivated by divergent reasons, some Indo-Trinidadians will continue to learn Hindi with varying degrees of commitment and competence. In brief, while Hindi may develop as a language among Indo-Trinidadians, Indo-Trinidadians are not likely to become a distinctive speech community.

Acknowledgement

The information and insights presented in this paper were gathered during the author's sojourn as Visiting Professor of Indian Studies at The University of West Indies, St. Augustine, Trinidad, in 1994-96. The assistance and affection received from Dr. Brinsley Samaroo are gratefully acknowledged. Thanks are also due to the anonymous referee for her/his useful comments.

NOTES

1. There is not a single reference on this theme in the Special number of *Sociological Bulletin* on Indians Abroad' guest edited by Sharma (1989); Jain's (1993) survey of literature on Indian diaspora lists only one study on this subject.
2. Bhojpuri is the westernmost member of the Magadhan family of Indo-Aryan languages spoken in northeastern India (see Grierson 1919: 125-26).
3. The virtual babel of Indian tongues was, however, welcomed by the plantocracy: 'The proprietors or managers of sugar estates purposely choose men speaking three or four separate and distinct languages not understood by each other, in order to prevent combination in cases of disturbances among them', observed Baptist Missionary Reverend Bronkhurst (1888: 18).
4. In her study, Mohan (1978: 12 and 35) found 'evidence of this initial diglossia in the pockets of variation in present-day Trinidad Bhojpuri where the formal options correspond to features which are functionally equivalent in the different dialects of Indian Bhojpuri'. She noticed 'the lexicon and the Present/Optative forms of the copula' to be the aspects manifesting 'the highest degree of dialectal variation (due to differences between the Indian parent varieties rather than to Creole contact)'.
5. Unlike in British Guiana and Trinidad, where Bhojpuri formed the basis for dialect-levelling, in Surinam (Dutch Guiana) the evolution of Sarnami was largely influenced by Avadhi (Damsteegt, 1988).
6. Long after Grierson (1919) classified Bhojpuri as a Magadhan language rather than as an eastern variety of Hindi as was previously assumed, there is a tendency among some scholars to mistake it (as also some other languages/dialects) as a dialect of Hindi. For instance, Tinker (1993: 53) refers to Bhojpuri (the language spoken by people of Shahabad) as 'a form of Hindi'. Similar misrepresentation is also noticed with reference to south Indian languages. For instance, 'the Malabar language'[Malayalam?] is identified as Tamil (*Ibid.*:77).

7. In British Guiana, Reverend William English had pleaded with the Wesleyan Methodist Missionary Society in London to 'send a missionary to us who is able to speak the language of India'. This resulted in Reverend J.E.S. Williams, who had worked with Tamils in Ceylon [Sri Lanka], being sent to British Guiana in 1852 (Ruhomon 1947: 207).
8. Reverend Morton uses the word 'Hindui' as including the Urdu dialect (Morton 1916: 67).
9. Mohan (1978: iii), who studied the morphology of Trinidad Bhojpuri in 1970's, notes: 'Ajie, my grandmother, who taught me this dying language from my earliest childhood in solitary defiance of convention, and, more recently, helped me to decipher and transcribe all my recorded data'.
10. Following Freed (1982: 1) we may broadly define language attrition as the loss of any language or any portion of a language by an individual or a speech community. It may refer to the declining use of mother tongue skills by those in bilingual situations or among ethnic minorities in (some) language contact situations where one language, for political or social reasons, comes to replace another. Mohan and Zador (1986: 293) refer to 'a community-wide shift to a new native language, in such a way that the community of native speakers ceases to be self-renewing, and/or the speakers cease to be native' as language death.
11. Significantly, in the 1940's the Franchise Commission had proposed that universal adult suffrage should be restricted only to those who were competent in the English language.
12. Trinidad Creole English (Trini) and Standard (Trinidadian) English are lexically related. They coexist 'not as discrete codes but as a continuum of speech forms exploited according to the communicative intent of members of the speech community' (Sealey, 1983: Intro-4). For a more general theoretical statement on 'cultural continuum', see Drummond (1980).
13. See the dictionaries compiled by Mahabir and Mahabir (1990) and Sookhoo (1985). It is noteworthy that in compiling *A Dictionary of Common Trinidad Hindi*, Mahabir and Mahabir have relied on 'purely oral' sources and have not consulted any existing Hindi-English Dictionary or glossary. Sookhoo's *Hindi-English Dictionary*, which cannot claim such an originality of sources, has in addition, however, proverbs and 110 pithy sayings. *A Dictionary of Hindi Names* has been compiled by Orie (1994).
14. Polite routines such as *Sitaram* (Greetings) and *Kaisen hai* (How are you?), and routinised sequences such as *Shabas, beta!* (Bravo, son!) and *Wha-wha* (exclamation) are still in use in Trinidad.
15. Sometimes an expression used by a public figure becomes a catchword: For instance, the expression *Nemackharaam* (Ingrate) used by Basdeo Panday (the then Leader of Opposition in Parliament and now the Prime Minister of Trinidad and Tobago) in 1986 to refer to some of his erstwhile cabinet colleagues in the then National Alliance for Reconstruction government has become so popular that even people of non-Indian descent use it now.
16. For instance, Sookhoo's (1985:iii) 'ajie' could not speak English. She told stories in Hindi, and someone had to say *Han* at the end of each sentence.
17. Visiting Hindu missionaries from India such as Pandit Hariprasad Sharma (in 1914) and Pandit Kunj Beharry Tiwary (in 1917) had commented on the loss of

native language among Indians and its adverse impact on Hinduism. The arrival of Pandit Jaimini Mehta (1928) marked a milestone in the development of Hindi as he assisted in the establishment of a Hindi school in Marabella. Also, even before their establishment/incorporation, the Hindu organisations had been in the vanguard of the effort to retain or revive Hindi. According to Forbes (1984:156), 'whereas many Sanatanist Hindi schools were extremely ephemeral, the Arya Samaj schools were maintained, during the 1930's and early 1940's, in a semi-institutional manner.

18. Sanskrit is the sacred liturgical language of Brahmanic Hinduism in India. Traditionally, Brahmans, the priestly caste group, held a monopoly over it. In Indian diaspora, however, it is Hindi which has taken the place of Sanskrit, from which it is derived, in Hindu liturgy. The credit for rendering the famous Hindu epic *Ramayana* into Hindi, so that laypersons can understand it, goes to Acharya Tulsidas, whose *Ramacharita Manas* is a popular religious text among the Hindus in Trinidad.
19. Forbes (1984:157-58) highlights the point that Pillai was a 'Madrassi' and a Christian, and Hindi was not his parents' native tongue nor did it have direct cultural import for him. 'His interest in the language was motivated by broader cultural nationalism, similar to that of Swami Dayananda, the Arya Samaj founder, who learned Hindi late in life because he recognised it to be the language of Indian unification'.
20. Ramlakhan also has to her credit *Smaran*, a compilation of Hindi Bhajans in Nagari script with transliteration in Roman alphabets and translation in English. Incidentally, in his collection of poetry in Hindi written by people of Indian origin abroad, Pandey (1985) has included the poems of two Trinidadians, both of whose mother tongue is English. They are Karmchand Ganesh, teacher at the Bharatiya Vidya Sansthaan, and Tara Vishnudayal Singh.
21. About 13 per cent of the indentured immigrants who came from India were Muslims. According to the 1990 Census, Muslims constitute 5.8 per cent of the population of Trinidad and Tobago. Like Trinidad Bhojpuri, Urdu, a language which most Muslims spoke, has faced attrition. There are a few elderly Muslims who can converse in Urdu. Observations made about language attrition, retention and survival will thus hold good for the rest of the Muslim population. Currently, under the auspices of the Anjuman Sunnatul Jamaat Association (the major organisation representing the Indo-Trinidadian Muslims), the Haji Ruknuddeen Institute of Islamic Studies, offers a course in Arabic, *not* Urdu, as part of a Diploma in Islamic Learning.
22. Tinker (1993:211) refers to an instance in British Guiana in the colonial era: 'When the allegation was made in Demerara that the interpreters of the Immigration Department could not speak Hindustani, the Agent-General defended the proficiency of his staff, though he admitted that they spoke a "literary" form of the language'. He quotes the following communication (dated 14 March 1883) from Robert Mitchell, Immigration Agent-General, British Guiana, to the Governor: 'I remember Sir Richard Temple (Lieutenant-Governor of Bengal) addressing a Bengali return immigrant at the Transit Depot in Calcutta in his native tongue, which he spoke fluently, and the man asked me in Creole French what His Honour had said'.

23. That this impact is not necessarily positive has been stressed by some Indo-Trinidadian commentators. Maharaj (1995:31-32) speculates that the Indo-Trinidadians would be more creative if they had not started imitating the packaged Hindi film culture and music. He bemoans that Indo-Trinidadian drama has become almost extinct, and at ceremonies like *matikor, barahi, chathi,* and weddings, folksongs are, by and large, replaced by loud speakers providing film music.
24. It is interesting to note that a key objective of Hindi Nidhi's newly designed Hindi courses for beginners is to help them 'comprehend dialogues and songs from Hindi films' and 'read and understand Ramayana' (Hindi Nidhi's advertisement in *Trinidad Guardian*, 8 September 1995).
25. The People's National Movement (PNM) is the political party founded by Dr. Eric Williams in 1955. It has always been perceived, not only by Indo-Trinidadians but also by Afro-Trinidadians, as a party mainly representing the interests of Afro-Trinidadians.

REFERENCES

Berko-Gleason, Jean (1982). 'Insights from child language acquisition for second language loss', in Richard D. Lambert and Barbara F. Freed (eds.): *The loss of language skills* (13-23). Rowley, Mass.: Newbury House Publishers.

Bronkhurst, Reverend H.V.P. (1888). *Among the Hindus and Creoles of British Guyana.* London: T. Woolmer.

Campbell, Carl (1992). *Colony and nation: A short history of education in Trinidad and Tobago, 1834-1986.* Kingston, Jamaica: Ian Randle Publishers.

Damsteegt, Theo (1988). 'Sarnami: A living language', in R.K. Barz and J. Siegel (eds.): *Language transplanted: The development of overseas Hindi.* Wiesbaden: Harrassowitz.

Domingue, Nicole Zuber (1971). *Bhojpuri and Creole in Mauritius: A study of linguistic interference and its consequences in regard to synchronic variation and language change.* Unpublished Ph.D. dissertation, University of Texas (Austin).

Drummond, Lee (1980). 'The cultural continuum: A theory of inter-systems', *Man* (NS), 15: 352-74.

Durbin, Mridula Adenwala (1973). 'Formal changes in Trinidad Hindi as a result of language adaptation', *American anthropologist,* 75 (5): 1290-1304.

Forbes, Richard H. (1984). *Arya Samaj in Trinidad: An historical study of Hindu organisational process in acculturative conditions.* Unpublished Ph.D. dissertation, University of Miami (Florida).

Freed, Barbara F. (1982). 'Language loss: Current thoughts and future directions', in Richard D. Lambert and Barbara F. Freed (eds.): *The loss of language skills* (1-5). Rowley, Mass.: Newbury House Publishers.

Gambhir, Surendra K. (1981). *The east Indian speech community in Guyana: A sociolinguistic study with special reference to koine formation.* Unpublished Ph.D. dissertation, University of Pennsylvania (Philadelphia).

——. (1986). 'Mauritian Bhojpuri: An international perspective on historical and sociolinguistic processes', in U. Bissoondoyal and S.B.C. Servansing (eds.): *Indian labour migration* (189-206). Moka, Mauritius: Mahatma Gandhi Institute.

Gamble, Reverend. W.H. (1866). *Trinidad, historical and descriptive: Being a narrative of nine years' residence in the island*. London: Yates and Alexander.

Grierson, George A. (1919). *Linguistic survey of India* (Vol. I, Part 1). Calcutta: Government of India.

Jain, Ravindra K. (1993). *Indian communities abroad: Themes and literature*. New Delhi: Manohar.

——. (1997). 'A civilisational theory of Indian diaspora and its global implications', *The eastern anthropologist*, 50 (3-4): 347-55.

Klass, Morton (1961). *East Indians in Trinidad: A study of cultural persistence*. Prospect Heights, Illinois: Waveland Press.

Laurence, K.O. (1971). *Immigration into the West Indies in the 19th century* (Chapters in Caribbean history 3). Aylesbury, Bucks, UK: Ginn and Co.

Mahabir, Kumar and Sita Mahabir. (1990). *A dictionary of common Trinidad Hindi*. El Dorado, Trinidad: Chakra Publishing Co.

Maharaj, Ashram B. (1995). 'Impact of Indian movies', in *The Indian review* (Commemorating the Sesquicentenary of the Arrival of Indians to Trinidad, 1845-1995) (31-32). Couva, Trinidad: Indian Review Committee.

Moag, Rodney F. (1979). 'The linguistic adaptations of the Fiji Indians', in Vijay Mishra (ed.): *Rama's banishment: A centenary tribute to the Fiji Indians, 1879-1979*. Auckland: Heinemann Educational Books: 112-38.

Mohan, Peggy Ramesar (1978). *Trinidad Bhojpuri: A morphological study*. Unpublished Ph.D. dissertation, The University of Michigan (Ann Arbor).

Mohan, Peggy and Paul Zador (1986). 'Discontinuity in a life cycle: The death of Trinidad Bhojpuri', *Language*, 62: 291-319.

Morton, Sarah E. (ed.) (1916). *John Morton of Trinidad: Pioneer missionary of the Presbyterian Church in Canada to the East Indians in the British West Indies (Journals, letters and papers)*. Toronto: Westminster Company.

Naipaul, Seepersad (1976). *The adventures of Gurudeva and other stories*. London: Andre Deutsch. (First published in 1943 as *Gurudeva and other Indian tales*).

Niehoff, Arthur and Juanita Niehoff. (1960). *East Indians in the West Indies*. Milwaukee, Wisconsin: Milwaukee Public Museum.

Orie, Siddartha L. (1994). *A dictionary of Hindi names: Towards a new consciousness*. Freeport. Trinidad and Tobago: Hem Publications.

Panday, Trilochan (1993). 'Trinidad mein Hindi' (in Hindi), *Gagananchal* (Indian Council for Cultural Relations, New Delhi), 16 (4): 109-22.

Pandey, Raj Kishore (ed.) (1985). *Videsh ke Hindi kavi* (in Hindi). Hyderabad: Hindi Prachar Sabha.

Ruhomon, Peter (1947). *Centenary history of the East Indians in British Guiana, 1838-1938*. George Town: The Daily Chronicle.

Sealey, W. (in collaboration with P. Aquing). (1983). 'A socio-linguistic profile of Trinidad'. Paper presented for the Caribbean Lexicography Project, June 1983 (Mimeo).

Sharma, S.L. (ed.) (1989). *Sociological bulletin*: Special Number on Indians Abroad, 38(1).

Siegel, Jeffrey (1975). 'Fiji Hindustani', *Working papers in linguistics* (Honolulu: University of Hawaii), 7 (3): 127-144.

Singh, Kelvin (1985). 'Indians and the larger society', in John La Guerre (ed.): *Calcutta to Caroni* (33-60). St. Augustine, Trinidad and Tobago: Extra Mural Studies Unit, The University of the West Indies.

Sookhoo, James R. (1985). *Hindi-English dictionary: Build your Hindi vocabulary through English*. St. Augustine, Trinidad: Trinidad Industrial Laboratories Research Ltd.
Sperl, Savitri Rambissoon (1980). *From Indians to Trinidadians: A study of the relationship between language behaviour, socio-economic and cultural factors in a Trinidad village*. Unpublished M.Phil. dissertation, University of York (Toronto).
Tinker, Hugh, (1993). *A new system of slavery: The export of Indian labour overseas, 1830-1920*. London: Hansib Publishing Limited.
Vertovec, Steven (1992). *Hindu Trinidad: Religion, ethnicity, and socio-economic change*. London and Basingstoke: Macmillan.
Winford, Donald (1972). *A socio-linguistic description of two communities in Trinidad*. Unpublished Ph.D. dissertation, University of York (Toronto).

17

India in Thailand: Explorations of a Sandwich Culture

RUCHIRA MISHRA (NEE ATAL)

From time immemorial, the peoples of different cultures have come in contact with each other in a variety of ways, and in the process have enriched their cultures through "gives" and "takes" of cultural patterns, traits, and complexes. However, the adoption process has taken various forms. In some cases, it leads to the process of assimilation through a merger of two cultures and emergence of a new culture containing the traits of both the interacting cultures but in an indistinguishable form. In other cases, one cultural group dominates over the other cultural group, resulting mainly in one-way traffic of adoption of traits by the dominated group. This process is called acculturation. The same is true of migrant groups. When people migrate, they come in contact with other cultural groups, and in a variety of ways. In the process, the migrants adopt many traits of other groups which gradually become a part of their culture. They also contribute to the cultural fabrics of the host country.

The pattern of mingling of the traits of two cultures has differed from country to country and the study of such interactions and the resulting configurations is an interesting and sociologically important area of investigation. To learn about this phenomenon, the researcher conducted a study among the Punjabis settled in Thailand. The choice for Thailand was due to many factors. Historically and culturally, there are many links between India and Thailand. Moreover, while studies of Indian migrants settled in other countries of Southeast Asia—particularly Malaysia and Singapore—exist, there is very little on Thailand.

Thailand and India: Cultural Interface

Thailand or *Prathet* Thai is a country that has long been known to India by its original name Siam: Located in the same continent, and forming part of Southeast Asia. Thailand is separated from India by Myanmar (Burma). It is bordered by Malaysia in the South, Laos in the Northeast, Cambodia in the East, and Myanmar in the West. The sprawling Bay of Bengal and the Indian ocean touch its shores on the West and the South. Both from the sea route and the land route, the people of India and Thailand have come in contact with each other for several centuries. Many names of the place and rivers of Thailand provide concrete evidence of the contact between the two cultures. To quote Desai "It was, however, from the Khmers, then the elite of Southeast Asia, that the Thai inherited a legacy of Hindu traditions, rituals, ceremonies and literature. This took place during the Ayuthia period after the conquest of Cambodia in A.D. 1431. It is here that the Hindu influence are predominant. King Rama Tibodhi, the founder of the Ayuthia dynasty, promulgated the Thai law. Later the war with Burma brought certain Hindu elements from Burma to Thailand. The most significant of these was the adoption of the Burmese law, the dhammathat (SKT. Dharmasastra) by the Thai" (Desai, 1980: 20).

The interaction of Indians with Thailand continued to grow during the British colonial period. A treaty was signed between the British crown and the Thai monarchy granting rights to the British ships to trade at Thailand's ports. This brought several Indians to Thailand. Indians also arrived in Thailand to work as labourers in plantations and some of them were enrolled in police force.

Many Indians settled in Burma migrated to Thailand because of the anti-India policy of the Burmese. Many Hindu and Sikh, refugees from the newly created Pakistan came down to Thailand for settlement. Similarly, Indians settled in the indo-Chinese countries sought shelter in Thailand after the communist take-over of those countries. Since then, there has been a speedy rise in the Indian population in Thailand.

Indians in Bangkok

A detailed breakdown of the Indian population in Thailand is not available. According to the Hindu Samaj association, there are approximately 60,000 Hindus in Thailand. The Sri Guru Singh Sabha cites 15,000 Sikhs in the country. The highest concentration of Indians is found in its primate city of Bangkok which is the capital of the kingdom. These Indians can be classified into three categories: 1. Sindhis and Punjabis, mainly engaged in business, 2. Migrants from Uttar Pradesh , Bihar and South India , mainly engaged in petty jobs, and 3. Indians working in joint ventures, International organizations and at the Indian Embassy.

Indians are scattered over most of Bangkok, though there are some areas of concentration, such as *phahurat*, Oriental Hotel (new road), etc. It is interesting to note that the residential pattern follows ethnic lines. *Phahurat* is essentially a Sikh locality, whereas the Oriental Hotel area is inhabited mostly by Muslims and Tamils.

In Bangkok there are several landmarks of Indian culture. These may be classified broadly into following categories: 1. Temples and shrines, 2. Eating places, 3. Shopping areas, 4. Clubs and associations.

Temples and Shrines

The city of Bangkok has an important Hindu temple of Laxmi Narayan. A beautifully constructed temple in the midst of a locality inhabited by most of the long time Indian residents serves as an important meeting place. Some years ago the Indian community decided to import from Jaipur a huge idol of Vishnu and installed it on one of its thorough fares. This statue and its temple was gifted to the city of Bangkok by the Indian community.

The other temple of significance is that of a goddess Uma Devi at the Silom road. During navaratri, the temple is visited by hundreds of thousands of people, both Indian and Thai. Recently the Sikh community got a magnificent Gurudwara built in the *phahurat* area. The town also has several mosque which are visited both by Thai Muslims as well as Muslims from the Indian subcontinent. The Thais themselves are worshippers of the Hindu God Brahma, whose statues and temples are found in different parts of the town. The major Hindu and Sikh gurudwara in *phahurat* are, Kali Mandir, Ashoke Gurudwara, Namdhari Gurudwara, Guru Singh Sabha, Hindu Samaj, Laxmi Narayn Mandir, Radha Swami Temple and Silom Mandir.

Eating Places

Over the years, there has been a phenomenal rise in the number of Indian restaurants. In 1975-76, there were three popular restaurants in the town: Gaylord at the Siam centre, Royal India in *phahurat*, and another one near the Oriental Hotel on the new road. Today, there are at least 15 well-known restaurants in different parts of the town, besides several small Dhaba or Hatti type in the *phahurat* area.

Shopping Areas

As was mentioned before, most of the Indians, both residents and visitors, go to *phahurat* for shopping. This area provides a full range from vegetables of daily consumption to clothes and ornaments. For the locals, all the provisions are easily available. A large number of restaurants and snack corners cater to the shoppers.

For the resident, shops for provisions are also available on Sukhumvit Soi 21, 71, 77 and on Soi Charoenchai linking Soi 63 and 71.

Occasions for get together of Indians

The celebration of the Indian Independence Day (15th August) and the Republic Day (26th January) provide occasions to the Indian community to come together. On these days, the Indians embassy issues an open invitation to all the Indians, be they the residents with Thai Nationality or those temporarily settled in the country.

The festivals of Diwali and Holi also provide opportunities to Indians in Thailand to renew their links with parent culture. These are the functions which are celebrated both by Hindus and Sikhs. For example, the local business community arranged a Holi gathering on 6th March 1988, two days after the actual date since that day was Sunday. Many families gathered together in a compound and played colours. After the play a feast was arranged. It is clear that migration and permanent settlement in an alien land has not eroded the cultural ties, occasions such as the above serve to reinforce the links with their parent cultures.

Indians Migrants: A Sample Survey

The above description reveals that Indians in Thailand are constantly exposed to various aspects of Indian culture which mitigates their chances of assimilation in Thai Society. Since, it is imperative for them to adopt some aspects of Thai culture at least, those traits which facilitates their continuation in Thailand. In the process, they are sandwiched between the host culture and the parent culture, and many develop. Sandwich culture (Atal, 1989). Atal has proposed the concept of Sandwich culture for the way of life of immigrants communities. A sandwich man, according to him bears two tags, one representing the country of his origin and the other, the country of his migration. The chances of creating a Sandwich culture are greater among conservative immigrants, who prefers to preserve their way of life. He further makes distinction between the

Sandwich culture of the permanent settlers and the *sojourners* and the temporary migrants. He has proposed two sets of factors which either facilitate or obstruct the process of formation of Sandwich culture. His two sets of factors are aperture openings and the insulatory mechanism. Among apertures Atal includes inter-marriage, adoption of names, language and food habit of the host society, religious conversion and promotion of inter-commensality. Among insulatory mechanisms he includes, pratice of endogamy, retention of mother tongue, separate educational facilities, concentration in certain occupations, pursuit of parental religion, continuation of food habits and taboos associated with eating, formation of voluntary organizations frequent visits, exposure to media (books, music, films), concentration of living quarters and so on.

In order to find out whether Indians in Thailand have become sandwiched between the two cultures or have insulated themselves from the host culture or have assimilated in Thai, a random sample of 100 Indians was selected for intensive study. In this study we concentrated only on Punjabi migrants settled in Thailand. A questionnaire was administered to collect data.

Socio-Economic Background

Most of the respondents included in the study were in the age-group of 30-50 years. All of them were educated, though 60 per cent were very well qualified, some of them were post-graduates and 44 per cent were graduates.

The average size of the family is 4.25. The 100 families are composed of 127 children and 298 adults (total 425). Among these, 212 are males and 213 females. The composition of the majority families (89%) is nuclear. All marriage in this group have taken place within the traditional endogamous groups. Search for spouse had taken some of them to India when they could not find suitable partners within their community in Thailand. Thus, in terms of martial tiles, they have maintained their traditional boundaries. In this regard, the Indians in Thailand differ significantly from the Chinese settlers who freely inter-marry with the Thais.

The survey reveals that higher education is not given a priority in this group. The educational level of most of the people in the family is high school or below. This is understandable as the sample consists of business families which ensure self-employment in family business.

It merges that there is a high concentration among respondent in the business category. Even the people who have professional education such as medicine or C.A. are to be found engaged in business. There is none in the service category who does not possess a B.A. degree. Of the 10 per cent in the service category there are three with M.A., two with degree in chartered accountancy, two with technical training, two with B.A. and one diploma holder. Those engaged in money lending also show a scatter on the educational variable similar to those in the business category. Women in these households were reported as non-working. However, it was seen that they quite often assist their husbands in their shops. Even daughters are occasionally asked to assist in business. Among the younger girls, there is a trend to do secretarial courses and to seek jobs in firms and companies as typists and shop attendants.

The average monthly income of the household sample comes to around Baht 8000; per capita income is around Baht 2000 per month. Thus, the sample families belong to the middle class. It must be said that the average income is not a good indicator as there are wide variations; there are families in the sample which earn as high as Baht 120,000 per month. Most of our respondents engaged domestic help, generally they hire maids of Thai nationality. Sixty per cent of the sample own their houses which is an indication of their permanent settlement. Nearly one-third of the respondents have some members of their immediate family such as mother, father, brother, etc., who reside in India and to whom they owe some financial or social obligations. In addition their married daughters and sisters also reside in India and they keep in constant contact. Despite these connections, visits to India by the respondents are not so frequent. The occasions when such visits are undertaken are: to see an ailing relative, to attend some family function, to arrange marriage, to escort children to the boarding schools, and to conducts business. Some even go for pleasure trips.

Induction and Integration into the Thai Society

(i) History of Arrivals

The respondents were asked about the history of their migration. As was said earlier, the sample consisted of people who were either born in Thailand, or who arrived themselves. The people in the latter category can be further divided in terms of the duration of their stay. Those who were born here may also, depending on their present age, belong to different types of families based on the time when their families moved here.

In the sample, There are 60 respondents who told that they were born here. Table 1 gives distribution of the population by their age and by the duration of their stay in Thailand.

Table 1 shows that there are only six cases of people who could be regarded as recent arrivals; among them two are above 50 years of age and the remaining four are between 26 and 40 years of age. 94 others are such whose stay in Thailand has been for more than 5 years. Among the respondents who were born here, there is representation from all age groups. However, the cases of those who have stayed from 5 to 15 years are generally located between the age-group of 36-50 years. There is only one respondent who is above 60 and was born here.

Table1: Duration of Stay by Age-Group

Age Group	*I was born here*	*More than 20 years*	*15-20 years*	*10-15 years*	*5-10 years*	*Less than 5 years*	*Total*
Below 25	5	0	0	0	0	0	5
26-30	6	0	1	0	0	2	9
31-35	16	2	1	1	0	1	21
36-40	6	2	1	7	4	1	21
41-50	18	2	3	2	3	0	28
51-60	8	1	0	0	3	1	13
Above 60	1	0	1	0	0	1	3
Total	**60**	**7**	**7**	**10**	**10**	**6**	**100**

Our sample suggests that there is a long history of Indian migration to Thailand. In the case of 8 respondents, their families arrived in Thailand four generation back—their great grand fathers (*i.e.*, Father's Father's Father) migrated here mostly with a view to settle here, this suggests that there were cases of migration even five generations ago. Partition of India on the eve of its Independence in 1947 resulted in mass migration of Hindus and Sikhs from those areas which became part of Pakistan. Leaving their parental homes as refugees, several of these sought shelter in other parts of India, but some also left for other countries where they had their kinsmen. Hong Kong, Thailand, Malaysia, Indonesia, and Singapore, attracted several such migrants. In our sample, there are nine cases of migration which were mainly prompted by partition. Once arrived, they also entered as business partners with other previous settlers or started their own enterprises. In all the cases of migration, irrespective of generation differences, there is high incidence of those who were motivated by better business prospects in Thailand. Thus, in terms of purpose of migration, one gets this profile by generation (Table 2).

Table 2: Pattern of arrival of families of those who were born in Bangkok

	Pattern of Arrival	Reason for Migration			Total
		Business	Partition	In-laws	
Father	1. He came alone and the brought the family	6	0	0	6
	2. He came with the family	5	0	1	6
	3. He came got married here, and settled	2	1	6	9
	Sub Total	13	1	7	21
Grand Father	1. He came alone and then brought the family	6	6	0	12
	2. He came with the family	8	2	1	11
	3. He came, got married here, and settled	8	0	0	8
	Sub Total	22	8	1	31
Great Grand Father	1. He came alone and then brought the family	3	0	0	3
	2. He came with the family	2	0	0	2
	3. He came, got married here, and settled	2	0	1	3
	Sub Total	7	0	1	8
	Grand Total	42	9	9	60

(ii) Religious Observances

Although living in Thailand, the Indians have not given up their religion and their cultural practices. There were only two cases of no response to the question regarding the festivals of Hindu/Sikh religious calendar that they regularly celebrate. The festivals and the frequencies of their mention is given in Table 3.

Table 3: Observance of Religious Festivals

	Name of Festival	Frequency
1.	Diwali	90
2.	Baisakhi	22
3.	Rakhee	29
4.	Lohri	1
5.	Gurpurab	5
6.	Holi	3
7.	Guru Nanak's birthday	13
8.	N.R.	2

It is interesting to observe that the most commonly mentioned festival is Diwali. While the sample consisted of 86 Sikhs, only 13 of them mentioned Guru Nanak's birthday, which is rather intriguing.

On the question about the places of worship the respondents mentioned the following which are frequented most: Ashoke Gurudwara, Namdhari Gurudwara, Guru Singh Sabha, Hindu Samaj, Radha Swami Temple, Silom Mandir, Wat Dorn Mandir. However, not all people visit them with equal frequency. Thirteen of the respondents confessed that they seldom visit a temple, only 28 are regular visitors; nine go quite often, and 50 visit them occasionally. The non-visit to a public place of worship is, however, not to be taken as an indicator of lack to religiosity. There are two reasons for a lower frequency of visits to a temple: one, the time constraint because of business engagements and; two, having a religious corner within the house itself for purpose of daily worship, thus avoiding going to a public temple.

The observations by the investigator attest to the fact that womenfolk, particularly in the middle ages and the older age group, go more often to the public places of worship. Visits to the house of many migrant families revealed that all houses had hung pictures of gods and goddesses and of religious saints and leaders. Moreover, all families observe the traditional *Rites de passage*—that is, rites and rituals connected with birth, initiation, marriage, and death. The families of Namdhari Sikhs observe strict vegetarianism and teetotalism in the house. Of course, this does not rule out deviation from these norms by some in outsides contexts. Sikhs males continue to respects the five Ks, Kangha (comb), Kesh (hair), Kachchh (underwear), Kada (bangle), Katar (dagger) and wear the turban in the traditional manner as a diacritical mark of their identity. It was observed that among the non-Namdhari Sikhs there is high incidence of non-vegetarian eating and consumption of alcohol and liquor. One can easily notice this behaviour either in the planes or in the restaurants.

(*iii*) *Adoption of Thai Cultural Elements*

It is generally observed that migrant groups attempt to strike a balance between maintenance of their separate cultural identity and adoption of elements from the host culture. In this process, those elements of the host culture find easy acceptance which are not in conflict with their original culture and which are perceived as similar or identical. Since Thai culture has received considerable impact of Indian culture and civilization there are many elements in it which lend themselves to easy acceptability. For example, Thai language has heavily drawn on Sanskrit vocabulary and the Dev Nagri script. Many of its dishes resemble those in the Indian cuisine. Modernization in the realm of dresses and fashion has provided many commonalities, under the impact of modernity, even the Thais wear their traditional costumes only on special occasions. In day-to-day living, they have adopted western style dresses, particularly among men. Among women, cosmetics, jewellery and ornaments have a common clientele. The non-vegetarian among the Indians only avoid beef as religion forbids, although, beef and pork are commonly eaten by the Thais despite their being Buddhist in religion.

Against this general background we may analyses the language competence, food preferences and media behaviour of our respondents.

(iv) Language Proficiency

The respondent were asked question about their proficiency in language, including Thai. The respondent mentioned Hindi, Punjabi, Thai and English as the language in which they are able to communicate. However, the degree of proficiency in different languages varies from respondent to respondent. This degree of proficiency was assessed in terms of whether they could speak the language only, speak and read, or speak, read and write.

In our sample, as high as 64 per cent respondents claimed to have competence in speaking, reading and writing Thai, 12 others could speak and read; 19 could only speak, whereas the remaining 5 confessed their poor grasp of the language. The latter are obviously the people who have migrated in the past five years.

Although, Hindi and Punjabi are the mother tongue of our sample population, proficiency in them in terms of speaking, reading and writing was lower than that of Thai (64%) and English (79%). Only 57 per cent possessed proficiency in Punjabi and 51 per cent in Hindi. If we regard competence in speaking only then the number of people who could speak these languages is as follows:

Thai: 95, Hindi: 66, Punjabi: 86, English: 87.

The details are given in Table 4.

Table 4: Language Proficiency

Language	*Speak only*	*Speak & Read*	*Speak, Read & Write*	*NRR*	*Total*
Thai	19	12	64	5	100
Hindi	12	3	51	34	100
Punjabi	22	7	57	14	100
English	4	4	79	13	100

We also inquired about the language generally spoken at home. As the data suggests, Punjabi is spoken in most (58%) of the homes, followed by Thai (18%), Hindi (12%), a mix of language (6%), and English (5%). Only in one case no response was given.

(v) Food Habits

Thirty five per cent of the respondents said that they like food of their country. Fifteen per cent liked Thai food. Half of the respondents like both kinds of food.

Table 5: Food Preference

	Response	*Food Preference Frequency*
1.	Food of my country	35
2.	Thai food	15
3.	It varies	50
	Total	100

There are many Indian restaurants in Bangkok. The investigator enquired about the restaurant business. She was told that, Indians cannot buy land over here unless and until they have a Thai nationality. Secondly, they are required to deposit one million Baht in advance and have to prove that this money has come from abroad, before starting restaurant business. When asked about the liking of restaurants, 26 people said that they like Chinese restaurants, 24 people like mixed, 20 people prefer Thai, 11 Indian and 5 prefer western restaurants, 14 people did not show any preference.

Indian music stood out as the most preferred accounting for a rich influence over 73 per cent of the sample. Western and Indian mix is 14 per cent only, western is 8 per cent, Thai music is 5 per cent, Indian and Pakistan mix is only 4 per cent. One person did not show any interest in music and did not respond to the question.

Video is very common these days. In our sample also, 81 families own a video. There are many video libraries in Bangkok. Enterprising operators of these libraries pirate several films. Even those films which are not yet released in India are easily available here in the video libraries. The owners of these video libraries have started side business by making Indian dishes like Samosa, Gulabjamun, Rasmalai, etc. and they deliver them at home, along with video cassettes. The preference for video movies was as follows: 31 per cent of the sample likes to watch Hindi movies, 8 per cent English movies, and only 2 per cent like to see Punjabi movies. When asked about the combination, following pattern emerged: English and Hindi 21 per cent, Hindi and Punjabi 8 per cent and all the three languages 11 per cent.

(vi) Self-Assessment of Adjustment and Perception of Attitude of Thais

We enquired from the sample about their adjustment in Thai society and culture. Forty three per cent of the sample said they were very well adjusted, 53 per cent said they were adjusted. Only 2 per cent confessed of their ill adjustment. When asked why were they not able to adjust themselves they mentioned recency of their arrival as the main cause; they were still feeling alien and ambivalent. Other two persons did not respond; they were also recent migrants (Table 6).

Table 6: Adjustment in Thai Society

	Adjustment	*Frequency*
1.	Very well adjusted	43
2.	Adjusted	53
3.	Not at all adjusted	2
4.	N.R.	2
	Total	100

When asked how do the Thais behave towards Indians, 65 per cent said that they were very friendly and hospitable, 24 per cent said that they were indifferent; only 10 per cent of the sample said that they were hostile. One person did not respond (Table 7).

Table 7: Perception of Behaviour of Thais Towards Indians

	Perception	*Frequency*
1.	They are very friendly and hospitable	65
2.	They are indifferent	24
3.	They are hostile	10
4.	N.R.	1

(vii) *Indian Migrants: A Sandwich Culture*

With such a profile of the Indian community settled in Thailand one may ask about their integration into the Thai society. Are they Indians or the Thais? What is the crucial thereshold the crossing of which results in the merging of the identity? In other words, when does a migrant cease to be a migrant and become a native? Students of the history of demographic movements are coming round the view that migration is a phenomenon which characterizes all individuals and groups in most of the societies and is becoming increasingly important element in socio-cultural change with growing modernization. Such a situation leads to considerable interchange of cultural elements. However, there exist clearly identifiable migrant groups in different societies and several forces operate to establish an equation between the opposing culture of the migrant. The same is true of the Indians in Thailand. It appears that the concepts of the "*sojourner*" (C.P. Siu, 1952) or of "Marginal man" (Stonequist, 1937), or of "Middleman minorities" (Bonacich, 1973) do not answer the description of the Indian community in Thailand. In our view, the concept of Sandwich culture recently offered by Yogesh Atal (1989) seems to have greater applicability in this case. The paradigm given by Yogesh Atal has been tested against the data from our sample to ascertain the extent to which Indians in Thailand can be described as bearers of a Sandwich culture.

As mentioned earlier Atal has talked of the twin processes of "Aperture opening" and of "insulatory mechanisms". He has defined "aperture opening" as, "Efforts made by the outsiders to become insiders so as to merge their identity and gain certain degree of acceptance by the host society". Let us see how the Indians settled in Thailand involve in the aperture opening process.

	Apertures	*Migrant Behaviour*
1.	Intermarriage (or break down of endogamy)	No, they still practice endogamy.
2.	Adoption of names of the host society	Yes, they have to keep Thai name as well as Indian name.
3.	Adoption (or use) of language of the host culture	Yes, they speak Thai very fluently.
4.	Religious conversion	No
5.	Promotion of inter commensality	Commensal relations exist
6.	Adoption of food habits and developing taste for host cuisine.	Yes, they eat Thai food quite often.

"Insulatory mechanisms" are defined by Atal as "Efforts made by the in-coming groups to conserve its identity and maintain some distance from the host culture".

The operation of insulatory mechanisms in the Indian migrant group are outlined below.

	Insulatory Mechanisms	*Migrant Behaviour*
1.	Retention of Mother tongue and use of the native script.	They speak both mother tongue (Punjabi and Hindi); speaking reading and writing capacity in Thai varies.
2.	Concentration of living quarters to promote greater interaction with the members of the in-group.	Yes, there are areas which show heavy concentration of these people.
3.	Provision of separate educational facilities.	Yes, they have recently opened a Sikh school.
4.	Practice of Endogamy.	Yes, they do not inter many with Thais.
5.	Concentration in certain occupation.	Textile business, mostly retail, and are thus occupationally identifiable.
6.	Formation of voluntary organizations.	Thai Bharat Cultural Lodge, Indian Chamber of Commerce, Hindu Samaj, Indian Women's Club.
7.	Pursuit of parental religion.	Yes.
8.	Continuation of food habits and tattoos associated with eating.	They eat both Indian and Thai food, but refrain from eating beef.
9.	Retention of cultural diacriticals particularly in the manner of dressing.	They wear Indian dress. Sikh men continue to wear turban and women also wear Indian dress.

(*Contd.*)

Insulatory Mechanisms	Migrant Behaviour
10. Racial features.	Indian, because they still practice endogamy.
11. Keeping apertures open to the parent culture: *e.g.*	
(i) Frequent visit to India.	Rare; frequency among younger people is reducing.
(ii) Schooling of children	Yes, in Indian or international schools.
(iii) Affinal relations	Yes.
(iv) Exposure to media (books music, films, videos)	Yes.
(v) Postal and tele-communication.	Yes.

The checklist of the Sandwich culture paradigm clearly reflects the fact of guarded assimilations. In fact, there has been more of transculturation which has helped the Indian community in maintaining its identity.

Since 80 per cent of the respondent belong to the business class their materialistic orientation and liking for worldly comforts is easily noticeable. Their attitude towards life seems to be single tracked, thinking only in terms of money and material gains. Their urge for accumulating money in an easier, secure and comfortable manner reinforces their motivation to continue to stay in Thailand and to get settled permanently. Given such an orientation, it can be assumed that this group has not consciously tried to promote Indian culture. It has shown considerable degree of adaptability and flexibility in regard to cultural norms of the host society.

This study was conducted just after the assassination of Mrs. Indira Gandhi, the then Prime Minister of India. Her assassination shook the entire country and further created tensions between the Sikhs and the rest. Happenings in India did affect the morale of Indian people in Thailand, and many worried parents from the Sikh community brought back their children studying in India. Some even went as far as disposing off their property in India, and bringing their close relatives to Thailand to settle down. Thailand is viewed by them as a safe place.

Cultural similarities between Thailand and India also provide incentive to Indian people to stay. Basically, Thai culture is influenced by Buddhism which originated in India. Thus, adoption of Thai culture does not pose any serious problems to Indians. They do not feel alienated. The fact that Indians are not treated as farangs (foreigners), but as khaek (guests) adds to a positive orientation towards acculturation of the Indian in Thailand.

Our respondents claim to have adopted and adjusted in Thai society but occasionally they do yearn for things Indian and show a liking for the Indian customs and ways of life, which they have inherited. They do want to move in their own community as the Indians in Bangkok are generally ethnocentric. There is also however, some degree of reservedness even between Indians of different origins because of occupational competition. At times, they look upon each other with envy and distrust. They have the feelings of lack of brotherhood and cooperative life-style. Some of the people are nostalgic about India because they still have their relatives living there. They are thus ambivalent towards India. But for a few handful people who carry such a myopic attitude towards life, Bangkok provides to most Indian migrants with sufficiently good reasons to continue staying.

In Bangkok it is easier to make money. Food is very cheap, business is easy, and most of the luxuries of life can be bought there at a throw-away price. Financially, life is quite secure, easy, and better off in comparison to India. Old generation Indian are very orthodox. They observe all sorts of rituals during the time of marriage as well as death. After the death, for 17 days, family members observe mourning and abstain from going out. At the end of the mourning period, the family members take an early morning bath and perform puja after which they return to a normal status.

The contrast in behaviour is to be found among the younger generation, most of whom have not yet visited India. But they follow the instruction of their elders; as regards the observance of rituals. These people believe in ostentation and conspicuous consumption. They are part of Thai economy but they live Indian culture.

(*viii*) *Final Comment*

The Indians in Thailand, in short, have a distinct identity of their own unlike the Chinese settled in Thailand. Modernity in their way of life is beautifully combined with continuation of tradition.

India continue to be their reference point. But Thailand is their new found home, which they would hate to abandon in favour of a return to the ancestral place in India. They have brought India of their choice to Thailand, and created a Sandwich culture of their own with a judicious mix of the Thai and Indian cultural elements, traits, and complexes.

REFERENCES

Atal, Ruchira (1988). "*Punjabis in Thailand*", unpublished M.Phil Thesis, Punjabi University, Patiala.

Atal, Yogesh (1989). "Outsiders as Insiders: The Phenomenon of Sandwich Culture" in *Sociological Bulletin*, Vol. 38, No. 1.

Bonacich, Edna (1973). "The Theory of Middleman Minorities" in *American Sociological Review* Vol. 38, pp. 583-594.

Desai, Santosh N. (1980). *"Hinduism in Thai Life"*, Bombay, Popular Prakashan.
Gupta, Surendra K. (1999). *"Indians in Thailand"*, New Delhi, Books India International.
Siu, Paul C.P. (1952). "The Sojourner" in *The American Journal of Sociology*, Vol. 58, pp. 34-44.
Stonequist, E. (1937). *"The Marginal Man"*. New York, Charles Scribeners Sons.

18

Indian Diaspora: A Comparative Study of Punjabis and Gorakhpuris in Thailand*

SURENDRA K. GUPTA

People of Indian origin constitute one of the largest groups among the diaspora and are found in all the continents of the world. The history of their migration to distant land is old and varied. Different migrations have different causes that prompted their movement out of the country of their origin. During the colonial period, many Indians went as indentured labour to places such as Fiji in the Pacific and Trinidad and Guyana in the Caribbean. There were other Indians who migrated on their own to the countries of the West specially to Britain, USA and Canada, either to pursue higher studies and/or to seek gainful employment. Another stream of Indian migrant settled down in the neighbouring countries of South Asia and Southeast Asia. Still another group of Indian migrants includes those people who went to the Middle Eastern countries in recent year to meet the rising demand of labour—skilled and unskilled—from the petro-dollar rich countries. The different categories of the Indian Diaspora represent different linguistic and sub-cultural group adding to the diversity and multi-culturalism of the host countries. They are also carriers of Indian culture and tradition to the countries of their settlement. Their adjustment in an alien land may depend on number of factors. But each group of immigrants may have some common and also some different problems.

* This article is a part of the book *Indians in Thailand* Surendra K. Gupta, 1999, New Delhi, Books India International.

A comparison of their adaptation and adjustment in different countries and the impact of cultural, contextual and situational factors may provide some interesting sociological insights.

Cultural conditions which affect the adaptation process in an alien society may include economic and political condition of the society of the immigrants, motivation for migration, attitude of migrants towards member of the host society, culture of the immigrants and other social factors as immovable property such as land etc. as well as kinship groups back at home. The contextual factors which may affect the process of adaptation can be listed as social, economic and political condition of the host society, attitude of the host society towards migrants in general and toward Indians in particular and culture of the host society. The situational conditions which may influence the adaptation process are personal experiences of the immigrant, institutions, and associations formed by immigrant group and their length of stay in the host society.

Several scholars have given various indicators to determine the status and the degree of assimilation of the migrants in the host society. Some have discussed the characteristics of the migrants to determine the status, whereas others have given certain indicators to determine the degree of assimilation. Paul C. P. Siu (1952) and Turner and Bonacich (1980) have given certain characteristics of the 'Sojourners" and the "Middlemen" respectively to determine the status of the migrants. On the other hand S. N. Eisenstadt (1954), M. M. Gordon (1964) and Yogesh Atal (1989) have given certain indicators to determine the process and degree of assimilation of the migrants. J.S. Furnival (1948) had used the concept of plural society where people with different cultural backgrounds live side by side without mingling with each other.

While studying the absorption of immigrants in Israel S. N. Eisenstadt (1954) used three indices of institutional integration, acculturation and personal adjustment and integration of the immigrants. Of the three indices, Eisenstadt has given least importance to the index of personal adjustment as it refers to individual immigrants. However, for group assimilation the other two indices of acculturation and institutional integration are crucial. Gordon (1964) on the other hand while discussing the assimilation of immigrants in the American Society used seven basic sub-processes to determine the degree of assimilation of the immigrants in the host society. The seven types or stages of assimilation proposed by Gordon are cultural assimilation, structural assimilation, marital assimilation, identificational assimilation, attiude receptional assimilation, behaviour receptional assimilation and civic assimilation. Gordon came to the conclusion that cultural assimilation is likely to be the first of the types of assimilation to occur when a minority group arrives on the scene. But according to him the structural assimilation is most important. If structural assimilation has not taken place other processes will not follow.

Yogesh Atal (1989) while developing his insulator and aperture model has proposed the concept of Sandwich culture for the way life of immigrant communities. His Sandwich man bears two tags, one representing the country of his origin and other the country of his migration. According to him the chances of Sandwich culture are more at among the conservative immigrants who prefer their own way of life. Atal also makes a distinction between the Sandwich culture of the permanent settlers and the Sojourners and the temporary settlers. He lists two sets of factors *i.e.* aperture opening and insulatory mechanisms which either facilitate or hinder the process of formation of Sandwich culture. In the present study I have used the Sandwich culture model.

The Problem and the Methodology

In the present study an attempt has been made to analyze the acculturation process of Indians settled in Thailand. Historically and culturally there are many links between India and Thailand, secondly while studies of Indian migrants settled in other countries of South-east Asia, particularly Malaysia and Singapore exist, there is no worth while study of Indian migrants in Thailand.

The specific questions answered through this study are:

1. What is the history and pattern of migrantion of various Indian communities in Thailand?
2. What aspects of Thai culture have been adopted by various Indian communities?
3. What traits of Indian culture have been retained by them?
4. What links have they maintained with the people back at home?
5. How have the cultural, contextual and situational factor affected their adoption process.

Some of the hypotheses which have been examined in this study are give below.

The chance of Sandwich culture will be more among those migrants who:

(*i*) maintain continuous contact with people back home,
(*ii*) accept the girls of the host society as brides but do not marry their daughters to the males of the host society,

(*iii*) accept only those elements of the host society which are necessary for their economic and other day-to-day activities,

(*iv*) form their own associations, run educational institutions and religious centres, and

(*v*) lower the socio-economic status, more the chances of Sandwich culture.

There were various group of Indians living in Bangkok in 1989, when the field work was done. But due to the time constraint it was decided to select only two groups, *i.e.*, Punjabis both Hindus and Sikhs and Gorakhpuris. Both these groups of people migrated to Thailand almost at the same line, *i.e.*, about a hundred year back. Therefore, it was thought that the comparison of these two groups would make interesting study. The data was collected by participant observation and informal interviews.

History of Migration

Indian influence in South-east Asia began in the first century AD and ended with the emergence of Thais as one of the major powers after 1300 years. The Indians who migrated to the region during this period assimilated themselves with the local people by marrying their women folk. The second wave of Indian migration to Thailand started in the 19th century when the Britishers were granted permission to trade at Thailand's port in 1826. Since Indians were British subject, they also started migrating to Thailand.Tamilians, both Hindus as well Muslim, were the first group of Indians to come to Thailand. They were engaged in various occupations. Another group of Indians who migrated to Thailand almost at the same time were Muslim Bohras from Surat and Bombay. These people were engaged in textile business.

Punjabis came to Thailand in 1884 A.D. and in the beginning there were only 20 families of Punjabis. Kiraparam Madan was the first Punjabi to settle in Thailand and he came from Bhadewal village in Sialkot district (now in Pakistan). His wife belonged to the Narula Sikh family of village Philloke in Gujaranwala district. She had five brothers and all of them gradually migrated to Thailand and settled there. All of their descendants are at present engaged in successful business in Bangkok. Gradually, other Sikhs and Hindus of the village Philloke started migrating to Thailand and by 1910 a large number of Punjabis, both, Sikhs and Hindus, had settled in Thailand. In the beginning, the Punjabis of three district of the then Western Punjab (now Pakistan), namely Gujaranwala, Sekhopura and Sialkot migrated to Thailand. All of them belonged to the Arora caste and three sub-castes, namely Madans, Narulas and Chawlas. Among them, Madans were the first to migrate followed by Narulas and Chawlas. Most of the Puinjabi migrants of the first wave were related to each other, as at that time there was no distinction between a Hindu and a Sikh. In fact, it was a common practice for a family to offer one of the sons to Sikhism.

Gorakhpuris also started migrating to Thailand around the late 19th century. After the first war of Indians independence in 1857, some Gorakhpuris first went to Burma, due to fear of prosecution by the British for their role in the revolt. Burma being a part of India at that time, was not considered as a safe place, therefore the Gorakhpuris migrated to Thailand. In the beginning there were about 20 families of Gorkhapuris and all of them were dairymen. Since the atmosphere in Thailand was congenial, they decided to settle there and gradually brought their families. There was spurt in migration of Gorakhpuris to Thailand from 1960 onwards. Most of them migrated with the sole purpose of making money and did not mind doing any kind of work.

Quite a large number of Punjabis and Gorakhpuris migrated to Thailand during the second world war. There were many army personnel who were fighting for the British in Malaysia and Singapore and were not happy by the discriminatory behaviour of the British officers in matter of promotion and other facilities. Some of these officers deserted the British army and joined hands with Indian revolutionaries to form Indian Independence League which later on was redesignated as the Indians National Army. At that time Bangkok was the centre of the Indian Independence League.

History and pattern of arrival of Indians in Thailand reveals that there are two kinds of migrants. In the first category are those who were lured to migrate mainly by their relatives and the second category is that of self-inspired migration. There is also a distinct pattern of migration among Punjabis and Gorakhpuris. Punjabi migration is chain migration as one member has been followed by others and gradually the whole family migrated. But among Gorakhpuris, there are very few cases of chain migration, the common pattern is relay migration. In relay migration, only one member migrated at a time and when he went back, was replaced by another member.

Vocational Activities of Punjabis and Gorakhpuri

Indians in Bangkok are engaged in various types of vocations, but the majority of them are self-employed, engaged in some kind of business, small or big. Some of the occupations in which Indians are engaged include textiles, precious stones, export and import, travel agency hoteliering, tailoring, watchman, newspaper distributors, nut/bread hawking and dairying. There are some occupations such as that of watchman, milkman, newspaper distributor and hawking which are generally pursued by Gorakhpuris. Punjabis are engaged mostly in textiles, hoteliering, tailoring and import and export.

The establishment of Europeon and British commercial and business firms in Thailand in the 20th century provided job opportunities to many Indian immigrants. In the early stages, all companies used to hire Indians especially Gorakhpuris as watchman due to their rudimentary knowledge of the English language. They were also preferred due to their honest nature. But now, Indian watchmen have been replaced by local Thais or Chinese. One can still find some Indian watchman but all of them are working with Indians firms.

Till 1950s the selling of milk and milk products was the monopoly of the Gorakhpuris, but after the introduction of the modern dairy companies, most of them have given up this occupation, and took to nut, newspaper and roti hawking, and very often one can come across these hawkers in the various business centres of Bangkok. Since this occupation needs little capital, and knowledge of local language not necessary, most of the new migrants from Gorakhpur go in far such activities. Quite a few Gorakhpuris are engaged as sales persons by Punjabis running wholesale and retail business of textiles. Some are also working as caretakers of the Guest Houses owned by Punjabis. Some Gorakhpuris also sell Pan (betel leaf).

Till a few years ago, money lending was one of the very popular occupation among Indians, especially among the Sikhs. Now, there are very few Sikhs doing this business.Another occupation which is quite popular among Indians is NGOEN-SOD. In common terminology it is called as *unq-phong* or *ding-dong*. This occupations is pursued by many Gorakhpuris as well as Punjabis including ladies. In this, Indians supply various items to local Thai by visiting them at their homes and take payment on a daily instalment basis. For instance, if some one wants to own a colour T.V., these people will supply the item but will charge almost double this amount to be paid in daily instalments. The amount to paid daily can be decided by the parties concerned.

The analysis of the Telephone Directory of Indian Residents in Bangkok revealed that most of the Punjabis are engaged in textile and tailoring business, and come in the category of leading businessmen of the country. Quite a large number of Sikhs also owned restaurants and guest houses. Other shops owned by Punjabis include ready-made garments, cassettes of Indian music and video-cassettes of Indian films. Some Punjabis also owed a travel agency.

Cultural Adaptation of Punjabis and Gorakhpuri

Three different trends of adaptation of host culture by Indians abroad have been identified by Sharma (1989). The trends are assimilation, cultural preservation with economic integration and ethnic politicization for power cultivation. Jamaica and Grenada have been cited by him as the countries where Indians have assimilated with the locals. In Mauritius, Guyana, Trinidad, Fiji and Sri Lanka Indians have formed strong political lobbies. However, the most predominant pattern found among Indian diaspora is cultural preservation with economic integration. Though the Indians in Thailand fall in this category, but they are at the different level of cultural preservation and economic integration. They can be placed at different points of an assimilation scale with completely assimilated at the top of the scale and completely segregated at the bottom of the scale. This means that those who have not assimilated in the host society must have been sandwiched between the two cultures for their continuation in the host society. In this section, we will see where Punjabis and Gorakhpuri fall on the assimilation scale.

Indians in Thailand are at the various stages of the acculturation process. Some have maintained their cultural identity by insulating themselves from the Thai culture, whereas others have adopted some cultural elements of the host society. A comparative picture of the acculturation process of Punjabis and Gorakhpuris may help us to examine our hypotheses proposed earlier.

It is generally known that expatriate Indians cling to their mother tongue. This is true of Indians in Thailand. In all, intra-group communications, whether at home or in public, all Indians use their mother tongue. In inter-group communication, when Punjabis interact with Gorakhpuris, or when Gorakhpuris interact with other Indian groups, generally Hindi is used. All religious ceremonies in Gurudwaras and temples are performed in Punjabi or Hindi. Thai words are sometimes intermingled with these languages.

Since communicating in Thai is essential for their survival in Thailand, it is invariably spoken by all the Indian communities. However, age, sex and community-wise differences in the intensity and extent of erudition of Thai are quite discernible. Though a large number of Punjabis have acquired proficiency in the three Thai R's most of the older generation people give preference to Punjabi.The younger generation among Punjabis, both the Hindus and the Sikhs, who have been born and brought up in Thailand generally prefer the Thai language. They are fluent not only in speaking Thai but also in reading and writing. These younger generation people also prefer to listen to Thai music and watch Thai films.

Learning of the Thai vocabulary is also essential to carry out their vocational activities in Thailand. Moreover, the learning of the language of the host society does not create any conflict with the parent culture. The only exception to this are aged Gorakhpuri females who generally do not interact with local Thais. In fact, very few Gorakhpuri have brought their womenfolk to Thailand. Even those Gorakhapuri females who live in Bangkok are generally confined to the four walls of the house. Whenever the Gorakhpuri females go out, they are always accompanied by their men folk including visits to the temple.

All Indians are nostalgic about Indian food, and look for Indian food wherever they go. Despite great regional variation in cuisine, there are certain strong flavours and smells associated with Indian food. It is also typified by the generous use of spices. Indians, therefore find Thai food insipid and bland on their palates. Besides not liking the flavour and smell of Thai food, the Gorakhpuri are prejudiced against Thai food because they believe that it is polluted and unclean. Being basically vegetarians or eating chicken and eggs, they suspect that food cooked in Thai restaurants is contaminated by meat dishes or cooked in lard. They generally prefer to cook their own food, because it is economical as well as in their opinion, unadulterated and pure. Hindu Punjabis and Sikhs do not have any such biases and do not hesitate to eat Thai food. The younger generation of Hindus and Punjabis have develcped a taste for Thai food. On the other hand, Gorakhpuris send their grown up children back to India for education and marriage and thus they do not get much exposure to Thai culture.

Indians migrating to the West sometimes changer or adapt their names not out of compulsion but for convenience. But anyone opting for Thai citizenship has compulsorily to acquire a Thai name. But this is only a superficial acquisition because they also retain their original name and are generally known by their Indian nomenclature.

Among the extrinsic cultural traits retained by Indians in Thailand, dress is the most visible. Most Indian females, old and young, stick to their saris or salwar kameez, though young Punjabi girls may occasionally wear jeans or skirts. All Gorakhpuri males cling to their traditional dress of dhoti/kurta or payjama/kurta. A tilak on the forehead of Gorakhpuri Brahmins confirms that living in an alien country has not affected the exteriors of their life. Similarly, most Sikhs, old and young, retain their long hair and wear turbans. Since it is an essential part of their religious ethos, they have not changed even after many decades and generations of migration.

Thus, we see that of the various elements of the Thai culture, almost all Indians including Gorakhpuris have learned their language but not all have been able to develop the taste for Thai food. Learning the language of the host society does not create any conflict with the parent culture, whereas the adoption of Thai food may pollute Gorakhpuris.

One important indicator of assimilation in an alien society is marital assimilation. "If marital assimilation... takes place fully the minority group loses its ethnic identity in the larger host or core society, and identificational assimilation takes place. Prejudice and discrimination are no linger a problem, since eventually the descendants of the original minority group become indistinguishable."(Gordon, 1964:80). This is another area where Indians, generally, do not compromise. Intrareligious and intracaste marriages are still the dominant pattern among Indians in Thailand.

The marriage pattern of Indians in Thailand shows that they prefer to marry their wards to Indians only. Generally, an attempt is made to find a suitable match from the same caste for their wards from India, failing that they try to find someone from the Indian community settled in Thailand, sometimes even ignoring the caste factor. Very few marriages have taken place between Indians and the local Thais. Most of such marriages have taken place among Punjabi boys both Hindu and Sikh and Thai girls. Secondly, most of such marriages have taken place among third and fourth generation migrants. This has also been confirmed by Zakir Hussain (1982) in his study of Indians in Thailand. According to his analysis, there were no mixed marriages among the first generation, and 47 per cent of the third generation Indians in his sample have marriages with Thais. He further shows that in such marriages the culture influences in 60 per cent of the families is Thai. In 19 per cent cases the influence of the culture of both the parents was there, whereas in the remaining 21 per cent the predominant pattern was Indian.

Among Gorakhpuris the cases of mixed marriages are very few. In some cases, Gorakhpuris males live with Thai females without marrying them. Generally, there is more social pressure on Gorakhpuris against such marriages as compared to Punjabis. Gorakhpuris on the whole do not encourage their children to intermingle with local Thais.

This confirms that the third and fourth generation migrants have better chances of assimilation in the host society as compared to first and second generation migrants. But at the same time their chances of assimilation in Thai society are less as they are not accepting the local Thai boys as their sons-in-law. So far some of them have accepted Thai girls as their daughters-in-law.

Differences in the pattern and intensity of maintaining contact with the parent country have also been observed. The majority of the Hindu Punjabis and Sikhs migrated to Thailand for permanent settlement and therefore migrated with their entire family. Some of them first came alone and later on brought their family while there were others who were bachelors when they migrated but later on got married in Thailand and settle there permanently. Our observation has been supported by Ruchira Atal's (1988) study conducted among Punjabis in Thailand. Out of 100 cases she interviewed, it was found that 60 were born in Thailand, whereas the other 40 cases were of first generation migration. Of the 60 cases who were born in Thailand, the families of 8 have been living in Thailand for the last four generation. Whereas as the other 31 have been there for the last three generation and the remaining 21 for the last two generations. The father of 20 of these 60 cases were bachelors when they arrived in Thailand but go married and settled permanently in Thailand. The rest of the 40 cases migrated with their families. Since these people brought their primary and secondary relatives from India and thus reduced their chances of maintaining frequent contact with the people in India. But there were some Punjabis both Hindus and Sikhs who maintained contact by sending their children for education to India. Almost all of them tried to get a suitable match for their wards from India, and some of them visited India for sightseeing. However, there are many Hindu Punjabis and Sikhs who have not visited India for many years and the children of some of these people have only heard of India but never visited.

The majority of the Gorakhpuris migrated to Thailand with the sole purpose of earning money and have no intention of settling permanently in Thailand. As a consequence, most of them are living alone and very few have brought their families to Thailand. The families of some of the Gorakhpuris visit them during the summer holidays when educational institutions in India are closed. All Gorakhpuris, whether their families are in Thailand or not, maintain regular contact with their people back at home. Most of them frequently visit India. Almost all Gorakhpuris remit money to their family members back at home and this money is used for the marriages of their wards, and also for the construction of houses and sometimes for buying agriculture land. It can be said that by living in Thailand they help their family members living back at home to raise their standard of living. Zakir Hussain's (1982) study shows that the first generation migrants visit India frequently, whereas the frequency comes down among second generation migrants. Among third generation migrants, the visits to India become very rare.

An important source of maintaining contact with the parent culture is the mass media. It plays a pivotal role in "...bringing the geographical distance and establishing cultural continuity between an immigrant group and the parent culture" (Yogesh Atal, 1991). The cinema plays a crucial role in dissemination of Indian culture in Thailand. Indian music and films are also popular among Indians in Thailand. Till the 1970s Indian films dubbed in Thai were regularly shown in the cinema halls of Bangkok. Cultural values, like respect for elders, etc. shown in Indian films, matched with Thai values and therefore they were popular even among local Thais. Once a month, on a holiday, an Indian film was shown on Thai T.V. and F.M. radio played the original sound track for the benefit of Indians. (*c.f. ibid.*) But all these have become outdated with the advent of video. Video cassettes of Indian films are available in Thai and almost simultaneously with their release in India and now, the majority of Indians watch Indian films in the comfort of their homes. The young are exposed to the parent culture through these films. Thus "a new image of India is getting registered on the minds of the young. International schools in a foreign land trend to alienate the children from their parent culture, through video, they are bought back home...New information technology has created apertures to tear off the political insulation of individual countries." (*ibid.*) Most of the Hindu Punjabis and Sikhs own video sets. Among Gorakhpuris, only those who live with their families own videos. Others watch Indian films in public places like the ATM department store or visit their friends for the purpose. Thus, we find that all Indians including the Punjabis, both Hindu and Sikh, maintain regular contact directly or indirectly with their parent culture which reduces their chances of assimilation in the host society.

India is a multi-cultural country. The occurrence of regional, ethnic and linguistic movements frequently "...have compelled frequent reiteration of the need to maintain the country's cultural diversity and ensure that the individual identities of different ethnic groups and communities do not get eroded" (Dube, 1992: 29). Indian immigrants maintain their cultural, regional, ethnic and linguistic diversities wherever they go. This has been emphasized by many scholars. S.L. Sharma in his article "Perspective on Indian Abroad" has observed that "...while dealing with the non-indians they tend to take on pan-Indian identity. But when it comes to interacting among themselves their regional, linguistic or religious identities take precedence" (1989:5). Indians in Thailand follow this pattern and distinctly maintain their linguistic, religious and regional identities. They may be identified as Indians by the local Thais, but while interacting amongst themselves, the distinction of region, religion and linguistic identity are uppermost in their minds. They are, thus, structurally separated not only from local Thais, but also amongst themselves. Their social interaction with other Indians as well as with local Thais are held to a minimum. However, necessary contracts on the job and on the business front and other impersonal contacts are maintained with locals and other Indians.

The immigrants generally keep alive their parent culture through various associations, educational institutions and religious centres which come in the way in their assimilation process in the host society. Indians in Thailand are no exception. Indians in Thailand have formed various associations based on religion, region and language. On the basis of religion, there are associations of Hindus, Sikhs, Namdhari Sikhs and Arya Samajis. Among Hindus, further distinctions can be made on the basis of region and language. In this category we can include the associations of Hindu Punjabis, Gorakhpuris, Marwaris, Sindhis and Tamils. Hindus, Sikhs and Namdhari Sikhs also run their religious centres, but only Sikhs and Hindu Punjabis run educational institutions.

These associations organize and celebrate various social cultural and religious functions which provide an occasion to meet each other and also expose the younger generation to some aspects of parent culture. One significant characterstic of these functions including the marriage ceremony is that such functions are celebrated in public places like temples and Gurudwaras, and an open invitation is given to all in the assemblies. All religious festivals are jointly celebrated by the members of the various associations. Non-members also attend such functions. For instance Sikhs celebrate Baisakhi and birthdays of various gurus, especially that of Guru Nanak Dev, the founder of the Sikh religion and Guru Gobind Singh, their last guru in a big way. Such functions are also attented by Hindu Punjabis who are not members of Sikh associations. Similarly, Hindus also celebrate their festivals like Durga Puja, Shivaratri, Holi, Dussehra and Deepawali with gaiety and solemnity. Since these functions are organized in temples, even non-members participate in these functions. All these functions are preformed in their mother tongue.

The various associations, educational institutions and religious centres form major receptacles of culture. Their activities not only reinforce religious and cultural values among its members but are also transmitted to the younger generations. They provide opportunities for frequent social interactions, enhance the feeling of social and cultural cohesiveness and also provide psychological support to new migrants.

Economic status of the migrants plays a significant role in enhancing or hindering the process of integration and assimilation in the host society. It has been observed that the migrants who have achieved higher economic status in the host society generally identify themselves with the elites of the host society. Their economic activities also provide them with more opportunities of interaction with the people of the host society. On the other hand, all those who have not gained economically, generally distance themselves from the people of the host society and interact with them whenever it is unavoidable. Their interaction is limited to the economic activities only. These people do not participate in the social and cultural activities of the host society. There might be two reasons for that. Firstly, they might be conscious of their lower economic status and secondly, they may feel more social pressure if they deviate from their normal life. Most of the time this social pressure may not be real but may only be a figment of their imagination.

In Thailand, a clear cut distinction has been observed in the behaviour of Hindu Punjabis and Sikhs on the one hand, and the Gorakhpuris on the other hand. Quite a large number of Punjabis, both Hindu and Sikh have gained economically and they do not hesitate in participating in social and culture activities of the Thais. Gorakhpuris, on the other hand, who are not well off economically, generally avoid mixing with the local Thais. Moreover, the Gorakhpuris have no intention of staying permanently in Thailand since their main purpose of staying in Thailand is to make money. This attitude affects their interaction with people of the host society which reduces their chances of assimilation in the host society.

A comparative picture of the acculturation process of two communities reveals that the aperture mechanisms are more operative among Hindu Punjabis and Sikhs, and the insulatory mechanisms are strong among Gorakhpuris. The presence of apertures nevertheless does not make these communities more susceptible to assimilate in Thai society in the immediate future. Eisenstadt (1954) and Gordon (1964) have pointed out that acculturation or cultural assimilation is only the first step to complete assimilation in the host society. The latter is not possible without institutional integration (Eisenstadt) or what Gordon calls structural and marital assimilation. Hindu Punjabis and Sikhs are inching towards institutional or structural and marital assimilation. The learning and internalization of some aspects of Thai culture have paved the way for their better adjustment in Thai society. At this stage Hindu Punjabis and Sikhs have a *double identity* and are sandwiched between the host culture and the parent culture. Though the Punjabis have taken some concrete step towards assimilation but unless they open more apertures, further assimilation will not be possible.

The presence of more insulatory mechanisms among Gorakhpuris makes them less vulnerable to assimilations. Gorakhpuris are happy to be "sojourners" who live as aliens in an alien society always maintaining their "separateness" and mingling only with the host society where it is absolutely necessary. After they have saved enough or are tired and old they go back to India and may be replaced by another batch of immigrants.

Variations in the adaptation process of Thai culture in two Indian communities may be attributed to differences in cultural, contextual and situational factors. Hindu Punjabis and Sikhs hail from the same region, *i.e.* Punjab and the cultural background of both these communities is more or less the same. Their level of acculturation in Thailand is also similar. They have created more apertures and are open to new influences. A distinctive feature of Punjabi culture is their adaptability and openness to change. This is due to the fact that most alien cultures came to India from the North-West and Punjab being geographically closest to the border had the maximum impact. Thus Punjab became a melting pot of various composite cultures, indigenous and foreign, which gradually were incorporated in what came to be known as Punjabi culture. This cultural co-mingling between people of different regions, with different social systems, gave birth to a culture with a liberal outlook. Immigrants with this kind of cultural background would certainly be more adaptable in a different society. Since both Hindu Punjabis and Sikhs migrated to Thailand with their families, it establishes the fact that these people went with the intention of settling there permanently. This intention has perhaps played a crucial role in their positive attitude towards the adaptations process. One of the best indicators of their receptive approach is that they have started accepting Thai girls as their daughters-in-law. Though the number of such cases is small, the first dent has certainly been made.

As compared to Punjabis, Gorakhpuris are more rigid and traditional. They hail from a region in India which is insulated and has not been exposed to other cultures. In Thailand they have isolated themselves and "shy away" not only from local Thais but from other Indian groups also. They have accepted only the language of the Thais, since it was necessary for their existence in Thailand. The majority of them went to Thailand not to settle permanently but to make their fortune or at least eke out a living. This has influenced their attitude towards the Thais. A large number of them migrated alone and never carried their families along. Old members went back and were replaced by younger ones. The majority has their primary and secondary relatives in India and close links are maintained with them. They have kept themselves aloof and did not make any attempt to assimilate in Thai society. They are also very critical of the social structure of the host society. For instance, they are very critical of the freedom and emancipation of Thai women. Such an attitude creates psychological barriers and does not allow them to make any attempt for assimilation in the host society.

Final Comments

There are very few cases where Indians, especially the Hindus and those who belong to these religions which are offshoots of Hinduism such as Jainism and Sikhism, have really assimilated in the host society. Indians generally adopt those cultural traits of the host society which helped them in continuation in an alien society. Most of the time they are sandwich between the two cultures. This may be due to the factor of basic personality structure. According to Kardiner, "certain culturally established techniques of child treatment had the effect of shaping basic attitude...and that these attitudes enjoyed a permanent existence in that mental equipment of the individual." (Kardiner, 1945:III). The seeds of basic personality are shown in the early stages of the socialization process. The values learned in the family become a part of the basic personality structure of an individual and these values are nurtured and nourished by various ethnic, religious and linguistic networks in a foreign country. Children born and brought up in these alien countries develop these values directly or vicariously and retain cultural identity, which prevent them from assimilating in the host society. As a consequence, the majority of the Indians become sandwiched between the parent culture and the culture of the host society. The same is true in case of Punjabis and Gorakhpuris in Thailand, however, they are at the different levels of sandwich culture.

REFERENCES

Atal, Ruchira (1988). *Punjabis in Thailand* unpublished M.Phil Thesis, Patiala, Punjabi University.

Atal, Yogesh (1989). "Outsiders *versus* Insiders. The phenomenon of Sandwich culture" in *Sociological Bulletin*, Vol. 38, No. 1.

Atal Yogesh (1991). "Indian Cinema in Thailand. Lost in video's Black hole" in *The Telegraph*, 27 September.

Coughlin, Richard J. (1960). *Double Identity: The Chinese in Modern Thailand*, Hongkok, Hong Kong University Press.

Desai, Santosh, N. (1980). *Hinduism in Thai Life*, Bombay, Popular Prakashan.

Dube, S.C. (1992). *Indian Society*, New Delhi, National Book Trust. (Second edition)

Eisenstadt, S.N. (1954). *The Absorption of Immigrants*, London, Routledge & Kegan Paul.

Furnival, J.S. (1984). *Colonial Policy and Practice a Compartive Study of Burma and Netherland*, India, Cambridge.

Gordon, M.M. (1964). *Assimilation in American Life: The Role of Race Religion and National Origin*. New York, Oxford University Press.

Hussain, Zakir (1982). *The Silent Minorities: Indians in Thailand*, Bangkok, Social Research Institute, Chulalongarn University.

Kardiner, A. (1945). "The Concept of Basic Personality Structure as an Operation Tool in Social Science" in *Science of Man in the World Crisis* (ed.) Ralph Linton, New York, Columbia University.

Sharma, S.L. (1989). "Perspectives on Indians Abroad" in *Sociological Bulletin*, Vol. 38, No. 1.

Siu, Paul C.P. (1952). "The sojourner" *The American Journal of Sociology*, Vol. 58.

Turner, J.H. and Bonacich, Edna (1980). "Towards a Composite Theory of Middlemen Minorities" in *Ethnicity*, Vol. 7, No. 2.

Part III

Exploring India

19

Social Science Activity in India and the IASSI

A. K. DASGUPTA

Yogesh Atal retired from UNESCO in the last quarter of 1997 and soon joined the Indian Institute of Education (IIE), Pune as its Director-General. From that position, he was elected as a member of the Executive Committee of the Indian Association of Social Science Institutions (IASSI). He was also then made the Chairman of IASSI Programmes Committee, which is responsible for the academic activities of the Association. When he left the IIE, he offered to resign from the IASSI bodies. The IASSI, however, prevailed upon him to continue. He was kind enough to remain associated with the IASSI.

Yogesh served as the Principal Director of the Social Sciences Sector at UNESCO and was responsible for promoting social sciences in the Asia-Pacific region. He executed his responsibility with a great deal of enterprise and succeeded in building up a social science consciousness in the countries of this region, most of which did not have much experience in this regard. When he returned to India, after serving UNESCO for more than two decades, IASSI was in the process of reforming its activities. The direction that IASSI took for its programme of reformation was parallel to the line of work pursued by UNESCO under Atal's leadership. Thus, having him in the IASSI bodies was a great comfort.

I have personally known Yogesh since 1960s when both of us joined the Panjab University at teachers—he in the department of Anthropology and I in the department of Economics. But we picked up friendship that never broke, though we moved to different worlds afterwards. Fortunately, we came together again at the IASSI, and thereafter, I have been at pains to see that we do not drift apart again. My personal interest remained at the back, which was to exploit his fund of knowledge and experience to the maximum in the work of IASSI's reformation.

IASSI has significantly reformed its programme during the last 4-5 years, thanks to support provided by Yogesh. I am also convinced in my mind that there is need to bring out the details both for public use and for presenting Yogesh's involvement in India for improving the state of social science activity in the country. This is what I wish to do in the following pages.

IASSI: ITS FORMATION AND OBJECTIVES

The Indian Association of Social Science Institutions was founded in 1979 by a galaxy of eminent persons, which included among others Shri K.R. Narayanan, who later became the President of India; Shri Tarlok Singh, who guided the preparation of the first three Five-Year Plans; Dr. Malcolm Adiseshiah, who served as the Deputy Director-General of UNESCO; and Shri J.P. Naik—an eminent educationist—who served as the first Member-Secretary of the Indian Council of Social Science Research (ICSSR). All of them were social scientists of the highest order and were convinced that social sciences have great role to play in the development of the society. As senior bureaucrats they an eminent educationist understood the significance of social institutions in the developmental process.

IASSI was, thus, formed to complement the work of institutions, like the ICSSR and the University Grants Commission, which were associated with the social science activities in the country. The founders of IASSI felt the need for bringing closer the universities, research institutions, and professional bodies for reorienting the social science activity in the country with a view to making them socially useful. Thus, an Association of such bodies was formed. It found easy acceptance as is evident from the large membership of institutions it enjoys.

India adopted comprehensive socio-economic planning as a means for bringing about rapid development in the society. With the feeling that for preparing the Plans, varieties of socio-economic studies could be necessary, a Research Programmes Committee was set up at the Planning Commission for encouraging researches in the academia in these areas. Later, the Indian Council of Social Science Research was formed for taking over the functions of the Research Programmes Committee of the Planning Commission.[1]

In the meantime analysis of data generated by the National Sample Survey brought out how great was the percentage of population living in abject poverty. It also revealed that slow growth of economy, which a comprehensive economic Plan could be expected to yield, might never succeed in lifting the people living below the poverty line to a reasonable state of living. A need for direct action for alleviating poverty was thus stressed. In the process, varieties of special programmes were developed and implemented in different parts of the country. These programmes also followed the mission-oriented approach that needed only monitoring and evaluation and very little input by way of social science research.

All these special programmes were included in the various Plans with the result that, over time, special schemes and programmes began to constitute the core of the Five-Year Plans. The licensing requirements were relented steadily and finally abolished. The core of the Soviet type of planning, with which developmental activities in the country started, vanished in the process, leaving only special schemes and programmes. Gradually, other economic and social policies became the responsibility of the departments and special institutions like the Reserve Bank of India and various councils and institutes. With these developments, bureaucrats and technocrats assumed all the responsibilities that required social science expertise; thus, the significance of social science research was considerably undermined.

The IASSI started working in such a milieu. The character of research in the social science areas began, therefore, to be formed in an environment of growing social engineering without the use of information and insights from the social sciences. The IASSI, in such circumstances, became involved in organizing seminars and conferences on matters of social interest, bringing together social scientists from diverse disciplines and the administrators and planners. In the absence of genuine multi-disciplinary researches only discipline-centred papers could be presented for discussions at these events. The discussions consequently could not throw new light and therefore no claim could be established for according due social significance to social science research.

The impetus for reformation of IASSI's programme was received from this experience. In particular, it began to be felt that there was a need for examining the character of social science research in the country for finding out what was required to be done for improving the significance of social science activity and for organizing further activities accordingly.

CHARACTER OF SOCIAL SCIENCE RESEARCH IN THE COUNTRY

Research Agenda and Support System

Empirical research in the social science area, particularly the survey-based research, is expensive, whereas there is an increasing realization that knowledge cannot progress without basic data and information. In the past, fieldwork was confined to anthropological and archaeological work, and for conducting and supporting work in these areas institutions like the Anthropological Survey of India and Archaeological Survey of India were established. Offices of Survey of India for making maps, and of Registrar General for population census work were also established.

With respect to other areas of social science research it was believed that facilities of a good library and proper documentation could be enough. After independence, when planning was introduced, the need for varieties of economic data arose. For meeting the needs, the National Sample Survey Organization (NSSO), the Department of Economic Affairs, the Economic Research Unit under the Reserve Bank, and offices of Economic Advisors under the Economic Ministries were formed. These agencies collected the necessary information for supporting economic administration and planning. The Ministry of Agriculture also supported a large number of Agro-Economic Research Centres for conducting farm management studies and estimation of cost of producing different crops.

The data collected by these agencies were also made public in suitable tabular form. In the area of economics a body of empirical research developed involving analysis of the data provided by these agencies. In the sociological area also some work in this direction was carried out. The work associated with published data did not involve further fieldwork and could be done sitting in-doors, aptly described as "armchair research".

The official agencies collect data and tabulate them primarily for meeting administrative needs. These are needed for evaluating some official policies and programmes; for building up concrete programmes by the departments; and for further use like preparing official estimates of GDP. These data, in effect, did not emerge as a part of social science research endeavour, correlated with theoretical and analytical thinking of the sciences. Thus, further use of the data in academic framework is very limited. Moreover, the data having been collected and tabulated for supporting administrative and planning related work fully enter into policy-making and evaluation. Therefore, the possibility was limited of the subjecting the data to further analysis for gaining any additional policy-related insights. The result has been that most researches by social scientists based on such data have not been utilized.

Some money is spent by agencies like the UGC and ICSSR towards support of social science research. UGC provides some money for supporting field surveys to the universities. Most expenditure of the ICSSR towards social science research is made up of grants to the institutes created under the ICSSR umbrella. These institutions obtain their basic grant from the ICSSR and the state governments. The amount of such grant available to each institute is barely sufficient for meeting its establishment needs leaving very little for researches involving field investigation.

Besides the ICSSR related institutes, there are many other institutes that are funded by various ministries and departments. Grants to these institutes are also barely sufficient for meeting establishment costs with very little funds available for field investigations. Thus all these institutes, including the ICSSR related ones, primarily involve in desk studies and additional analysis of data published by official agencies. By and large, therefore, the support available from public sources for social science research in the country is very meagre. Rarely provision for field-based researches are made with the result that most studies concentrate on the analysis of published data. As has been mentioned earlier, such studies, in the Indian context where data are produced for official use, rarely produce additional insights to gain social significance.

Field survey based studies are, nevertheless, conducted in the research institutes and centres and such studies have acquired great significance in these institutes. The studies are commissioned by different national and international agencies including government departments. The commissioning bodies specify the objectives and foci of these studies. The studies commissioned by the government departments are largely for evaluation of programmes. In such cases the commissioning body specifies the aspects to be examined, and some times also the method of examination. The reports on these studies are presented to the sponsoring agencies and are rarely disseminated for public use. Strictly speaking, therefore, the endeavours associated with such studies rarely contribute to the existing stock of knowledge.

Methods and Techniques

Empirical researches in social science areas take two forms. In one, attempts are made to prepare estimates of different magnitudes. In the other, individuals or households are distributed according to various characteristics. In cases where information is gathered on more than one characteristic of individuals/households cross-classification of the units is also done. In studies aimed at preparing estimates sample units are divided into various groups and estimates of the desired magnitudes are prepared for different groups.

Researches in the area of economics are largely focussed on preparing estimates of various magnitudes. Population distributions are also worked out and in many cases, the percentage of the population exposed to given characteristics, like unemployment, is also worked out. In most other social science areas population distributions are worked out.

Researches in India are carried out at two levels—large-scale national surveys, and micro-level studies. Large-scale national surveys cover almost all dimensions of socio-economic life. Each such survey is repeated at periodic intervals and the estimates prepared on the basis of each survey are used for study of changes over time. Due to limitations of sample size the cross-classified tables are usually available only at the national level; at the state level, only estimates of characteristics are prepared.

India is a large country with widespread variations. Geographical and physical characteristics, population composition, socio-economic features, political, social and economic institutions, and similar factors widely vary from one part of the country to the other. The national surveys, aiming primarily at obtaining aggregate estimates of different magnitudes, never bring out the correlates of these estimates and thus rendering the surveys of little analytical use. Mostly, such surveys are used for checking the effects of different policy measures.

At the other level, studies covering small regions—village, tehsil, block, district, urban centre, etc.—are conducted routinely by research institutions, university centres, and departments. These studies also aim at producing estimates of magnitudes and population distribution by characteristics. Cross-classifications are also attempted taking into account multiple characteristics of individual units.

These studies generally have theoretical orientation: either hypotheses are tested, or attempts to develop new hypotheses are made. The studies are usually directed by professional social scientists and, thus, a degree of rigour characterizes all these studies. Estimates of magnitudes and also various distributions are obtained through these studies. In many cases, estimates of statistical parameters like correlation coefficients and regression coefficients are developed. Significance of these coefficients is also tested rigorously using statistical techniques.

The environmental factors, which vary in intensity over the different parts of the country, affect the results of statistical investigation. For example, the geographical and soil characteristics influence the response of particular input complex on agricultural productivity. Similarly, characteristics of social and economic institutions in different regions affect the behavioural response of individuals. Thus, if studies similar to each other in all respects are conducted in different parts of the country a part of the variation in the results could be due to variation in the environmental factors. It could also be difficult to separate the effects of environmental factors in the overall variation in the results of the study. Because of this, results of individual studies lose social significance and applicability.

In a way, researches in social science areas in India in the present time do not generally satisfy basic objectives of research in any science. The results of researches should be expected to add to the stock of knowledge either in information terms or in terms of insights. Secondly, results should be expected to be useful socially. Research is a costly affair and the expenses for it are borne by the society. Therefore, concern for a proportional social benefit should also be borne in mind. From both counts present-day social science activity in India might not pass as relevant and significant. In a way, the development is surprising. The IASSI undertook to investigate the matter.

The Initial Years of Social Sciences

Social sciences began developing in Europe during the 18th and 19th centuries in a formal manner. Before that, political philosophers and political scientists began writing on aspects of polity, human rights, and equality as exemplified by the works of, for example, Bodin, Hobbes, and Locke. Their writings influenced the formation of modern states and development of democratic institutions for governance of the states, keeping regard of the aspects of liberty and equality of individuals.

In this process, works by economists, sociologists, and anthropologists also contributed considerably. Economic reforms, changing the earlier protectionist regime to a system of free trade and *laissez-faire,* came about largely through the influence of classical economics, developed by Adam Smith.

The Industrial revolution that started in England and spread subsequently to all parts of Europe was sustained, to a very large extent, by the structure of the State that evolved consequent on the pressures generated by the writings of these social scientists. Sensitive persons also noticed the dark sides of the rapid industrial progress. The horrendous exploitation of the working population, the distress suffered by the child labour, conditions of living in the slums, and extreme poverty which afflicted the majority of the people were too glaring. It was also noticed that democracy with the rule of majority over others, which all the countries adopted, could not maintain individual liberty and freedom in the same way as expected.

These matters also attracted the attention of social thinkers of the time. They started working on the parameters for state action. The liberal thinkers, who championed the cause of democracy, liberty, and equality, found that these do not progress harmoniously. Bentham worked on the legislative reforms needed for establishing bits of harmony among these.

His biggest contribution lay in the development of the idea of utility and the greatest happiness of the greatest number as the basis for judging the significance of state action.

Equally significant has been the contribution of John Stewart Mill. He was critical of the idea that the evolution of the government from tyranny to popular self-rule necessarily solved the problem of liberty. He saw that society might practice a social tyranny that may be more formidable than many kinds of political oppression, because social tyranny left fewer means of escape.

Mill, who grew up with a strong faith in *laissez-faire*, slowly abandoned what was dogmatic in the economic philosophy of *laissez faire* and adopted a position that was closer to that of Fabian Society, founded only a decade after his death. He was convinced of the need for state intervention for alleviation of problems that resulted from rapid industrialization in England, much against the principles of classical political economics.

Bentham also developed a critical and empirical method of investigation of concrete problems of law and government and extended the experimental method of reasoning from the physical branch to the moral. The Fabians took over his investigative method, applying factual research to concrete problems that affected the lives of ordinary men and women. They worked on nursery education, parish councils, community feeding and employment, under the strong influence of Sydney and Beatrice Webb.

The great concern for equity and justice expressed in the writings of social thinkers of the time also led, to a significant extent, empirical work in England, France, Germany and other countries. These were stimulated by pressing practical needs, and the need to gather information in response to rapid growth of towns and urban population and the consequent decline in the standard of living, polarization of wealth and poverty, pauperisation, and rising incidence of crime.

In England, investigations were directed to study the position of workers and poor strata of the urban population. Statistical societies were founded in many cities that brought together enthusiasts of empirical social studies. The British Association for the Advancement of Science set up statistical section. In France and Germany also empirical studies were conducted to understand the difficulties and deprivations suffered by the working population.

In a significant way the works by the social thinkers, particularly those with a socialist orientation and empirical studies complemented each other. A great deal of social pressure also evolved affecting the minds of the policy makers and the legislators. In the process, the states of almost all

European countries acquired a social welfare orientation. Legislations regulating working hours, employment of child labour, minimum wages and safe working conditions, education, health and other public services were adopted in almost all countries.

Decline of Relevance of Social Science Research

In course of time, however, empirical work in the social science related area became less and less significant as all the states started working for improvement of the quality of life of the people. Appropriate institutions were also formed in the European countries, which collected relevant data and analysed them. Thus, work in this area dried off.

In course of time the weight of theoretical work in the social science area began to increase. It was dominated by the philosophy of Natural Law. There was a strong belief that the universe was fully deterministic, governed by the operations of natural laws. It was also believed that the discovery of these laws was the primary objective of science. For aiding this process, a theory of knowledge was developed, giving predominance to reason than to experience.

A part of this ideology consisted of the belief that the universe being wholly deterministic, it could be possible to know everything through reason, provided one could start with a few basic postulates and build up a system of *a priori* hypotheses and theories by logical means. The empirical part of the work then consisted of finding evidence for testing the hypotheses. Following from the above, the primary emphasis in the area of social sciences was laid on developing theories in the form of hypotheses and testing them empirically.

The empirical work was, thus, largely confined to testing of hypotheses. The data and information gathered under such a programme did not aim at improving the stock of knowledge. These did not also possess qualities to function as a sufficient basis for policy and other uses.

Empirical work in the area of economics provides the best illustration of this development. Most economic magnitudes are defined in quantitative terms; therefore the system is amenable to quantitative analysis. The theories are largely formed in macro-terms and have significance in a macro setting, *i.e.*, at the level of national economies. Most magnitudes are measured in terms of money, whose value changes as price of products changes from year to year, whereas theories largely deal with changes in values of the basic magnitudes over time. Thus, a degree of abstraction is involved in building up the measures in real terms, *i.e.*, at prices prevalent during a given period of time. The results are also obtained at the same price whereas the current money prices may be different. Thus, by and large, no empirical verification of the results of an empirical economic exercise is logically and practically tenable.

The magnitudes used for macro-analysis, such as income, capital, saving rate etc., cannot be estimated for a part of a country or even a segment of the economy. Thus, analysis of economic events in any part of the country using the laws developed for macro analysis is not possible. The result is that micro-and macro-level empirical works follow altogether different lines. Separate theories applicable to regions or sectors of the economy are not developed generally and thus micro-level empirical work is not very popular, except in the area of agricultural economics. In such studies, mostly simple or multiple correlation and regression estimates are made. Such studies are not programmed to generate hypotheses by inductive means, with the result that these exercises remain illustrative without any contribution to the stock of knowledge and information.

Education in social sciences has been organized in the universities in a mono-disciplinary framework. Each discipline, as part of its work, produces definitions of its subject, its scope and coverage, the objects for investigation, the methodology of investigation and methods for verification of hypotheses. These constitute the bulk of discussions. Theories are also propounded and investigations aim at verification of these theories.

The writings are largely addressed to professionals of respective disciplines and rarely constituted a body of knowledge for socially enlightened people in the country. In a way, this area of work did not have the extent of social significance that the initial work in the social science area possessed. There have also been studies on matters of social concern. In particular, the subject of poverty has been studied in many social science disciplines. In economics, the study of this aspect has attracted great attention and constitutes the bulk of empirical work in recent years.

Poverty in India is ubiquitous and is visible all around. Before independence also the issue of poverty was raised repeatedly and a general feeling developed that alleviation of poverty should be the central focus of all our developmental programmes. Study of poverty, consequently, has become very important and the research efforts came to be directed towards this aspect in increasing order.

In England also empirical researches in the area of social sciences were directed largely to the study of the conditions of living of the working population and the slum dwellers. A large number of studies, under the rubric "study of social hygiene", were conducted bringing out the misfortunes and deprivations suffered by these people. The character of poverty, which the people at the lower level suffered, came out vividly in these studies and helped in stirring the conscience of the people. In India, political leaders and social thinkers raised the issue of poverty and the need for its redressal was well appreciated much before the country acquired independence. Here also the need for producing insights and information was well appreciated and rightly the matter became a primary focus of socio-economic studies.

However, the study of poverty in India was not done in the manner it was done in Europe during the 19th century. With macro-economic focus of economic theories, the studies in India were done in macro-terms. Efforts began to be made to estimate the proportion of the people who spend on living less than what could be considered as essential for their survival. With great degree of sophistication, estimates were prepared of what could be considered "essential" for survival. Since, the requirement was conceived in physical terms, this was taken as a physical constant, called "poverty line". As the prices of products keep on changing, a part of effort in poverty related studies consisted of preparing estimates of money value of the poverty line at different points of time, including working out what conditions such estimates should satisfy.

Another part of the effort consisted of preparing estimates of average expenditure by individuals on their living at different points of time and of the number of persons whose average expenditure was less than the level established by the fixed poverty line. A comparison of the ratio of persons below the poverty line at different points of time was expected to bring out how much poverty has been alleviated over time in India.

The Government of India has been carrying out, through the NSSO, a periodical survey of consumer expenditure. The data available from these surveys provide periodical estimates of per capita expenditure, at prices relevant for the period of survey. Thus, for the survey years estimates of number of persons spending less than the minimum required expenditure could become available, provided the money value of the poverty line, at the same prices could be produced.

Obtaining money value of the poverty line at different periods of time needed price adjustment, through use of price deflators. At one time, only national level deflators could be produced and, thus, estimates of poverty ratios only at the national level were produced. Now, deflators—though of dubious validity—at the state levels are available and thus estimates of poverty ratios at the state level are also produced. In all cases, however, many subjective assumptions are needed for producing the estimates with the result that though the estimates are produced with a great deal of sophistication, all resulting figures are of dubious validity and call for periodical revisions which are also done with a further set of assumptions[2].

The estimated poverty ratio turned out to be more than 50 per cent at one stage and this came down to around 15 per cent over the last 30 years. A large part of the developmental programmes in the country is aimed at alleviating poverty so that the estimates of poverty ratios, so available, constituted an evaluation of the effectiveness of these programmes. Nevertheless, a reduction of the poverty ratio to such an extent, was difficult to absord in the absence of other supporting information. An expert Committee formed for reviewing the methodology, found way to push up the ratio to arround 25 per cent, which is the currently accepted state.

It does nothing more than the above. One even finds it difficult to correlate the picture of a rapid decrease of poverty, indicated by these figures, and the near unchanging depressed picture of the quality of life of the people of this country, evident all around in a stark manner. The deprivations suffered by the bulk of the people in all such matters as health, nutrition, education, housing, drinking and other water supplies, drainage and sewerage, communication, power supply, employment etc.—over the ages, all of which constitute veritable parts of civilized and decent quality of living—find no place in such poverty related studies. Most importantly, the steady decrease in poverty as brought out by these studies in utter disregard of sensible facts and giving publicity to these figures, draws the attention of the people away from the basic issues of social concern.

The figures produced by these exercises could also have very little social significance. It has now been established that changes in the estimated poverty ratios are related largely to changes in growth of national product[3] and agricultural output,[4] whereas one never knows from these studies how other structural features, like distribution of land holding, tenancy system, occupation and industrial distribution of the working force, educational distribution, character of social and economic infrastructure, and similar others affect the behaviour of the poverty related figures. Thus, these exercises do not also lead to policy and programme directions.

Thus, one finds that while poverty related studies in Europe in the 19th century stirred the public conscience to such an extent that the states received an altogether new orientation, in India no worthwhile force could be developed for working towards establishment of a civilized society.

Gulbenkian Commission

Declining significance of social science related activity has been a universal phenomenon. An international commission was formed with Immanuel Wallerstein as Chairman for finding ways to restructure the social sciences.

The Gulbenkian Foundation of Portugal provided support to the Commission. The report has identified reasons why social sciences began to lose significance.

The Commission highlighted in its report the following aspects:

(i) Eurocentrism.
(*ii*) Colonization of Social Sciences.
(*iii*) Cause and effect relationship and natural order, and belief in universality of relations.
(*iv*) Neglected groups: gender, depressed sections.
(*v*) Objectivity and rationalism and deductive methodology.
(*vi*) Complex reality and approach from mono-disciplinary side.

The Commission looked at ways for restructuring social sciences and made many suggestions. The suggestions are valuable and need looking into favourably by all countries.

Investigation of Indian Situation by IASSI

After the Gulbenkian Commission's report was published, IASSI organized a seminar on State of Social Science Research in the Country to bring out specific problems in this context faced in India. The Seminar discussed the following four issues:

(*i*) Quality of research with focus on character of analytical tools and concepts, the form of linkage with reality, methodological approach,
(*ii*) Relevance with reference to focus of research, uses of the results of research (prediction, application and information generation),
(*iii*) Information content, dissemination and application with reference to field of reference (geographical area, population class etc.), mode of dissemination of results and uses,
(*iv*) Finance and organization of teaching and research focusing on quantum of support, supporting agencies, manner of distribution etc.

The significant conclusions of the seminar were:

1. While social phenomena consist of complex of factors—social, cultural, political and economic—the way disciplinary research activities are organized, there is little possibility of insights from various areas converging on social issues under investigation.

2. Most empirical studies are carried out as validation of hypotheses; this feature, in the framework of social sciences, does not generate quantitative information. In economic studies, the estimated coefficients, obtained through the use of mathematical/statistical tools, are useable for checking whether the direction of change implied in the application model is consistent with the direction of change implied in the theory. The numerical values of the coefficients obtained from the exercise are never given significance, nor are used as pieces of information.
3. In other areas of social sciences, quantitative work has not been of the same nature as in economics. But in those areas also empirical work is largely carried out as tests of hypotheses. The check is largely dependent on the observed distribution of some variates. In these cases also the observed distribution, used for checking the hypothesis, is not usable as pieces of information.
4. Disciplinary orientation of researchers in the area of social sciences has led to development of ideas in the mind of researchers that social problems could best be understood viewed from their respective disciplines. This has produced partial pictures of the reality. Any such picture derived from the individual disciplinary perspective may not yield information capable of use for analysis of complex social problems. Even in those cases where interdisciplinary teams are set up for study of complex social problems quite often individuals belonging to a discipline are put to work on only such aspects that fall in their area of disciplinary specialization. The result has been that interface areas between different disciplines remain unattended; and more importantly, the benefit which a genuine interdisciplinary approach could yield is lost.
5. Concepts are essential tools in the pursuit of knowledge. Most concepts used in the area of social sciences originated in the West. Applicability of these concepts in the Indian situation is rarely judged before using them.
6. Search for universal relations, which has been the agenda for research in Europe has also dominated the thinking of Indian researchers in a general way. Thus, research themes have rarely dealt with specific social problems and in cases where investigation was carried out in small local areas attempts have usually been made to obtain generalizations.
7. Research support from the Government departments has been available largely for evaluation of policies and programmes. In most cases, the departments also indicate what should be checked

under the programme of evaluation. In such works, no problem is studied. They focus on the effect of the policy measure.

8. In recent years, there has been a rapid proliferation of non-governmental organizations (NGOs), which engage in development research. Most of the studies carried out by these agencies address specific issues with the object of policy advocacy. Funds are also provided by bilateral and multilateral donors in the form of consultancy work. Large dependence on funds from such agencies creates a research priority in the society, which might not be an appropriate social priority.
9. There has occurred an increase in policy related research but policy makers have taken little interest in utilizing research for policy-making purposes. Serious effort is also not made to fill up research gaps by engaging research institutions for improving the quality and outcome of policy.
10. Many research studies are not directly concerned with policy like those on caste, religion or social movement. The consequent knowledge, however, could be extremely valuable for understanding many developments which shape the state of policy and also the effects policies have on people, if the studies are integrated and further analysed in the framework of existing and a desirable policy frame.
11. The donor agencies, including the government departments, being the principal source of funding of research organizations, in a way set the research agenda and priorities for the nation. There occurs, in the process, withdrawal of support for studies in certain areas, and also added support for studies in certain other areas. In a way, short-term interest is allowed to overwhelm research priorities to the neglect of research topics that are likely to deepen the knowledge about the structures and processes in society. In this way, significant gaps emerge in the structure of knowledge.

The IASSI also organized one National Symposium on Significance and Relevance of Social Science Activity in the country, inviting eminent social scientists as panellists. The Symposium, by and large, echoed the points made at the seminar and stressed the need for reviewing the system of research, education and training in the area of social sciences.

IASSI'S PROGRAMME FOR REFORMATION

Reforming an educational system is a difficult work in a big country. Many universities, research institutions and professional associations, all of which are nearly autonomous, are components of the system. In the universities, research and teaching are managed by mono-discipline centred departments, which have also reasonable degree of autonomy. Thus, bringing about a patterned structure in the teaching and research activities could be difficult.

The framework of suggestions provided by the Gulbenkian Commission could constitute a meaningful guideline that the individual departments and universities might slowly adopt, as it has been going on in the United States. The IASSI is making every effort to bring these matters to the notice of academicians and academic planners for considerations through organization of seminars and symposia. Organizing such meets has been adopted as a sort of routine programme as a means to sensitise concerned parties all over the country.

With respect to the special problem affecting social science activity in India, brought out in course of seminars and meets organized by IASSI, three action programmes have been developed.

Social science activity has three components—research, education and training. As has been noted earlier, the present depressing state of research in the social science area in India is associated with the structure of funding. It has been felt that a structure of funding needs to be established that might ensure conduct of researches results of which could add to the stock of knowledge and be socially useful and relevant. With respect to education and training, a need also came to be felt for working on the proper objective of social science education, currently and in future, and for exercise of a degree of coordination, with due regard to the autonomy of the institutions, for ensuring consistency between the social objective and the work objectives of the different agencies. For taking care of all the above functions a need for developing appropriate social institutions also began to be felt. Thus one of the programmes adopted by the IASSI relates to impressing the government about the need for making a national social science policy statement that will contain the governments' intention of supporting development of social science activities in the country. The IASSI has been organizing many regional meets at different universities and research institutions to prepare suitable inputs for such a policy statement, which could be held out as the corporate view of the community of Indian social scientists.

Under the second programme, a series of workshops are being organized by the IASSI, separately for economy-related, polity-related and society-related researches, for developing uniform standards for presentation of research results in the reports and for working out the classificatory details. India is a large country and empirical researches, on specific issues are carried out in many places. Without some sort of standardization, results of such researches are incomparable. Moreover, there is a wide degree of confounding of results as the conditions under which studies are conducted are not similar. The IASSI is working on the guidelines, which can be included in the research methodology programme offered by the different universities. It is hoped that if the research results are presented in a standardized form uses of the research reports might improve considerably.

Under the third programme, the IASSI is promoting formation of IASSI Local Chapters involving social scientists and others associated with social science related activities and encouraging them to organize seminars and discussions on matters of social concern. It is expected that such efforts would bring together social science related professionals for research and discussions on matters of social concern and help building up appropriate focus for researches in social science areas.

In the development of these programmes at the IASSI and also in their execution Yogesh has been intimately associated and I have no doubt that without support from him, both as an expert in his professional area, and as the Chairman of the Programme Committee, crystallization of IASSI's efforts would have been very difficult.

NOTES

1. It is important to mention that Yogesh Atal was the first Research Director to be appointed by the ICSSR to assist J.P. Naik in the new mission. Thus, Atal's contribution to the development of social sciences in India has a long history.
2. Depending on the coice of database and the methodology for producing the price indices many estimates of money value of the poverty line for a particular year are possible. in a paper by Amaresh Dubey and Shubhasish Gangopadhyay, three catagories of poverty lines have been estimated for particular years. The paper also gives estimates of poverty ratios for all states using the three categories of measures. The three categories provide distincly different measures of poverty ratios for each state. There is no basis for choosing any one estimate, whereas confronted with all the three one would not know the exact state of affairs. Ref.: Dubey and Gangopadhyay: *Counting the Poor in National Income Accounts and Data Syatem*, edited by B.S. Minhas (Oxford University Press, 2002).
3. Ravallion and Datt, using NSS Data, examined the relationship between growth in average consumption, and corrspondingly also average income, and poverty ratio. They found a high value of elasticity (negative) of poverty ratio with respect to average consumption both for rural and urban areas. The information has been taken from the paper by Bhaskar Dutta, referred in the following note.

4. In a paper by Bhaskar Dutta estimates have been provided of elasticity of rural poverty ratio with respect to availability of cereals in the country. It is observed that poverty ratio has a tendency to decrease as net availability of cereals in the country. Bhaskar Dutta: Economic Reforms and the Poor; published in *Poverty and Employment*, Edited by K.Raghavan and Leena Sekhar, New International Publication.

20

Theoretical Trends in Post-Independence Ethnographies of India

GIRI RAJ GUPTA AND SATISH KEDIA

In this paper we explore the theoretical trends and boundaries of ethnographic writings in post-Independence India. The focus of the paper reflects an attempt to understand shifts in scholarship on India and its possible antecedent in the rapid social transformation in Indian society after Independence. We discuss selected ethnographic works in terms of extent to which they embody contemporary theories in anthropology and sociology. The main purpose of this endeavour is to initiate discussions of ethnographies on society and culture in India within the context of theoretical development in the West. India's Independence also coincided with what L. P. Vidyarthi (1978) has characterized as a transition from a descriptive to an analytical period in Indian anthropology and sociology.

The facilitators of the departure from the descriptive to the analytical were dissatisfied with prevailing single-village studies that assumed the autonomy of rural Indian society. Many of these studies lack an emphasis on both institutional (rural-urban, peasant-elite, and caste-class) and conceptual (historical and political economy) linkages and led to the emergence of a movement toward the indigenization of culture concepts. Increasing contact with the West during the early 1950s exposed Indian social scientists to the works of British and American anthropologists. The British influence included the works by E.E. Evans-Pritchard, Meyer Fortes, and A. R. Radcliffe-Brown. The first wave of American scholarship in India boasts Morris E. Opler, Oscar Lewis, David G. Mandelbaum, Robert

Redfield, Milton Singer, Bernard S. Cohn, and McKim Marriott. By this time, a number of Indian anthropologists were graduating from universities in England, reflecting the growing influence of British social anthropology in India—primarily the functionalist and structure—functionalist paradigms. The emphasis on empirical fieldwork, systematic analysis, and attention to theory accelerated. Despite these influences, most studies remained primarily descriptive and did not yield substantial methodological and theoretical innovations (Jha, 1983; Kolenda, 1985).

Inspired by the British and American schools of diffusionist thought, several scholars transplanted these ideas to the cultural canvas of India. Initial influences were the works of British diffusionists (Grafton Elliot Smith, William James Perry, and W. H. R. Rivers), who argued that cultural similarities among people in distant areas are due to a diffusion of traits rather than independent inventions. American thinkers (Franz Boas, Clark Wissler, and Alfred Kroeber), added the importance of historical particularities in the diffusion of cultural traits. Although M. N. Srinivas did not explicitly discuss the diffusionist influence on his concept of "spread," it is evident that he was certainly advancing a similar thesis. He opined that rituals and cultural forms of Hinduism spread from local, to regional, to peninsular, to the all-India level. To solve the puzzle of tribe-caste boundaries, scholars such as F. G. Bailey (1960), Surajit Sinha (1965), and N. K. Bose (1953) advanced the notion of a "tribe-caste continuum" to explain how tribes in various parts of India are being pulled toward the caste system through adaptation of agriculture and Hindu rituals and value systems of the caste society.

By the middle of the 20th century, a few Indian anthropologists trained by British anthropologists brought the structural-functional influence to Indian works. M.N. Srinivas' work on *Religion and Society among the Coorgs of South India* (1952), is considered a turning point in easing into the analytical phase. In his work, he applies Radcliffe-Brown's theory of structural-functionalism and shows the close inter-connections between religious institutions, family and kinship systems, and the laws of inheritance and succession. Srinivas devised the notions of "Sanskritization" and "Westernization". Sanskritization explained how a section of a lower caste over a period of time emulated the customs, rituals, and life-style of a higher caste, which was also critical in absorbing individual tribes into the Hindu fold. Westernization was used to explain the process of westernizing life-styles by the higher castes. Iravati Karve's *Hindu Kinship System* (1953) extended the functional argument linking kinship and marriage with the caste system. F. G. Bailey's *Caste and the Economic Frontier* (1971) is influenced by a structure-functionalist analysis.

This interest in kinship and economy was echoed in the works of many other anthropologists (S. C. Dube and D. N. Majumdar), who were exploring the nature and functions of castes and the caste-rankings to understand the social structure of Indian villages.

Interest in Indian studies by many American anthropologists was instrumental in incorporating theoretical paradigms into ethnographic works in India, especially in village studies. The emphasis on the village studies brought into question whether a village satisfactorily reflects the whole in itself and leads to an understanding of the greater society in which it is embedded. This approach required a dramatic leap from the little tradition to the great tradition, and left a hiatus in comprehending a historically complex civilization.

As the interest grew from the village level to a more Pan-Indic level of analysis, American anthropologists began to make some compelling arguments regarding Indian civilization, which Robert Redfield explained in terms of social structure of the culture, the cultural influences coming from outside the village are part of the "great tradition", while those coming from the local areas are called the "little tradition". McKim Marriott (1955) developed this argument further with his study of the Kishangarhi village community, and presented related concepts of "universalization" and "parochialization". The idea of universalization signified a forward movement of materials that the little tradition already possesses, while the devolution of the great-traditional elements and their integration with little-traditional elements is called "parochialization". Also, drawing his inspiration from Redfield, Singer described Indian civilization as a cohesive network of rural and urban areas that were linked with great and little traditions and a continuum of tribes, castes, and linguistic groups.

Some anthropologists, even though they work within the rubric of structuralism, embrace a cognitive-historical approach. Dumont's *Homo Hierarchicus* (1970) offers several leading perspectives analyzing the cognitive and ideological structure of the Indian social system. Apart from ideology and dialectics, the notion of 'hierarchy' has a pivotal place in Dumont's analysis. Reflecting on the facts of representation and facts of behaviour, Dumont perceives the caste system in India as a product of tradition and the ideology of inequality. He states that the spirit of the caste system has three tendencies: repulsion, hierarchy, and hereditary specialization. In order to have a complete picture of a caste, one has to understand the dynamics among all three tendencies. Dumont establishes the relationship between abstract and concrete aspects of the caste system. Dealing with the idea of abstraction he states that opposing civilizational modes of equality and hierarchy are purely relative. He emphasizes a search for entities and structure rather than processes and functions.

Dumont argued that the structure of the caste system arises from the idea of a logical predilection that is religious in nature, thus emphasizing that notions of ideology and tradition are intrinsic to the Indian psyche. Dumont's definition of ideology operates on two separate levels: specific and global. Indian civilization represents a 'specific' ideology that has components of binary opposition. These components include purity and impurity, idea and action, equality and hierarchy, and individualism and holism. For Dumont, 'global' ideology is shared by a larger group of people; it can be a linguistic group or the entire world.

One of the distinctive features of Dumont's structuralist approach is that it is grounded in substantive observation. As a result, he is able to make the distinction between facts of representation and facts of behaviour. Hierarchy implies opposition between pure and impure, which in turn determines the dialectics of superiority of the pure over the impure. According to Dumont, it is important to keep pure and impure separate. The whole is founded on the necessary and hierarchical co-existence of two opposites. Hierarchy also implies the relationship of encompassing and being encompassed—the pure encompasses the impure.

According to Dumont, even though the West accepts the notion of equality as its social ethos, hierarchy is represented in the form of racism. Indian society is holistic, contrary to the atomistic nature of Western society. In India, primacy is given to the whole—the structured hierarchy—whereas in the West, individualism of "Homo economicus" prevails. There is a dialectical confrontation of "Homo hierarchicus" of the traditional society and "Homo aequalis" of the modern society. Although the theoretical significance of Dumont's work cannot be undermined, it has limited application in the rapidly changing Indian society where binary or dichotomous oppositions of purity-pollution, high-low ritual status, and individualism and holism are challenged in everyday life. Little effort has been made by Indian anthropologists and sociologists to carry forward or to critically examine these structural arguments (Khare, 1990) that are the distinguishing themes of Indian studies. Considering the limitations of Dumont's dualism, Marriott envisaged a new ethno-sociological view of India, explaining Indian society as a unique system that demands conceptualizing various categories in the context of its own ethno-history and culture. Marriott sees the absence of appropriate concepts in Western social sciences that are able to explain the reality found in Indian society. Many concepts of Western social science do not 'fit' well and fail to represent the intrinsic meanings of the terms commonly used by people in India. Marriott's ethno-sociology is better grounded in his substantial empirical work. Exceptions are B. N. Saraswati's (1977) work *The Brahmanic*

Ritual Traditions and Makhan Jha's (1982) work on *The Civilizational Regions of Mithila and Makakoshal*. These two works extrapolate the civilizational modes of similarities and diversities while addressing the factors responsible for continuity and change in socio-religious systems in India. Pauline Kolenda's (1985) work *Caste in Contemporary India* is clearly different from the Dumontian tradition, and it marks a shift in anthropological perspective on Indian society.

Marxist paradigms influenced a handful of Indian scholars, but as a whole, they failed to develop a rigorous tradition of research using these ideas. The early Marxist-influenced social scientists emphasized a dialectic-historical approach. For D. P. Mukerji (1948), a dialectical relationship between Indian tradition and Western ways brought contradiction and conflict, particularly with regard to cultural values. Yet at the same time, there was a synthesis of these two seemingly opposing cultures to form the rise of the middle-class. A.R. Desai (1959) argued that nationalism was a product of material conditions created by British colonialism. While the British rule caused economic disintegration and threatened the continuation of the caste system, the colonial-induced economic relations created a new class structure and a new social consciousness, which in turn created Indian nationalism. The strength of this approach is that it provides a framework for analyzing various processes of change and conflict in India. However, this proposition needed further empirical verification and analysis from various parts of the country. On another front, Chauhan (1967) explains how a Rajasthan village transformed from its feudal past and adapted to the new system of administrative links after the Independence of the nation. A few studies have followed up on the themes of the rehabilitation of the former princely rulers and their role in the participatory democratic system.

The challenge of linking the theory to empirical data continues for subsequent Marxist-influenced ethnographers. For example, Mencher's (1978) study in Tamil Nadu compiled detailed information on the agricultural system, but her method of linking this data to the economic forces "above" and "below" and her argument for more equitable land re-distribution to increase agricultural productivity remained unconvincing. Kathleen Gough (1978) analyzed Dravidian kinship and modes of production. Many ethnographies after the advent of community development programmes in India have development orientations. Majumdar's ethnography, *Himalayan Polyandry* (1963), focuses on impacts of community development programmes on the Khasa tribal community in Himalayas. Morton Klass's *From Field to Factory* (1996) deals with the impacts of industrialization on agriculture. Other prominent works are

Wayne Broehl's *The Village Entrepreneur* (1978) and Kusum Nair's *In Defense of the Irrational Peasants* (1999).

Cultural ecology has been the motivating force for many recent ethnographic studies in India. Alan Beals (1974) in *Village Life in South Asia: Cultural Design and Environment Variation* explains the variation in Southern Indian villages as the result of adaptations to particular social and physical environments. Murray Leaf (1984) in his famous work *Song of Hope: The Green Revolution in a Panjab Village* traces the history of successful agricultural intensification involving technological, economic, and social characteristics of a Punjab village. Another work that comes to mind is Morgan Maclachlan's *Why They Did Not Starve: Biocultural Adaptation in a South Indian Village* (1983).

A relatively recent ethnography *The Poison in the Gift* (1988) by Gloria Raheja explains the semiotic aspects of gift giving and receiving among different segments of the population in a Gujjar village in Uttar Pradesh. Hermeneutic paradigm is not evident in many Indian ethnographies with the exception of Ostor's and Khare's works. In a review article, Marcus and Cushman (1982) described Ostor's *The Play of the Gods: Locality, Ideology, Structure, and Time in the Festivals of a Bengali Town* (1980) as an exemplary ethnographic work from India. Khare in *The Untouchable as Himself* (1984) has allusions to works by Bourdieu, Marshall Sahlins, Victor Turner, and Clifford Geertz. While Fox's work "The Lions of the Punjab" (1985) is driven by political economy and a Marxian analysis of world systems, colonialism, and social class, his interest in the " Akali Movement" focuses on action in human agency and historical contingency.

Veena Das's work on violence and ethnic identity and communal politics, *Mirrors of Violence: Communities, Riots, and Survival in South Asia* (1990), is highly interpretive in its orientation. Cynthia Keppley Mahmood's on terrorism among the Sikh separatist militants in Punjab deconstructs the myth of terrorism in favour of reasonable ethnographic assessment as the first step toward curbing such violence in the future.

A number of ethnographers examine the position of women in Indian society. Several described the roles of women in the family (Susan Seymour, Purnima Mankekar, Yuko Nishimura, and Patricia Caplan), including the tensions that arise among kin, marriage and dowry, and recent changes in families. Several ethnographers describe women in India as having a subordinate position in relation to men under a system of patriarchy (Kelkar and Nathan, 1991; Shiva, 1988). However, Nishimura describes married women in the Nagarattars of Tamil Nadu as protected by the kinship system and by their property rights (1998). Because India is very diverse, women do not hold an established position in India; gender roles vary by ethnic group, region, and class and caste, and family. Caplan (1985) notes the relationship of gender to the formation and reproduction of class in capitalist societies using the example of upper-class women's voluntary social welfare organizations in Madras. She argues that these upper-class women perpetuate and maintain a division of classes as well as participate in the perpetuation of an ideology that subordinates women.

Sunil Khanna articulates his re-study of the Karimpur in the context of William and Charlotte Wiser's *Behind Mud Walls* (1963) and Susan Wadley's *Struggling with Destiny* (1994), both earlier ethnographies on Karimpur , in terms of current debates on post-modernist skepticism and feminist assertions of agency, involvement, and advocacy. Wadley interprets the life stories of Karimpur respondents and examines lives, feelings, images of Gods and Goddesses, and negotiations and struggles with destiny. It also represents an indulgence with women's issues, their role in the family, their health, and their religious power. Mindful of the tension between the scholarship of "detachment" and that of "activism, " Sunil Khanna (1995) opts to focus on the ways in which patriarchal ideologies that devalue women contribute to discriminatory attitudes in North India that are manifest by practices such as female infanticide, neglect in health care and food allocation, and more recently female feticide.

Another theme appearing in works on gender and women in India has been women's adjustments to economic change, including modernization, economic development, urbanization, and changing economic relations. Kelkar and Nathan (1991) argue that women in the Jharkhand region in East India have a deteriorating position caused by economic changes associated with economic development. Accompanying these economic changes were pressures for an engendered division of labour in which men obtained power by being dominant over and exploitative of women. Several authors, including Bhatt (1989) and Rao and Rao (1988), studied urban women and noted their poverty and lack of opportunities to earn monetary remuneration for their work.

Seymour (2000) examines change on a different front—the impact of increased education and delayed marriage age on women's roles in the family. Mankekar (1999) also investigates the change of women's place in the family as well as in the community and nation, but in her case, she focuses on changes brought about from the influence of television programming and how the messages on TV affect not only gender but also caste, class, and politics. Indian ethnographies also reflect the feminist movement within anthropology. Fruzzetti's *The Gift of the Virgin* (1982) analyzes the worth of women's rituals in Indian society. Vatuk (1972) provides a compelling account of women, their world, worries, gossips, kinship tensions, and dowry and marriage concerns.

Ethnographic work on aging in India is scarce. As often as Western popular culture mythologies aging experiences in India, there have been few serious or successful attempts to conduct ethnographic research on these lived experiences in all their diversity and richness, especially in times of rapid urbanization and a rapidly growing elderly population in India. Two exceptions to this void are the recent works of Lawrence Cohen, *No Aging in India: Alzheimer's, the Bad Family and Other Modern Things* (1998), and Sarah Lamb, *White Saris and Sweet Mangoes: Aging, Gender, and Body in North India* (2000). Another interesting text is John van Willigen and Narender Chadha's book, *Social Aging in a Delhi Neighbourhood* (1999). Blending heuristic devises to paint a picture of an elderly middle-class neighbourhood, van Willigen and Chadha have produced a work that is fresh in many ways: in its intellectual interweaving of the traditions of anthropology and psychology, in its straightforward ethnographic descriptions enriched with analytical strategies to untangle difficult constructs such as 'disengagement' and 'power', and in its combination of quantitative data with observational and reflective narratives.

A recent trend led by Ramchandra Guha and modern historiographers is encapsulated under the umbrella of subaltern studies. The idea of subaltern is borrowed from Gramsci's notion of 'subordinate by hegemony or dominated classes which include class, gender, age, ethnicity, and religion. Subaltern studies became a compelling voice, beginning with early 1980s, led by a group of historiographers including but not limited to Ramchandra Guha, Shahid Amin, David Arnold, Partha Chatterjee, David Hardiman, Giyatri Spivak, and Gyanendra Pandey who reinterpreted the colonial history of India from the perspective of politics of the people and not from the perspective of the elites. Cohn (1987) argued that this emergent "post-colonial anthropology" may help us formulate the cultural categories and the process of their construction in the context of power relations of colonial history. This thinking permeated the guises of the historiography to sociology and anthropology in works such as "Caste and Subaltern Consciousness" (1989) by Partha Chatterjee, which voiced the subaltern concerns to the understanding of Indian society and culture.

Practice theory studies relationships between human action and social systems. Bourdieu's idea of habitus is similar to Sahlin's idea of cosmological drama. Bourdieu's works *Outline of Theory of Practice* (1977) and *Logic of Practice* (1990) have been instrumental in advancing these ideas. Sahlin's *Culture and Practical Reason* (1974) is also along the same genre. According to the practice school, society is not the sum of *ad hoc* responses to stimuli or adaptation to a specific environment but is governed by organization and evaluative schemes called "systems". Society cannot be broken into base and superstructure. Giddens argues that we must study temporality, paradigmatically (invoking instantaneous structure), and spatially. Practice theorists seek to understand the social system through people's doing by unfolding events They are also interested in the way the system is reproduced and changes over a period of time. There is no doubt that culture constitutes reality, but it is always looked at with critical eyes. Agents' aspirations have the same objective limits as the system. So practice generates, reproduces, and changes the system.

There are considerable gaps in current ethnographic writings on Indian culture. Reflective ethnographic traditions have not completely entered the mainstream of ethnographic scholarship by native researchers. Most hermeneutic, phenomenological, and interpretive traditions have not been able to fully gain a foothold in Indian scholarship. Contemporary anthropology is going through an unprecedented change, especially in the field of ethnography. Anthropologists are trying to reformulate their ideas about ethnographic practices and the construction of cultural concepts. Their interest is in ethnography within the framework of historical and political economy and in the form and rhetoric of writing. Marcus and Fischer (1986) consider it an experimental moment in human science. Interpretive anthropology focuses on understanding the natives' point of view by gaining knowledge of their social systems. The thrust is on epistemological bases of the account and meta-interpretation—interpretation of how natives interpret their culture. Paul Willis's work, *Learning to Labour* (1981), and June Nash's ethnography, *We Eat the Mines and the Mines Eat Us* (1993) are good examples of this tradition. Geertz brought the idea of authority, which is an act of self-reflection and protrudes our works through rhetoric, textual organization, and analysis.

Given the historical circumstances, Indian cultural studies transcended the conventional disciplinary boundaries of social anthropology, sociology, history/historiography, and so-called ideology, albeit the distinction among these disciplines remains blurred. No doubt, native anthropologists with training in Indian universities, native anthropologists with training in Europe and the United States, and Western and American anthropologists have all equally contributed to the development of the intellectual wealth of Indian ethnography. However, a lack of enthusiasm remains among Indian scholars for rigorous and systematic methodological and theoretical innovations or even indulgence with the theoretical advances in the West. The problematic aspect of the works of Indian anthropologists is their *laissez-faire* attitude about methodology. We have rarely encountered any serious attention to research design or systematic data collection techniques or analysis. Similarly, collaborative work is considered to taint or compromise individual scholarship. The prevalence of academic elitism in Indian universities discourages independent thinking on the part of the budding professionals and gets in the way of open dialogue with colleagues elsewhere in the world. Equally challenging is the lack of resources in the Indian universities, which inhibits concerted research efforts.

Ethnographic practice in India can be enriched in many ways. Social scientists may consider incorporating dialogue and reflect on how knowledge develops in the course of dialogue. One needs to be more sensitive to the historical and political economic forces in order to understand specific circumstances in which a social system and cultural configuration develops. One also should not loose sight of the need to situate Indian communities in the context of colonial and post-colonial history and politics as well as in the context of local and national responses to the forces of globalization. There is no doubt that India's extensive cultural diversity provides immense potential for classic ethnographies.

REFERENCES

Amin, Shahid (1995). *Event, Metaphor, Memory Chauri Chaura,* 1922-1922 Berkeley: University of California Press.

Arnold David (1984). "Gramsci and Peasant Subalternity in India" *Journal of Peasant Studies,* 11(4) : 155-1777.

Bailey, F.G. (1960). *Tribe, Caste and Nation.* Manchester, U.K.: Manchester University Press.

——(1971). *Caste and the Economic Frontier: A Village in Highland Orissa,* Manchester: Manchester University Press.

Beals Alan (1974). *Village Life in South Asia: Cultural Design and Environmental Variation.* Chicago: Aldine Pub. Co.

Bhatt, Ela (1989). "Organizing Self-employed Women for Self-Reliance." In Carla M. Borden. Ed. *Contemporary Indian Tradition.* Washington: Smithnosian Institutions Press. 203-219.

Boas, Franz (1911). *The Mind of the Primitive Man.* New York: Macmillan.

Bose N.K. (1953). *Cultural Anthropology and Other Essays.* Bombay: Asia Publishing House.

Bourdieu, Pierre (1977). *Outline of a Theory of Practice.* Cambridge: Cambridge University Press.

——(1990). *Logic of Practice.* R. Nice, transl. California: Stanford University Press.

Broehl, Wayne (1978). *Village Entrepreneur: Change Agents in India's Rural Development.* Cambridge: Harvard University Press.

Caplan, Patricia (1995). Class *and Gender in India: Women and Their Organizations in a South Indian City.* London: Tavistock Publications.

Chatterjee, Partha (1989). "Caste and Subaltern Consciousness." *In Subaltern Studies No. 6 Writings on South Asian History and Society*. R. Guha, ed. pp. 169-209, Delhi: Oxford University Press.

Chauhan, B.R. (1967). *A Rajasthan Village*. New Delhi: Vir Publishing House.

Cohen, Lawrence (1998). *No Aging In India Alzheimer's, the Bad Family and Other Modern Things*. Berkeley, California: University of California Press.

Cohn, Bernard S. (1987). *An Anthropologist among the Historians and Other Essays*. Delhi: Oxford University Press.

Das, Veena, *ed.* (1990). *Mirrors of Violence: Communities, Riots and Survivors in South Asia*. New York: Oxford University Press

Desai, A.R. (1959). *Social Background of Indian Nationalism*, Bombay: Popular Prakashan.

Dube, S.C. (1955). *Indian Village*. London Routledge and Kegan Paul.

Dumont, Louis (1970). *Homo Hierachicus: The Caste System and Its Implications*. Chicago: University of Chicago Press.

Epstein, T.S., A.P. Suryanarayana and T. Thimmegowda (1996). *Village Voices, Forty Years of Rural Transformation in South India*. New Delhi: Sage.

Evans-Pritchard, E.E. (1951). *Social Anthropology*. New York: Free Press.

Fortes, Meyer (1945). *The Dynamics of Clanship among the Tallensi*. London: Oxford University Press.

Fox, Richard G. (1985). *Lions of the Punjab: Culture in the Making*. Berkeley: University of California.

Fruzzetti, Una M. (1982). *The Gift of the Virgin: Women Marriage and Ritual in a Bengali Society*. New Jersey: Rutgers University Press.

Geertz, Clifford (1973). *The Interpretations of Culture*. New York: Basic Books.

Giddens, Anthony (1979). *Central Problem in Social Theory: Action, Structure, and Contradiction Social Analysis*. Berkeley: University of California Press.

Gough, Kathleen (1978). *Dravidian Kinship and Modes of Production*. New Delhi: Indian Council of Social Science Research.

Guha, Ramachandra (1995). "Subaltern and Bhadralok Studies" *Economic and Political Weekly* 30:2056-2058.

Gupta, Dipankar (1985). "On Altering the Ego in Peasant History: Paradoxes of the Ethnic Option." *Peasant Studies* 13(1) : 5-24.

Hardiman, David (1986). "Subaltern Studies' at Crossroads". *Economic and Political Weekly* 21:288-290.

Jha, Makhan (1982). *The Civilizational Regions of Mithila and Mahakoshal*. New Delhi: DK Publishers.

——(1983). *An Introduction to Anthropological Thought*. New Delhi: Vikas Publishing House Pvt. Ltd.

Karve, Iravati (1953). *Hindu Kinship System*, Bombay: Asia Publishing House.

Kelkar, Govind and Dev Nathan (1991). *Gender and Tribe: Women, Land and Forest in Jharkhand*. New Delhi: Kali for Women.

Khanna, Sunil (1995). *Gender Discrimination. Maternal Health. and Pregnancy Outcomes in North India*. PhD., Syracuse University.

Khare, Ravindra (1984). *The Untouchable as Himself: Ideology. Identity and Pragmatism among the Lucknow Chamars*. Cambridge: Cambridge University Press.

——(1990) "Indian Sociological and the cultural other". *Contributions to Indian Sociology* 24, 177-200.

Klass, Morton (1996). *From Field to Factory: Community Structure and Industrialization in West Bengal*. Lanham: University Press of America.
Kolenda, Pauline (1985). *Caste in Contemporary India: Beyond Organic Solidarity*. Prospect Heights: Waveland Press.
Kroeber, Alfred (1944). *Configurations of Culture Growth*. Berkeley: University of California Press.
Lamb, Sarah (2000). *White Saris and Sweet Mangoes: Aging, Gender, and Body in North India*. Berkeley, California: University of California Press.
Leaf, Murray (1984). *Song of Hope: The Green Revolution in Punjab Village*. New Jersey: Rutgers University Press.
Lewis, Oscar (1958). *Village Life in North India*. Urbana: University of Illinois Press.
Maclachlan, Morgan (1983). *Why They Did Not Starve: Biocultural Adaptation in a South Indian Village*. Philadelphia: Institute for the Study of Human Issues.
Mahmood, Cynthia Keppley (1997). *Fighting for Faith and Nation: Dialogues with Sikh Militants*. Philadelphia University of Pennysylvania Press.
Majumdar, D. N. (1963). *Himalayan Polyandry Structure Functioning and Culture Change. A Case Study of Jaunsar Bawar*. Bombay: Asia Publishing House.
Mandelbaum, David (1991). *Society in India*. 5th edition. Missouri: South Asia Books.
Mankekar, Purnima (1999). *Screening Culture, Viewing Politics: An Ethnography of Television, Womanhood, and Nation in Post-colonial India*. Durham: Duke University Press.
Marcus, George E., and Michael M. J. Fischer (1986). *Anthropology as Cultural Critique: An Experimental Moment in the Human Sciences*. Chicago, IL: University of Chicago Press.
Marcus, G. E. and D. Cushman (1982). "Ethnographies as Texts". *Annual Review of Anthropology* 11:25-69.
Marriot, McKim (1955). *Village India*. Chicago: Chicago University Press.
——(1991). "On 'Constructing an Indian Ethnosociology'" *Contributions to Indian Sociology* 25: 295-308.
Mencher, Joan P. (1978). *Agriculture and Social Structure in Tamil Nadu*, Bombay: Allied Publishers Private Ltd.
Moffat, Michael (1979). *An Untouchable Community in South India: Structure and Consensus*. Princeton University Press.
Mukerji, D. P. (1948). *Modern Indian Culture*. Bombay: Hind Kitabs.
Nair, Kusum (1999). In *Defense of the Irrational Peasants: Indian Agriculture after the Green Revolution*. Chicago: University of Chicago Press.
Nash, June (1993). *We Eat the Mines and the Mines Eat Us: Dependency and Exploitation in Bolivian Tin Mines*. New York: Columbia University Press.
Nishimura, Yuko (1998). *Gender, Kinship and Property Rights: Nagarattar Womanhood in South India*.
Opler, Morris. E. (1956). "Extensions of an Indian Village". *Journal of Asian Studies* 16:5-10.
Ostor, Akos (1980). *The Play of the Gods: Locality, Ideology, Structure, and Time in the Festivals of a Bengali Town*. Chicago: University of Chicago Press.
Pandey, Gyanendra (1991). "In Defence of the Fragment: Writing about Hindu-Muslim Riots in India Today": *Representations* 37:27-55.
Perry, William James (1923). *The Children of the Sun*. London: Methuen.

——(1927) *Gods and the Men*. London.

Raheja, Gloria (1988). *The Poison in the Gift: Ritual, Prestation and the Dominant Caste in a North India Village*. Chicago: University of Chicago Press.

Radcliffe Brown, A. R. (1952). *Structure and Function in Primitive Societies*. E.E. Evans-Pritchard, ed. London: The English Language Book Society and Cohen and West Ltd.

Rao, V. V. Prakasa and V. Nandini Rao. (1988). *Marriage, the Family and Women in India*. New Delhi, India: South Asia Books.

Redfield, Robert (1947). "The Folk Society" *American Journal of Sociology* 52:293-308.

——(1973). *The Little Community and Peasant Society and Culture*. Chicago: The University of Chicago Press.

Rivers, William Halse Rivers (1906). *The Todas* New York: Macmillan.

——(1914). *The History of Melanesian Society*. Cambridge: Cambridge University Press.

Sahlins, Marshall (1974). *Culture and Practical Reason*. Chicago: University of Chicago Press.

Saraswati, B. N. (1977). The *Brahmanic Ritual Traditions*. Simla: Indian Institute of Advanced Studies.

Seymour, Susan C. (2000). *Women, Family and Child Care in India: A World in Transition*. Cambridge: Cambridge University Press

Shiva, Vandana (1988). *Staying Alive: Women, Ecology and Development*. London: Zed Books.

Singer, Milton (1972). *When a Great Tradition Modernises*. New York: Praeger Publishers.

Singh, Yogendra (1983). *Image of Man-Ideology and Theory in Indian Sociology*. Delhi: Chanakya Publications.

Sinha, Surajit (1965). "The tribe-caste Continuum." *Man-in-India* 45(1).

Smith, Grafton Elliot (1928). *In the Beginning: The Origin of Civilization*. New York: Morrow.

——(1933). *The Diffusion of Culture*. London: Watts.

Spivak, Gayatri (1987). *In Other Worlds*. New York: Methuen.

Srinivas, M. N. (1952). *Religion and Society among the Coorgs of South India*. Oxford: Oxford University Press.

Turner, Victor (1957). *Schism and Continuity in an African Society of Ndembu Village Life*. Manchester: Manchester University Press.

Van Willigen, John and Narender Chadha (1999). *Social Aging in a Delhi Neighbourhood*. Westport, Connecticut: Bergin & Garvey.

Vatuk, Sylvia (1972). *Kinship and Urbanization: White Collar Migrants in North India*. Berkeley, California: University of California Press.

Vidyarthi, L.P. (1978). *Rise of Anthropology in India* (2 volumes). New Delhi: Concept Publishing House.

Wadley, Susan (1994). *Struggling with Destiny in Karimpur, 1925-1984*. Berkeley, California: University of California Press.

Willis, Paul (1981). *Learning to Labour: How Working Class Kids Get Working Class Jobs* New York: Columbia University Press.

Wiser, William H. and Charlotte Wiser (1963). *Behind Mud Walls* 1930-1960. Berkeley, California: University of California Press.

Wissler, Clark (1929). *An Introduction to Social Anthropology*. New York: Holt.

21

Jayaprakash Narayan: From Gramdan to Sampoorna Kranti

PARTHA NATH MUKHERJI*

So much has been said and written about JP, and so much will be said about him in future, that I have decided to share my understanding of him, from the time that I came to know him personally as a young academic, interested in social movements and social change, until the time we suffered his grievous loss. I had the privilege of knowing him through the study of social movements that he tried to give shape to, courageously and selflessly, only with the intention of building a strong, democratic and egalitarian India. This is the period that JP traversed from *gramdan* to *sampoorna kranti* (Total Revolution). Such was his unique and towering personality that he could relate spontaneously with everyone with mutual respect and warmth, no matter how young or old, high or modest his/her position or status in life. My task in this paper is broadly to project JP through the movements he symbolized and embodied, as well as through my personal interactions with him, including those little things about him that mark out the great from the lay. The exposition is part anecdotal, part sociological, and part historical. I hope this will result in a sketch of the man that JP was, through the personal eyes of an academic. You will have to forgive me for being a poor, clumsy novice at his first, and perhaps last, such attempt. The portrait, however, is done with passion by one, out of many, who had the rare good fortune and privilege of close association with him, Prabhavatiji and the sarvodaya parivar since 1961. In this

* Reprinted from *Think India*, Volume 5, No. 4, October-December 2002, pp. 1-25, with the kind permission of the Editor.

presentation, the biography of JP will necessarily intersect with the minimum autobiographic essentials of an insignificant author and admirer[1]. You will have to excuse him for this unavoidable intrusion.

I come from a modest middle class family in Bihar that was in the 'background' of the freedom struggle. My Late father Narendranath Mukherjee, was one of JP's sincere friends, and in the thick of the Total Revolution days, his routine task was to read out to him the reporting on the movement from the Bengali paper Ananda Bazar Patrika. My mother Bijoya Mukherji was very close to Prabhavatiji, and when Mahatma Gandhi visited Patna in 1947 she had demonstrated to him her skill at spinning on the charkha with cotton grown in her small garden, as part of the swadeshi efforts of the Mahila Charkha Samiti, enough to draw an appreciative comment from the Mahatma.

Fresh from my Masters in Sociology from Patna University[2] in 1961, as one enamoured by the sarvodaya movement, with its radical egalitarian programme of transformation of society through non-violence, when I went to seek JP's advice on my Ph.D research, I was more than welcome. The second generation had begun relating with him. His enthusiasm with my research proposal led to my registering for Ph.D on *Gramdan in Bihar: A Sociological Analysis,* in 1963. I was given a Research Assistantship by the Gandhian Institute of Studies at Varanasi, of which JP was the Chairman. Out of nearly hundred gramdan villages, I chose to study nine—four in north Bihar and five in the south.

I had done fieldwork in four gramdan villages, when the next meeting of the Bihar Sarvodaya Sammelan was slated in the idyllic rural setting of Simaltala (a health resort close to the religious complex of Deoghar). JP called me and with a charming smile said 'You should present a brief report on the villages you have already been to'. I would have to do the presentation in Hindi before an audience of over hundred sarvodaya workers who would assemble for the annual stock taking of the constructive work and the challenges faced by the bhoodan-gramdan movement in Bihar. This was held sometime in late 1963 or early 1964.

My sarvodaya friends and I reached Simaltala two days before JP and Prabhavatiji were to arrive. On the early morning of his arrival, I jogged through several villages in the area. Out of my researcher's curiosity, I would stop at places to enquire whether they knew about his coming, and wanted to gauge how they were responding. I was shocked to find that the message had gone round that JP would come and ask them to hand over their lands in bhoodan! I shared this with concern with my sarvodaya friends, who too were taken aback by the misleading propaganda. The result was, our expectation of a large crowd waiting impatiently for JP's arrival, was belied.

When he and Prabhavatiji alighted from the train in the twilight evening, there were hardly a hundred people from the villages! I was thinking how disappointed JP would feel. As they alighted from the train, two chairs were placed just outside the small station for them to occupy. JP was his normal cheerful self as he spoke for nearly an hour to the meagre audience. He spoke with the same composure and candour as he would to an audience of 100,000! He spoke about gramdan and bhoodan and the potential this movement had for ushering in a transformed society, with their will and effort, which would be for the welfare of all. His language was informal, direct and sincere. His exposition was masterly as he translated complex abstractions into people's everyday language with simple homilies. He could do this because his fundamentals were clear. That was my first taste of his greatness. He was equally at ease, when the turnout was abysmally small. *For him audience-size made not the slightest difference, it was the message that was all-important.*

The conference was held in the house of a well-known Bengali film director Probhat Chatterjee. All the three days JP and Prabhavatiji sat together listening carefully to the reporting from all parts of state, keeping the meeting enlivened by their avid interest and inimitable sense of humour. Everyone in the audience felt they were part of a mission for a revolutionary transformation that sought to change the face of Bihar and India. At the end of the three days when JP began summarizing and making his final comments, giving direction to the workers about the work ahead, I was stunned. Even the minutest details that were relevant were not missed. The exposition knit all the sessions into one organic whole. The presentation was simple, lucid, analytical, comprehensive and above all, logically consistent. I wondered how he could do this without taking a single note during the three-day proceedings! I said to myself, he is of the intellectual stuff that would have qualified him as a National Professor had he been in the university. He had won the admiration and respect of a budding academic. This admiration grew the more I interacted with him. It was amazing how he found the time to keep abreast with the latest readings in his fields of interest. We had to be careful whenever we went for any discussion for he could raise intricate questions for which there could be no lay answers. *JP was a rare intellect.*

Coming to my part of the participation, I need to provide a brief background. The sarvodaya movement began in Pochampalli, in the present Andhra Pradesh, with Vinoba Bhave conceptualizing bhoodan (land-in-gift) in the fiery fields of Telengana armed struggle for agrarian revolution in April 1951[3]. The bhoodan momentum spontaneously evolved into gramdan in village Mangroth in Uttar Pradesh in 1952[4]. JP while visiting Mangroth for the first time exclaimed ecstatically, 'It was thrilling to visualize the great moral, economic, political and social revolution that would sweep over the country if Mangroth were repeated in every village'.

Among the gramdan villages I had studied, was the internationally exposed model village of Berain in the district of Monghyr. The village had embraced gramdan in 1956. JP was closely monitoring the forces of 'directed' change that were being released in Berain. For him it was a 'laboratory' in which a sarvodaya society was being fashioned. It was an experiment close to his heart. Underlying this experiment was his passion for ushering in a new egalitarian society. It was for this that he had chosen to make his progression from socialism to sarvodaya.

Within a short period of two to three years Berain had the distinction of attaining total adult literacy. Besides, a variety of village industries had taken root and found an immediate market. The mustard oil, the jaggeries (gur), the milk, the ghee, and all such products produced in Berain earned the rare public testimonial of being unadulterated, and therefore were sought after. Children's education was taking place in the community centre of the village, where irrespective of caste status, they were staying and eating together! Something unheard of in those days. They were introduced to the Nai Talim brand of Gandhian basic education of 'learning by doing', as they tended the flower garden and produced vegetables, along with routine studies. Many of the village construction projects found ready voluntary labour (*shramdan*) from the village. Every earning had a small component of contribution to the Sarvodaya Sahayog Samiti (Sarvodaya Cooperative Society, henceforward SSS), for capital accumulation.

There were few landowners, but all except three had pooled their lands (by making a gift of all their lands) in bhoodan. These lands were cultivated collectively. Even tenant cultivation followed a collective principle. Any landlord desiring to get his/her land cultivated by tenants from Berain had to approach the SSS, which in turn, allocated the tenancy to households in accordance with a roster system. Visitors from afar, from within and beyond the country, came and stayed in the village to witness the amazing spectacle of development carried out in the Gandhian model of rural reconstruction. Economists from the Patna University had done surveys to highlight the model of development (For details see Mukherji 1966: 33-41). Needless to say, JP and the entire sarvodaya fraternity held the two elderly veteran and respected sarvodaya leaders who had dedicated their lives to this 'successful' experiment, in great esteem. My study confirmed all these achievements, and also earned in the process the special affection of these venerated leaders for the young researcher who could relate well with the rural people and their concerns.

However, I had *two* extremely important critical observations to make, which I feared would be very embarrassing, coming as it would from a young raw research assistant. I was wondering how to put across the two points, especially when Berain had earned such international acclaim, and my audience was justifiably proud of the recognition it had brought to the movement. The *first* related to the three 'substantial'[5] landowners who had refused to pool their lands by donating them to the statutory, Bhoodan Yagna Committee, unlike all the other lesser petty landowners who had done so. These landowners were averse to taking the risk of donating their lands, so they agreed to a conditional pooling of their lands without transferring their right of ownership to the Committee. The conditions were in the form of a guarantee of supply of certain fixed quantities of paddy yield (irrespective of a good or bad harvest), and a few others, which insured more than their risks.

The village level sarvodaya leadership, found this a fit case for an experiment in 'change of heart' of these landowners. They appealed to all others, in the *gram sabha* meetings (meeting of all adult males and females), to grant them these extra concessions, so that their magnanimity would produce a change of heart in these landowners. This would eventually lead to their joining gramdan like the rest of them, making gramdan total. The gramdan villagers in deference to the wisdom of the sarvodaya *karyakartas* (workers) granted these concessions. When I visited the village, the *gram sabha* was discussing the same issue over again, as the landowners were still not prepared to give in, after several years of enjoying these concessions. The views were getting polarized, with the sarvodaya leadership appealing for giving more time to the experiment, and many villagers quite cynical that this would not work. The cynics were of the definite view that these landowners were exploiting the rest in their own narrow self-interest. Clearly, the application of the Gandhian concept of 'change of heart', in the otherwise egalitarian framework, which was introduced with gramdan, was unintentionally perpetuating class differentiation. This could do irreversible damage to this extraordinary experiment.

The *second* point, to which I wished to draw the attention of the sarvodaya members, was the well-meaning but 'patriarchal' style of operating village accounts. Although the funds that were accumulating through diligent economy were being operated with all good intentions by the venerated village level leadership, it left a latent scope for differing interpretations of how and on what items they should be spent. There was need for formalizing the operation of village accounts, and making it more transparent. I did the reporting with a frank appreciation of the great transformation that was taking place in Berain, and at the conclusion, cautioned them with respect to the two vulnerabilities to the experiment. Decades later, JP was to provide a reformulation of the Gandhian concept of 'change of heart' while steering the movement for Total Revolution[6].

Except for one or two mature senior level grassroots sarvodaya leaders, this led to anticipated emotive reactions, particularly from the two venerated sarvodaya leaders in Berain. JP was swift at responding to the situation. He explained that the observations that were made came from the objective sociological understanding of a young and well-meaning scholar, which was meant for the good of the movement, and should be taken in that spirit. He then followed up by taking the decision that the accounting system should be rationalized. *JP was a rare combination of scientific temper and had the courage of self-criticism.*

The tardy progress in the increase in the number of *gramdan* villages led Vinoba to give a clarion call for *gramdan toofan* (literally the spread of gramdan like a storm). Vinoba felt that unless an enveloping environment was created for gramdan and bhoodan, the revolution would be stalled[7]. He somehow felt strongly that the existing conditions laid down for declaring a village gramdan[8] was too stringent to attract large numbers of landowners. So he simplified these conditions and reconceptualised *sulabh gramdan*[9] (literally gramdan simplified). He made a whirlwind walking tour (*padyatra*) of the states of Assam, West Bengal and Bihar, beginning from 1965. This resulted in numerous *promissory* gramdans and bhoodan declarations. Such was the euphoria that accompanied the saint on the march that entire Development Blocks (*prakhand dan*), even entire districts (*zilla dan*) and to crown it all, by October 1969 the entire state of Bihar (*Bihar dan*), were declared as having been gifted *on the basis of just pledges*! As someone perceptively remarked, whichever way the saint passed, the storm blew the dry leaves sky-high, only to settle down after he left and the storm had subsided.

This was the biggest farce that was perpetrated on the people in the name of Gandhi and sarvodaya. It was the final undoing of the sarvodaya movement. For, after this neither were lands being gifted nor were gramdans forthcoming in any perceivable numbers. On the contrary, the movement was on reverse gear, as village after village that had embraced or pledged gramdan reverted to *status quo ante* and thousands of acres of lands obtained in bhoodan remained undistributed. The sarvodaya movement that provided a non-violent alternative to bloody agrarian conflict for bringing about rural transformation just seemed to sap.

JP, initially, seemed to suffer from a sense of perplexed ambivalence. During this period of Vinoba's stormy *padyatra*, I had several times attempted to discuss with him the bizarre nature of this programme and its sociological impracticability. I felt distressed apprehending what damage this could cause to the movement. He wouldn't contest my reservations nor would he disown the programme. He was, quite regretfully, avoiding any discussion on the topic. This was very uncharacteristic of JP. I could sense that his conscience did not permit him to share his real thinking. He seemed to have prepared himself to act as a disciplined sarvodaya worker/leader, who once having been a party to the decision was disinclined to raise the issue and would work only for its accomplishment. My impression in my interactions with his close associates was that he did express his serious reservations about the implications of diluting the concept of gramdan, but failed to convince the dominating view of Vinoba, whose charisma was overwhelming. JP's scientific and sensitive mind could anticipate the damage this programme could bring about to the movement. However, in his mind and heart he still assigned himself a position only as second in command to Vinoba, and presumably gave him the benefit of doubt. While Vinoba was simplistically attempting to simplify complex propositions, JP was searching for opportunities that would revive the sarvodaya movement. This was a period of catharsis for him, as he struggled within himself between his own rational understanding and Vinoba's intuitive spiritual and moral perception of the course that garmdan movement had to take. He had to find out for himself, empirically and scientifically, as he would later, in Musahari. *This was the Himalayan weakness of a gentle revolutionary.*

While the drama of gramdan toofan was in full swing, the bloody agrarian conflict reincarnated itself in the form of the Naxalite movement, drawing revolutionary ideological inspiration from Mao tse-tung. Just as the communists had to face the sarvodaya solution to agrarian conflict of Vinoba in Telengana in the early fifties, the Sarvodaya movement was faced with the challenge of communist revolutionaries in the sulabh gramdan fields of Musahari in the district of Muzaffarpur, in north Bihar in May 1970. The Maoists had served notices of death to two sarvodaya karyakartas[10]. The opportunity that JP was searching for was provided by this traumatic event. He decided to position himself in Musahari with Prabhavatiji, study the whole situation objectively, and engage directly in action research. Reacting to sensationalized press and radio reporting, he declared 'I look upon what I am doing not as a fight *against* anybody but as a fight *for* social and economic justice' (Narayan, 1971: 6). To him the emergence of such danger appeared as a 'Godsend' opportunity to test out sulabh gramdan on the field. He confessed:

> I had been feeling for quite sometime past that our movement was losing its fire, and we, its workers, were becoming stale and flabby of spirit. One of the reasons for this seemed to be that our work was so bland that it involved no personal danger to us, nor demanded any great sacrifice (Narayan, 1971: 6-7).

His was a competitive approach. He wished to demonstrate that the Gandhian non-violent approach was superior to the violent approach of the Naxalites. The 'ends' were not so much the bone of contention as the 'means'. There was his appreciation of the fact that the certain 'objective conditions' had led to Naxalism. He observed:

> It is not the so-called Naxalites who have fathered this violence, but those who have persistently defied and defeated the reform laws for the past so many years—be they politicians, administrators, landowners, or money-lenders. The big farmers who cheated the ceiling law through *benami* and fictitious settlement; the gentlemen who grabbed Government lands and village commons; the landowners who persistently denied the legal rights of their share-croppers and evicted them from their holdings or those who underpaid their labourers and threw them out from their homestead; the men who by fraud or force took the lands away from weaker sections; the so-called upper-caste men who looked down upon their harijan brethren and ill-treated and socially discriminated against them; the money-lenders who charged usurious interest rates and seized the lands of the poor and the weak; the politicians, the administrators and all others who aided and abetted these wrongs—it is they who are responsible for the accumulated sense of injustice, grievance and hurt among the poor and downtrodden that is now seeking its outlet through violence' (Narayan, 1971: 15).

It is not surprising that JP after his first hand study of agrarian conditions in Musahari would be interacting with the Naxalites in Bihar and West Bengal in the Total Revolution phase. He visited them in the jails in Jamshedpur and in West Bengal and pressed the two governments to treat them more humanely.

In the mid-seventies, the Maoist movement attracted my attention. I recall when JP was under virtual house arrest at the Mahila Charkha Samiti, I wished to meet Satya Narain Sinha (henceforward SNS), who was a member of Charu Mazumdar's original politburo of the Communist Party of India-Marxist Leninist (CPI-ML). By then he had his own splinter Central Committee. It was open secret that he was in regular communication with JP, visiting him surreptitiously at the Mahila Charkha Samiti. The Inspector General of Police at that time was a family friend of ours. When I casually sought to know about SNS and how best to contact him, he smilingly said, the best place to meet him was at JP's residence!

I got to know about what was going on between the two from my one of my sarvodaya friends who was facilitating these meetings. SNS was trying to impress upon JP that he was wasting his time experimenting with sarvodaya as nothing would come out of non-violence, that instead, if he took up the Naxal cause, the revolutionary gains would be immense. JP on the other hand was inducing them to join him and abjure violence! JP's proposal was clear and simple. It ran something like this, 'you give me your wholehearted support for five years. If during this period I am unable to convince you all of the superiority of non-violent action, I will have no moral authority to restrain you from going your own way'. At times, JP would even empathise with him on the lines, 'if I were in your position what I would have chosen to do'. (Which, apparently, nót being in his position, he would not do.) SNS had confided his frank admiration of JP to my sarvodaya friend. He had confessed, little did he know how great a revolutionary he was at the time they were contemplating whether or not to annihilate him in Musahari! *JP knew no fear, nor did he ever consider anybody his enemy. He had the extraordinary capacity to empathise with anyone.*

The Musahari experience of ground realities provided the real watershed of the gramdan sarvodaya movement. While JP had flung himself to personally supervise and direct the transformation process of sulabh gramdan, he soon discovered that most of the sulabh gramdan pledges were bogus as those who signed them were least inclined to honour the pledge. Within four months of his study he observed:

> As is apparent our progress has been rather slow. In many respects, this is a difficult area; yet we would have moved faster had the earlier work of obtaining gramdan pledges been properly carried out. So far we have not come across a single village where we have found the two requirements of 75 per cent of the population and 51 per cent of the land to have (been) fulfilled. So we have to telescope both the stages of obtaining and implementing pledges into one (Narayan, 1971: 26).

If the chance experience of JP in Musahari revealed this fatal flaw in obtaining sulabh gramdan, one can well imagine how gifts of entire prakhands, zillas and even states made a mockery of the gramdan movement! It is therefore, no wonder that JP in the Bhopal session of the Sarva Seva Sangh in October 1971, after satisfying himself of the truth, declared 'that the decision to pursue sulabh gramdan was a mistake'. Dada Dharmadhikari, the most respected sarvodaya philosopher opened up the issue of the mode of decision-making in the Sarva Seva Sangh, insisting that 'too rigorous an insistence on consensus was wrong, as it only served to give a veto to the minority'[11]. He was against making 'a fetish of non-violence' and urged that they 'should not be afraid of class war', and as a future strategy, urged the movement to organize the landless and the small holders, isolating the rich (Church, 1973: 11; also see Allan and Wendy Scarfe, 1997: 241). This was presumably an implicit reference to JP's difference of view with Vinoba on gramdan toofan in the Sarva Seva Sangh, which was overridden by a consensus. Hereafter, the differences between Vinoba and JP started surfacing, as also within the rank and file of the sarvodaya leaders and workers. *JP was no longer second in command.*

Much has been written on the Total Revolution phase. I do not wish to enter into this well-trodden terrain, suffice it to say that JP had transcended the gramdan sarvodaya phase of the movement and had pitch forked it to the plane of Total Revolution, where he willy-nilly became the 'revolutionary authority' in command. I shall confine myself to relating *three* little-known experiences. The *first* relates to JP's campaign prior to his pro-state surgery in Vellore (*i.e.* 29th April 1974), when he was not in a position to urinate and his urine got automatically collected in a bottle tied round his waist through a surgical perforation in the urinary tract. Inspite of his frail health he was exerting himself to a good deal lecturing, in and around Patna, travelling by car, causing us a great deal of anxiety.

Many will not know that JP never possessed a car. It was only from some few select close admirer-friends that he would request for a car when needed. My father's only car was one such with me as the chauffer as long as I was located in Patna or on occasions when I came to Patna to stay with my parents[12]. However, among them there were a few who had more than one car. So the demand on our car was only when there was a difficulty or when he wished to ride with me Illustratively, several times I took him to Sadaquat Ashram, originally the head quarters of the Indian National Congress Party, where he was personally supervising the construction of the house where President Rajendra Prasad would be staying after his retirement. At times he would ask me to take him to the Polo Grounds behind the Raj Bhavan for a walk[13] There were numerous instances when he chose to bother none and hired a rickshaw. A dentist friend of mine once related to me how he found JP sitting along with others in his clinic waiting for his chance in the queue! He had come on a rickshaw[14].

To come back to the movement scene, I felt very strongly that it was high time that JP should have a transport of his own. The need for physical mobility had increased manifold and sometimes I felt it odd that he should be travelling in some one else's car, particularly when this some one else was a well-to-do person about whom some people carried, rightly or wrongly, negative stereotypes. It occurred to me that a transport could be purchased for him, which could be so designed that he could address a public meeting sitting in it through a built-in public address system. Also, it could have enough space for him to take rest lying down, with medical emergency fittings as in a hospital ambulance. The money for this could be collected through countless (equal) small contributions ranging from rickshaw pullers to the wealthy from all parts of Bihar and India. It would be quintessentially a people's car for JP, a strong symbol for a people's movement, with the man-in-the-street having the satisfaction of a contribution, however modest. I shared this concept with my sarvodaya friends and others, who found it exciting. When I discussed this in detail with JP he was visibly moved. I said, 'you give us the green signal, and we will produce the people's car for you'. He quietly thought for a while and then said, 'not now, when the time comes, I will tell you'. I thought the whole idea was forgotten, as JP got busier by the day, moving in and out of Patna. Quite some time after, when his memory was being taxed and becoming very select, I met him in Gandhi Peace Foundation in Delhi. If I remember well, he had come for a meeting of 'Citizens for Democracy'. There was a very heavy demand on his time. The meeting lasted for about 15 minutes as I briefed him on several matters that he wished to know. When I was about to leave, he held me back with an unexpected question, 'Parth, didn't you once suggest that I could have a people's car?' When I nodded in the affirmative, he just kept quiet. I took leave. His silence spoke more than words. He knew it would have been good for the movement, but perhaps it was too late. He still couldn't give me the green signal! *JP was never swayed by cravings for personal acquisition and believed in simple, clean and efficient living.*

I chanced to be in Patna on 5th June 1974 listening to JP in the Gandhi Maidan. The whole atmosphere was surcharged as news spread of the Indira Brigade having fired upon the peaceful procession injuring 21 people. On that day JP gave expression to the concept of *Sampoorna Kranti* (Total Revolution) and assumed spontaneously the role of a 'revolutionary authority'. It all happened on its own. In an awe inspiring masterly speech he warned his people not to respond to violence with violence. He, at times, used pathological imagery to describe the condition of the society and its people, as 'rotten' (sada),'decomposed' (gala), invoking his more than half-a-million audience to recreate a new, strong, democratic non-violent society, and be prepared for sacrifices. He expressed his serious apprehension that he may be arrested any time after the day's events, but the tasks of this revolution should continue unimpeded no matter what obstacles came in the way. All the socialist and sarvodaya stalwarts were present in the audience. One-by-one he took the names of Karpoori Thakur, Ramanand Tiwary, and others. In the electrified atmosphere, each of them stood up one-by-one, as if mesmerized. To each JP assigned specific responsibilities, in case he was put behind bars. Each vowed that he would obey his command. The spectacle had to be seen to be believed. JP personified the living embodiment of a charisma par excellence. He announced *two* major programmatic decisions. *First,* was the programme of peaceful *satyagraha* from June 7 to July 12 in front of the Assembly gates, demanding its dissolution; and *second,* was the establishment of a parallel people's government (*Janata Sarkar,* henceforward JS) in the villages. The former was urban-centred, the latter, dispersed in the rural areas. The role of the youth was paramount with a vanguard role to perform. *JP was now in full command.*

I decided then and there to focus my research interests on both these programmes. During this period the persistent critique of the JP movement by the Congress Party and the Communist Party of India was that the Bihar movement was totally reactionary. They claimed that the social base of the movement was urban, upper caste and extremely narrow. Hence this movement was anti-democratic, even fascist. I decided to examine the social composition of the movement participants. JP's call for peaceful *satyagraha* before the Assembly provided the opportunity.

Soon after the commencement of the *satyagraha,* with the cooperation of one of JP's closest lieutenants, Tripurari Sharan (presently Adhyaksh, Shokhodeora Ashram, JP's ashram in Bihar), a so-called bio-data form (*Jeevan Parichay*) was designed. The idea was to get the satyagrahis 'kind of' registered with this form, by asking them to fill it up. They arrived in batches from various parts of the state in the evenings. On the morning following their arrival, they were given orientation on how they were expected to conduct themselves non-violently no matter what the instigation, while offering satyagraha. Then they were asked to fill up the *Jeevan Parichay* forms before proceeding to the Assembly site. Some 1260 forms could be filled up in 25 days, out of 36 protest days. The analysis made interesting reading.

The satyagrahis converged into Patna from all districts of Bihar, except West Champaran. They were demographically very young with more than 50 per cent below the age of 21 and over 75 per cent below 26 years. Female participation was only 6.6 per cent. They were overwhelmingly Hindus (90 per cent), a little over two per cent declared themselves non-believers and 6.6 per cent maintained silence on this. Only 17 Muslims and two Christians participated. Of the 55.8 per cent who revealed their caste identity, 22.5 per cent were upper castes (including 5.1 per cent Brahmin; 6.2 per cent Bhumihar Brahmin; 3.2 per cent Kayastha; Rajput 8 per cent) and the rest 32.3 per cent were Backward and Scheduled Castes.

Interestingly, more than half of them (54 per cent) had received school, college or university education. A substantial number were illiterate (35.4 per cent). Even if we discount the student population of 50.4 per cent, an impressive 20 per cent came from the rural areas. Sixty per cent of the students reported their father's rural-based occupations. Thus the movement composition had an agrarian bias. The working class and the poor sector constituted 17.3 per cent. In comparison the response of the professions and business sector was not high. When it came to landownership, only 53 per cent declared their asset status. Of these, 55 per cent had land in excess of 1 acre, but 32 per cent owned land between 1-5 acres, whilst about 11 per cent had between 6-10 acres of land. The landless and the marginal landowners (less than one acre) constituted a meagre 2.9 per cent. Those with household incomes less than Rs.1000 per annum were 33.5 per cent, while those earning between Rs.1000-2000 were 14.1 per cent. Nearly 35 per cent did not declare their incomes (See Mukherji, 1986: 261-62).

Thus the satyagrahis were young, mostly students; they were rural based and male-predominant; they were mostly literate or educated; they came from all over the state and even beyond; they were heavily drawn from the Backward and Scheduled Castes. The movement participants spanned a broad spectrum—higher income groups and illiterates; agrarian classes and urban professionals; working classes, middle classes and owners of the means of production; upper and non-twice-born castes. Conspicuous by their absence were the tribals and the urban-industrial working class. The mobilization was urban-centered but not urban-centric (Mukherji, 1986: 262-63).

The ideological persuasions of the movement participants suggest that nearly 63 per cent had no clear ideological position. Of the 37 per cent that did have a political background, 31.9 per cent were of socialist or Gandhian persuasion, less than 5 per cent identified themselves with the Jana Sangh, whilst less than one percent was Marxist (Mukherji, 1986: 264-65). It was the youth, largely apolitical (in the sense of not being attached to any political party) and yet politically conscious, that emerged in the vanguard role as a mobiliser of general discontent and initiator of protest under the overall leadership of JP. This study was reported by the Hindi weekly *Dinman* and the English paper *Everyman*, while the movement was in its full heat.

It was not until 10th September 2000 that the full implications and significance of this study was brought to my knowledge. I was allowed special hospitality by the Gandhi Sangrahalaya, Patna, by its esteemed Director, my good friend Razi Saheb, on condition that I give a talk on JP.

I chose to speak on 'JP Today'. The talk was presided over by Hemant, a distinguished journalist of the Times of India group of papers, himself a product of JP's movement for Total Revolution. He gave the welcome speech, in which he revealed, to my great and pleasant surprise, that he was one of those who had filled up the *Jeevan Parichay* and courted arrest outside the Bihar Assembly! He then narrated what followed after his arrest with hundreds of others. All the jail inmates used to read the newspapers, hear the news on the radio and engage in constant and animated analysis about the prospects of the movement. The criticisms about the movement that appeared in the papers were more or less along the lines I have already described earlier. They could see clearly that the government was employing a repressive strategy of containment consistent with the assumption that there was not much to worry about the movement as it was localized to the urban areas with a narrow urban social base. Hemant and his group was confused about how to assess the depth and extension of the movement. It is at such a juncture that the report of our study appeared in *Dinman*. The report brought a sudden surge of elation among them, as well as apprehensions of dim forbodings. They now came to learn that the movement had indeed penetrated the rural areas extensively, a calculation that the government had so far dismissed. The group came to predict that with the movement having snowballed with such great rapidity, the forces of transformation were getting stronger with the day and would continue to do so. So, the revolutionary moment for which they were waiting with impatient expectation and suspense had actually arrived. The time to take the plunge with all one's non-violent might and resolve was at hand. It could wait no longer. On the other hand, they were very sure that repression of the state would be mounted manifold in a desperate move to stall this snowballing before it consumed them. There was no guarantee that the fire would not engulf the other states as well. Having shared this inside story in the prison camps, Hemant proceeded to present the data of my study and analysed it in detail. I was awe-struck, as too were the large audience gathered on the occasion[15].

The concept of *Janata Sarkar* (henceforward, JS) also evoked a lot of criticism and misgivings. JP was at pains to explain that this did not constitute a parallel government in defiance of the existing government of the state. It was aimed, more positively, at developing and institutionalising the people's organ of power at the grassroots level, to combat corruption, help resolve disputes outside law courts, engage in rural reconstruction through *gram sabha*, act as a watch dog of the developmental activities, help people to nominate potential candidates for electoral office, and so on. Perhaps in today's jargon it would be more appropriately fitting to call this *parallel governance* rather than parallel government.

Since time was a constraint, I requested my sarvodaya friends to name one JS experiment that I could study and learn from, in terms of the potential it had. They were unanimous in suggesting Raghopur in the district of Saharsa, in north Bihar. It is important to know a little about the background of Raghopur. At the time that JP had parked himself in Musahari, in September 1970, at its Paunar meeting, the Sarva Seva Sangh selected Raghopur for concentrating their efforts in *gram swarajya* and gramdan work. Sarvodaya luminaries like Dhirendra Mazumdar, Nirmala Deshpande and Krishna Raj visited the area exhorting people to respond to *sulabh gramdan*. By February 1974, disappointed with the overall impact of Raghopur, Vinoba declared that it be given one more month to prove its efficacy, or else the programme could be 'terminated'. Interestingly, Raghopur still recalled with collective nostalgia its role in 1942 when JP and Ram Manohar Lohia, the two socialist stalwarts conducted the underground movement during the freedom struggle. So when JP visited the village in 1974 and observed that not much had changed since then and exhorted them to have faith in the youth for bringing about true democracy, it was like a shot in the arm of a people who felt like re-living the past. The *Janata Sarkar* had come into being in Raghopur by January 1975.

I was in Raghopur sometime in June 1975. Subh Murti, of the Tarun Shanti Sena, who was engaged in gram swarajya work of the Sarva Seva Sangh, provided the main leadership as coordinator (*Sanyojak*) of the (a) Executive Committee (*Karyapalika*), and (b) the Finance Committee (*Artha samiti*) of the newly established JS. There was also a judiciary (*Nyayapalika*) and corresponding to it, a People's Court (*Janata Adalat*). By the time I had reached, the effect of parallel governance was palpably visible. By January 1975, as many as 150 cases of dispute were orally disposed off to the satisfaction of the contending parties. Thereafter, the procedure became formalised. Complaints were now invited in writing. The *Sanyojak* would then put it across to the Nyayapalika, which was constituted of seven members. The parties in conflict would sit with the members of Nyayapalika. If the matter were resolved the 'judgment' would be awarded then and there. If not, it would be referred to the *Sanyojak* and other members. The process would continue in this fashion in an attempt to resolve the problem to the mutual satisfaction of both the parties. Even if this did not work out, only then, would the matter be referred to the Court of Law.

By March 23, the JS presented a 'rate chart' of essential commodities (passed on from Muzaffarpur to Saharsa to Raghopur) to the Block Development Office. This led to certain essential commodities like Sunlight soap, match boxes, etc. becoming unavailable for a time. However, the prices and supply of rice and wheat could be firmly maintained. Contraband rice coming from Nepal was impounded by the JS and sold in the market at the fixed rates in the presence of the owners, and the proceeds of the sale handed over to them. The foodstuffs produced in the area would have to be sold in the area first, then the surplus would be allowed out for trade. Vigilance committees were attached to each panchayat to watch and monitor the behaviour of subsidised government Fair Price Shops[16]. Earlier, diesel was supplied only to pump owners for irrigation, now at the instance of the JS it was also supplied direct to those who rented pumps. Corrupt practices of senior and petty officials alike were effectively checked with firmness. They were able to perfect an elaborate intelligence system with amazing penetration into the government offices and all other institutions in the area, which was an indicator of the positive environment created by the movement for Total Revolution. Even heavy weight Congress leaders like Lalit Narayan Mishra and Jagannath Mishra, who belonged to Saharsa, could not face up to the activism of the JS[17].

Notwithstanding these remarkable achievements within a very short span of time, the JS, constituted of the Chhatra Sangharsh Samiti and Jan Sangharsh Samiti, experienced its share of problems. The ideologically weak members occasionally became victims of actions not easily condonable. Occasional incidents of violence and financial irregularities tarnished the fair image of JS. The well-trained and mature leadership of the Tarun Shanti Sena swiftly responded by self-criticism and retributive/corrective action. Apart from these inevitable costs of the movement, the main problematic was the sustainability of the JS, in the absence of a stable resource base. However, this dilemma was short lived with the unleashing of the repressive hand of Emergency.

The growing influence of the JS in Raghopur under the very nose of Lalit Narayan Mishra, only confirmed the analysis of Hemant and his group, that the Congress Party in power could ill afford to ignore the menacing spread of the movement. JP could not be taken for granted any longer. In Delhi he drew a crowd of one million. Wherever he went, the aura of the revolutionary personality attracted the common people in large multitudes. The only way to hold on to power was by invoking the Emergency[18], not allowing him even the electoral opportunity to prove his credentials with the masses through a challenge that the Prime Minister had herself thrown at him with contempt.

The movement praxis witnessed the resurrection of non-violent direct action and the philosophy of Gandhian *satyagraha*. The movement participants had to be socialized into a long forgotten style of militant non-violent protest, which knew no defeat, which brought success through self-suffering, without inflicting physical harm to the opponent. It was a contest in which, ideally, the vanquished did not suffer from a sense of humiliation and victory was for a cause.

JP was released from Chandigarh ultimately on 12th November 1975, under mounting public pressure about his failing health. He was straight away admitted to the All India Institute of Medical Sciences in New Delhi. I remember vividly visiting him along with my dear colleague Late Professor (Mrs.) Urmila Phadnis. As we entered the floor of the Special Ward where he was allotted the last room on the eastern side of the corridor, two policemen were sitting there with a register to record the names of visitors I was already in a sad and bad mood. This arrangement incensed both Urmila and me. I refused to enter my name and sign. I told the policemen, I am going to meet our foremost citizen, any objection? They were merely performing their duty, they remarked, in a voice of regret and deference, and did not insist on our signing. When our turn came, we again encountered another policeman outside his door, at whom also I flung a remark. He quietly nodded looking remorseful. The spectacle that met our eyes simply overwhelmed us. JP was weeping incessantly, uncontrollably, and murmuring incoherently about the tragedy that had overtaken the country. As I extended my hand, he put it on his chest. Urmila was simply aghast and stupefied. We uttered a few words of encouragement. But it was he who was weeping and talking all the time. Finally, the words just came to me and I said slowly and deliberately, meaning every word that I uttered 'JP, once a lion, always a lion. You are a lion. What will happen to us if you break down? We are waiting for you to play your historic role. All is not over yet'. He gave a faint smile and pressed my hand even more firmly. Then we left wishing him speedy recovery. The next day, I shared this mortifying experience with my friend Sudhir Kakkar, who was then a Senior Fellow of the Indian Council of Social Science Research, attached to our Centre for the Study of Social Systems in Jawaharlal Nehru University. Is he going to lose his mental health in this state of acute depression? I felt somewhat relieved when Sudhir assured me that it was, on the contrary, good for him that he was letting out his long accumulated, pent up emotions. Fortunately, for us Sudhir's diagnosis turned out to be more than correct. JP gave a pulverizing reply to Mrs. Indira Gandhi in the general elections soon after the Emergency was lifted. I am reminded of two events after the Emergency, which I would like to record. Both these occurrences took place when I was in Patna continuously for two weeks at the instance of Mr. J. P. Naik, the then Member-Secretary of the ICSSR. I used to be with him from morning till evening at his insistence at the Mahila Charkha Samiti, trying to be generally helpful. Consequently, I became a party to almost all that happened during this period.

Karpoori Thakur was already the Chief Minister of Bihar. JP, during this period was undergoing dialysis at home three days a week. On the days he was on dialysis the entrance to the first floor, where he stayed would be locked. Again on JP's and Prabhavatiji's wish, the massagist, who used to loosen his cramping muscles when on dialysis, was relieved as I volunteered to combine this function by his bedside. Such was the state of his memory that he would not be able to recall in the afternoon, whom he met in the forenoon, or what he had spoken to whom during the day, except very very selectively. His 'immediate memory recall' had become extremely weak. But, astonishingly, whenever he discussed anything, politics or political history or anything, he spoke with his usual consistency recalling everything relevant to the subject. This was something extraordinary, and political and social luminaries kept on meeting him during the time periods permitted by the physician.

On one such occasion, Karpoori Thakur[19], then Chief Minister of Bihar, accompanied by Pranab Chatterjee (who was then the Speaker of one of the Legislative Houses), came to meet with JP and was closeted with him for some time. Immediately after their departure, JP told me that both came to take his signature on a statement, purportedly by him, but drafted by them, on the reservation policy that was on the anvil. This was going to be released to the press for the next morning edition of the news. Then he showed me the statement he had signed. I do not recollect the exact content of the statement, but I was greatly disturbed, because I knew instantly that this could not be JP's view. I also had the greatest regard for Karpoori Thakur and his integrity. I sensed that he might be acting under political compulsions. I sincerely felt that what was going to happen might not be good for either him or JP. I immediately asked JP if what he had signed was truly his honest view? It was apparent that he had either not read the statement carefully, or did not give it much thought. Extremely close as he was to Karpoori Thakur and Pranab Chatterjee, and in his given state of health, he had not exerted himself over the contents and its implications.

Now it was his turn to feel extremely worried and uncomfortable. His close associate Devendra Prasad Singh was immediately summoned. When he arrived with another friend, we discussed the statement in detail. Clearly, the publication of the statement would create an embarrassing situation. He asked Devendrababu to rush to the press with a letter from him to get the statement withdrawn. This was done and Karpoori Thakur was informed. To the best of my knowledge, JP did not give any statement on this issue. What is known now as Karpoori Thakur formula for Backward castes reservation policy, I conjecture, must have given some credence to the perspective of JP.

There is another incident that is worth sharing. Normally, with every dialysis, the first couple of hours would be very discomforting, with muscle cramps in the calves and thighs. The last two hours he would be in deep sleep. Then he would wake up and listen to some recorded music or poetry. On one of these dialysis days, the tape recorder played a long poem on the great Mahabharat characters Karna and her mother Kunti. I never knew that the great Hindi poet Ramdhari Singh Dinkar had rendered Tagore's *Karna Kunti Sangbad* in Hindi with such meticulousness, evoking emotions no less than Tagore's poem. Basically, a mortified Karna asks Kunti, why he was deprived of the knowledge that he was her son. The poem ends with Karna agreeing to sacrifice himself for Arjuna. Karna was Tagore's hero, not so much Arjuna. I was stunned to see tears rolling out of JP's eyes when the recitation was nearing its end. Quietly, he exclaimed, 'What a great character!'

I would like to conclude with one more event (to which I was not a witness). This was Indira Gandhi's meeting with JP at the Mahila Charkha Samiti. She, now out of power, went to visit him at the Mahila Charkha Samiti, after a humiliating defeat at the hustings. JP, as mentioned earlier, was being dialysed three days a week after the irreparable damage that was done to his kidneys during his imprisonment, for which none else than she was responsible. She had gone to seek his blessings. JP blessed her and even expressed his opinion that if she acted with maturity and honesty in the interest of the people and democracy, she had a bright future ahead! Many, who had been aggrieved by Mrs. Gandhi during the Emergency and shared the pain of JP's incarceration, did not take kindly to this act of JP. *This was the stuff in JP that made him what he was.*

Witnessing the contemporary scenario, one may be prompted to ask, 'what is the relevance of JP today and his movement for *Sampoorna Kranti*? What good did it bring to the country?' There could be many answers to this, and no less counter questions. But I would only make *two* points. *First*, that the movement for Total Revolution exposed the vulnerability of Indian democracy at that time, but also at the same time, provided its safeguard for the future. Constitutional subversion of democracy will no longer be easy in this country, at least for quite some time. *Second*, any social movement, particularly of a transformatory dimension, leaves a residual deposit in the collective memory of a society, which continues to exist in a state of latency. Objective conditions and historic conjunctures can witness their repeated manifestation, over the infinite expanse of time, albeit not in exactly the same form. The Gandhi—Vinoba-JP inspired movement for social revolution is one of this genre.

NOTES

1. I am doing this at the request of the editor, who seriously feels that all that we can document on JP must not be lost.
2. JP was instrumental in introducing Sociology at the Master's level in Patna University, He himself had a Master's in Sociology from the University of Ohio in 1929 (Prasad 2002: 3).
3. One Ramchandra Reddy created history by donating 100 acres of land to Vinoba in response to his appeal.
4. Bhoodan literally means land-in-gift, and gramdan means village-in-gift.
5. These were 'substantial' landowners only in a relative sense. All three of them owned lands below 4 acres. In a village of 88 households, the total pooled land was about 20 acres. It was a village of landless and marginal peasants with very smallholdings.
6. Decades later, he came to the conclusion that 'change of heart' in persons did not take place on its own, there was need to build an environment of social or political pressure. When he proposed the organization of the 'oppressed', to bring about a 'change of heart' among the oppressors through non-violent action, many in the sarvodaya movement felt uncomfortable, thinking he was relapsing into Marxist language.
7. Vinoba realized, 'if the people would not take the big step to economic equality all at once, the proper course was a more limited programme to which they could agree. The important point was to spread the *idea* so that it would lead to further acts of altruism and to change in the whole socio-economic atmosphere (Church, 1973: 7).
8. The definition of a gramdan village did not coincide with the government revenue village on the basis of which land records were maintained by the government. A gramdan village could even be a satellite settlement of a revenue village with a minimum of 10 households. Such a settlement (of 10 or more households) would qualify as a gramdan village provided: (a) 80 per cent of all such households in the settlement, including landowners and landless, decided to form a gramdan village; (b) if the number of such landowners who decided to declare gramdan were 80 per cent of all landowners of the village settlement; and (c) if at least 50 per cent of the total owned land of the settlement was gifted in gramdan.
9. In a sulabh gramdan village 'Proprietors of land, in addition to the regular contribution of produce, have to donate one-twentieth of their land in the village for re-distribution among the landless, and have also to surrender their legal title in their land to the Gram Sabha, retaining, however, the right of possession (except for the donated area), the right of usufruct (except for the contribution to the Gram Kosh), and the right of inheritance. Their right of alienation is limited by two conditions: (a) prior permission of the Gram Sabha; and (b) restriction of sale or mortgage only to Gramdan inhabitants of the village in question' (Narayan, 1971: 21-22).
10. These sarvodaya workers were Badri Narayan Sinha and Gopalji Mishra, President and Secretary of District Sarvodaya Mandal, Muzaffarpur.

11. All decisions in the Sarva Seva Sangh were taken by consensus.
12. I recall, once when I went to Mahila Charkha Samiti to take him somewhere, he was accompanied by an elderly VIP leader of Bihar. The VIP took the back seat and beckoned JP to sit next to him. JP smiled and simply said, 'I will sit with Parth', and sat next to the chauffeur's seat. Later he told me that I should not sit on the back seat when the driver had none sitting next to him, because that would reflect that you hold your status to be superior to the driver's. I learnt the lesson of a lifetime.
13. On one such occasion I remember to have asked him a question that had intrigued me often. For leaders of your stature, I asked him, wasn't it very difficult to learn the correctness of a situation through briefings? After all, how can you be sure that briefings were not motivated? Besides, those who could give you the truthful picture, and who you might have liked to hear, may not find access to you! He had remarked that indeed this was a real problem. The only way to go about it was to deliberately listen to persons holding different or opposing viewpoints and to have trustworthy friends who would not misguide you. In spite of all this, he admitted this risk was always there.
14. My friend related to me in detail that JP had dropped in without prior appointment. When he wanted to attend to him immediately after the patient-in-hand, he insisted that he would take his turn, as he had not come with an appointment. This episode left a lasting impression on my friend and he remained ever devoted to him, sharing this experience with countless others.
15. It is important to mention here that I did this study out of a small project grant of Rupees Five Thousand made available by the ICSSR. I had parked the project with the Gandhi Peace Foundation. Later on, during Emergency, the ICSSR was asked to explain why an academic staff of the Jawaharlal Nehru University was allowed to park the project in the Gandhi Peace Foundation! This only validates the observation of Hemant.
16. The Chhatra Sangharsh Samiti (Student's Struggle Committee), Jan Sangharsh Samiti (People's Struggle Committee) and Tarun Shanti Sena (Youth Peace Force) were organizational structures that came up with the Bihar movement. The former two were organizations directly recruited from civil society, whilst the last, was a wing of the sarvodaya movement. They had their decentralised units at the district, block and panchayat levels, wherever the movement had gained momentum. In the district of Saharsa, where the movement was fairly strong, these organizational bodies integrated with the Janata Sarkar operations in Raghopur. The Janata Sarkar functionaries in Raghopur were drawn from the Tarun Shanti Sena and the other two bodies.
17. Lalit Narayan Mishra was a cabinet minister in the Central Government, whilst Jagannath Mishra, later became the Chief Minister of Bihar. They were brothers and members of the Congress Party.
18. Emergency was declared on 26th June 1975.
19. I had known Karpoori Thakur since the time I was studying the Gramdan movement. He was then a socialist MLA and a dynamic young politician. One of the Gramdan villages, Bharadia, was in his Assembly constituency. He devoted a lot of time and energy for the development of the village. It was initially Bharadia which brought us close to each other.

REFERENCES

Church, Richard : *Vinoba Bhave, Jayaprakash Narayan and Indian Democracy*, Paper presented at the Canadian Society for Asian Studies, University of Guelph, May 23-26, 1973.

Narayan, Jayaprakash : *Face to Face*, Varanasi, Navchetna Prakashan, 1971.

Scarfe, Allan and Wendy: *JP His Biography*, New Delhi, Orient Longman Ltd., 1997.

Mukherji, Partha N.: *Sarvoday after Gandhi: Contradictions and Change*, in Ramashray Roy (ed.), *Contemporary Crisis and Gandhi*, Delhi, Discovery Publishing House, 1986.

Mukherji, Partha: *Gramdan in Village Berain, a Sociological Analysis*. Human Organization, Vol. 25, No.1, Spring 1966.

Prasad, Bimal : *The Making of JP's Vision*, Think India, Vol. 5, No. 3, July-September 2002.

22

India's Experiments with Decentralization: A Historical Account*

S.N. JHA

The need for decentralization in India has long been felt because of the size and the complexities (religious, ethnic, linguistic, cultural, agro-climatic etc.) of the Indian polity. However, the schemes of decentralization introduced from time-to-time differed depending upon the governing ideologies and requirements of the prevailing regimes.

In the last quarter of the 18th century, the colonial rule created District administration making the District Collector as the effective head of decentralized administration. By the time rule of the Crown was formalized in the middle of the 19th century, the need for more effective forms of local administration was emphasized by Ripon's Resolution of 1882 and more comprehensively by the Royal Commission on Decentralization in 1909. These schemes of decentralization were clearly administrative, governed by the requirements of the centralized colonial state.

Decentralization became important after Independence to meet the twin objectives of the Indian polity, namely, democracy and development. The early 1950s saw the introduction of the Constitution, the electoral process, and planned development. Different schemes to promote decentralization with a view to actualising the goals of an effective

* Some of the material included in this paper has been taken from my article in *Decentralization and Local Politics*, S.N. Jha and P.C. Mathur, eds. Sage Publications, New Delhi, 1999.

democratic process and planned development of all the regions were introduced since 1950.

This Paper attempts to present an overview of the various efforts at decentralization.

Local Self-government Institutions

Local institutions were introduced in India in the last quarter of the 17th century for the urban areas and, two centuries later, in the rural areas. The city of Madras (now renamed Chennai) was the first to have a Municipal Corporation in 1687 to be joined by the other two Presidency towns of Bombay (now renamed Mumbai) and Calcutta (now Kolkata) in 1720. These institutions were given 'municipal' status under the Acts of 1842 and 1850. By the time Mayo's Resolution of 1870 was put into force, there were about 200 municipalities throughout British India (Tinker 1954). Decentralization Commission and the Government of India Acts of 1919 and 1935 further strengthened the urban local institutions both in terms of functions as well as their popular base. Generally, there are four types of urban local bodies in India, namely, Municipal Corporations, Municipal Committees, Notified Area Committees and Cantonment Boards. With the expansion of the urban areas, the emergence of new areas branded as 'urban' by successive censuses, and the complexity of the 'urban phenomenon', some new institutions have come in the picture for specific purposes like urban land management, housing and management of public utilities. While the number of such organizations has grown with new challenges being faced by urban areas, most of these have been allowed to run parallel, with little attention paid to their integrated functioning.

While municipal organizations have languished under the mounting urban pressures, ever-increasing functions and receding finances, new organizations have emerged, often trapped by the same forces and factors that have been affecting the municipal bodies. There has been no effort to integrate the urban bodies into the planning process, though successive Five Year Plans have lamented the state of urban management. The Rural-Urban Relationship Committee (1966) pointed out the need for integrating urban and rural areas into comprehensive planning process and the National Commission for Urbanization (1985) reviewed the urban challenge faced by the country and suggested improvements.

For rural areas, the two institutions that took shape in stages were the District Board and the Village *Panchayat* (Jha, 1972). It was the logic of events and of necessity that was responsible mainly for the system of local administration in the earlier stages of British rule. Between the pressures of a section of public opinion and Parliament in England and the British officials serving in the 'outlying parts' of India, some welfare activities were undertaken, which included education, roads, bridges, ferries and hospitals. Local resources for such activities were sought from rich people of the areas where the facilities were provided. Such arrangement became more pressing because of 'the post-Mutiny financial embarrassment of the Indian Government' (Tinker, 1954: 5; Mishra, 1970: 596). This, in turn, gave rise to demands from the contributors for participation in the management of activities. The Local Rates Act of 1871 in UP created the Local Funds Committee to advise the District Collector. Ripon's Resolution of 1882 provided for institutions at the *Taluk* level, as also for the district board. The recommendations of the Royal Commission on Decentralization, and Government of India Resolutions of 1915 and 1918, strengthened the district boards, both in terms of functions and representation. By the time India became independent, district boards had become established institutions.

The Village Panchayat was another local institution that revived the tradition of Panchayat of ancient 'Village Republics'. The role of these Panchayat was mainly to settle disputes; where 'caste panchayats' existed this function was quite visible. While the consensual nature of these Panchayats provided a sound background, the Famine Commission and Ripon's Resolution of 1882 emphasized the necessity for a village Panchayat as an institution of local self-government. Decentralization Commission Report was more emphatic in this regard: '...it is most desirable, alike in the interests of decentralization and in order to associate the people with local tasks of administration that an attempt should be made to constitute and develop Village Panchayats for the administration of local village affairs'. Many provinces introduced Village Panchayats with limited functions and coverage. The institution got willing support from the leaders of the freedom movement and became an integral part of Gandhian ideology.

The two institutions of the district board and the Village Panchayat were in existence at the time of Independence. Alongside some other institutions like Land Management Committees of Gaon Samaj, Uttar Pradesh enacted the Zamindari Abolition and Land Reforms Act of 1951. All these institutions ran parallel to each other, covering almost the same area(s), but owing their existence to separate legal authorizations and often following different organizing principles. The requirements of planning, specifically of the elaborate programmes of rural development, made it necessary to have an integrated network of rural institutions.

Planning Imperatives

Commitment to planned development had become part of the Congress programme in the penultimate phase of the freedom movement. The Government of India set up the Planning Commission within weeks of coming into force of the Constitution. The planning process acquired a new thrust when the Second Five Year Plan was formulated setting the stage for the 'interventionist' Indian state that continued till the 1990s.

In terms of the complexity of the task of the planning process, it was necessary to have a broad framework of policies and institutions, as well as an effective machinery for implementation. The inclusive nature of planning also required integrated institutional network to carry out the programmes of development. Institutions of local self-government in the form of district boards and Village Panchayats had to be integrated for a unified working. These institutions came to be viewed as institutions of rural development, which broadened the institutional perspective.

From the administrative point of view, the 'districts' have been the basic units of local administration since they were introduced in the last quarter of the 18th century. Though some authors trace this local unit of 'territorial administration' to the Mauryan kings, the Gupta empire and later to the Mughal system of revenue administration (Rai, 1965: 644-46), the district as the basic unit of British administration had its beginning in 1772 with the appointment of a Collector at the District level (Mishra, 1965). The actual role of the Collector took shape as a result of the competing models of local administration in the form of the Cornwallis system and the Munro system (Sachidanand, n.d.: 7-13); it was stabilized as a powerful administrative unit of British administration after 1857. Subsequent exhortations by the Famine Commission and Decentralization Commission and increasing importance of 'law and order' with the progress of the freedom movement, made the district the hub of the territorial administrative unit concerned with the two major administrative objectives, namely, collection of revenue and maintenance of law and order.

Below the district, the taluk, or tehsil, the village were the revenue units. The urban areas had municipal agencies of different types depending upon the size of urban settlements. The District Collector was in charge of the 'line' administration. The power and prestige attached to the position of the collector and the importance that the civil servants themselves attached to their experience as 'district officers' was an indication of its pivotal position (Woodruff, 1953). These units of local administration remained almost intact after Independence.

While institutions of local self-government of district board and Village Panchayat, and the municipal institutions and the units of local administration like the district, the taluk (or the tehsil) and the village, evolved into full-fledged institutions, they remained parallel to each other. So long as the concept of management of local matters remained dominated by considerations of revenue collection and maintenance of law, the overall control of the Collector worked well. With increasing participation, and even control of local institutions (like the district boards and municipal bodies of urban areas) by leaders of the freedom movement, there were many instances of conflicts between the local self-government institutions of local administration (Jha, 1979).

The logic of decentralized institutions changed significantly in two directions. One, the logic and rationale of local administration changed from 'revenue collection' and 'law and order' to development, making new demands and requiring new orientations. Two, the process of planning required integration of the institutions of local self-government and of local administration. This was by no means an easy task. Issues like the position and role of the District Collector and selection of the primary unit of decentralization between the district, the village and the intermediate units like the taluk or the tehsil or the block, occupied a central place in discussion on decentralization.

Planning for Rural Development and the Emergence of Panchayati Raj

Rural development had received priority since the 1920s. Several programmes and experiments in different parts of the country were 'carried out by charismatic leaders with or without outside resource support (and those) executed through individual initiatives generally but with the resource support of the state' (Ray, n.d.: 2). Mention may be made in this regard of programmes such as: Tagore's *Sriniketan* experiment, Hatch's *Martandam* experiment in Kerala, Gandhi's *Wardha* and *Sabarmati* experiments, Bryne's *Gurgaon* experiment, Krishnamachari's *Baroda* experiments and *Firka Development Scheme* in the then Madras Presidency. While these experiments influenced the form and programme of rural development that was started in 1952, Albert Mayer's *Etawah Project* and S.K. Dey's *Nilokheri Experiment* were coterminous with Independence. In fact, the Etawah Project proved to be a 'trial run' for the Community Development Programme that was launched in a big way in October 1952, on Gandhiji's birthday.

The Community Development Programme (CDP) became part of the First Five Year Plan and was implemented with assistance from the Technical Cooperation Programme Agreement between the Government of India and the United States of America, which was signed in May 1952. The philosophy and the organization of the Programme have been extensively analyzed in the vast literature on the subject. The Programme was initiated with a great deal of enthusiasm and hope. By May 1953, when the Community Project Administration presented its first report to Parliament, work had started in 417 blocks covering 43,350 villages affecting the lives of almost 35 million people. A complete coverage of the country with Development Blocks by October 1963 was mentioned in the Third Five-Year Plan. The programme and the network of National Extension Service Blocks was by far the most extensive decentralized scheme of administration for rural development in India. Writers (Taylor, Ensminger, Johnson and Joyce, 1965) have ably discussed the features of this Programme that marked significant departure from the accepted system of administration in India. Three such features that are relevant for the present discussion are: the style and orientation of administration, the structure of new development administration and the element of people's participation that was a part of the basic assumptions and objectives of the Programme.

The CDP marked a departure from earlier attempts of rural reconstruction in two directions. First, with regard to its orientation, the method to be adopted was 'extension' in place of 'executive methods' (Dube, 1967: 159). The government officers were to act as agents and persuaders for change, rather than officers to administer laws. Second, the Programme advanced a structure of integrated administration, especially at the block level, emphasizing horizontal coordination of different activities in place of the vertical command structure of 'line' administration. Indian bureaucracy felt uncomfortable about this 'administrative innovation' from the beginning and in course of time, 'horizontal co-ordination' gave way to 'vertical line control' of government departments, with emphasis on special programmes (*e g.*, food production under IADP) and programmes aimed at specific target groups (*e.g.* programmes for the poor, for backward areas, for rural employment and for ecologically disadvantaged areas). The existing government departments alongside of those that were created, bypassing the CDP network, administered these programmes.

The Block level was actually new introduction in the administrative structure of development: the district and the village, the other two levels, had existed for long. Blocks at the intermediate level were especially created, though little is known as to how this delimitation was actually done (Dubhashi, 1963: 191-261). In 1966, the Madhya Pradesh government announced the abolition of the post of Block Development Officer; other states like Haryana, Punjab and Bihar followed suit. By the 1970s the Block machinery was in shambles. Since democratic decentralization was introduced in 1959 as a supplement to the CDP, the eclipse of the latter was coterminous with 'the phase stagnation (1965-69) and the phase of decline (1969-77)' of the Panchayati Raj (Asoka Mehta Committee Report 1978: 4).

The CDP was subjected to rather frequent evaluation and within five years of its introduction, the blame for its lapses was placed squarely at the doors of the 'people' who, it was pointed out, did not 'participate' in the Programme. The Balvantrai Mehta Committee appointed in 1956 to examine this problem, felt that:

> Development cannot progress without responsibility and power. Community development can be real only when the community understands its problems, realizes its responsibilities, exercises its necessary powers through its chosen representatives and maintains a constant and intelligent vigilance on local administration. With this objective we recommend an early establishment of statutory elective bodies and devolution to them of the necessary resources, power and authority.
> [Asoka Mehta Committee Report, 1978: 2-3].

The National Development Council endorsed the three-tier scheme of Democratic Decentralization in 1958. The states of Rajasthan and Andhra Pradesh took the lead in establishing the Panchayati Raj (PR) institutions in 1959. Other states followed soon.

By the time another review was undertaken in 1978, the total number of gram panchayats, covered 90 per cent of the rural population; 4,974 blocks had 4,033 samitis, since some had opted for districts and taluks as the key unit. In 399 districts a total of 262 zilla parishads were created with varying degrees of actual power (Asoka Mehta Committee Report, 1978: 3).

The Village Panchayat, Panchayat samiti and Zilla parishad constituted the three-tiers of PR, located in the village, the block, and the district levels respectively. While the village panchayats and district boards were already functioning units of local government, the block development committees that existed as advisory bodies at the block level, were converted into Panchayat samitis. Since the scheme of decentralization was conceived as a means to facilitate programmes of development, the middle tier of

Panchayat samiti at the block level was to be 'the basic institution in the entire scheme of Panchayat Raj' (Mehta, 1962: 472).

The three-tier structure was largely accepted, but there were some variations. Some states like Gujarat and Karnataka, placed their middle tier at the taluk level; Assam had a virtual two-tier structure with Mohkuma Parishad at the sub-division; and Tamil Nadu had its top tier of District Development Council at the level of Development District rather than the Revenue District. There were variations also in terms of functions and the importance accorded to different tiers. In most of the states, the middle tier of Panchayat samiti at the block level was the pivotal unit with wide executive functions. Gujarat made all the three-tiers equally strong and Zilla parishad was the strongest unit in Maharashtra. Andhra Pradesh gave certain executive functions to the Zilla parishad in the field of education.

The states also followed different models for the constitution of PR bodies. While the members of Village Panchayats were directly elected, the Panchayat samitis were constituted of members/chairmen of the Village Panchayats. Zilla parishads, similarly, included members/chairmen of Panchayat samitis, except in Maharashtra where parishads had directly elected members as well. Organizational integration was sought when members at higher levels, *e.g.*, Zilla parishad, members of state legislatures and of Parliament, were included in the PR bodies in their respective areas. Such interlinking was an aspect of major emphasis.

The PR scheme, both in terms of its conception and evolution combined the development imperative with an attempt to provide democratic administration at local levels. Balvantrai Mehta scheme combined the past experience of local bodies and the new functions of development (Lele, 1965: 18-19). The middle tier from the CDP structure was added to the already existing local bodies at the district and village levels. The emphasis placed on the middle tier, the method of interlocking membership at the three levels, place of importance to the bureaucracy and, above all, the functions placed in their charge indicate a clear preference for the developmental role of PR. Elections, both direct and indirect, did introduce the democratic element, which brought about changes in the complexion of their membership in course of time. The rationale and the effect of different types of elections on the working of PR bodies were subjects of elaborate discussions (Santhanam Committee Report, 1963). But the prevailing conception was that 'politics' is divisive and that PR institutions should be 'non-political'. The PR institutions were not regarded either as a 'political means' to bring about change in rural India, or as part of the overall political process in the country, or as institutions reflecting social divisions in society. But the logic of a democratic process at different levels affected changes on all the three counts and the 'Second Generation' of PR institutions in West Bengal, Andhra Pradesh and Karnataka brought in the new role of PR as 'political' institutions.

By the 1970s, the strategy of field administration for rural development had changed, undermining both the CDP and PR. The intensive area development (IADP) strategy, the 'target group' approach and the assertion of the 'line' administration of departmental handling of development, coincide with the eclipse of the scheme of democratic decentralization. The Asoka Mehta Committee declared in 1978 : "A number of developments in the past have conspired to undermine the Panchayati Raj structure and made them ineffective".

The Asoka Mehta Committee Report represented a landmark insofar as it (a) treated the PR clearly as 'an extension of democracy' and recommended 'establishment of democratic bodies below the state level'; (b) declared 'the need of providing constitutional sanction to Panchayati Raj'; and (c) suggested 'to transfer substantial quantum of powers from the State Government to the local bodies'.

Changes in Indian Politics and PR

Indian politics in the 1970s showed a shift towards centralization of power on the one hand, and, on the other, an effort on the part of the central leadership to reach out to the people directly. A detailed analysis would show that the two tendencies were part of a coherent strategy to bypass the state level institutions, processes and leadership.

Centralization of power at the level of the Prime Minister was perceptible in the 1970s both within the Congress Party and in government (Kochanek, 1976; Zins, 1988). Elections for Parliament and the State Assemblies were delinked in 1971, creating two arenas of politics. The Centre started special programmes of development for specific 'target' groups, to reach the people directly. The new style of 'plebiscitary' politics had little place for PR institutions that were already strained under the impact of several other factors. Also, the agricultural strategy of green revolution, as also other processes of change in Indian society (Frankel and Rao, 1989) brought in an ascendant class representing the agrarian interests, that wanted a share in the political power. Institutions of democratic decentralization were seen as 'opportunity structures' to gain such power. There was thus a push from below for more decentralization (Mathur, 1997).

The first non-Congress government at the centre in 1977 was constituted of parties and leaders who had consistently criticized centralization of power culminating in the 1975 Emergency. The Asoka Mehta Committee appointed by the Janata government heralded new emphasis on democratic decentralization. The Left Front government that came to power in West Bengal in 1977 (and has continued since then) gave a new meaning and direction to PR institutions. Hegde's Janata Party government in Karnataka and N.T. Rama Rao's Telugu Desam government in Andhra Pradesh reformulated the PR statutes in their respective states.

The bifurcation of the two arenas of politics at the centre and in the states became fully operative in the 1980s with the emergence of regional parties that came to power in many states. The non-Congress chief ministers introduced 'a new level of intensity in the debate on federal restructuring' (Arora, 1992: 6). They became assertive especially after the formation of a joint forum that met at regular intervals raising substantive issues of centre-state relations. The *Report of the Sarkaria Commission on Centre-state Relations* appointed in 1983 gave a place of importance to democratic decentralization. The Economic Advisory Council appointed by the Prime Minister in 1983 (under the chairmanship of Professor Sukhamoy Chakravarty) pleaded for 'functional reasons for decentralization' (Economic Advisory Council, 1983).

Rajiv Gandhi took up the issues of the decentralization on a different note of providing 'responsive administration' and effective planning. He 'spent practically the whole of 1989 in having his reform package discussed at a series of meetings' (Arora, 1992:18) with district officials, district council presidents and chief ministers. The effort again was to reach out to the districts directly, but with due realization of the importance of PR institutions. A comprehensive 64th Constitution Amendment Bill passed by the Lok Sabha by a two-thirds majority fell through in the Rajya Sabha in October 1989 by a margin of two votes. The Congress government revived the proposal and democratic decentralization finally received constitutional status in 1992 with the 73rd and 74th amendments, extended to the Scheduled Areas by an Act of 1996.

Constitutional Status for PR

The tiered structure of local government originating at the level of the Village Panchayat and integrating with the successively higher levels going up to the Centre was a part of the Gandhian Constitution for Free India formulated in 1946 (Agarwal, 1946). The scheme was debated in the Constituent Assembly and was referred to the Constitutional Advisor. The arrangement did not find favour mainly on tactical grounds that it would mean a complete revision of the Constitution, which was at the final draft stage (Panchayati Raj as the Basis of Indian Polity, 1962: 79-80). Finally Gram Panchayats found a mention among the Directive Principles of State Policy. Again, almost coinciding with the Balvantrai Mehta Committee Report, Jayaprakash Narayan came up with a Plea for the Reconstruction of Indian Polity representing his 'organic' or 'communitarian' view of Indian society (Mathur, 1991). First formal proposal for 'providing constitutional sanction to Panchayati Raj' was put forth by the Asoka Mehta Committee which contains a Draft Constitution Amendment Bill with a view to making the PR "an organic integral part of our democratic process and that they should be accorded appropriate constitutional status and recognition" (Asoka Mehta Committee Report, 1978: 207). The Sarkaria Commission underlined the urgent need for decentralization below the state level and mentioned "amendment of the Constitution" as one of the alternatives for attaining "uniformity of... laws throughout the territory of India" (Sarkaria Commission Report, Part 1, 1988:543-44). The Constitution (64th Amendment) Bill proposed in 1989 could not be passed. A somewhat revised Bill was introduced in September 1990, but remained unattended. The Bill was introduced again in 1991 and was passed in December 1992. After ratification by more than half the state assemblies, the Constitution Amendment Act came into force in April 1993. All the states covered by the Act have passed the conformity Acts and almost all have constituted the PR bodies in accordance with the Act. The 1992 Amendment categorically excluded from its jurisdiction areas that are covered by the Fifth and Sixth Schedules of the Constitution. Thus, Nagaland, Meghalaya, Mizoram and Manipur were excluded and certain sections of the Act were not to apply 'to those districts in West Bengal that are covered by the Darjeeling Gorkha Hill Council'. The special characteristics and requirements of the Scheduled and Tribal areas were considered by the Bhuria Committee and based on their recommendations, the Panchayats (Extension to the Scheduled Areas) Act, 1996 was passed in December 1996. Clause 5 of this Act stated clearly that it would come into force after the 'expiration of one year'. Andhra Pradesh, Gujarat, Himachal Pradesh, Maharashtra, Madhya Pradesh and Orissa passed conformity legislations (Institute of Social Sciences, 1998).

The Constitutional Amendment of 1992 along with the extension to Scheduled and Tribal Areas has been hailed as important landmarks in the system of decentralized governance. To accord constitutional guarantee to PR institutions by itself is a major step, which has long been demanded from various quarters. A fixed tenure for the Panchayats and holding of elections at the proper time under the supervision of an independent Election Commission appointed in the states is a major step.

Besides reservation of seats for the SCs and STs in proportion to their population, the Amendment provides for the reservation of one-third of the seats of members, as well as of chairmen of PR institutions, for women. These provisions are rightly regarded as important steps towards 'empowerment' of women—an issue debated forcefully in the last two decades (see *Seminar,* 1997). There is also an important provision for setting up a Finance Commission in the states to ensure the financial viability of PR. These provisions go a long way in providing a sound basis to PR, ensured by the highest law of the land. Many of them are aimed at correcting the often mentioned malaise arising out of the reluctance on the part of the states to accord to the PR, a place of 'political' importance and to devolve power and finances to these institutions. Scholarly analysis of the Amendment and the Conformity Acts, however, conclude that 'functional and financial devolution have been more to satisfy the letter of the law than keeping to the spirit of self-government' (Oommen, 1995:32).

Since the introduction of PR under the Amendment, various issues have been discussed. Certain lacunae that have been discovered in the implementation of legal provisions call for 'further Amendments' (Meenakshisundram, 1977). A detailed review of the working of PR in different states', undertaken by the functionaries at the countrywide workshops held under the aegis of the Rajiv Gandhi Foundation has discussed problems in the 'effective implementation' of the Amendment and useful and interesting suggestions have been made (Rajiv Gandhi Foundation, 1997).

The third phase of democratic decentralization after the 1992 Amendment extended to the Scheduled Areas by the Act of 1996 provides for measures of decentralization that present vast promises though not without complex multiple problems in operational terms. Decentralization is no longer left to the changing preferences of the state governments. The question of ensuring adequate resources and the required administrative support, however, have to be attended to so that these institutions act as decentralized units of effective governance.

Multi-Level Federalism

Convinced by the argument that there is 'nothing in the federal idea or in various theories of federalism, which limits its application to two levels of government only', writers on the Indian federal system have talked about multi-level federalism in view of the uneven size of the states and districts with different levels of complexities (Mukerji and Arora, 1992: 17). They have argued that 'since multi-level federalism is the institutionalized expression of popular participation in a democratic context, partisan politics is inextricably woven into a framework which seeks to distribute political power among multiple centres' (Arora, 1997: 44). In fact, the 1980s have experienced 'a clear shift in orientation...in the direction of an increased willingness to re-discover and explore flexible federalism' under diverse pressures faced by the Indian federal system (*ibid*: 78). The PR scheme provides 'The Third Stratum' of the Indian federation and 'a more radical change is difficult to visualize' (Mukarji, 1993: 859). Another writer goes further to add that the 'two constitutional amendments have radically changed the character of Indian polity' (Mathew, 1997: 276).

The experience of the 'two-tier' federalism (*i.e.*, the centre and the states) in the changing context of Indian politics has been complex and enriching with several experiments. The additional stratum of PR has added enormous complexity to the Indian federal system, which will have to be managed not only structurally but politically as well. The euphoria about 'the Third Stratum' needs to be tempered with great deal of caution and maturity.

Decentralized Planning

Planning in the India, as indeed in many countries, has been primarily a central activity though the process has always been conscious of the dynamics of the federal system. Imbalances and inadequacies in the administration of development programmes have often been analyzed in terms of the problems at the state level. 'Fiscal federalism' has been a subject of much discussion and it is emphasized that the meaningful participation of the states and local institutions will help the process of 'cooperative federalism'. The Sarkaria Commission has put forth extensive recommendations for the effective participation of the states in the process of planning (Sarkaria Commission Report Part I, 1988:385-88).

Decentralized planning refers specifically to the involvement of institutions below the state level, necessitated both by the administrative-developmental exigencies and the constitutional status of local institutions after the 1992 Amendment. Decentralized planning with reference to their institutional levels is the subject matter of our discussion.

The need for decentralized planning has been emphasized for many reasons. The historical-ideological grounds for 'planning from below' were provided by the aspects of Indian society emphasized during the freedom movement, the Gandhian ideals of village community and the Nehruvian vision (Hanson, 1966: 394-96). Another compelling need for decentralized planning has been the vast territory with social, cultural, administrative and agro-climatic specificities, calling for special emphases. The predominantly bureaucratic model of plan implementation constantly complained about the lack of 'people's participation' in development programmes, and it was mentioned by administrators as well as researchers that involvement of the people should really begin with planning. Such plans would also be more sensitive to the local needs. The PR institutions derived much of their justification on the basis of such involvement.

The process of national planning does have a tendency to be a centralized exercise, both because of its concerns as also of finances. Planning in India from the 1950s has shown this tendency, though the need for 'planning from below' has always been emphasized. The Planning Commission undertook detailed exercises, especially since the Second Five-Year Plan to involve the village, the block and the district with plan formulation.

There has been no dearth of academic interest in such exercises. The National Institute of Rural Development undertook some detailed worthwhile exercises of preparing district plans. Maharashstra's efforts after the setting up of the district planning boards in 1972 have been a much discussed subject (Inamdar and Kshire, 1986). Such attempts in the second-generation PR states like Andhra Pradesh, Karnataka and West Bengal are often cited as successful attempts at decentralized planning. The experience of 'planning from below' in Karnataka has been fraught with problems, both 'transitory' and 'others (that) might persist' (Crook and Manor, 1998: 49-50). Official (Sundram, 1984) as well as academic evaluations of decentralized planning, however, agree with this limited effort: 'The planning exercise at the local level continues to be confined to compilation of schemes in specified sectors according to the guidelines issued from above' (Mathur, 1995: 2706). The overall conclusion of the mid-1960s that "attempts to give the plans 'grass-roots' have achieved little success" (Hanson, 1966: 442) has been echoed thirty years later: "Local level planning has not yet taken roots" (Mathur, 1995: 2705).

Decentralized planning has faced both conceptual and operational problems. With regard to the 'domain' of local plans, the initial emphasis on planning of agricultural activities was enlarged in its scope in the context of multi-level planning or regional planning (Mundle, 1977). Such widening of the scope of local plans brought in its turn, a greater need for planning expertise and inter-and intra-level coordination and integration. But lack of technical expertise at the local level has been a persistent problem. The groups of functionaries, which were supposed to plan at the local level, were the hierarchy of officials including the 'subject matter specialists' and the elected representatives in local institutions who were supposed to provide the important inputs of 'local requirements', local initiative and involvement. The planning exercise, however, needed expertise of a different and comprehensive kind that was not available at local levels. Neither was it feasible to provide the network of such specialized planning expertise in the vast country. Major responsibility for the planning was left to the bureaucratic structure and was thus caught in the usual routinized sector-wise perception, allowing limited amount of initiative, imagination and specialized perceptions.

Another area of much debate has been the proper unit at which local planning is useful and feasible. Though the purist notion of 'grass-roots planning' always emphasized the importance of the village as a unit, because of administrative convenience and strategic location of the block and the district, these were often regarded as effective units for local planning (Mundle, 1977; Government of India, 1978, 1984). The block was supported on the basis of its strategic location between the village and the district and as the hub of the scheme of implementation of development programmes, especially during the earlier Plans. Some kind of local planning was already a part of the Community Development approach. The block also had a group of subject matter specialists and a 'coordinator' in the form of the Block Development Officer. The district had all these characteristics and in addition, it was supported by the strong tradition of district administration that had gained historical legitimacy. The ambivalence about the proper unit was reflected also in the structure of PR institutions where in some states the Panchayat samiti at the block level was the strategic unit, while in some the Zilla parishad was the unit with powers and finances. PR with Zilla parishad at the district as the main unit (or the Maharashtra model) often found favour with writers as well as with various committees of the government.

Besides the existing units of the villages, the block and the district as units of planning, there have been some suggestions from important quarters that 'there is a strong case for introducing an intermediate tier of executive authority (between the district and the state level) for development purposes' (Economic Advisory Council, 1983: 18). This proposal recommends restructuring of development planning on the basis of agro-climatic regions in the country.

A major problem of any 'planning from below' is the integration to lower level plans into those at higher level: village to block to district to state and finally to the national plan. This is a massive task requiring technical expertise and matching resources of appropriate levels. Activities that can be handled at the local levels and those that have to be planned at higher levels with reference to larger coverage and 'economies of scale' (*e.g.* power and communication) have to be properly balanced.

The institutional framework for local planning has been another issue that has attracted discussions, suggestions and experiments. Besides the obvious administrative structures of the block and the districts and the 'popular' elements added on in the form of the PR institutions, special agencies have been evolved in some cases, *e.g.* District Planning and Development Council (DPDC) in Gujarat. The District Rural Development Agency (DRDA) also took up local planning sometimes, though it has been primarily an agency for overseeing the implementation of the programmes of rural development. There have been, thus, three organizational structures in this field: (a) the regular administrative structures, *e.g.*, the block and the district, (b) the PR institutions, and (c) specially created structures like the DRDA, DPDC (in Gujarat) and District Planning Boards. These institutions mostly run parallel to each other, though there are always attempts at interlocking of membership. The bureaucratic structure being the more entrenched is by far the more enduring with greater effectiveness.

The 1992 Amendment define the 'Powers, Authority and Responsibilities of Panchayats' to include 'preparation of plans for economic development and social justice' (Article 243G). The Amendment also provide for the Constitution 'in every State at the district level a District Planning Committee to consolidate the plans prepared by the Panchayats and the Municipalities in the district and to prepare a draft development plan for the district as a whole' (Article 243ZD). The details of the constitution of the District Planning Committee, with necessary linkages with other institutions have to be worked out carefully (Hooja n.d.).

The most serious problem of decentralized planning has been lack of financial autonomy of the local institutions. The local planning bodies do not have much financial autonomy as they are in the unenviable position of being the guardian of funds, which are already pre-empted for various departmental programmes' (Sarkaria Commission, 1988: 385). While most of the schemes are centrally sponsored, some are sponsored by the states.

Oommen points out that "... that local government expenditure in India as a percentage of total union, states and local expenditure was as low as 6.4 per cent (rural sector still lower at 2.9 per cent) in 1986-87" (Oommen, 1995: 9). Inter-governmental transfer of financial resources in the context of federal relations, especially the local institutions, has been a persistent problem. Writers on fiscal federalism have repeatedly emphasized the necessity of proper distribution of resources.

The 1992 Amendments have shown sufficient awareness of many of these problems. Additions of the Eleventh Schedule in the 73rd Amendment and the Twelfth Schedule in the 74th Amendment including

29 and 18 items respectively detailing the specific functions of Panchayats and municipalities, has not only expanded their functions but has also made them specific. Amendments to Article 280 direct the Union Finance Commission to 'supplement the resources of Panchayats' by 'augmenting' the Consolidated Fund of states on the basis of the reports of the State Finance Commissions. The Tenth Finance Commission made an *ad hoc* provision of Rs. 4,381 crore for Panchayat institutions for the years 1996-2000 (Institute of Social Science, 1998). With the Constitution of the State Finance Commissions and the submission of the reports by most of these state commissions (*ibid*), the Eleventh Finance Commissions managed 'to recommend measures to augment the Consolidated Funds of states in order to supplement the resources of Panchayats and municipalities'. An effective recommendation of the Eleventh Finance Commission 'can alter significantly the nature and character of fiscal federalism, inter-governmental financial relations and public finance in India' (Oommen, 1998: 3231).

A difficulty that is often mentioned with reference to the involvement of local institutions in the planning process has been the abstract and technical nature of the planning exercise that the people's representatives do not find easy to comprehend. Consequently, the bureaucrats dominate whatever local planning is done. With the new thrust to the PR institutions after 1992, the state of Kerala has undertaken a massive programme for 'participatory planning' (with the help of the Planning Commission) and has started a campaign to provide training to local functionaries who are estimated to be about 400 at the state level, 15,000 at the district level, and about one hundred thousand at the Panchayat and Municipal Ward Levels' (George, 1997: 9-10).

The 1992 Amendment has certainly provided the required thrust to the PR institutions with fairly well worked out institutional support (*e.g.*, State Finance Commission and District Planning Committee) for undertaking decentralized planning. Its success, however, will depend much upon the shape that the institutions take and the way in which the problems are tackled.

PR as a Political Institution

The Asoka Mehta Committee pleaded for 'an integrated democratic polity': "As an end, it [PR] is an inevitable extension of democracy to the grass-roots, which, in turn, makes it the base of the democratic pyramid in the country. The extension should encourage a two-way system of political linkages from bottom upwards through the state ...and *vice versa* with built-in potential for reinforcing responsiveness and accountability of the representatives to the people on the one hand and encouraging mobility, circulation and broad-basing of the political and the ruling elite on the other" (Asoka Mehta Committee Report, 1978: 35). The three states of West Bengal, Karnataka and Andhra Pradesh that organized the PR as a sequel to this vision shaped and 'used' PR institutions as 'political' institutions.

Political 'Use' of PR

Political parties and leaders were quick to note the political potentialities of PR institutions. The Congress Party had no difficulties in gaining control of the PR in the early years because of its mass base. In the first two decades after Independence the Congress organized its political support base mainly on their 'patronage' network resting heavily on the dominant castes and classes in society. This also helped these social categories to gain control of PR institutions and thus have control over the programmes of development with funds and facilities that flowed through developmental agencies. The PR institutions proved to be a reliable forum to build such network.

The Maharashstra Case

PR in Maharashtra was often quoted as a success story in the PR experiment. An important aspect of this phenomenon was the way in which PR, along with other local institutions like the cooperatives was effectively made a part of institutional network that Rosenthal calls 'opportunity structures' (Rosenthal, 1977). The Maratha-Kunbi caste cluster that had consolidated itself as a major block in Maharashtra politics (Lele, 1990) mostly controlled the network of power and patronage. While control over development funds helped the political elite in the mobilization of other social groups, it also made available to the ever-expanding aspiring social groups positions in these institutions. Thus, PR helped the mobilization of the rural population in general and of the aspiring intermediate elite in particular. This helped the state leaders like Y.B. Chavan to maintain dominance 'by skilfully manipulating the extension of opportunities to ambitious men'. The Congress Party in Maharashtra succeeded in developing 'a set of interlocking institutions which integrated the political demands of village, taluka and district elites with the ambitions of state and even national level leaders' (Rosenthal, 1977: 50). The secret of Congress dominance in Maharashtra for a longer period after Independence was attributed to the efficient management of political network through local opportunity structures.

The West Bengal Case

The Left Front government came to power in West Bengal in 1977, and it started to build a wider support base with the help of a revitalized PR. Besides the legal institutional measures, it was the vigorous implementation of land reforms that provided a strong base to the Front as well as to the Panchayats. Operation Barga concentrated on quick recording of names of sharecroppers, government land beyond the permissible limits was distributed, benami land was identified and the old revenue system was revised (Ray, n.d.: 58; Bandopadhyaya, 1980). The Bargadars were organized and were encouraged to take up the critical issues of the community. These 'class-based' organizations were involved in the development process and Panchayat activities, and they were instrumental in effective people's participation in the administration of development programmes (Westergaard, 1986). As a 'political' strategy, the Left Front mobilized the poor without alienating 'the small and middle peasant' (*ibid.* 1992: 229). These measures provided a wider and stable support base from the grass-roots to the party and also changed the membership complexion and the working of the Panchayats.

Other states like Karnataka and Andhra Pradesh, which introduced PR in the 1980s, had a clearly worked out political agenda. The changing fortunes of political parties in PR elections are indicative of the close links between the PR and the state level political processes.

Leadership in PR

The institutions of PR have introduced changes in the structure of rural leadership that has been a subject of discussion from the beginning (Narain, 1964). Elections to PR bodies opened up the hinterland for recruitment of leadership that was represented by the 'limited elite' in the beginning and turned into 'expansive elite' in course of time to include leaders from diverse social categories. In the meantime the increasing frequency and intensity of electoral politics as well as various movements in the countryside, and the 'decline of the traditional social order' under diverse impacts, brought in new groups in political competition. These developments forced marked changes in the nature of leadership. Some regions like West Bengal, Kerala, Karnataka and Andhra Pradesh made conscious efforts to bring about changes as a part of their long-term political strategy.

After the 1992 amendments with 33 per cent of seats reserved for women, studies on women's leadership emphasize a new category of leaders and a new set of issues. As part of the 'empowerment' measures, some states like West Bengal have some Panchayats where all the members are women (Mukhopadhyay, 1995). Such Panchayats exist in other states as well.

Thus, PR as a part of the democratic process has certainly opened up opportunities for different groups, especially the deprived, to join the leadership in the local institutions, which have in many cases been used as springboards for social mobility and movement to institutions at higher levels.

The combining of PR institutions with the programmes of development planning brought forth some discussion on the type and style of PR leadership. Henry Maddick talked about 'the new breed of politicians'; Rajni Kothari described the 'new leaders' as 'pragmatic men' (Maddick, 1970: 309; Kothari, 1970: 127). The development activities and the available funds from governmental sources brought in entrepreneurial leadership and a group of 'fixers' and 'facilitators' who acted as links between the rural population and the government bureaucracy, always known for the maze of rules, regulations and procedures (Ram Reddy and Hargopal, 1985).

New social groups have either forced their way to leadership positions as a result of socio-economic changes in society, or have come to occupy leadership positions as a result of reservations in the system of representation. Attitudes, values, motivations and styles of leaders from these social categories have a distinctive characteristic and are in a state of constant flux. A comparatively less explored field has been the institutional behaviour of the 'new' leaders in the context of the 'new' PR as well as municipal bodies that have gained 'status' and 'powers' under the 1992 Amendments. The reservations of seats for women in local institutions and seats for the SC and ST in proportion to their share in population have 'empowered' these social groups. It will, however, be interesting and worthwhile to see whether this change in the composition of leadership has left any distinctive mark on the functioning of these institutions in the context of their professed goals and social impact.

REFERENCES

Agarwal, S.N. (1946), *Gandhian Constitution for Free India*, Allahabad, Kitabistan.

Arora, Balveer (1992), "India's Federal System and the Demands of Pluralism: Crisis and Reform in the 80s", in Choudhury, Joyopaul eds. *India's Beleaguered Federalism: The Pluralist Challenge*, Tempe. Arizona: Centre for Asian Studies, Arizona State University.

——, (1997), "Federalism and Inter-Governmental Relations in India: Bibliographical Essay" in Bhatnagar, S. and Pradeep Kumar (eds). *Some Issues in Contemporary Indian Politics*, New Delhi, Ess Ess Publishers.

Asoka Mehta (1978). *Report of the Committee on Panchayati Raj Institutions*, Government of India, Ministry of Agriculture & Irrigation, Department of Rural Development.

——, (1962) *Panchayati Raj as the basis of Indian Polity: An Exploration into Proceedings of Constituent Assembly*, Association of Voluntary Agencies for Rural Development, New Delhi.

Bandopadhyaya, D. (1980), *Land Reforms in West Bengal*, Calcutta.

Crook, Richard C. and Manor, J. (1998), *Democracy and Decentralization in South Asia and West Africa*, Cambridge University Press.

Dube, S.C. (1967), 'Communication, Innovation Planned Change in India', in Lerner, D. and W. Schramn, *Communication and Change in Developing Countries*, Honolulu, East-West Centre Press.

Dubhashi. P.R. (1963). 'The Basic Administrative Unit for Development in Mysore State', in *Case in Indian Administration*, New Delhi, The Indian Institute of Public Administration.

Economic Advisory Council (1983), 'Decentralization of Development Planning and Implementation Systems in the States', *Mainstream*, 21 January 1984.

Frankel Francine R. and Rao, M.S.A. (eds.) (1989), *Dominance and State Power in Modern India: Decline of a Social Order*, Vols. I and II, Oxford University Press.

Government of India (1978), *Report of the Working Group on Block Level Planning* (Chairman M.L. Dantwala), Planning Commission, New Delhi.

________(1984), *Report of the Working Group on District Planning* (Chairman: C.H. Hanumantha Rao), Planning Commission, New Delhi.

Hanson, A.H. (1966), *The Process of Planning: A Study of India's Five Year Plans, 1950-1964*, Oxford University Press.

Hooja, Rakesh, (n.d.) *District Planning: Practice and Theory with Special Reference to the 'How To' Aspects* (Mimeo).

Inamdar, N.R. and Kshire, K.V. (1986), *District Planning in India*, New Delhi; Oxford and IBH.

Institute of Social Sciences (1998), *Panchayati Raj Update*. July, August and October, New Delhi.

Jha, S.N. (1972), 'Historical Determinants of the Structure of Panchayat Raj in Uttar Pradesh', *The Indian Journal of Political Science*, Vol. XXXIII, No. 4. October-December.

______(1979), *Leadership and Local Politics: A Study of Meerut District in Uttar Pradesh*, Bombay: Popular Prakashan.

Kothari, Rajni (1970), *Politics in India*, Orient Longman.

Kochanek, S.A. (1976), 'Mrs. Gandhi's Pyramid: The New Congress" in Hart, Henry (ed.), *Indira Gandhi's India: A Political System Reappraised*. Boulder (Colorado): Westview Press.

Lele. Jayant K. (1965), *Role of Local Government in Rural Development*. Ph.D. Thesis, Cornell University.

—, (1990). 'Caste, Class and Dominance: Political Mobilisation in Maharashtra', in R. Frankel, Francine and M.S.A. Rao, (eds), *Dominance and State Power in Modern India*, Vol. II, Oxford University Press.

Maddick, Henry (1970), *Panchayati Raj: A Study of Rural Local Government*, Orient Longman, New Delhi.
Mathew, George (1997), 'Institutions of Self-government in India: Towards Multi-level Federalism', *Review of Development and Change*, Vol. II, No. 2, July-December.
Mathur, Kuldeep (1995), 'Politics and Implementation of Integrated Rural Development Programme', *Economic and Political Weekly*, 14-21 October.
——, (1997), 'Challenges of Decentralization: The Politics of Panchayati Raj', *Social Action*, Vol. 47, January-March.
Mathur, P.C. (1981), 'Local Politics: A Trend Report' in Indian Council of Social Science Research: *A Survey of Research in Political Science, Vol. Two, Political Process*, New Delhi: Allied Publishers Pvt. Ltd.
——, (1991), 'Rural Local Self-government in India: Ideological Nuances from Ripon to Jayaprakash Narayan. 1882-1964', *Journal of Rural Development*, Vol. 10, No. 5, September.
Meenakshisundaram, S.S. (1997), 'The 73rd Constitutional Amendment: A Case for further Amendment', *Journal of Rural Development*, Vol. 16, No. 4, October-December.
Mehta, B. 1962, 'The Panchayat Samiti at the Block Level as the Basic Unit of Panchayati Raj', *The Indian Journal of Public Administration*, Vol. VIII, No. 4, October-December.
Mishra, B.B. (1965), 'The Evolution of the Office of Collector (1770-1947)', *The Indian Journal of Public Administration*, Vol. XI, No. 3, July-September
—, (1970), *The Administrative History of India, 1834-1947: General Administration*, Oxford University Press.
Mukarji, Nirmal (1993), 'The Third Stratum', *Economic and Political Weekly*, 1 May.
Mukarji, Nirmal and Balveer, Arora. (eds.) (1992), *Federalism in India: Origins and Development*, Vikas Publishing House.
Mukhopadhyay, Asim (1998), 'Kultikri: West Bengal's only All Women Gram Panchayat', *Economic and Political Weekly*, 3 June.
Mundle, Sudipto (1977), *District Planning in India*, New Delhi, Indian Institute of Public Administration.
Narain, Iqbal (1964), 'Democratic Decentralization and Rural Leadership: The Rajasthan Experiment', *Asian Survey*, Vol. IV, No. 8, August.
Oommen, M.A. (1995), 'Panchayat Finance and Issues Relating to Inter-Governmental Transfers', in Oommen, M.A. and Datta. A., *Panchayat and Their Finance*, Concept Publishing House.
——, (1998), 'Eleventh Finance Commission and Local Bodies" Tasks and Options', *Economic and Political Weekly*, Vol. XXXII, No. 3, July-September.
Rai, Haridwar (1965), 'Institution of the District Collector', *The Indian Journal of Public Administration*, Vol. XI, No. 3, July-September.
Rajiv Gandhi Foundation. (1997), *Revitalising of Panchayati Raj in India: Problems and Prospects*, Task Force on Panchayati Raj, New Delhi.
Ram Reddy, G. and Hargopal, G. (1985), 'Pyraweekar "The Fixer" in Rural India'. *Asian Survey*, Vol. 25, No. 11, November.
Ray, C.N. (n.d.), *Rural Development Programmes in India: Overview of Their Organizational Form* (Mimeo.), Lucknow: Giri Institute of Development Studies.
Rosenthal, D.B. (1977), *The Expensive Elite: District Politics and State Policy-making in India*, University of California Press.

Sachindanand (n.d.). *The District Officer in Bihar during British Rule* (Mimeo), Patna: A.N. Sinha Institute of Social Studies.

Sanathanam (1963) *Report of the Committee on Panchayati Raj Elections*. Ministry of Community Development and Cooperation, Government of India.

Sarkaria Commission (1988), *Commission on Centre-State Relations: Report, Part 1*, Government of India Press.

Seminar (1997), *Empowering Women: A Symposium on Political Reservation for Women*. September.

Sundaram, K.V. (1984), *Decentralised Planning to Sub-national Levels: Rhetoric and Reality* (Mimeo) quoted in Sarkaria Commission Report, pp. 384-85.

Taylor, C.C., Ensminger, D., Johnson, H.W. and J. Joyce (1965), *India's Roots of Democracy: A Sociological Analysis of Rural India's Experience in Planned Development since Independence*, Orient Longman, New Delhi.

Tinker, Hugh (1954), *The Foundations of Local Self-government in India, Pakistan and Burma*, London: University of London.

Westergaard, Kirsten (1986), *People's Participation, Local Government and Rural Development—The Case of West Bengal*, CDR Research Report No. 8, Centre for Development Research, Copenhagen.

—, (1992), 'Local Government in Bengal: Steps towards Democracy?' in Rudebeck, Lars ed., *When Democracy Makes Sense: Studies in Democratic Potential of Third World Popular Movements*, Upsala, University in Sweden.

Woodruff, Philip (1953), *The Men Who Ruled India: The Guardians*, London: J. Cape.

Zins, Max Jean (1988), *Strains on Indian Democracy: Reflection on India's Political and Institutional Crisis*, New Delhi: ABC Publishing House.

23

Half a Century of Urban Sociology in India*

RANVINDER SINGH SANDHU

In December 2001, Indian Sociological Society (ISS) celebrated its golden jubilee year at Guru Nanak Dev University Amritsar during 27th All India Sociological Conference. The theme of the conference was Half a Century of Sociology in India (1951-2001): The Challenges, Responses and Expectations and a special symposium was devoted to The State of the Profession: Indian Sociology—Yesterday, Today and Tomorrow. But in the symposium, the main focus remained on sociology in general in India and there was no mention of urban sociology. Keeping this fact in mind and being a student of urban sociology especially when we are living in the urbanizing world and India has the second largest urban population in world, I thought it is an appropriate occasion to share my views on the state of urban sociology in India in the last five decades. The present paper is an attempt to know the major trends in research and teaching in urban sociology.

The most striking feature of India's urbanization is its long tradition. The emergence of early urban life here is associated with the evolution of Indus Valley civilization around 2500 B.C. (Dunbar, 1951:2). Some temporal and spatial discontinuities in urban growth and spread notwithstanding, the urbanization process diffused to other parts of the country under the

* This is the revised version of the paper presented at the special session on *Themes in Indian Sociology: Coming Challenges*, organized by the Indian Sociological Society at 15th World Congress of Sociology held at Brisbane (Australia), 7th to 13th July, 2002.

impact of varied forces operating during the ancient (early times to 1206 AD), medieval (1206 to 1757 AD) and modern (1757 till date) periods of Indian history. For that reason, India's urban pattern is a mosaic of segments belonging to the pre-colonial, colonial and post-colonial periods (Rajbala, 1986 and King, 1976).

Despite its long urban history spanning over nearly five millennia, India remains one of the less urbanized countries of the world. At the onset of 20th century it was one-tenth urban; and it was around one-sixth urban at the time of Independence in 1947 (Krishan and Nina Singh, 1993). During the first half of the 20th century, the process of urbanization was slow, registering an increase in the level of urbanization from 10.84 to17.29 per cent only, on the other hand during the second half urban population increased two and a half times *i.e.* it increased from 25 millions to 62 millions. The latter half of the 20th century has been the era of urbanization in the developing countries in general and India in particular. During this period, although the level of urbanization in India increased from 17.29 per cent to 27.8 per cent, the total increase in urban population is about four and a half times *i.e.* from 62 to 285 millions (Singh, 2001). It has second largest urban population among the countries of the world. Although, there are 285 million urbanites and 35 metropolises in India, yet the urban phenomena have not received due attention from sociologists.

It is very difficult to have a comprehensive view of urban sociology at the international level and at all-India level because its status has intimate relationship with the level of development and level of urbanization of a particular nation. In the United States of America, the subject got recognition in 1925 when American Sociological Society devoted an annual meeting to urban sociology. The papers from this meeting were published under the editorship of E.W.Burgess entitled *The Urban Community*. Prior to this volume Park, Burgess and Mckenzie published a volume, *The City* (1925), which contained essays they had published in the previous decade. These two works laid the foundation of the subject which was further enriched by the students of Park and Burgess at the University of Chicago, which is very well known as the Chicago School of Urban Sociology. On the contrary in India sociology is a relatively young discipline. It was only in 1920 that the first department of sociology was established at the University of Bombay by Professor Patrick Geddes. Although, during the decade 1914 to1924 he made diagnosis and treatment surveys of some 50 Indian urban areas which included his two volumes of *Town Planning Towards City Development* for Indore in 1918 (Boardman, 1976) yet unlike Park and Burgess his work could not lay the foundation of the subject. The field of urban sociology remained unheard in Indian universities till 1960 (Ganguli, 1965).

M.S.A. Rao (1974) considered two main reasons for this neglect: First, the predominant view among the sociologists that distinction between rural and urban sociology is not meaningful in India due to its lower level of urbanization and second, the argument that in the Indian context, there was no dichotomy between the traditional city and village as both were the elements of same civilization. Satish Saberwal (1977) observed in his paper on "Indian Urbanism: A Socio-historical Perspective", appearing in a special issue of *'Contributions to Indian Sociology.'* Over sixty years ago Patrick Geddes wrote his *Report on re-planning of six towns in Bombay Presidency* (1915), prior to his appointment as the first Professor of Sociology in the University of Bombay. Geddes occupied the Chair only briefly; and G.S.Ghurye, his successor, wrote on the *'Cities of India'* in the March 1953 issue of *Sociological Bulletin*. During the years in between and since, sociologists and others have off and on referred to urban phenomena in India; but this terrain has until recently remained singularly devoid of decisive intellectual landmarks: the key ideas which cutting through thickets of data, clearly show the road ahead.' (Saberwal, 1977:1).

The three trend reports or surveys (D'Souza, 1974, 1985 and Kosambi, 1994) commissioned by the Indian Council of Social Sciences Research which have reviewed the literature on urban studies from 1950 to 1988, reveal the major trends in the field of urban studies in India. It is important to note that field of urban studies has been subjected to multi-disciplinary research involving disciplines like economics, geography, history, political science, demography and social anthropology, besides sociology. On the other hand, urban sociology has a specialized field which forms a part of urban studies. The present survey reports have been undertaken only from sociological point of view. The contributions in the field of urban studies belong to all disciplines mentioned above. These surveys have divided the field in a number of subject matter areas to learn how far each area has been covered; and in each area, the studies are further examined to see if they provide adequate explanation of the problem involved (D'Souza, 1974:115). The subject matter has been considered under the following categories: urbanization, city and region, urban functions, urban internal structure, emerging urban systems, urban social organization, urban community development, urban social problems and urban planning.

D'Souza (1974) observed that there was already accumulation of a huge mass of urban data and number of studies based on this data. But these studies were mainly descriptive, revealing only the magnitude of the phenomena concerned and did not aim at giving the explanation of the problems or came out with some generalizations. Some comparative studies had been undertaken but they mostly aimed at showing the differences among cities with regard to certain variables. Some important studies are by Mitra (1961), Amrit Lal (1962) and V.L.S.Prakasa Rao (1964) and these are mainly based on census data. Other comparative studies are conducted under the aegis of Research Programme Committee. Bert F. Hoselitz (1961) studied cities of Calcutta, Kanpur and Jameshedpur. V. Pethe (1962) compared the socio-economic conditions of Hyderabad, Poona, Sholapur, Baroda, Hubli, Cuttack and Puri to indicate the overall levels of inequalities between the different strata in the communities. Bulsara (1964) also made a comparative study of four metropolises *i.e.* Bombay, Calcutta, Delhi, and Madras. All these studies are very useful but are lacking in analysis.

D'Souza writes in his first survey of urban studies, "To summarize the major trends that have become evident in urban studies, it may be pointed out that social scientists began to take real interest in urban studies only after the 1951 census which revealed a high rate of growth in urban population. Therefore, the history of serious urban studies in India covers a span of about twenty years only. At first the emphasis was on finding out the dimensions of urban problems through descriptive studies based on census publications as well as collection of first hand data. This has resulted in cumulation of large body of facts but not in a commensurate growth of theoretical knowledge"(1974:140-41).

The 1971 census recorded that the high rate of growth of urban population had continued resulting in the massive number of 109 million with all the problems that it entailed. The interest of scholars in urban studies continued unabated during 1970's and consequently, urban sociology gained importance, and problems of rural urban migration, urban development and other related areas such as demography, neighbourhoods, slums, stratification, education, ethnic conflict and movements, kinship, religion, politics, economy, social problems and impact of urbanization on rural areas attracted the attention of the sociologists and social anthropologists (M.S.A. Rao, 1982). Many well-known slum studies were conducted (Desai and Pillai, 1970, 1972; Wiebe 1975, Alfred Dsouza, 1978; V.S D'Souza, 1979 and Singh and Alfred Dsouza, 1980). During this period studies were mainly based on census data and several edited volumes of papers on urban themes published as the proceedings of the conference or special number of journals devoted to urban issues. Asish Bose (1970 and 1973) brought out two important guides to source material. The important feature of this decade was the absence of city surveys. The studies were not based on primary data but were more problem oriented and analytical in their approaches. D'Souza (1985: 184) again concluded in his second survey report that the studies so far have accumulated large number of empirical generalizations about the urban phenomena. But, most of the generalizations lack the rigour of scientific method.

Kosambi (1994) conducted the third survey of literature on urban studies covering the period from 1979 to 1988 and reviewed 900 items which included books and articles culled from about 50 journals and printed doctoral theses, which appeared during the period 1979 to 1988 in India and elsewhere. This number itself is an indication of growth of literature in the field because D'Souza reviewed 250 and 350 items only for the first and second survey respectively. During eighties there were many studies on urbanization pattern and trends but issues pertaining to metropolitization and regional planning remained inadequately explored. Migration studies also highlighted the all-India trends as well as regional variations in terms of male and female socio-economic differences. The spatial structure of cities has not been systematically explored and theoretical contributions in the field were relatively meagre. Among the various urban problems, there was some fresh thinking on the concept of urban poverty. Like the previous decade, studies on different aspects of slums and squatter settlements received due attention and later on this trend continued during eighties also, *e.g.*: Misra and Gupta, 1981; Rao and Rao, 1984; and Jha, 1986. Kosambi also found that a set of definitive theoretical statements about the urban impact on the traditional institutions or about the important relationship between the caste and class in urban areas lacking. During eighties sociologists still favoured sample surveys with interview schedules and questionnaires; social anthropologists continued to prefer the study of small communities; while demographers, economists, and geographers used sophisticated quantitative techniques in analyzing the data. The sociologists had, by and large, shied away from the advanced statistical methods

Like previous decade, urban studies remained attractive for scholars during nineties. The National Commission on Urbanization (NCU) report published in five volumes highlighted the problems of urbanization at the grass-roots, sub-state and state levels. NCU noted that our nation is gradually beginning to realize that the process of urbanization is much more than just "breakdown of Calcutta"... rather it is a phenomenon of unique scope and dimension, one, which is joining to change fundamentally the nature of our lives. This decade has also seen some valuable studies on slums and squatter settlements such as: Kaldate, 1989; Dhadave, 1989; Sandhu, 1989; Rao R.N., 1990; Das, 1994; Desai, 1995; De wit, 1996; Purewal 2000 and Lobo and Das, 2001. In addition to this many other publications appeared as conference and seminar volumes on different aspects of urbanization such as: human settlements, urban poor and sustainability of human settlements some of the important works are; Mohanty, 1993; Diddee and Rangaswamy, 1993; Ray and Das Gupta, 1995; Kundu, 2000; Sandhu, Singh and Sandhu, 2001 and Sharma and Sita, 2001.

After United Nations Centre for Human Settlements (UNCHS) Habitat 1996 Istanbul conference, like Research Programme committees of sixties, Government of India encouraged city studies for the preparation of National report on the state of Indian cities. This report based on ten city studies (Government of India, 2001) was presented at the special session of United Nations General Assembly (commonly known as Istanbul +5) held in June 2001 in New York. On the same line Government of India under its National Urban Observatory, which has been recently established in Town and Country Planning Organization New Delhi, has identified four universities for more city studies according to the framework of UNCHS urban indicators programme. They are also planning to promote urban database at city level as a part of the local urban observatories in accordance with the UNCHS guidelines and suggestions. All these efforts would provide more congenial environment for the urban studies in India and urban issues would be better known than before. The future of urban studies looks bright.

The preceding analysis reveals the overall development of urban studies in India in the last five decades. But, when we try to assess the contributions of sociologists to the body of literature, we are surprised to note that their contributions are not keeping pace with the growing body of literature. The urban studies are dominated by geographers, economists, planners and other social scientists. This fact is also evident from articles on the subject that are published in the *Sociological Bulletin* since its inception in 1952.The *Sociological Bulletin* is the official journal of Indian Sociological Society and it has brought its 51 volume recently. If the entire period of *Sociological Bulletin* is divided into three phases namely, first phase from 1952 to 1967, second phase from 1968-1983 and third phase from 1984 onwards, then it can be seen that out of the total 41 articles published on the relevant subject as many as 23 were published in the first phase whereas only 10 and 8 in the second and third phase respectively. By the numerical criterion such a trend would appear to be at variance with the overall growth of the urban studies and urban population in the country. This may be due to the fact that urban studies include contributions from several disciplines including sociology and the *Sociological Bulletin* mainly published Sociological Studies.

The different phases also vary according to the geographical areas covered and the range of topics dealt with in the articles published. During the first phase the majority of the articles dealt with Bombay and its surrounding areas and only two with Delhi. These articles covered a wide range of topics such as cities: their history, growth, development and ecology; social problems, social stratification, neighbourhood relations, migrants, impact of urbanization on family and rural areas and rural urban continuum. The articles during the second phase covered wider geographical area than the area covered in the first phase. But, unlike the first phase, they were mainly focused on caste, class, migrants and rural urban differences in India. During the third phase also articles published covered wider geographical area as in the second phase but varied in themes. In addition to a theoretical paper on urbanization as a perspective, three papers were on migrants and one each on social ecology, family law, ideology and ethnicity. The diminishing coverage of urban studies during the seventies onwards also coincides with the appearance of articles in some new areas in sociology such as; gender, social movements, globalization, liberalization, environment and civil society.

If publication in the *Sociological Bulletin* is any index of status and importance of the subject then it can be concluded that urban sociology has failed to attract the notice of the journal at a critical juncture just at a time, when urbanization and its impact on the society has become more and more vital and complex with ever increasing levels of urbanization and rapidly multiplying numbers of the urbanites and their problems in the country. The problem is getting worse because an aging, decaying and neglected urban India cannot keep up with exploding urban population, one-third to one-half of which, live in slums, with basic necessities such as safe water and sanitation at a premium. The 21st century is the century of urbanization and we must realize that within next 20 years only, *i.e.* between 2001 to 2021, India's urban population would more than double itself to reach the figure of 618 million (Government of India, 1996).With the doubling of population, problems of urban India would multiply many folds. Therefore, it would be a great challenge for us to understand and tackle these problems before they overtake us. In the era of globalization, the cities are undergoing tremendous change: social, economic, political and physical. Socio-economic inequalities are increasing, so also the aspirations of the urban dwellers. There is lack of good governance leading to many law and order problems and fiscal problems of cities, which consequently are leading towards low quality life. Cities are becoming unsafe and unlivable. Here is big challenge for the urban sociologists to understand the urban phenomena and foresee the future problems and this requires usable research for planned development. In order to do so, urban sociologists should focus more on the design of their studies—both at the micro and macro-structure levels—that should be aimed at showing causal connections between variables in an interdisciplinary perspective. Knowledge in that form can then be used in planning projects for the transformation of urban society and environment. The existing knowledge although focussed mostly on understanding urban society is still indispensable for designing explanatory studies on social change in urban India.

There are many universities in India where urban sociology is being taught at the post-graduate level. A recent survey conducted by Curriculum Development Committee (CDC) constituted by University Grants Commission revealed that urban sociology is being taught in 30 to 39 universities out of 50 universities from where they collected the information. But it is being taught as an elective subject. Further it was noted that it is not treated as the thrust area in any university in India. It seems that urban sociology has become less important for the sociologists because of new emerging areas such as sociology of development, gender studies and environment. This lack of interest in the subject is also reflected in publication of books in the subject. There are very few books that directly cater to the needs of students and researchers. Except M.S.A. Rao's *A Reader in Urban Sociology* (1974, 1991 revised version), there is no other Indian book, which could cover major part of the syllabus and students have to glean the material from different sources.

REFERENCES

Agnihotri, Pushpa (1994). *Poverty amidst Prosperity: Survey of Slums*, New Delhi: M. D. Publications.

Boardman, P.L. (1976). 'Patrick Geddes and His many Worlds', in Ferriera J. V. ed S.S. Jha (eds), *The Outlook Tower: Essays on Urbanization in Memory of Patrick Geddes*, Bombay: Popular Parkashan.

Bose, Ashish (1970). *Urbanization in India: An Inventory of Source Material*; Bombay: Academic Books.

Bose, Ashish (1973). *Studies in India's Urbanization 1901-1971*, New Delhi: Tata McGraw-Hill.

Bulsara J.F. (1964). *Problems of Rapid Urbanization in India*, Bombay; Popular Parkashan.

Burgess, E.W. (ed.). (1926). *The Urban Community*, Chicago: University of Chicago Press.

Das Biswaroop (1993). *Socio-Economic Studies of Slums in Surat City*, Surat: Centre for Social Studies.

Desai A.R. and S.D. Pillai (eds.) (1970). *Slums and Urbanization*, Bombay: Popular Prakashan.

—— (1972). *A Profile of an Indian Slum*, Bombay: University of Bombay.

Desai, V. (1995). *Community Participation and Slum Housing: A Study of Bombay*, New Delhi: Sage.

D'Souza, V. S. (1974). 'Urban Studies: A Trend Report', in *A Survey of Research in Sociology and Social Anthropology*, Bombay: Popular Prakashan.

—— (1979). 'Socio-Cultural Marginality: A Theory of Urban Slums and Poverty in India', *Sociological Bulletin*, 28 (1-2): 9-24.

—— (1985). 'Urban Studies', *in Survey of Research in Sociology and Social Anthropology*, 1969-1979, Vol. I, New Delhi: Satvahan (Sponsored by ICSSR), Vol. I: 139-209.

De wit, J. (1996). *Poverty, Policy and Politics in Madras Slums: Dynamics of Survival Gender and Leadership*, New Delhi: Sage.

Dhadave, M. S. (1989). *Sociology of Slum*, New Delhi: Archives Book.

Dunbar, G. (1951). *India and the Passing of Empire*, London: Nicholson and Waston Ltd. Cited from Krishan G. and Nina Singh *op.cit.*

Fox, Richard G. (ed.) (1970). *Urban India: Society Space and Image*, Duke University Program in Comparative Studies on Southern Asia.

Ganguli, P.G. (1965) 'Need for a National Policy on Urbanization', *Economic Weekly*, July 29,13:1215. Quoted from D'Souza 1974 (*ibid*).

Government of India (1996). *Indian National Report: Second United Nations Conference on Human Settlements-Habitat II*, Ministry of Urban Development.

—— (2001). *India:Report of Urban Indicators, State of Indian Cities*, Istanbul +5 UNCHS (Habitat) Conference 2001, Ministry of Urban Development and Poverty Alleviation, New Delhi.

Hoselitz, Bert F. (1961). 'Indian Cities,' The Surveys of Calcutta, Kanpur and Jamshedpur,' Economic Weekly, Special Number, 13: 1071-1078.

Jha, S. S. (1986). *Structure of Urban Poverty: The Case of Bombay Slums*, Bombay: Popular Parkashan.

Kaldate, Sudha (1989). *Slums and Housing Problem*, Jaipur, Printwell.

Kantesbovskaya, I.V. (1976). "Some definitions of Urbanization in Geographic Literature and the Relevant Ideas" in S. Manzoor Alam and V.V.Pokshishevsky (eds.) *Urbanization in Developing Counties*, Hydrabad: Osmania University Press.

King, Anthony D. (1976). *Colonial Urban Development: Culture, Social Power and Environment*, London: Routledge and Keagan Paul.

Krishan,G. and Nina Singh (1993). 'The Political Economy of Indian Urbanization', in Diddee Jayamala and Vimla Rangaswamy (eds.), *Urbanisation: Trends, Perspective and Challenges*, Jaipur: Rawat Publications.

Kosambi, M. (1994). *Urbanization and Urban Development in India*, ICSSR, New Delhi.

Kundu, Amitabh (ed.) (2000). *Inequality Mobility and Urbanisation: China and India*, New Delhi: ICSSR and Manak Publications.

Lal, Amrit (1962). 'Age in sex structure of cities of India', Geographical review of India, 24 (1): 7-29. Quoted from D'Souza V. S. 1974 (*ibid*)

Lobo, Lancy and Biswaroop Das (2001). *Poor in India*, Jaipur: Rawat Publications.

Majumdar T.K. (1983). *Urbanising Poor A Sociological Study of Low Income Migrants Communities in the Metropolitan city of Delhi*, New Delhi: Lancers Publishers.

Mishra, Asok (1967). 'A Functional Classification of India's Towns, in Ashish Bose (ed.) *Pattern of Population Change in India 1951-61*, Calcutta: Allied. Quoted from D'Souza V. S. 1974 (*ibid*).

Misra, G.K. and Gupta R. (1981). *Resettlement Policies in Delhi*, New Delhi: Indian Institute of Public Administration.

Mohanty, Bidyut (ed.) (1993). *Urbanisation in Developing Countries: Basic Services and Community Participates*, New Delhi Institute of Social Sciences.

Ôyen, Else., (1996). 'Poverty Research Rethought' in Else Ôyen, S.M. Miller and S. Abdus Samad (eds.), *Poverty: A Global Review*, Oslo: Scandinavian University Press.

Park, Robert E., *et al.* (1925). *The City*, Chicago: University of Chicago Press.

Prakasa Rao V. L. S. (1964). *Towns of Mysore State*, Calcutta: Statistical Publishing Society. Quoted from D'souza V. S. 1974. (*ibid*).

Pethe, V. P. (1962). "Income Inequalities in Urban Communities", *A.I.C.C. Economic Review*, April 22, 15: 26-29. Quoted from D'Souza V. S. 1974 (*ibid*).

Purewal, Navtej K. (2000). *Living on the Margins: Social Access to Shelter in Urban South Asia*, Aldershat, Burlington, Singapore, Sydney: Ashgate.

Ranga Rao, K. and M. S. A. Rao. (1984). *Cities and Slums: A Study of a Squatters' Settlement in the City of Vijaywada,* New Delhi: Concept.

Rajabala (1986). *Trends in Urbanisation in India*, Jaipur: Rawat Publications.

Rao, M.S.A. (1974). *A Reader in Urban Sociology*, New Delhi: Orient Longman.

—— (1982).'Sociology in the 1980s: Retrospect and Prospect' in P.K.B.Nayar (ed.),*Sociology in India: Retrospect and Prospect,* Delhi: B.R. Publishing Corporation.

—— Chandrashekar Bhat and Laxmi Narayan Kadekar. 1991. *A Reader in Urban Sociology*, New Delhi: Orient Longman.

Roy, Prodipto & S. Das Gupta. (1995). *Urbanization and Slums*, New Delhi: Har-Anand Publications.

Saberwal, Satish (1977). 'Indian Urbanism: A Socio-Historical Perspective', in Satish Saberwal (ed.), *Process and Institution in Urban India: Sociological Studies*, New Delhi, Vikas.

Sandhu R. S. (1989). *The City and Its Slums: A Sociological Study*, Amritsar: Guru Nanak Dev University Press.

Sandhu R S. (ed.) (Forthcoming) *Urbanization: Sociological Perspectives*, New Delhi, Sage.

Sandhu, R. S., Sarup Singh and Jasmeet Sandhu (2001). *Sustainable Human Settlements: The Asian Experience*, Jaipur: Rawat Publications.

Sharma, R.N. and K. Sita (eds.) (2001). *Issues in Urban Development: A Case of Navi Mumbai*, Jaipur: Rawat Publications.

Singer, Milton and Bernard S. Cohn (eds.) (1968). *Structure and Charge in Indian Society'* Viking Fund Publication in Anthropology No. 47.

Singh, A.S. and Alfered, Desouza (1980). *The Urban Poor: Slum and Pavement Dwellers in the Major Cities of India*, New Delhi: Manohar.

Singh, Inderjit (2001). *Provisional Population Totals: Rural-Urban Distribution of Population (Paper-2 of 2001)*, New Delhi, Controller of Publications.

Smets P. 1996 *Informal Housing Finance in Hydrabad*, Urban Research Working Papers, No. 40, Amsterdam: Vrije Universiteit.

24

Involuntary Resettlement and Voluntary Organisations: Some Emerging Issues

HARI MOHAN MATHUR

Development is undertaken to generate benefits for the society at large, but the process has often led to the forced relocation of millions of people, uprooting their communities, and shredding to pieces their essential social fabric. In India, the construction of dams, power plants, highways and such other infrastructure development projects has led to the displacement of around fifty million people during the last five decades. Subsequently no more than one-fourth of them could be assisted to regain their livelihoods. (Roy, 1999) The majority, reduced to poverty from the loss of land and other means of making a living, continues to face an uncertain future.

The disruptive potential of development projects is now well documented. (Mathur and Marsden, 1998; McDowell, 1996) The World Bank (2001) acknowledges it in the opening lines of its recently updated policy on involuntary resettlement:

> Bank experience indicates that involuntary resettlement under development projects, if unmitigated, often gives rise to severe economic, social and environmental risks: productive systems are dismantled; people face impoverishment when their productive assets or income sources are lost; people are relocated to environments where their productive skills may be less applicable and competition for resources greater; community institutions and social networks are weakened; kin groups are dispersed; cultural identity, traditional authority, and the potential for mutual help are diminished or lost.

People who are impoverished are often poor to start with. Such impoverishment is in direct conflict with the goals of development. The key problem with development projects requiring resettlement is that the costs are unequally shared. Those who bear the cost may not be those who enjoy the fruits of development, and those enjoying the fruits of development may not be those who bear the costs. For example, electricity generated in the Singrauli region is available in homes or industrial uses in north Indian cities hundreds of miles away, but the people in that region who gave up their lands for the erection of power plants often have no access to it. (Mathur, 1999) Conflicts between wider societal interests and interests of the people adversely affected by development projects are therefore increasingly coming into the open.

The Resettlement Debate

Involuntary resettlement, triggered by development projects, is an issue that now is high on the development agenda. Because of its adverse effects, involuntary resettlement has become a highly contentious issue, and voluntary organisations (commonly known in India as NGOs, a short form for non-governmental organisations) have not remained undivided on this issue either. The NGO intervention in development induced resettlement issues has taken place in two ways. (Pandey, 1996)

On the one hand, there are NGOs who regard development as some kind of a sinister device to promote interests of the rich and the powerful at the expense of the poor and the weak. They are vehement in denouncing development projects because they displace poor people, and are opposed to the current development paradigm itself that often gives rise to problems of resettling the displaced people. They see no use in continuing with this destructive process in the name of development, and would want it to come to a halt to save people from preventable disruption to their lives. In their view, governments and donor agencies that assist them in their development plans alone are accountable for disruption to the lives of the affected groups. Such NGO groups are active in mobilising project-affected people against their impoverishment due to developmental activities and are getting wide support in their struggle against development projects. With support from the academia, the media, the environmentalists, the human rights activists and the others concerned, these NGOs have successfully built up strong protest movements against mega-projects. (McCully, 1996; Roy, 1999; Udall, 1995) By putting pressure on international development agencies and aid establishments in donor countries, they even succeed in some cases stopping the flow of funds for projects that they regard as harmful.

However, not all NGOs react to the resettlement problem created by development projects in a similar hostile manner. Those on the other side of the fence, too, are critical of the mindless pursuit of development that instead of improving the quality of life only adds to the woes of large numbers, but they are not in favour of abandoning development altogether. They recognise that without planned development no government can hope to meet the rising expectations of its peoples for better living conditions. What they definitely want, however, is that the previous neglect of the displaced people should be replaced with policies and programmes that assure them a future better than their past, not promise them a return merely to their 'good old days.' Their role has been significant in highlighting the plight of the uprooted people, and in lobbying for a fair deal for those who lose from the development process. In fact, such NGOs are even willing to work with government agencies in the planning and implementation of resettlement operations. Their primary goal is to see that the hardships of project-affected people are mitigated as much as possible.

The fact is that NGOs are not a homogeneous group, all united in the way they perceive the resettlement problem, and the manner in which they wish to deal with it. Perhaps nothing illustrates better the sharp differences in the NGO community than the situation of NGO movements in this area. (Dhagamwar, 1997) While some NGOs are supportive of the resettlement plans and are willing to lend their helping hand to such initiatives, there are others whose confrontational stance in effect tends to obstruct the resettlement process (unintentionally hurting the very people whom they wish to help).

Development Agencies and NGOs

Development agencies are now increasingly turning to NGOs to seek their help in dealing with the problems of involuntary resettlement. A large number of NGOs have been contracted to carry out resettlement operations by several major public sector organisations, especially those being funded by the World Bank and other external donor agencies. The Coal India Limited (CIL) and the National Thermal Power Corporation (NTPC) are among the major Government of India undertakings that took an early lead in using the NGO resources in their resettlement activities, especially their expertise in generating new income opportunities for the displaced people. Many other organisations are now following their example. Indeed, the last few years have been a boom time for voluntary organisations working in the area of involuntary resettlement.

Only a decade ago the NGO involvement in resettlement activities at the present level would have been inconceivable. For long, NGOs have generally been viewed as troublemakers by government agencies. Partly their campaigns against development projects, often conducted with international support, strengthened such negative perceptions about them. Government agencies in the face of protests have even been forced to roll back their development plans in some cases. Donor agencies too have withdrawn their support in such situations. One well known case is the campaign launched by the Narmada Bachao Andolan (NBA) which resulted in the withdrawal of the World Bank funding support for the Sardar Sarovar Project. (Dreze, *et al:* 1997) The Koel Karo Jan Sanghatan (KKJS) also successfully challenged the might of the state and saved 150000 tribal lives in 256 villages from displacement. Their sustained pressure forced the government to cancel the laying of the foundation stone of the project on 5 July 1996 by the Prime Minister of India. (Sekhsaria, 1996)

What has, then, brought about this turnaround in the outlook of development agencies? The pressure of external donor agencies is not the whole answer. Other factors have also been at work. The fact is that government agencies themselves have now become more aware of their limitations in managing resettlement. This is a task that requires live contact with the people to be resettled on an almost daily basis, and NGOs known for their closeness to the people definitely appear better suited for it. A major factor that has changed the attitude is, however, the impressive track record of many NGOs in the fight against poverty. Here development agencies see for NGOs a useful role in the difficult task facing them—the challenge of reconstructing livelihoods of the affected people, and seeing that at least they do not end up worse off than before due to development activities, as has often happened in the past.

Government agencies have necessarily to choose NGOs that have the right credentials. Such NGOs are still small in number. NGOs with expertise in generating new income and employment opportunities for the displaced people are also generally unwilling to come forward. Resettlement has nowhere been an east task, and the risk of failure that may boomerang on their credibility has held back many NGOs. The choice before development agencies interested in working with NGOs is thus very limited.

The friction between project officials and NGOs contracted to work for the project is not uncommon. In some cases this results in project authorities terminating the contract, and NGOs retaliating with withdrawal from the project in the middle of the implementation process. For government agencies the reasons of dissatisfaction with the NGOs are many. A large number of NGOs are city-based organisations, often with no knowledge of local conditions where they are supposed to work. Many such NGOs rarely move into the project area, preferring to operate from their offices in the city. Their presence in the project is minimal. Poorly paid and inadequately qualified staff is usually assigned to the project area. The staff turnover is then too rapid to provide any continuity in service to the people.

The potential for government-NGO collaboration in resettlement is enormous. Much, however, remains to be done. The collaboration has not proceeded on a completely smooth course, but both governments and NGOs are rapidly learning the ways to pool their skills, and to organise their action plans in ways that prove beneficial to those most in need. (Bhat, 1992) So far the results of this collaboration have been mixed. While NGOs have been helpful in managing relocation, the main resettlement task, namely the restoration or improvement of incomes and livelihoods, is proving to be an uphill one. As Morse and Berger (1992: 130) noted "it is one thing to persuade people to move, and provide them with a house and some land at a resettlement site; it is another thing to ensure their long-term rehabilitation".

Closeness to people gives NGOs a distinct advantage in assisting the project-affected people. Barring those who on ideological considerations wish to steer away from government programmes, the NGOs are now increasingly coming forward to work with development agencies. They are also recognising the need to have good working relationship with the project authorities. (Das, 1998) Although there is still a long way to go, the results of this cooperative activity are beginning to bear fruit. In Gujarat the resettlement process has been greatly facilitated by NGOs. Morse and Berger (1992) noted that the identification of land, its purchase and selection by oustees, and many other aspects of the relocation process were greatly assisted by the collaboration between non-government organisations and Nigam officials.

The NGO Strengths

The common perception is that NGOs are by their very nature participatory, gender sensitive, flexible and transparent, while government carries the baggage tack of red-tapism and rigidity. In addition, NGOs are believed to provide important lobbying functions, to ensure greater compliance with newer and stronger policy guidelines, at local and international levels through emerging global linkages.

NGOs also tend to view themselves as pursuing a participatory approach that is uniquely their own, giving them particular strengths which the government agencies are believed to lack. It is due to these distinct advantages they possess that, in comparison with government agencies, NGOs are regarded as better suited to: (1) reach the poor; (2) obtain true, meaningful participation of intended beneficiaries; (3) be flexible and responsive in their work; (4) strengthen local level institutions; (5) achieve outcomes at less cost; (6) experiment with alternative ideas and practices; (7) utilise indigenous knowledge and other local resources. (Fowler, 1990:11)

How far this depiction of their self-image is a true account of the NGO strengths remains debatable. Experience has shown that there is a great variation among NGOs themselves and within government. Government is not a monolith. Some government programmes function with remarkable sensitivity, transparency and accountability and the instances of rigidity in NGO operations are not unknown. (Ramachandran, 1996) As participants at a Royal Tropical Institute seminar held in Amsterdam observed: "The stereotyped way of thinking often encountered—that NGOs 'can do' and government departments 'cannot'—is an oversimplification." (Jaeger, 1986: 64)

Corruption, manipulation, power and control are not the exclusive preserve of government institutions. NGOs are not free from it. Given shrinking employment opportunities, people register charitable or service organisations as a means of livelihood. (Ramachandran, 1996) Contractors who were earlier engaged in construction work have set up voluntary organisations to make a fast buck. Many political leaders and retired civil servants also set up their own NGOs to make money for themselves, using their contacts for easy access to government funds without being pestered with awkward questions. It is public knowledge that many NGOs function as family establishments with the majority of governing board members and organisational leaders drawn from one family. The organisation's assets are also treated as family property with unwritten inheritance rights.

The NGO views about themselves have, in fact, given rise to many myths.

On the basis of their studies, Gazelius and Millwood (1988) are unable to confirm that NGO-supported participatory projects are more effective than government-supported ones. While it is true that the examples of NGO experiences are in general more positive with respect to participation, this does not mean that NGOs are always more disposed towards and effective in participatory development. Commenting on the anti-dam movement launched by the Narmada Bachao Andolan (NBA), Singh (1997: 13-14) stated: "It has been less successful in developing a truly democratic representation of the people's interests, and of the diversity of these interests. The oustees have never really been their own spokespersons, nor have they been incorporated in the top leadership of the NBA. In fact, as the momentum of the movement grew, the functioning of the NBA became somewhat less democratic and participatory."

In a number of cases NGOs have been rather paternalistic in their approach. (Uphoff, 1989:9). People have even been prevented from getting information about resettlement package available to them. One observer noted that NBA "did not want people to be informed about the resettlement offered under NWDT Award, as this information would probably induce the potential oustees to think of accepting resettlement, which in turn would weaken the movement". (Dhagamwar, 1997: 95)

The NGO claims of giving voice to the people are being increasingly questioned. As people become better aware of their own situation, they are able to see things for themselves. They are becoming critical of the NGOs that claim to speak on their behalf. In some cases people have even begun campaigns against such NGOs. As recently reported in the press, the people affected by the Maheshwar Hydel Project in Madhya Pradesh even went as far as submitting a memorandum to the National Human Rights Commission accusing the widely respected Narmada Bachao Andolan (NBA) of violating human rights and their right to development. They stated in the memorandum that though they were in favour of speedy implementation of the Maheshwar project, the anti-development forces led by NBA activists were creating hurdles in completion of the project. The affected people alleged that NBA was intimidating the government officials and their activists were bringing anti-social elements from outside to create law and order problems. (The Hindu, April 1999; and The Observer, 1998).

The concept of voluntary work appears to have changed, with NGOs becoming a source of income and employment generation for people sitting in plush, air-conditioned offices in the capital, or other major cities, hopping from country to country for conferences around the globe, and doing 'advocacy work'—a fancy term for churning out reports that put you to sleep by the time you reach page three. (Dhillon, 1997) NGOs are in the throes of a credibility crisis; a crisis brought about by racketeers amongst them. The examples of their misdemeanours now abound. The Council for Advancement of People's Action and Rural Technology (CAPART), a Government of India organisation that supports the projects and activities of NGOs, recently blacklisted 400 such organisations. The Central Social Welfare Board (CSWB), which funds NGOs on behalf of the Department of Women and Child Development, has a long blacklist of 3,000 NGOs.

Limitations of the NGO Approach

One major limitation is that NGOs often do not operate in areas where their need is the greatest. Then there are places where there is a heavy concentration. In Singrauli region, efforts of the NTPC to involve NGOs in resettlement activities proved largely unsuccessful. Most local NGOs were neither professionally equipped nor very willing to come forward to collaborate on resettlement tasks. This led the NTPC to set up their own NGO, called 'Chetna', which is managed by their staff in its spare time.

NGOs tend to get rooted at one place and they find it difficult to expand their operations in other places. For example, an NGO that has done successful work in resettlement in Bombay may also not necessarily be equally effective in Calcutta, and may be reluctant to move over to a new place. The NGOs in Calcutta too may not much welcome an outside NGO on their home turf.

The management capacity of NGOs is often a great limitation, hindering their overall effectiveness. Generally NGOs are without adequately equipped staff to deal with day-to-day problems of management and accounting. With a tight budget they tend to economise on such activities.

While NGOs have played an important role in resettlement, often their outreach has remained limited. People served are usually a fraction of the affected population. When asked about the role of NGOs in their communities, most people rank the contribution of the NGOs to their development as secondary to the government efforts. Even in areas where they operate, the people are often unaware of their existence.

NGOs are willing to work with government agencies under contract, but quibble over the use of term 'contractor' to describe their legal status. Although contracting is one of the important functions of NGOs, the term 'contractor' evokes a negative perception of their role. (Partly this may be due to the fact that the expression 'contractor' is not felicitious in India.) Some NGOs choose a confrontational stance. They see no use in any collaborative relationship with development agencies. The presence of NGOs with an adversarial outlook proves a hindrance to agencies providing resettlement assistance to those affected by development projects. Such NGOs tend to keep away from government agencies, and this prevents a potentially productive relationship from developing.

Recognising the limitations of the NGO approach in the context of resettlement, Morse and Berger (1992, 131) observed: "But there is a limit to what non-government organizations can achieve. They may be effective at the level of community mobilization and policy design; they may have the ability and experience to shape policies in a way that no one else could; and they may be able to help the process of implementation. But their resources do not allow them to achieve all this for thousands of families spread across several hundred villages...Nor should they be expected even to attempt so vast an undertaking."

Growing Disenchantment

NGOs can play a useful role, providing much needed support to development agencies responsible for resettlement management. But many NGOs, those based in the capital and other big cities in particular, tend to steer away from resettlement work. Apart from the remoteness of rural areas, what seems to hold them back is the difficult nature of this task. Success in resettlement operations is often hard to achieve. In case of failure, they may lose their credibility, and this is a risk they are unprepared to take. Instead, they find it more rewarding networking with their counterparts in capitals of the developed world. There is a growing feeling among development agencies that NGOs are generally reluctant to come forward to do field jobs (implementing income generation schemes for the displaced people, for example). Their preference is clearly to stay back in their offices and do research and such desk jobs.

Many NGOs simply lack the experience necessary to perform their job. Galab and Reddy (1998) report one scheme of income generation for displaced people from the Singoor project that did not work due to the NGO's lack of familiarity with local traditions and conditions. Despite reluctance of the people, this NGO went forward with its plan to distribute high milk yielding Jersey cows, little aware of the fact that these people had neither experience of nor inclination for rearing cows. The NGO did not even bother to check the local demand for milk. As people could not take due care of cows or feed them properly, many cows died. A few that survived the neglect, turned largely unproductive.

Often, NGOs arrive on the scene with the project. They would not be around if there were no projects. Many NGOs have sprung up from almost nowhere simply because there is money in resettlement. They are game for anything that promises to be lucrative. "NGOs are getting into event management, media management and business planning for better returns. Today, heading an NGO is almost like running a business. These organisations sell everything—gender sensitisation, sanitation, AIDs awareness, palliative care, education, policy research, legal advice, water management, tree plantation and housing". (Kaul, 2000: 1)

The cash compensation is never adequate to enable the displaced to rebuild their livelihoods, yet the NGOs in the Singrauli region have often negotiated with the NTPC for just cash payment. Perera (2000: 62) reports: "NGOs and rural activists also contribute to the 'compensation bias' in the resettlement process. Many of them believe that high compensation would help PAPs (project-affected persons) to improve their living standards and 'fight' for higher compensation rates. As a result, they hardly show any interest in income rehabilitation strategies or in helping the PAPs to develop such strategies. For instance, they could have helped in identifying suitable land to purchase and suggested some investment programmes." For NGOs getting higher compensation for the displaced people is an attractive proposition. It is the easiest way to organise them and to win quick battles (though in the long run cash compensation may prove inadequate for proper resettlement).

A major criticism against NGOs is their reliance on government funding support. Increasingly, the NGOs are becoming mere contractors for government agencies, middlemen who take money for a job, and often do it indifferently. In this context, Slim (1997, 210) made a very apt remark: "Increasingly dependent on government funding, it is becoming commonplace to question the appropriateness of the 'N' in the NGO acronym".

The anti-development slant of some NGOs has provoked wide criticism. As Singh (1997) reported, the campaigning against the construction of Sardar Sarovar Dam on Narmada river, the Narmada Bachao Andolan (NBA) went as far as preventing all project officials and other government officers from entering the project area villages. This put the tribal people of the valley in a position of total dependence on the NBA for information and leadership. The people earlier deprived of basic information about the prospect of displacement now received incomplete information on resettlement opportunities, and—more importantly perhaps—on possibilities of negotiation for improved resettlement. Gill (1995) goes as far as to speak of the 'reign of terror' unleashed by the NBA on government officials as well as on those oustees who preferred to negotiate with the government in the light of a revised resettlement policy. He questions the NBA claim that the oustees are against the dam *per se*, and determined to oppose displacement no matter what the government offers them. He also cites the cases where oustees have had to resist the NBA's pressure tactics in order to establish contact with the government to discuss resettlement. He also criticises NBA's disinformation activities.

Once established at any project site, NGOs seem to be in no hurry to finish the job and get out of it. On one pretext or the other, they tend not to phase out, ensuring that local capacity building does not take place. They conveniently forget that "the goal should be to decrease dependency of relocatees on all outside organisations, not simply replace dependency on government agencies with dependency on NGOs". (Koenig Dolores and Tieman Diarra, 2000: 353) Far from turning communities into self-reliant entities, they themselves are becoming dependent on them for 'doing development' in perpetuity. While nobody suggests the withdrawal without first preparing people to take full charge of their affairs, yet the reluctance to hand over local affairs to people's own local organisations is not desirable.

The NGO Viewpoint

The NGO list of complaints against development agencies, and the way they manage resettlement, is also a long one. A major complaint is that when they are asked to do resettlement, it is to ask them to do work that can hardly be successful, the failure for which NGOs will then have to take responsibility. A related complaint is that usually they are brought into the picture too late, and are then expected to produce results magically.

In the Singoor Project where NGOs were associated with income generating schemes for the displaced people, the NGO experience with government agencies has not been a very happy one. (Galab and Reddy, 1998) In implementing resettlement activities the NGOs faced certain difficulties in working with the resettlement and rehabilitation authorities. While NGOs were given a relatively free hand in the preparation of resettlement action plans, the same kind of autonomy was not allowed during the implementation phase. This often resulted in frictions between NGOs and the authorities. In some villages, this led to great delays in programme implementation. The required level of co-operation from officials (particularly those at the grass-roots) was lacking. Although purchase committees were constituted comprising the displaced people, the officials and the NGO representatives, officials on many occasions did not agree with the choice of the displaced people related to the purchase of the asset. On many occasions purchases could not take place due to the authoritarian attitude of some officials. In animal husbandry related schemes, the displaced people were given no voice in selecting the places from where to purchase animals. Project-affected families were forced to travel to places as far away as 500 kilometres, undergoing much hardship. It is true that some displaced people were involved in fictitious purchases at one point of time, but selecting the purchase locations at such far off places was unwarranted. In the circumstances, the NGOs could do nothing to help the poor people. Still, involvement of the NGOs improved the process substantially. Had the project authorities given more discretion to NGOs, the economic rehabilitation programme would have proceeded much more effectively in mitigating the hardships to the people affected.

NGOs are not oblivious to some of their own weaknesses and are, in fact, quite concerned about the rapid loss of their popularity. Their protests against development projects do not seem to evoke the kind of response that they should. Analysing the reasons why NGO protests do not enjoy adequate hearing space or acquire the necessary momentum and political clout (Sethi, 1995: 9) observed: "that they have, in the main, been marked by weaknesses and schisms in the mobilisation of different players. For instance, in the case of the Narmada Valley Project, differences between those who were arguing for appropriate relief and rehabilitation for the displaced and those who articulated a blanket 'no dam' position: between those who favoured a greater mobilisation of the project affected people and those who sought to lobby and influence the concerned officialdom, did not help in conveying a sense of cohesion. It also helped the Government to play off one set of activists against another. Secondly, all such movements have so far been led by NGOs, which to put it mildly, have enjoyed an antagonistic relationship with political parties."

Summing Up

The number of NGOs engaged in resettlement work is rapidly rising, and their role is now being more fully acknowledged. The fact is that many of the constituent activities of resettlement management are better suited to organisations in the NGO sector. As Cernea (1996) noted, many NGOs have proven themselves very effective in designing resettlement plans and realistic options, acceptable not only to the people but also to governments, and in mobilising the energies of the resettlers for better implementation and monitoring of those plans. Morse and Berger (1992) found commendable the role played by NGOs in relocating people affected by the Sardar Sarovar Narmada Project in Gujarat and observed that without Arch Vahini and Anand Niketan the resettlement process would have been little short of disastrous.

The NGO presence in many project areas has made people more vocal in demanding their rightful claims. As (Marsden, 1998: 24) pointed out, "the emergence of large number of organisations of civil society has meant that poor performance is increasingly visible, and more easily translates into pressures for action and change. It is no longer easy for powerful organisations to ride roughshod over the interests of the weak and marginalised, or to impose solutions which have not been publicly debated and agreed to by all the major stake-holders."

On the other hand, where there are no NGOs, the displaced people are often unable to get resettlement assistance to which they are entitled. Parasuraman (1999) found the absence of NGOs in the Upper Krishna Project to be an important factor contributing to the unsatisfactory performance of resettlement programme. The absence of advocacy groups had serious negative consequences for the welfare of the displaced people. The multiplicity of castes, the numerical predominance of backward castes and the strong economic differences within and between the caste groups effectively prevented the people from organizing themselves to bargain for better R&R provisions. At the same time, the intervention of advocacy groups from outside the affected villages was also absent. In Punjab, too, the NGO activity is minimal, and there is much that the affected people have lost due to this lack of NGO support. (Judgem, 1997)

NGOs have been lobbying for a national R&R policy for a long time. When the draft national policy, prepared in the Government of India's Ministry of Rural Development, found its way into the hands of some social activists, NGOs took it as an opportunity to reflect on it, organise discussions around this theme and to come up with their own alternative policy paper. Accordingly three national meetings were held for the purpose in 1995-96 which over 1500 NGOs attended from all over the country. They also looked at the Land Acquisition Act of 1894 and suggested a reformulation. (Fernandes, 1998) The NGO contribution to the process of policy formulation is indeed very significant, though it is a different matter that the national policy on resettlement is still at a draft stage. (Cernea, 2000)

NGOs have been in the forefront in warning the governments and international donors against neglecting resettlement dimension in the development process. It is the NGO pressures that have led to recent improvements in resettlement planning and implementation processes, and much better resettlement packages are now being increasingly offered to assist the affected people to improve their previous levels of living. Recognising the many achievements of NGOs in the difficult and sensitive area of resettlement. Mathur and Marsden (1998: 20) succinctly summed up their contribution as follows: "If involuntary resettlement today figures prominently on the development agenda, much credit for it must go to the voluntary organisations. Their persistent campaigns, giving a voice to the people marginalised by development projects, have done a lot to bring about a perceptible change in the way the resettlement task is now visualised."

REFERENCES

Bhatt, Anil. (1992). *From Adversary to Collaborator: The Role of an NGO in Rehabilitation and Resettlement of Tribal Oustees*. IIAS, Brussels (mimeo)

Cernea, Michael. M. (1996). "Understanding and Preventing Impoverishment from Displacement: Reflections on the State of Knowledge", in Christopher McDowell (ed) 1996. *Understanding Impoverishment: The Consequences of Development-Induced Displacement*. Providence/Oxford: Berghahan Books.

Cernea, Michael M. (2000). "Resettlement Scene in India: Some Thoughts on Research Priorities" *The Eastern Anthropologist (Special Resettlement Issue)* Vol. 53, Numbers 1 and 2, January-June 2000 (pp. 3-12).

Das, Achyut, Das. (1998). "Role of NGOs in Rehabilitation and Resettlement", *in* Pyarimohan Mohapatra (ed) 1998. *Development Induced Displacement and Rehabilitation*. New Delhi/Bhubneswar: Prachi Prakashan.

Dhagamwar, Vasudha. (1997). " The NGO Movements in the Narmada Valley: Some Reflections", in Jean Dreze, Meera Samson and Satyajit Singh. (eds) 1997. *The Dam and the Nation: Displacement and Resettlement in the Narmada Valley*, New Delhi: Oxford University Press.

Dhillon, Amrit. (1997). "Anti-social Service: The Government and Non-governmental Organisations Face a Financial and Credibility Crisis as Racketeers Masquerading as Voluntary Outfits Siphon Off Funds"' *India Today*, Vol. XXII, Number 34, 11-17 November 1997. (pp. 58-59).

Dreze, Jean, Meera Samson and Satyajit Singh. (eds). (1997). *The Dam and the Nation: Displacement and Resettlement in the Narmada Valley*, New Delhi: OxfordUniversity Press.

Fernandes, Walter. (1998). "The National Draft Policy for Rehabilitation: Principles of the NGO Alternative" in Hari Mohan Mathur and David Marsden (eds) 1998. *Development Projects and Impoverishment Risks: Resettling Project-Affected People in India.* New Delhi: Oxford University Press.

Fowler, Alan. (1990). "Doing it Better? Where and How NGOs have a 'Comparative Advantage' in Facilitating Development", University of Reading. 1990. *AERRD Bulletin*. (28 February 1990, pp. 11-20).

Galab, S. and M. Gopinath Reddy. (1998). "Displacement, Resettlement and Rehabilitation: A Case of Singoor Project in Andhra Pradesh", *ASCI Journal of Management*, Volume 28, Number 1, September 1998 (pp. 120-144).

Gazelius, Helena and David Millwood. (1988). *NGOs in Development and Participation in Practice: An Initial Inquiry*. Stockholm: University of Stockholm (Department of Social Anthropology).

Gill, Maninder. (1995). "Resettlement and Rehabilitation in Maharashtra for the Sardar Sarovar Narmada Project", in William F. Fisher (1995) *Working Towards Sustainable Development?: The Damming of the Narmada River in Western India.* New Work: M.E. Sharpe.

Jaeger, D. (1986). "Organising the Framework for a Large and Small Scale Rural Policy", in Martyn Keith Kingdon Morris (ed) 1986. *Rural Development for Poverty Alleviation* (Jubilee Symposium on the Effectiveness of Cooperation in Rural Development) Amsterdam: Foris Publications.

Judge, Paramjit S. (1997). "Response to Dams and Displacement in Two Indian States", *Asian Survey'* Vol. XXXVII, No. 9, September 1997 (pp. 840-851).

Kaul, Malvika. (2000). "Corporate Makeover for NGO Jholawalla", *The Sunday Times of India Review,* New Delhi, 21 May 2000 (p. 1).

Koenig Dolores and Tieman Diarra. (2000). "The Effects of Resettlement on Access to Common Property Resources", in Michael M. Cernea and Christopher McDowell (eds.) 2000. *Risks and Reconstruction: Experiences of Resettlers and Refugees.* Washington DC: The World Bank.

Marsden, David. (1998). "Resettlement and Rehabilitation in India: Some Lessons from Recent Experience", in Hari Mohan Mathur and David Marsden (Eds). 1998. *Development Projects and Impoverishment Risks: Resettling Project-Affected People in India.* New Delhi: Oxford University Press.

Mathur, Hari Mohan. (1999). "The Impoverishing Potential of Development Projects: Resettlement Requires Risk Analysis", *Development and Cooperation (D+C),* No . 6/199, November-December (pp. 24-26).

Mathur, Hari Mohan and David Marsden (1998). "Introduction and Overview", in Hari Mohan Mathur and David Marsden (eds). 1998. *Development Projects and Impoverishment Risks: Resettling Project-Affected People in India.* New Delhi: Oxford University Press.

Mathur, Hari Mohan and David Marsden (eds). (1998). *Development Projects and Impoverishment Risks: Resettling Project-Affected People in India.* New Delhi: Oxford University Press.

McCully, Patrick. (1996). *Silenced Rivers: The Ecology and Politics of Large Dams.* London: Zed Books.

McDowell, Christopher. (ed) (1996). *Understanding Impoverishment: The Consequences of Development-Induced Displacement.* Providence/Oxford: Berghahn Books.

Morse, Bradford and Thomas Berger. (1992). *Sardar Sarovar: The Report of the Independent Review.* Ottawa; Resource Futures International (RFI) Inc.

Pandey, Balaji. 1996. "The Role of NGOs in Effective Resettlement and Rehabilitation of the Displaced", in A.B. Ota and Anita Agnihotri (eds). 1996. *Involuntary Displacement in Dam Projects.* New Delhi: Prachi Prakashan.

Parasuraman, S. 1999. *The Development Dilemma: Displacement in India.* London: Macmillan.

Perera, Jayantha. 2000. "Compensation *versus* Rehabilitation in the Singrauli Resettlement Projects," *The Eastern Anthropologist (Special Resettlement Issue)* Vol. 53, Numbers 1 and 2, January-June 2000 (pp. 53-71).

Ramachandran, Vimla. 1996. "Committed and Crooked: NGOs Need a Code of Conduct", *The Times of India.* New Delhi, 29 November 1996 (p. 10).

Roy, Arundhati. 1999. *The Greater Common Good.* Bombay: India Book Distributors (Bombay) Ltd.

Sekhsaria, Pankaj. 1996. "The Struggle of Koel Karo", *The Ecologist Asia,* Vol. 4 Number 1, January/February 1996 (pp. 37-40).

Sethi, Harsh. 1995. "Inherent Weakness: NGOs Can Only be Irritants to Vested Interests", *The Pioneer,* New Delhi, 24 June 1995, Saturday (p. 9).

Singh, Satyajit. 1997. "Introduction", in Jean Dreze, Meera Samson and Satyajit Singh (eds.) 1997. *The Dam and the Nation: Displacement and Resettlement in the Narmada Valley.* Delhi: Oxford University Press.

Slim, Hugo. 1997. "To the Rescue: Radicals or Poodles?", *The World Today*, Volume 53, Numbers 8-9, August/September 1997 (pp. 209-12).

The Hindu. 1999. "Villagers Submit Memo Against NBA", *The Hindu*, New Delhi, Thursday 22 April 1999 (p. 4).

The Observer. 1998. Campaign Against Narmada Bachao Andolan, *The Observer* (of Business and Politics), New Delhi, 14 July 1998 (p. 8).

Udall, Lori. 1995. "The International Narmada Campaign: A Case of Sustained Advocacy", in William F. Fisher (ed.) 1995. *Towards Sustainable Development? Struggling Over India's Narmada River*. New York: M.E. Sharpe, Inc.

Uphoff, Norman. 1989. *Approaches to Community Participation in Agriculture and Rural Development*. Washington DC: Economic Development Institute of the World Bank.

World Bank. 2001. *Operational Policies 4.12. Involuntary Resettlement*. Washington DC: The World Bank.

25

Brain Drain or the Migration of Talent*

T.K. OOMMEN

The Issue

For many years there has been some concern about the migration of skilled people from the Less Developed Countries (LDCs) to the developed and rich countries of Western Europe, North America, and Australia. Much of the views expressed in the past were based on ill-defined concepts and inadequate quantitative data. But more recently, there have been some studies which have contributed towards a clearer perception of this phenomenon.

Two contrasting views appear to be prominent in the debate on 'brain drain'. The first assumes that the enormous investment of scarce resources on higher education in the LDCs is lost through the migration of skilled people from their countries, and this problem (migration) is reaching crisis proportions. The other view suggests that the LDCs are exaggerating the problem of the migration of the skilled, and only a few of their professionals are actually migrating at any point of time. Thus there is not much of an impact on their economies specially when they cannot even employ all the skilled manpower that they generate through their educational institutions.

The main concern with 'brain drain' is that an inordinate number of professionals, including scientists, engineers and allopathic doctors are

* Originally printed in International Migration, 1989, Vol. 27, No. 3

seen to migrate from LDCs. These skills can be utilized in any country, unlike professions such as law which calls for knowledge of specific societies, cultures and norms, in addition to technical expertise. Lawyers, thus, cannot easily practice their profession in an alien cultural milieu. This essay concentrates on the migration of scientists, engineers and allopathic medical doctors from India to the countries of the West.

Only a relatively small number of scientists, engineers and medical doctors migrated immediately before and after Indian Independence, *i.e.* in the 1940s and 1950s (Misra, 1985: 1-10). An important reason for this was the racial proclivities of the host countries, which discouraged, and to a large extent prevented, immigration from Asian countries. For instance, Australia followed a 'whites only' policy till 1958 which encouraged immigration from countries such as Britain but discouraged immigration from Asia (London, 1970). There were quotas to restrict the number of Asian migrants who would be admitted into the United States of America, Canada and other countries. These quotas were relaxed in the U.S.A. in 1965 (see Gujral and Gupta, 1983:1-6); in 1958 and 1966 in Australia; in 1967 in Canada; and in 1962 and 1965 in Britain (Bhagwati, 1976 : 3-27). Till 1962, Britain had allowed relatively large numbers of migrants from the Commonwealth countries (see Misra, 1985: 1-10). The new immigration laws that these countries introduced removed the racist restriction on immigration, but the focus was shifted to the skills that immigrants could bring with them. Thus, highly skilled professionals were preferred, who would meet the requirement of specific skills which may be in short supply in the host countries. The largest migrations since then from India were to the U.S.A., Canada and Britain (Bhagwati, 1976 : 3-27).

In the literature on 'brain drain' from India, frequent references are made to the cost of education, incurred by the country, which is lost through the migration of professionals. For instance, the cost of training an engineer to graduate level in the Indian Institutes of Technology (IIT) is roughly computed at US$ 14,000, most of which is borne by the Indian Government. The IIT graduates are considered the cream of Indian engineers and the loss to India through their migration is not only seen in monetary terms, but also in terms of their possible contribution to the development of the Indian economy. Very often, Indian authors tend to stress the loss to India, but they do not consider the cost that host countries incur when these migrants study at their institutions and at their cost. For instance, the cost borne by the United States of America (the preferred country for advanced study) when Indian students study at U. S. universities at U.S. expense (see Bayer 1968 : 465-77), is ignored. Many of these students return to India, and this constitutes a loss to the U. S. (Baldwin, 1970 : 358-72). Trying to figure out who pays for what and how much each country gains or loses when professionals migrate, will lead to endless argument with no firm conclusions being reached. India does not totally lose its investment in education when professionals migrate, since they contribute to knowledge even when they are based in other countries and they also send remittances to their family members and relatives still in India (see Grubel, 1968 : 541-58). Some of these migrants do return to India after a few years in the foreign countries, and thus can make direct contributions through the use of their skills in India. 'Brain drain' is thus not an issue that can be considered a 'problem' without various qualifications. Certainly India would benefit from the skills of professionals who remain in the country but, perhaps, when professionals return to India after advanced training they would be of even more benefit to the country. The problem, therefore, would be in devising ways to attract the highly skilled professionals who are now based in other countries to return and settle down in India.

A point to be considered in any debate on the migration of professionals is about what they would be doing in India when they do not choose to migrate. If these professionals were just to join the considerable number of unemployed in the country, it will be a greater drain on the country's resources since they are virtually unproductive, and they have to be fed. Thus the migration of professionals has to be seen from various angles, from the point of view of the costs involved in their training, to the possible employment of their skills. The foreign exchange that they can remit if they were abroad, the fact that a democratic country cannot prevent professionals leaving if they wanted to, and so on. It cannot be said that there is no problem at all when professionals migrate, but a more pragmatic approach would be to consider the ways and means of having professionals get the best of advanced training in other countries (if such training is not available in India itself) and then return to India.

The Concept of 'Brain Drain'

The concept of 'brain drain' has been used rather indiscriminately by many, and to refer to all migration of people who are of a high educational level. But it carries some emotive and pejorative connotations, and therefore needs to be carefully qualified (see Adams, 1968: 1-8). In recent years the concept is more circumspectly used and has also gained some clarity. However, for our purpose, the phrase 'migration of talent' or 'migration of professionals' will be used rather than 'brain drain'. This is to take note of the fact that when professionals migrate from India, not all of them remain permanently in those countries. Some do, but many return.

'Migration of talent' indicates both migration from India as well as return to India, a two-way movement of professionals. 'Brain drain' on the other hand does not indicate this two-way movement adequately, but rather emphasizes only a one-way movement of professionals out of India (Ahmad, 1970 : 215-22). We need to consider also the return of professionals since they are a benefit to their own country: also that they may not have. been able to acquire an advanced training and experience if they had remained in their own country.

Studies on the migration of professionals suggest different perspectives from which the problem can be considered. The 'Internationalist' model proposed by Johnson (1968 : 69-91) suggests that the migration of professionals only reflects the operation of an international market for specialised human capital. The model considers the transfer of talent as mutually advantageous to both the sending as well as the host countries, and that a *laissez-faire* policy, *i.e.* non-interference with migration, should be followed. Opposed to this, is the 'Nationalist' model (Patinkin, 1968 : 92-108) which regards human capital, or at least a minimum level of human capital, as indispensable to a country's economic development. A loss of skilled persons will ultimately result in the economy being gravely affected and development programmes being jeopardised (Adams, 1968 : 1-8).

Baldwin (1970 : 358-72) makes the distinction between society's 'human needs' and the economy's 'effective demand' which is useful in placing the two models (Internationalist and Nationalist) in a proper perspective. The Internationalist model gives more importance to the 'effective demand' of the economy while the Nationalist model places more importance on the society's 'human needs'.

Who Migrates? Where To? and Why?

Most of the migrants from the LDCs are students (Ahmad, 1970 : 215-22). Through migrating, they hope or intend to avail themselves of the best possible facilities, get trained under professors of better standing and repute than are found in their countries, learn the latest developments in their fields, and use better equipment than that available in their own countries. In the more prestigious and better universities, particularly, the facilities are likely to be far superior to those available in their own countries (*cf.* Klaw, 1969). Moreover, outstanding scientists tend to be concentrated in a few institutions and laboratories, and these concentrations make it more likely that a small number of organizations provide evocative environments and are thus the sites of major scientific achievements. A further reason for students and scientists to migrate to advanced countries is that through studying and working with outstanding scientists and in prestigious institutions, they not only acquire superior training, but also gain some prestige through working in these institutions. This prestige could be converted into better jobs at home, when they return, or in the case of medical doctors, a more lucrative private practice in their home country. An added incentive to migrate is also the much higher scales of remuneration than in their own country.

A review of the available data shows that the students who had been awarded post-graduate and doctoral degrees and are now settled in India acquired them from a few preferred countries. From the United States there had been 40 per cent of all overseas doctorates and masters and in all the fields that Indians had studied abroad and returned. Thirty-five to forty per cent of the doctorates and masters degrees were acquired from British universities, and the remaining 20-25 per cent were awarded these degrees from other countries.

Table 1: Country Bias in Acquiring Foreign Qualifications (1971)

Country of Qualification	*All Fields*				
	Total	*Doctorate*	*Master*	*Bachelor*	*Others*
U K	33.4	35.2	39.5	23.7	38.8
USA	28.0	40.5	40.7	14.1	7.3
Canada	2.0	4.0	2.0	1.2	1.4
USSR	1.6	3.5	0.9	1.4	1.8
Germany	3.1	6.4	2.0	1.8	6.5
France	1.3	1.8	1.0	1.2	1.7
Other European countries	3.7	4.7	2.9	3.1	6.1
Australia and New Zealand	1.0	1.2	1.0	0.6	1.6
Japan	0.7	0.3	0.3	0.9	1.9
Others	25.2	2.4	9.7	52.0	32.6
Total	100.0	100.0	100.0	100.0	100.0

Magnitude of Migration from India

About 11,000 university graduates, which includes doctors, engineers and scientists, leave the country every year for advanced study and/or work. A conservative estimate suggests that, of this number, about 2,500 will remain abroad permanently, and the rest will return to India. In 1967, the annual migration of the highly educated was about 10 per cent of all university graduates. About 11 per cent of scientists migrated, and also about 20 per cent of the Indian Institutes of Technology (IIT) graduates of 1961-1965. The permanent loss each year is about 2.6 per cent of university graduates, 7 per cent of doctors, 7 per cent of engineers and 2.5 per cent of scientists. Many of the migrants are graduates of prestigious institutions including the IITs and the Indian Institute of Science (IISc, at Bangalore). About 50 per cent of the graduates from the IISc and about 60 per cent of the doctorates from the same institution go abroad every year (Domrese, 1970:215-57).

The largest number of professionals migrate to the U.S.A. and Canada. In the five-year period ending in June 1967 (*i.e.* 1962-1967) over 10,000 Indians are reported to have migrated to the U.S.A. out of which just over 5,000 were professionals and technical workers. This included 2, 141 engineers, 624 physical scientists, 174 physicians and 78 social scientists. In the same five-year period, about 7,000 Indians had migrated to Canada, and just about 2,000 were of the professional category and technical workers. This included 408 engineers, 206 natural scientists and 164 physicians (*Technical Manpower,* April 1970).

Between 1977 and 1979 the total number of professionals who migrated to the United States was 8,035 (scientists, engineers and medical doctors excluding social scientists). The total number of these three groups in each of the three years was: 3,298 in 1977; 2,673 in 1978; and 2,064 in 1979. The most noticeable trend was that over the years the number of physicians migrating to the U.S.A. has been declining. From a total of 1,984 doctors in 1977 to only 598 migrating in 1979 makes a considerable decline. One of the reasons for such a decline seems to be that there are not more than a few good residencies available to doctors from India. If the trend continues, the 'drain' of doctors to the U.S.A. will automatically 'dry up'.

While it is difficult to say exactly how many Indians among the professionals have left India to settle permanently in a foreign country, there were probably about 30,000 of this category who were abroad in 1971-1972, when in India the unemployed numbered about 110,000 (Banerjea, 1975:190-4). At this time (1971) the total number of Indian physicians working in the U.S.A. was 3,959 (see *Technical Manpower,* August-September, 1973).

Factors Promoting Migration

Unemployment

One of the most frequently asserted explanations to account for the high rate of migration of professionals is that the Indian economy cannot employ all the professionals produced by Indian universities and institutions of learning. As Usha Nayar (1985: 1-13) says, the number of graduates in science and technology produced by Indian universities is fewer than the number of graduates that American universities turn out every year. But the American economy needs even more highly skilled persons, whereas the Indian economy cannot absorb even the small number of graduates from Indian universities.

Grubel (1976 : 209-24) suggests that India over-invested in education since the end of the second world war. When one considers the available limited opportunities, this may well be the case. Moreover, there are only a few institutions that can employ the scientists that graduate each year. The Government of India has placed more emphasis on a few 'key institutions' to provide the impetus to research and high quality education. Private and public sector industries also employ scientists in their laboratories, but far less than the corresponding employment of scientists in research in the developed countries (see Research and Development Statistics, 1982-1983, Government of India, Department of Science and Technology, p. 30). Thus, of the total number of graduates in science produced every year, only a small proportion can be employed in these institutions.

Further, graduates at prestigious institutions prefer to work in high-paying and prestigious occupations and institutions. Thus, of the graduates of the IISc who enter the academic profession, about 10 per cent teach in the IITs (Domrese, 1970 : 215-57). Higher expectations among these graduates, and possible disappointment when they do not get the kind of high-paying and higher prestige jobs that they want, may be one possible reason for the migration to other countries. However, administrators of the five IITs blame Indian industry for failing to provide IIT graduates with jobs that are sufficiently challenging and also with more opportunities for advancement in their careers (see Neri, 1985 : 40-57).

Immigration Rules

Countries differ in culture, economic development, political systems, and so on, which could influence the migrant. An important condition for migration is the immigration laws that exist in various countries. Countries that favour immigration would obviously be more likely to attract more migrants than those that do not. The countries of the First World have by and large been in favour of attracting professionals to work in their countries. Socialist countries, on the other hand (the Soviet Union and countries of the Warsaw Pact) do not normally admit immigrants although they allow students to stay in their countries until their studies are completed.

The migration of professionals is to be seen as a temporary stay in any country abroad, and in some instances merely exploratory in nature. Most of them would return to their home country sooner or later. Their return could, however, be expedited if attractive conditions of work and suitable jobs are available in their own country (Glaser and Habers, 1978).

Compared to migrants from some countries such as Brazil and Pakistan, Indians appear to be more prone to emigrate. However, even among the Indians abroad, only a minority are definite in their plans to settle down in the country to which they had migrated. For example, the UNITAR survey found that of the Indians abroad, 34 per cent definitely planned to return to India, 14 per cent thought it was probable that they would return, 22 per cent were uncertain about their future plans, 21 per cent thought it was probable that they would emigrate and only 9 per cent were definite that they would stay abroad permanently (Glaser and Habers, 1978).

Colonial Links

Some of the nation-states from which there are much higher rates of migration as also of non-return are former colonies of such countries. For example, the migrants to Britain from India are much more familiar with the educational system of Britain since India closely follows the pattern established by the British. The majority of the professionals (probably all) in India are educated through the English language. Thus, it is likely that migrants prefer to go to countries of former colonial powers in the belief that their problems of adaptation will be much less, compared to another country with a different language and unfamiliar culture. That is why, for example, fewer Indians migrate to Japan compared to those who migrate to Britain (Glaser and Habers, 1978; Johnson, 1968:69-91).

Religious minorities, for example Christians from India, migrate in large numbers not because they face persecution in the country (Christians are rarely discriminated against or persecuted) but because there is a considerable number of schools and colleges, some founded by the British and managed by Christian institutions, to which they had easy accessibility and through which they are educated. These schools follow a system compatible with those countries where English is the dominant language, particularly Britain, which also have predominantly Christian populations. Language and religion thus make it easier for the migrants to interact with the people of those countries, and perhaps the Indian Christians can find the environment more congenial and less foreign than those of other religious groups from India.

Financial Incentives and Material Benefits

In India professionals are not paid enough to be able to maintain what they consider a respectable' standard of life. By this is meant better housing, good schools for their children, ownership of a car, a refrigerator, a television, etc. The cost of living has gone up considerably in the country and the inventory of things regarded as essential for a comfortable life-style has also increased.

The income that a highly skilled professional can earn in a Western country could be anything like 4-5 times what he would earn in India. By remaining in India many of the material benefits that he could get within a short time would be available to him only by investing all his savings, and probably only a couple of decades after beginning his career. An average middle class family in India would not be able to afford much of the technical gadgets and conveniences that most people in the West take for granted. This would be an attraction for those professionals who are eager to have these items, and could acquire them by migrating (see Chopra, 1985: 1-13; Glaser and Habers, 1978). Further, for those professionals who are expected to extend financial assistance to their kin (see Oommen, 1982: 57-93), employment outside the country is a great attraction as they can meet this obligation without sacrificing their own material requirements.

Professionals are an occupational elite in India. The status and prestige that are accorded to professionals such as physicians and engineers, are among the highest. But their income levels are not always commensurate with their high prestige and status. This is particularly true in the government institutions, which have fixed salaries. Private medical practice in urban areas is much more lucrative, and income levels may compare favourably with high ranking business executives of large private sector corporations. But such high incomes are limited only to a few of the professionals. High status and prestige may to some extent compensate for the lack of high salaries, but usually such attributes are achieved by professionals in India only after many years and in the latter years of their careers. Thus, the incongruence between high professional status and low income seems to be an important factor prompting the migration of professionals.

Higher Education

One of the most important factors that contributes to the migration of professionals from India is the lack of development in certain branches of knowledge. Much of the latest developments take place in the industrialized countries of the West, even as scientists from the Third World countries contribute to this. Most of the professionals from India travel abroad for higher studies as noted earlier. Some, however, may utilize 'study' as a means of going abroad and perhaps stay there permanently (see Ahmad, 1970 : 215-22; Fortney, 1970 : 217-32; Glaser and Habers, 1978).

The possibility of studying under, and working with, 'giants' in the field was an important reason for going abroad. The advantage of working with eminent persons abroad is easy recognition, and higher chance of getting entrenched in the system in the foreign country (see Zuckerman, 1977).

Working Conditions

Working conditions for professionals in the Western countries are considered far superior to those in India. Better facilities for research, better equipment and so on, encourage migration and also permanent settlement in foreign countries. Indians consider the professional milieu abroad better. Moreover, they do not feel particularly confident about making a professional contribution within the country (Glaser and Habers 1978).

Spectacular contributions to science in the last 50 years (*i.e.* between 1920 and 1970) from scientists in India are more likely to be found in the pre-Independence days than after Independence (Sudarshan, 1974 : 465-67). This, the author attributes to the system which does not discredit mediocrity, and does not have incentives for the exceptionals.

Many complaints are often made about the conditions of work in India. In scientific establishments such as the government laboratories and even within government departments, problems arise between administrators and technical experts. Very often the heads of departments are general administrators who are not likely to have the necessary expertise to make decisions on technical matters. They may not entirely rely on the engineers and scientists to provide recommendations towards policy making as well as in implementation, leading to much frustration among the experts, and to conflict between administrators and the technical experts (see Singh, 1975). The problem of 'protecting their turf' is not confined only to the general administrators but extends also to administrators who are themselves scientists.

Dissatisfaction is caused when directors of institutions, or heads of divisions in research laboratories, have a high degree of power concentrated in them. Lesser degree of professional autonomy, lack of professional recognition, and limited chances of promotion are other reasons for dissatisfaction in government institutions (see Aurora, n.d.). Naturally, the scientists who find the system not to their liking will probably choose to find more congenial surroundings in a foreign country.

It is possible that a 'patriarchal tradition' survives in Indian institutions. As Suri (1967 : 22-25) describes it, this involves, for instance, a literary tribute to a senior colleague (irrespective of his competence or achievement) who expects his juniors to include his name as author of the article that they write. It has become almost obligatory to pay such tribute. Such a system would give undue credit to persons who are highly placed in the institution's hierarchy and perhaps even deny credit to the person who had done the work. Suri considers this as a practice that would certainly upset a young researcher and may even prompt him to migrate. Writing recently about the Indian academic scene with reference to the social sciences, Oommen (1983: 111-36) found a similar persistence of patron-client ties.

Excessive Bureaucratic Procedures

A serious problem that scientists in India appear to face is the excessive amount of red-tape involved in the course of their work. Buying new equipment, getting old ones repaired, and even to acquire the barest essential and cheaper materials involve procedures which take up an inordinate amount of time and effort. What makes this worse is that on occasion the researcher has to justify expenses to bureaucrats who are not technically qualified to make such judgments. Homi Bhabha, who is considered as one of the most eminent scientists that India has produced in the 20th century, is said to have complained about this same problem in the 1950s. He had felt that as a consequence his scientific work suffered. When even a scientist of the standing of Bhabha had to put up with such bureaucratic controls, the plight of lesser scientists can well be imagined.

Conditions in other countries, especially the United States of America, are seen to be far better for scientific work, with less bureaucratric interference, and due recognition being given to talent, irrespective of age and status (see Chopra,1985 : 1-13).

Mismatch Between Indian Education and Employment

It has been suggested with reference to the training of allopathic physicians that Indian medical colleges turn out doctors who are more suited to Britain and the United States than to India (Jeffery, 1976 : 502-7). Jayaram (1977 : 207-20) goes even further and states that it is almost as if India maintains a certain number of medical colleges specifically for the benefit of other countries. The consumers of health services in Britain and the United States have their parallels in India only among the urban middle classes. The majority of Indians, who live in villages, and a large number of them very poor, do not have the resources to utilise the services of trained, allopathic physicians (see Mathur, 1971 : 58-96).

Soon after graduating, some of the doctors find themselves unemployed for varying lengths of time. This is because they cannot all be employed by government institutions, and neither can the urban middle classes provide enough work for them. Physicians find their working conditions unattractive in India, and this is specially when they know that they have the necessary skills to find employment in other countries (Jeffery, 1976: 502-7), which prompts them to migrate. The receptivity of host countries towards physicians is at least partly conditioned by the high cost and the comparable quality of training.

Reasons for Returning to India

Notwithstanding the many adverse conditions that exist in India, quite a few migrants do return. Some of these had returned as soon as they had completed their studies, and some had returned after working for a few years upon completion of their study. All those who return are well aware that the levels of income that they could hope for in India are far below what they were earning abroad or hoped to earn in foreign countries. Income and material benefits, while they are important factors which promote migration to western countries, apparently lost their importance to at least some of the professionals after some time, or other factors took precedence.

Panandikar's study (1971 : 46-57) found that there was a desire among the migrants to return home after a stay abroad of about 10-12 years. However, he also noticed that some of the returnees decided to return as their wives could not adjust to the foreign way of life.

Merriam's study (1969 : 52-82) also found that among the faculty of IIT, Kanpur, most of the foreign-trained would have returned to India even if the institution had not been laying down stringent conditions. Contributing to Indian development was a reason that many in that study had mentioned.

One of the reasons for their return was the racial discrimination that the scientists had experienced in the country where they had studied and worked. They felt that their being Indian was a major hurdle in not getting jobs and positions commensurate with their qualifications and experience. Although Indians in Britain considered this a major problem (see Schaefer,

1976 : 305-27), those in the United States were less concerned about racial discrimination (see Glaser and Habers, 1978).

Those who had been sponsored by the Government of India under various exchange programmes usually returned to India, as required according to the bond signed by them at the time of going abroad. Those who had gone on fellowships from foreign foundations also generally returned.

Inferences and Suggestions

In a brief essay such as the present one, it is possible to highlight only a few aspects of any problem such as the migration of professionals. We have pointed out the factors that encourage and induce migration, and those that further the return of the professionals. The basic assumption that has underlined our analysis is that any large-scale migration of professionals from a relatively less developed country such as India, with its enormous population, will have a detrimental effect on the total situation prevailing in the country. This detrimental effect is not sought to be gauged in terms of the monetary cost involved in training these professionals, but in terms of the long-term effects on the development of the country including distributive justice.

A better life for a majority of India's citizens calls for better health care, better education, better communication for the masses, and so on. While migration of professionals is to a certain extent inevitable—from the perspective of migrating individuals, given the underdeveloped state of the Indian economy, one has to consider the issue of migrating professionals also from the point of view of 'societal needs'. Indian society needs many things, not the least of which are the services of many more physicians, engineers and scientists.

The problem that many have recognized about Third World countries in general, and India in particular, is that there is too large a population in the country. The economy has to grow at a phenomenal rate to ensure any real increase in people's incomes and improvement in their standard of living. However, this has not taken place to any great extent and one finds that the income differences between those in the advanced countries and those in India are still very large. For the same level of skills, the professional could earn much more in an advanced country of the West. This factor is likely to be influential to a considerable degree in the foreseeable future, and there is no reason to expect that people will suddenly become less interested in their material well-being. Thus, there will always be some people who will find it an attractive idea to migrate to the western countries. It will not be easy to bring them back to India when the primary reason that motivated their leaving India was relatively higher income abroad.

Another category of migrants are those who had left the country with the intention of getting advanced training in their field of specialization; they are expected to return upon completion of their studies. Since they had no intention of remaining indefinitely in the foreign country, this group could be brought back to the country by attractive job offers and, other incentives such as new opportunities of using their skills through building up their areas of expertise in the country.

A third group of migrants leave the country because high quality research cannot be carried out in Indian laboratories. For such people ways must be found to bring them back. Indian laboratories do not seem to encourage the bright minds to explore new frontiers of knowledge. India's pre-occupation has been to educate the average and not encourage the gifted, leading to the nurturing of mediocrity to the detriment of the exceptionals. 'Not only have we eliminated hereditary royalty, but somehow suppressed intellectual aristocracy' (Sudarshan, 1974: 465). Recognizing that gifted individuals need a special kind of environment and expect preferential treatment, it will be to the advantage of the country to identify such individuals and provide them with as many facilities as possible so that their creative energies may not be wasted, and they do not choose to migrate instead (see Dhar, 1969:404-9).

Obviously the only way to employ more scientists is to increase expenditure on research and development. By investing only 0.85 per cent of the GNP on research and development, not more than a fraction of the annual turnover of science graduates could hope to find employment in scientific institutions and laboratories. On the other hand, the government, which is the major source of research funds, cannot devote more resources than it already does to research and development. However, it may be possible for the private industrial sector to invest more in developing indigenous products for the consumer market in the country. The private sector had spent only Rs. 161.382 crores compared to Rs. 997.29 crores spent by the government (Research and Development Statistics 1982-1983). By reducing the protective measures that the Government of India grants to Indian industries, it can make these industries more competitive, resulting in the manufacture of better products. This will be possible only if there is a greater investment in research and development which means a greater possibility of employing a large number of high quality scientists. Moreover, if the research products of the scientists are used in industry there is the greater chance that the scientists will find the work more rewarding and satisfying. This will result in scientists joining research laboratories in India, rather than thinking of leaving the country.

The possibility of travel to other countries to learn of the latest developments in their field, and to contribute to these developments through contacts and working with foreign scientists, should be open to Indian scientists too. This may be for short periods of time, such as in the case of the scientists who are sent to the International Centre for Theoretical Physics at Trieste, Italy (see Salam, 1966: 451-55). This kind of programme could be expanded to encourage a large number of scientists to periodically visit foreign laboratories and institutions for short periods. Such a programme will be beneficial to the country in the long run.

Finally, the conditions of research work should be made more conducive for creative effort. Getting bogged down with matters of procedure, in a typical bureaucratic style of functioning, is something that goes against the spirit of academic quest. Efforts should also be made to give proper and adequate recognition for scientific achievements. It has often been seen in the past that Indian scientists receive recognition in the country only after they have been honoured abroad. This may imply that talent is not intrinsically viewed in India, and there are not many incentives for the professionals to motivate them to do their best while they are in India. They usually produce outstanding results when they are working abroad. There does not seem to be any need or effort to realize one's potential fully in India, as if Indians could be satisfied by second best rather than striving for the best, while working for the country.

The migration of professionals from India in recent years has taken on the form of a collective exodus, and a pattern can be discerned in these migrations. That is, professionals do not migrate out of sheer individual impulse, but are also prompted through various conditions that exist in Indian society. Through the identification of some of these conditions, it is possible that solutions could be found to restrict the number of persons who choose to migrate, and also to bring back those who had already left. However, this involves drastic changes in the official policy towards scientific personnel, considering the fact that government measures already taken have yielded relatively less than impressive results. In this approach, one is required to jointly analyse two sets of factors—socio-economic and psychological attributes of the migrants and structural properties of the situation both at the points of departure and destination—in order to unfold the factors involved in migration and to prescribe remedies to moderate and/or prevent the exodus.

Perspectives on the Problem of the Migration of Talent

I would like to conclude this essay by suggesting that there are several hidden assumptions in the existing studies; unless one makes them explicit, one cannot unfold the full import and thrust of the conclusions arrived at by these studies. The problem of migration of talent can be viewed from at least three perspectives. These include: first of all, the perspective of the individual concerned, the professional who migrates. Secondly, one could look at the problem from the perspective of the nation-state. Thirdly, the problem can be considered from the point of view of developing a knowledge pool for the whole world.

From the point of view of the migrating individual, the fact of moving has many obvious benefits. The material benefits that an individual derives from working in a more prosperous country may be denied to him if he remains in his own country. Besides the material rewards he may also benefit in terms of working in an atmosphere more favourable for his scientific work. This makes him more cosmopolitan in outlook, and he begins to look at the whole world as his potential field of activity. This cosmopolitanism also fosters in him an individualism which transcends the claims of his country, region, cultural and kin group. This is not to suggest that all migrating professionals take an absolutely individualistic view. They are more likely to carefully consider different factors, weight them up, giving more importance to some and less importance to others. Ultimately it is the overall inference that he derives from these 'pros' and 'cons' that results in his decision to migrate.

A purely individualistic approach would consider migration of talent from the perspective of the benefits that accrue to the producer of knowledge, that is, the scientist. But once it is produced, it should not be constrained by artificial limits imposed on the people who possess knowledge from moving to any place they choose. Moreover, this free market economic orientation would probably go in favour of those with the highest hiring capacity, that is, the affluent countries.

From the point of view of the nation-state, the large-scale migration of professionals is not only a loss in terms of the knowledge that could be utilized in the country, but also that another nation-state that had not invested anything or very little in the development and training of the individual reaps the benefits that legitimately belong to the former. However, the problem of sorting out who benefits and who can automatically claim the loyalty of an individual is not so simple. When a scientist makes a contribution to knowledge in a country other than his native country, inevitably both countries stake the claim to their share of his success.

Besides claiming the loyalty of the scientists, the nation-state also strives to keep the knowledge produced by the scientist in question away from other countries. Knowledge, admittedly, has different values to different people. Scientists consider their contributions to knowledge as the property of the whole world, but the nation-state where they work, or the industrial corporation that sponsors their research, may consider these findings and discoveries as their private property, to be dispersed only at their discretion. This brings us to the third perspective, which is that the knowledge that is contributed by the scientist is considered the property of mankind as a whole. This contribution to knowledge is considered as an important aspect of a scientist's work regardless of his location and citizenship.

There could also be cases where a nation-state is perceived as indifferent to providing the necessary work environment for scientific research. However, that does not prevent it from showing pride in the achievements of its scientists. For instance, though much of the work by S. Chandrasekhar and Har Gobind Khorana was done while they were abroad, India shows a justifiable pride that they are of Indian origin.

Much of the problem of the 'brain drain' is due to a complex of attitudes about the migration of professionals. There is no single consistent view about such migration, and as we noted above, there can be different perspectives from which the 'problem' can be viewed, leading to a different conclusion in each case.

NOTES

1. 'Scientist' refers to specialists in the physical and natural sciences unless otherwise indicated.
2. One crore is ten million. The present exchange rate is (nearly) Rs. 15 to one US dollar.

REFERENCES

Adams, W. (ed.) (1968). *The Brain Drain*. New York: Macmillan Company.

Ahmed, A. (1970). Gain-Drain Ratio in the Global Exchange of Scientific and Technical Manpower. *Journal of Asian and African Studies*. 5, 3.

Atal, Yogesh and Luca Dall'Oglio (1987). *Migration of Talent: Causes and Consequences of Brain Drain*. UNESCO, Bangkok.

Aurora, G. S. n. d. *Scientific Community in India: the Organisational Context*. Report of a research project sponsored by the Ford Foundation, Hyderabad: Administrative Staff College of India (mimeo.).

Baldwin, G. B. (1970). Brain Drain or Overflow. *Foreign Affairs* 48, 2.

Banerjea, D.(1975). "Brain Drain: Its causes and remedies" *Science and Culture.* 41, 5.

Bayer, A. E. (1968). "The Effect of International Interchange of High-Level Manpower on the United States" *Social Forces.* 46, 4.

Bhagwati, J. N. (ed.) (1976). *The Brain Drain and Taxation: Theory and Empirical Analysis.* Amsterdam: North Holland Publishing Co., 2.

Chopra, S. K. (1985). "Bringing them Home—the Problem of Brain Drain" in *Seminar on Brain Drain.* New Delhi.

Dhar, M. L. (1969). "Creativity in Scientific Institutions" *Indian Journal of Public Administration.* 15, 3.

Domrese, R.J. (1970). "The Migration of Talent from India" in *International Migration of High-Level Manpower: Its impact, on the development process,* New York, Praeger Publisher.

Fortney, J. A. (1970). "International Migration of Professionals" *Population Studies.* 24, 2.

Glaser, W.A and C. Habers (1978). *The Brain Drain* (Findings of a UNITAR Multinational comparative survey of professional personnel of developing countries who study abroad). New York: Pergamon Press.

Grubel, H. G. (1968). "The Reduction of the Brain Drain: Problems and Policies" *Minerva.* 6, 4.

Grubel, H. G. (1976). "Reflections on the Present State of the Brain Drain and a Suggested Remedy" *Minerva.*14, 2.

Gujral, S. F. and S. S. Gupta (1983). "Indian scientific, technical and professional personnel admitted as immigrants to the U.S.A. (1977-1979)" *Technical Manpower.* 24, 8-9.

Jayaram, N. (1977). "Social Implications of Medical Education in India" *Journal of Higher Education.* 3, 2.

Jeffery, R. (1976). "Migration of Doctors from India" *Economic and Political Weekly.* I 1, 13.

Johnson, H. G. (1968). An 'Internationalist' Model, in Adams, Walter (Ed.), *The Brain Drain.* New York: Macmillan Co.

Klaw, S. (1969). *The New Brahmins: Scientific Life in America.* New York: William Morrow and Company, Inc.

London, H. I. (1970). *Non-white Immigration and the White Australia Policy'.* Sydney: Sydney University Press.

Mathur, P. N. (1971). "Demand and Supply of Doctors in India, 1951-1986" *Manpower Journal.* 7, 1-2.

Merriam, M. F. (1969). "Brain Drain Study at IIT Kanpur" *Manpower Journal.* 5, 1.

Misra, D. N. (1985). "Brain Drain: Consequences and Some Related Issues", in *Seminar on Brain Drain.* New Delhi.

Nayar, U. (1985). "Brain Drain: The phenomenon and its causes" in *Seminar on Brain Drain.* New Delhi.

Neri, M. (1985). "The Slow Decline of the IITs" *Business World.* September, 16-29.

Oommen, T. K. (1982). "The Urban Family in Transition" in Augustine, John S (ed). *The Indian Family In Transition.* New Delhi: Vikas Publishing House Pvt. Ltd.

Oommen, T. K. (1983). "Sociology in India: A Plea for Contextualization" *Sociological Bulletin*. 32, 2.

Panandikar, V. A. P. (1971). "Brain Drain—the Indian Myths". *Manpower Journal*. 7.1-2.

Patinkin, D. (1968). A Nationalist 'Model', in Adams, Walter (Ed.), *The Brain Drain*, New York: Macmillan Co.

Salam, A. (1966). "The Isolation of the Scientist in Developing Countries", *Minerva*. 4, 4.

Schaefer, R. T. (1976). "Indians in Great Britain". *International Review of Modern Sociology*. Autumn, 6.

Singh, B. H. (1975). *Conflict in a Formal Organization*. Chandigarh, Department of Sociology, Punjab University, (mimeo).

Sudarshan, E.C.G. (1974). "Science in India". *Economic and Political Weekly* 9,12.

Suri, S. (1967). "A case study", *Seminar*, April.

Zuckerman, H. (1977). *Scientific Ellite: Nobel Laureates in the United States*, New York: Free Press.

26

Contesting and Contested Self-Identities: Mathura's Chaubes*

OWEN M. LYNCH

Mathura city lies about 100 miles south of New Delhi, India. It is famous for the ancient Buddhist and Jain cultures buried in its soil and displayed in its museum; it is even more renowned among Hindus as the birthplace of India's beloved god, Lord Krishna, and as a sin-cleansing bathing spot, Vishram Ghat, on the banks of the holy river Jamuna. The city is one of the *saptamahatirthas*, Hinduism's seven great pilgrimage centres. Pilgrims come to Mathura throughout the year for a day or so to bathe in Jamuna's waters and visit temples including that erected over the site of Krishna's birth. Others come for the annual *Braj Chaurasi Kos Parikrama* (160 mile circumambulation around the land of Braj) a forty-day pilgrimage visiting many of the places where Krishna, as a child, performed his miraculous *leelas* (sports, play).[1]

Mathura is equally renowned for its Chaubes, a community of priests of the high-ranking Hindu category (*varna*) of Brahmans. Chaubes act as guides and ritual specialists (*pandas*) performing necessary rites for pilgrims at various holy stations. In Mathura a Chaube is hard to miss for they often have hefty, husky wrestlers' bodies and unfailingly confront unwary pilgrims with demanding offers of their ritual services.

---

* Reprinted with permission from: Owen M. Lynch 1996 "Contesting and Contested Self-Identities: Mathura's Chaubes" in: *Narratives of Agency: Self-Making in China, India and Japan* (Wimal Dissanayake ed.); Minneapolis: University of Minnesota Press, pp. 74-103.

The Chaubes densely inhabit an elevated part of Mathura known as Chaubiya Para whence they look down upon the river Jamuna. In 1882 Growse (1979 : 9) estimated their population to be 6,000, although Chaubes today say that their population is about 4,000. My own rough estimate puts their population resident in Mathura at 11,300 in 1978.[2] I, too, needed a *panda* for my study of Mathura as a pilgrimage centre and that need led me to ask them about themselves and who they were. I quickly learned that there was no simple answer enabling me to locate them in time and social space; all their answers were open to interpretation, sometimes seemingly contradictory, and as often contested. Such answers led me to abandon an approach of looking for who the Mathura Chaubes "really" were as a socially distinct, bounded group or caste and to concentrate instead on the narratives of their contesting and contested identities and what they might reveal. This paper, then, first asks what does a narrative perspective reveal about self-identity and social order in India?

My concern is narratives, rather than narrative, because in daily life the self is not experienced or displayed in one totalized whole, rather it is constituted through narratives of multiple identities in social situations, as Mead (1934) long ago argued. Self-identity, therefore, is not a fixed 'thing,' it is negotiated, open, shifting, ambiguous, the result of culturally available meanings and the open-ended, power-laden enactments of those meanings in everyday situations. (Kondo, 1990 : 24; see also Carrithers 1985 : 255) Thus, selves, as agents, in any society are constituted and experienced through multiple identities in the process of daily life.

Such a perspective of narrative as constitutive necessitates an appropriate theory of self as agent. I draw, then, upon Charles Taylor's (1985a; 1985b) theory of the self and only briefly and inadequately outline it here. Taylor understands an agent as one who can make life plans, hold values, and make choices. An important characteristic of such an agent is not consciousness, although that is involved; rather it is significances intrinsic to the agent. Intrinsic significances are constitutive in that the things humans experience, such as their identities, their feelings and their emotions, are inseparable from their understanding of them (see also Lynch 1990a); they are not, then, pure representations in consciousness of objects separate from the self as subject. Such significances are human beings' own and not the derivative ones of machines or artifacts whose purposes are ultimately given to them by human beings.

A second characteristic of such an agent is that significances involve the agent's awareness of self-definition and self-transformation, not merely awareness of purposes that can be sought. For that reason the significances agents seek are such that "our not choosing them reflects on us rather than undermining their status as ends" (Taylor, 1985a : 266); they are strong evaluations "concerned with the *qualitative* worth of our desires" Taylor, 1985b : 16). Thus, if I choose not to eat ice cream, it merely ceases to be an end for me; but if I choose to go to Hawaii rather than attend my daughter's wedding, my choice reflects poorly on my paternal identity on that occasion.

Finally, agency is characteristically connected with language or discourse, through which agents focus on significances, bring them into view, disclose them, acquire, and even change them and thereby their selves. Such focusing involves not just self but *other* in communication or conversation and, therefore, some *public space* for the disclosure of significances.

> We learn language in conversation, and hence the original acquisition of articulacy is something *we* do, rather than *I* do. Later we learn to do it to some extent on our own. But we do so in a language which is ours, and hence in principle our formulations should always be capable of being common formulations. That is why they are all in principle addressed to others, and open to criticism by others. And for certain key matters, the human significances among them, *the connection between the attainment of clarity and continuing conversation is never relaxed very far*. (Taylor, 1985a : 275 emphasis added)

I shall make use of Taylor's theoretical notion of a public or social space of disclosure through language, or discourse, in this paper. Theoretical space, when manifested in specific cultural form, I shall call place. My second question, then, is what does a narrative perspective through a space of disclosure reveal about how self is experienced and understood among the Chaubes of India?

The importance of Taylor's theory for purposes of this paper is threefold.[3] First, it is not representationist or internalist and, therefore, does not assume a culturally specific metaphor of an interiorized consciousness making agents self-evidently aware of themselves and their significances. That assumption involves "a total suppression of any recognition of a space of disclosure" (Taylor, 1985a : 280). The appeal of Taylor's theory is its decentering the subject/agent without eliminating it; agency remains. Because the subject/agent is not located in an interiorized consciousness, it is not phonocentrically self-present to itself, logocentrically aware of all meaning, and culturally limited by one language's metaphor for its conception. Rather, the subject/agent is theoretically located in the open-ended, public and social space given through language.

Second, agents become selves as interlocutors; they are "self-interpreting animals" (Taylor, 1985b : 226) whose identities involve significances, those strong evaluations fundamental to who selves are. Yet, because those identities are culturally contingent and articulated in the public space of language, the self is not a coherent, unique object or essence clearly known to agents.[4] The search for clarity and the conversation about the self is unending and expressed most often in narratives of self-identity.

Third, numerous studies (*e.g.* Hardgrave, 1969; Lynch, 1969; Barnett, 1973; Rao, 1979) of Indian castes in the process of change, particularly that of Sanskritization (Srinivas, 1966), have emphasized change of identity. Yet they all implicitly assume that a caste is a bounded, coherent, entity of individuals sharing some essence. Berreman (1972) does not share that assumption, but he shares with those studies the additional assumption of the interiorized self, such that change in the myths of caste identity is something epiphenomenal to or, like a mask, on the surface of the real interiorized self. Thus, language is not constitutive, but merely a medium for reference to things purportedly more basic. In taking a narrative approach, this paper argues against those assumptions.

Narrative, as a linguistic phenomenon, is characterized by *différance* (Derrida, 1973, 1976) such that self-identity bears the presence of absent other meanings, other identities. Derrida notes three aspects of *différance*: difference, deferral and dissemination. Difference refers to a signifier having a space between it and its signified; the two are not identical. Therefore, there is always some play allowing a difference between signifier and signified; a signifier is not tied to only one signified or referential meaning. Deferral concerns a temporal space between a signifier's present signified and its other possible signifieds at other points in time. Finally, dissemination refers to signifier's taking on new, as well as losing old, signified meanings. A signifier, then, is characterized by the presence of an absence, the *trace* of other things it can mean. It is not that signifiers have no meaning, rather they have contingent meaning; otherwise, there would be nothing to deconstruct.

Narratives composed of signifiers are caught in what Derrida calls "the play of difference;" as inter-texts, they carry the possibilities of multiple interpretations. Narratives of self-identity, then, are "strategic assertions which inevitably suppress differences, tensions and contradictions" (Kondo, 1990 : 10); they can be socially contesting and contested. Narratives form part of a discursive field that is a range of competing narratives focussed on an institution or central organizing concept, such as self. Discourses, such as those of law, medicine, rhetoric or scripture, are social frameworks of intelligibility enabling or constraining ways of thinking within a discursive field. Their use makes narratives seem natural and culturally appropriate (*cf.* Duncan, 1990 : 16; Foucault, 1972).

My paper is itself one more narrative resulting from a dialogue (see Daniel, 1984) with individuals and their writings in answer to my incessant questions and puzzled attempts to make sense of their narrative answers. My questions, then and now, are: What is your name, where do you live, and who are you? The answers received had more to do with self-identity in the Hindu world of *samsara*, the world of desire, attachment, change and the everyday, than with self-identities in the world of the individual soul (*jeeva*) as identical to the ultimate soul of the universe (*atma*). Thus, my concern is with self-identities in the world of *samsara*, which, I believe, tends to be overlooked in studies of the Hindu self. The narratives of self-identity that I heard are also "we" rather than "I" narratives; their narrators speak as though similarly named others identified and agreed with them. Unfortunately, they are also male narratives because I had restricted access to females. I shall discuss Chaubes' identities in the following order: Scriptural Identities, Historical Identities, Contesting Identities, Contested Identities, and Discussion and Conclusions.

Scriptural Identities

When I first began asking them about themselves, Chaubes adamantly asserted that their ancestors had been present in Mathura since its very foundation. They advised me to go to Mathura's museum, renowned for its collection of Buddhist and Jain sculptures, and to look at its stone sacrificial pillar (*yupa*) from the time of Raja Huviska (2nd Cent A.D.), upon which are inscribed the following words:

> In the 24th year of Vashishka on the 30th day of the fourth month of summer, Dronal, son of Rudral, a Bharadvaj Mathur Samvedi Brahman, after making a twelve-night sacrifice placed this sacrificial pillar here (V.K. Chaturvedi n.d.:14).[5]

V.K. Chaturvedi, as do other Chaubes, asserts that Dronal, the Mathur Brahman mentioned in the inscription was their ancestor. Dronal metonymically stands for all Chaubes today. The sacrificial pillar is for them, then, material proof of their ancestry and grounds them in the soil of Mathura itself; the pillar is proof of their identity as continuous with that of their Mathur ancestor. It *is* their past in the present; myth "transforms history into nature" (Barthes, 1972 : 129).

Some learned Chaube scholars (B.M. Chaturvedi, 1986; V.K. Chaturvedi n.d.; Y.K. Chaturvedi, 1968; R.P. Chaturvedi, 1981) trace their ancestry at least as far back as the *Satya* or *Krita yuga*, the first of the Hindu mythological ages when, in one version, it is said that they came from the sweat of Lord Vishnu in his incarnation *(avatara)* as Varah (*Varaha*), the boar, (Y.K. Chaturvedi, 1968 : 25; see also R.P. Chaturvedi, 1981). Varah settled the Chaubes in Mathura. An idol (*murti*) of Varah said to be from that age is today installed in a Chaubiya Para temple, once again giving concrete proof of their ancestral roots in Mathura. Vishnu Chaube told me another narrative from the Varah Purana that makes the same point:

"[6]Hiranyaksh [a demon] did *tap* [austerities giving magical powers] and through this got the power to take all of Prithvi [the earthly world] to hell, except for Mathura. Everyone was in great fear, so they asked God to help. He took the form of Varah [the boar], killed Hiranyaksh, took Prithvi, and put it on his tusk. Mathura had remained, because it is *teen lok se nyari* [separate from the three worlds of heaven, earth and hell]. Varah put Prithvi down behind Vishram Ghat and said to Prithvi:

There is no god equal to Keshav
There is no Brahman equal to Mathur Brahman [Chaube][7]
There is no pilgrimage place equal to Vishram Ghat
Oh Earth! This is the essence of truth

Chaturvedi Brahmans were, then, in Mathura even before Varah's time. That proves, say many Chaubes, that they, the Mathur Brahmans, resided in Mathura during the *Satya Yuga*. Thus, when they say that the name, Mathur, in the text refers to themselves, the Mathur Chaubes, they strategically use an ancient, yet living, Hindu scriptural discourse to locate themselves in a place of disclosure, Mathura itself continuous with and identical to the Mathura of the Varah Purana.

In the *Treta yuga* during which Lord Rama reigned, the Chaubes find proof not only of their residence in Mathura, but also of their honoured status and place in it. In the scriptural epic, the Valmiki Ramayana, it is said:

"A resident on the bank of the Jamuna, Nar Singh, was a happy person"

The above verse mentions the Mathurs by calling them Jamuna people, because it was unnatural for them to be unhappy while living on the banks of the Jamuna near Madhuvan [Mathura]. (V.K. Chaturvedi, n.d.:13). In quoting that verse the author identifies himself and other Chaubes with the holy river Jamuna, whom Chaubes consider a goddess (see Lynch,

1988). Chaubes say that they are "*Jamuna ke putra,*" children of the Goddess Jamuna; she is, among other things, one source of their livelihood as well as of their constantly renewed purity from daily lustrations in her holy waters. How, then, when living on her banks, could they have been unhappy, even while the rest of Mathura was under duress from the demon Lavanasur? Mukund Chaube narrated to me:

> Madhu's son was Lavanasur. He fought with the Chaubes because when his father died, he asked them to come and do *shraddh* (ritual of remembrance of ancestors) for his father. But they refused, because at the same time Durbasa *Muni* (sage)...asked them to give him food. They went and gave him [Durbasa] food. Lavan began to attack the Chaubes in anger for what they had done. Seven of them went from here [to Ayodhya] and spoke to Rama and asked his help. He sent his younger brother, Shatrughna, back with them and Shatrughna killed Lavan and founded [resettled] Mathura.

Thus, the Chaubes again locate themselves in Mathura during the time of the great god-king Lord Rama.

In the *Dvapara Yuga* of Vishnu's manifestation (*avatara*) as Lord Krishna, Chaubes' narratives of identity become more complex and more implicated in current concerns. Krishna was born in Mathura, but raised outside of it by foster parents. While still a young boy, Krishna returned to Mathura to slay demons sent by his wicked and oppressive uncle, King Kans of Mathura, whom, it had been prophesied, Krishna would destroy. Krishna prevailed over the demons, slew Kans, and liberated the city. Chaubes say that, as Krishna's friends, their ancestors assisted him in purging the world of one of its most ancient tyrants, Kans. They are, then, a brave and courageous people, a theme of their character iterated in other narratives of identity to follow.

Annually in Mathura on the 10th day of the bright half of the Hindu month of Kartik (early November) Chaubes celebrate *Kams Vadh ka Mela* (Festival of Kans's Destruction) by a victory parade through the Chhata Bazaar section of the city. Chaubes monopolize and control the entire festival.

On that day an image (*putla*) of Kans about two stories high is constructed using an inner frame of cane covered with a face and garments of brightly coloured paper. In the evening it is brought to Kans Tila, a Chaube hilltop garden (*bagicha*) (Lynch, 1990) where menacing Chaube young men wielding *saunta* (heavy wooden staffs) surround it. Then, two specially chosen Chaube young men dressed as Krishna and his brother, Balram, both mounted upon an elephant, march toward the hill. At an appointed moment in their approach, Kans is decapitated, his head impaled upon a staff, and his body destroyed, its battered remains tossed over the hill. The Chaube warriors followed by Krishna and Balram on the elephant then begin their victory procession through the Chhata bazaar section of the city. Carrying aloft Kans's impaled head, as well as other symbolic loot from his castle, they gleefully dance around the hapless head and sing the following song of victory:

> Ram was brave among Krishna and Baldev's friends.
> To Madhupuri [Mathura] marched slayers of Kans
> And trembled with fear his kin in castle.
> Parading to thunder of *lathi* (wooden staff) and dust-storm swirl
> They hoist aloft the impotent mustache.[8]
> Incense and sandalwood perfume the walls
> And fresh, green cow dung purifies courtyard floors.
> Friends embrace and chant auspicious songs
> Under victory canopy bedecked with elephant pearl and banana.
> Chajju dances with the looted bed.

Then, before arriving at Vishram Ghat on Jamuna's river banks, they halt at Kans Khar where they lower Kans's head to the ground and triumphantly pulverize it into confetti. Thereafter, they march to Vishram Ghat where the youths dressed as Krishna and Balram, each sitting in the lap of a Chaube elder, are worshipped and fed. All, thereafter, enter Jamuna's waters to purify themselves from the sin of killing Kans.

The festival of *Kams Vadh Ka Mela*, a celebration of Mathura's victory over a wicked ruler, is also a performative narrative that produces and reproduces Chaube identity; its participants metonymically stand for their ancestors' participation in the original event. Moreover, their agonistic display is not lost upon the non-Chaube audience for whom Mathura's Chaubes are a dominant and contentious presence to be dealt with cautiously, if not feared.

Recently Chaubes' domination of the festival has been contested. In 1980 the All India Yadav Conference was held in Mathura. The Yadavs are traditionally cow herders, as was Lord Krishna who is said to have spring from the Yadav clan. At their meeting, I was told, the Yadavs asked how were the Chaubes able to get control of the *Kams Mela* when the Yadavs were in Mathura long before the Chaubes. The implied Yadav narrative is that they, as Krishna's clan brothers, are the original and real heroes of the festival and that the Chaubes are poseurs and usurpers. The Yadavs also vowed that the following year's festival would be in Yadav hands. It was not.

Chaubes over and over again narrated to me their version of episode 10.32 from the Bhagavata Purana wherein they again identify themselves.

> Once Lord Krishna's helpers Subal, Satok, Shridan and others felt very hungry. Lord Krishna sent them to the Mathurs [in search of sustenance]. A Mathur Brahman named Angiras was engaged in a ritual, but for fear of breaking the Vedic rules he did not give them food even while knowing about the *avatara* [divine manifestation, here Krishna]. After the cowherds returned, Lord Krishna sent them to the Brahman women who recognized Lord Krishna, as a god beyond Vedic rules. They brought many things, soup, rice, etc., and fed Lord Krishna and his good friends. Thus, they brought home his blessings. (V.K. Chaturvedi n.d.: 15)

In gratitude, it is said, Krishna promised that from that day forward the Chaube women would be renowned for their fair-skinned beauty, as indeed they are today, and the Chaube men would control pilgrimage in the area of Braj, as they do today. Also said is that on that day Krishna bestowed upon them knowledge of all four Vedas rather than one, two or three, as among other Brahmans, and also gave them their name, Chaube or Chaturvedi, knower of the four Vedas. In narrating the episode Chaubes proudly tell how no one other than a cheeky Chaube would ignore Krishna's hunger and thirst.

Communities of Brahmans in India are many. The narratives of self-identity related thus far are signifiers of difference that constitute, as unique and separate from other Brahmans, all Chaturvedi Brahmans owing their origin to Mathura. Just as one cannot change one's blood, so too one cannot change one's place of origin. An original place of disclosure in the sacred soil of India permanently marks and constitutes the self through discourse. Thus, for the Chaubes these narratives, somewhat like social charters (Malinowski, 1948 : 101), are of strategic, vital importance. They assert an autochthonous identity as high status Brahmans; they discursively constitute their self-identities as different from others through location in a place of disclosure; and they claim social honour and political power through prestige of primordial origin in holy Mathura.[9]

The narratives to this point also hint at another essential characteristic of Chaube self-identity; they are happy-go-lucky, even in adversity, and warriors on behalf of their holy city and its soil. In short, they are *mast* (happy, carefree, intoxicated, lusty) an emotion that they say is *sattvik* (good, pure, virtuous) in moral significance (Lynch, 1990b).

Historical Identities

We come, then, to the *Kali Yuga*, the present age of decay and moral decadence as well as of more conventional history. Muslim conquerors and invaders beginning with Mahmud of Ghazni (997-1030), who in 1018 A.D. saw Mathura's opulent temples and bejeweled Hindu idols as abominations, sacked the city repeatedly. Although the Moghul emperor Akbar (1556-1605) had friendly and supportive relations with Mathura and its Hindus, they bitterly remember his great grandson Aurangzeb (1658-1707) as the city's worst despoiler.

Chaube narratives of self-identities for this age involve two important figures: the emperor Akbar and the saint Vallabhacharya, founder of the Pushti Marg Sect. Mukund Chaube told me the following version of the Akbar narrative:

> **Only for 400 years have we been doing this *Jajmani* system [priests holding individual pilgrims as patrons]. Before this all money was put in a common alms box (*dan patra*) and distributed to all by a headman. It was shared equally. Akbar used to go to Agra from Delhi by boat. When he passed by Mathura he asked "What is this place, who are these people, what are they doing?" [concerning Chaubes on Vishram Ghat]. He summoned them to him, but the Chaubes did not go because of fear. One Chaube,[10] Ujagar Chaube, got into a boat and went to see Akbar. He told Akbar that this is the place of Krishna and it is filled with his history. The box into which you see people putting money is for charity, alms (*khairat*). We take (*dan*) religious donations. Whether a person gives a cowrie shell [worth much less than a penny] or a *lakh* [100,000] of rupees, it is the same. Akbar gave Ujagar a [worthless] broken cowrie (*kani kauri*) into his hand. Ujagar returned to Vishram Ghat. The Chaubes on the Ghat asked him to put what Akbar had given him in the alms box, but he refused and said "No, because Muslims are not of our religion and I did not take it on the Ghat." They started to fight with him and he fled. Akbar sent his servant and called back Ujagar. Akbar asked what the fight was about. Ujagar told Akbar..." That is our custom." Akbar asked why he didn't give the cowrie. Ujagar said "I kept it in my fist so no one could see it. In this fist is your and my honour (*Ijjat*)" [that is, if he should show the worthless cowrie people would wonder what kind of emperor would give such a worthless thing. The emperor would be dishonoured]. Akbar then said, "What do you want?" Ujagar asked that he become the priest (*Purohit*) of the four [Hindu] sects and the fifty-two kingdoms around Mathura. Akbar gave a *Farman* (royal decree) in which this was done.

Chaube association with the saint, Vallabhacharya is different. It begins with Vallabhacharya's arrival in Braj to make a pilgrimage. He tried to do so, but lacking a guide he was unsuccessful. Arvind Chaube narrates one version of what Vallabhacharya then did.

> **He asked Jumunaji (the river goddess, Jamuna) what he must do to have success. He was told that it was important to have a guru from the Chaubes, and to get their blessing. So he went to [Ujagar] got his blessing and took him as a guru. After that he got success in his pilgrimages. Till today followers of Vallabhacharya must come to descendants of [Ujagar] to begin pilgrimage.[11]

From that day forward, all followers of Pushti Marg take one or another Chaube as their pilgrimage priest, and even today Vallabhacharya's descendants take their pilgrimage vows from Ujagar's descendants. It is important to note that Harirayji (1905) and other hallowed Pushti Marg hagiographers (see Chaube, 1967) have narratively inscribed that event, in essence although not in detail, in Pushti Marg scriptural discourse. The event was decisive for the Chaubes; the wealth of Vallabhacharya's followers has been a major source of their income and supported many of them in a prosperous style of life.

What do these two narratives have to do with Chaube self-identity? First of all, the narrative of Vallabhacharya, an authoritative figure, has him recognize Ujagar, his descendants, and synecdochically all Chaubes as Brahmans and as *Pandas* (pilgrimage priests). Today Vallabhacharya's descendants and the followers of his sect revalidate those identities whenever they utilize Chaubes' ritual services on pilgrimage. Second, that identity is confirmed by its appearance in the scriptural discourse of Pushti Marg. Third, the emperor Akbar, a Muslim, ironically and not without ambiguous consequences for the Chaubes, did likewise when he gave to Ujagar the *Farman* granting to him rights to the four sects and fifty-two kingdoms. Although I was never allowed to see it, the *Farman* has inserted, as we shall see, Chaubes' claim into a legal discourse and added legal authority to their strategic assertions of identity and rights.

In Hindu India, one of the traditional sources of valid knowledge (*Praman*) is verbal authority (*Shabda*), as in the scriptures or the words of some learned or holy person, such as Harirayji. Thus, by continuously finding their narrative identities in scriptural discourse and by asserting them in daily life, Chaubes implicitly and strategically base many of their identities on this taken for granted criterion of proof. Their narratives of self-identity are, then, implicated in power through constitutive scriptural discourse.

Moreover, as Appadurai (1981) has noted, the past is a scarce resource not only in political debate but also in problems of identity itself (see also Lynch, 1969). Such debate proceeds in India according to five cultural norms:

1. that *textual evidence* for the authority of any charter is superior to any other kind;
2. that the evidence for a charter ought to involve the ratification of a credible *external authoritative figure* (whether sacred or secular) in the past;
3. that the charter should be based on an authoritative document that encodes (in addition to the claims of the group in question) the *privileges of a maximum number* of other relevant groups;
4. that the evidence for the charter in question should be reflected, as far as possible, *continuously* in the documented past; and
5. that the greater the *antiquity* of the referents of the charter in question, the better the case for the rights in question. (Appadurai, 1981 : 204).

Chaubes in written and spoken narratives constitute their identity as "the" autochthonous Mathur Brahmans by using the discourse of *ancient scriptural texts* including that of the Museum's sacrificial pillar. The *Kams Mela* is a performative narrative text that recreates, or better re-realizes, another identity in which Chaubes actually become Krishna's friends and allies, as well as Mathura's ancient citizens. When the two youths portraying Krishna and Balram are crowned, they do not merely portray, rather they become, the two divine brothers and are worshipped as such. The *Kams Mela* is more than a festival; it is a ritual event that grounds its truth and Chaube identity in actual experience.

When the Yadav's contest Chaubes' control of the festival by asserting that it is theirs, they implicitly acknowledge the power of the *Kams Mela*, as a performative narrative socially producing and reproducing a Chaube identity in the present. Likewise, the ritual wherein Vallabhacharya's descendants take pilgrimage vows from the Chaubes is a performative narrative text producing and reproducing their identity as Brahman pilgrimage priests. The same is true whenever they act as pilgrimage priests for other pilgrims and members of the sects as granted in Akbar's *Farman*.

Chaubes cite Varah, Krishna, Rama, Vallabhacharya, Harirayji, Akbar, and British government officials, as *external authoritative* figures ratifying their identities and their claims to be the pilgrimage priests of Mathura in Braj. In 1901, British census officials listed the Chaubes in the third and last category among all Brahmans. The British, then, became another external secular authority recognizing a new Chaube census identity and privileges them among others, even though Chaubes rejected classification in the third category and submitted such proofs, as I have already presented, to claim classification in the first and highest category (Mathur

Mandli, 1964). In more recent days, as I describe later, some of their privileges, as pilgrimage priests *versus* other claimants, have been validated by judges in courts of justice. Thus, Chaubes today construct their identities using three recognized discourses: scripture, performance, and secular law including governmental classification. Each narrative using one of those discourses implicitly asserts the absent presences of all other Chaube identities.

The evidence, as Chaubes see and present it, is *continuously documented* in the past, and its *antiquity* stretches back to the beginning of the *Satya Yuga*. Thus, the *Kams Mela* victory song is crucially emphasizes the continuity of blood relationship between today's Chaubes and their ancestors. No clearer illustration of their metonymical turn of thought could be given.

My own narrative conceals the audiences, the others, for the Chaubes' narratives of self-identity: Hindu pilgrims, occasional interested anthropologists, and, in particular, other Brahmans for whom Chaube narratives strategically assert a charter constituting them as Brahmans, as autochthonous offspring of Mathura, its soil and holy river Jamuna, and as legitimate priests for the pilgrimage sites in the area, especially Vishram, Ghat. More important, their discourses—scriptural, legal and performative—are not merely political, they are also constitutive of Chaube self-identities, of the selves they know themselves to be.

Contesting Identities

Chaubes' vehemence and certainty in constructing their narratives of self also obscure and conceal the ambiguities, tensions, and uncertainties with which their self-identities are fraught; "their [Chaubes'] origin and history is riddled with controversy (*vivadgrast*)" (Bhagvandatt Chaturvedi, 1958 : 487). I came upon this when Chaubes began telling me about the Karua (*karua*—bitter, astringent) and the Mitha (*mitha*—sweet) which are more names summarizing contesting narratives of identity within the Mathur Chaturvedi community than they are units or groups of social structure. Yet, the names and the narratives they imply are felt deeply and contested bitterly because their significance involves honour (*Ijjat*). *Karua*, bitter, is a trope for bravery, courage, and truth, while *mitha*, sweet, is a trope for cowardice, evasiveness and duplicity.

During the centuries of various Muslim invasions and atrocities in Mathura there were different migrations of Chaubes to nearby villages, cities and states.[12] Marriage relations were broken off and a number of different sub-communities of Chaturvedis were established, one of which is the Mitha. From the Mathura Chaubes' point of view, those who remained in the city are the true Karua because they tasted bitter fruit of persecution and fought for the preservation of their religion and its holy relics. They talk as though *all* who left Mathura under threat of Muslim persecution are Mitha who fled like cowards, diluted their pure blood by intermarriage with other communities, and even took up polluting habits, such as smoking cigarettes. Most Mathura Chaubes date the Mithas' flight to the reign of Aurangzeb.

But ask many of those to whom the Mathura Chaubes give the name, Mitha, and they reverse the name saying that they are the Karua and the Mathura Chaubes are really the Mitha. Gopal Chaturvedi, an emigrant's descendant now resident in Mathura, told me:

> **We are the Karua because *karua* means to speak straightforwardly with truth. In the time of Aurangzeb some of his soldiers came here and took some of our women during a marriage. Some Chaube men resisted them and killed those attacking them and abducting the women. After this, they were forced to flee Mathura. They did not want to become slaves of the Muslims and to be affected by their teachings. They settled in the villages of Madhya Pradesh and the Chambal valley...even today we celebrate the interruption of the wedding....

Thus, they are courageous because they did flee and, thereby, preserved their Hindu faith in its pristine purity without taint of Islamic association and religious doctrine, and especially without becoming slaves to Muslims. The thrust of the narrative is that by remaining in the city the Mathura Chaubes degraded the purity of their blood by association with Muslims, sullied the orthodoxy of their Hindu faith with Islamic influence, and dishonoured themselves by becoming slaves to Muslims.

Mathura's Chaubes themselves will occasionally tell the narrative of the grave diggers in which only a few will dare to name as the protagonists Ali Datt and Kuli Datt, two Mathura Chaube ancestors. Mohan Chaube narrated the following version[13] to me:

> **Ali Datt and Kuli Datt were two famous Chaube wrestlers. One day Akbar [in almost all other versions it is Aurangzeb] came to Brindaban and he saw two fat (*mote*) Chaubes. He asked how they got so fat. They said, "because we eat till our bellies are full (*bharpet*)." He said, "I eat and am not as healthy as you two." So he said, "come and show me" and he took both of them to his camp, but then he forgot about them. Birbal [friend of Akbar] was partial to the Chaubes, so he got them out of prison, but they were told to dig graves. They then proceeded to dig many, but made two very big ones. The emperor saw these and asked what they were

> doing. They said" we are digging these two graves for you." The emperor then took fright because he thought he might die. So he dismissed Ali Datt and Kuli Datt immediately.

Most often the names of Ali Datt and Kuli Datt are not given in versions of this narrative, and mention of them is hard to come by. Mohan Chaturvedi's narrative cited above asserts not that some of those Chaubes who remained behind in Mathura were forced into slavery and grave-digging for the Muslims, but rather that the Chaubes cleverly outwitted even the Emperor's attempt to enslave them. Yet, some Chaubes were and are known as *gulmata* who, according to Govind Chaube, were "**those who stayed in Mathura and converted to Islam—at least openly so, if not in their hearts." For that they were outcasted, although they have now been accepted back into the community. Moreover, some Chaubes now live in a place called Gol Para, said to have been a burial ground for Muslims.

The factual historicity of these events and persons is not an issue here. In Mohan Chaube's narrative above, Ali Datt and Kuli Datt are clever, defiant heroes standing for all their Karua descendants in the present day Mathura. Indeed, one narrative asserts that Ali Datt was a very renowned and powerful wrestler during the Emperor Akbar's reign when that sport was more popular and more patronized than in the present (Jivanlal Chaturvedi, 1972 : 33). All such narratives are strategic assertions claiming an unblemished self-identity and heroic status. To some extent in the present and I'm told in the past also, marriage relations occur between Mathura Chaubes and different Chaturvedi emigrant communities, but not with the real Mitha. Thus, the actual "group" is not at issue; the name, Karua, and its constitutive narrative of self-identity, is. The identifying names disclose the significances, the moral evaluations, that the narratives are about, namely honour (*Ijjat*) for the Karua and shame (*Sharam*) for the Mitha.

Many Chaturvedis who emigrated from Mathura became prosperous village agriculturalists, and others became highly educated and well placed throughout northern India. Some of them are called *kulin* (see Y.K. Chaturvedi, 1968), a name that Mathura Chaubes often use for all emigrants, particularly those with western-style educations. *Kulin* means "of noble ancestry, educated." That name is opposed to the name *panda* identifying those in Mathura who work as pilgrimage priests. From the Mathura Chaubes' point of view, the Mitha Chaturvedis were and are *kulin* also and the words are often used interchangeably. Thus, some will stigmatize *kulin* identity, saying that *kulin* means "*kul heen*," of low caste, without proper ancestry. From the point of view of those labelled *kulin* and who claim to be true Karua, the *pandas* practice a demeaned and demeaning profession. Mukesh Chaturvedi, a *kulin* whose community emigrated many years ago, said to me, "**we hate that profession (*Pesha*) [of *panda*]."

What is the *panda's* profession and why do the *kulin* hate it? The role of *panda* as ritual mediator between gods and humans is as ancient as Hinduism itself and is restricted to Brahmans by birth. *Pandas* perform required rituals at pilgrimage places, as do Mathura's Chaubes. *Pandas* appear daily at Vishram Ghat where they dun pilgrims for alms (*daan*) and badger them to use their ritual services. Others go to Mathura railroad station in search of old clients scheduled to arrive or new arrivals to whom they can offer ritual services.[14] Patrons most often have hereditary *pandas* with whose family their own family has been liked for generations. Records of patrons are kept in registers (*bahi*) and a proud *panda* is one who can show a young person of today an ancestor's signature or thumbprint in his register.

If, as Marx says, humanity makes itself through work as *homo faber* and if work and identity are intrinsically linked, then the Chaubes' daily praxis constitutes one of their identities in performing *pandagiri* (*panda*'s work). It must also be remembered that the right to do this work is rooted deeply in religious tradition whereby it is inherited through their bloodline; purity of lineage is, therefore, crucial. But Brahmans who do that work, because they depend upon the good will and alms of others, have always suffered an ambiguous reputation, because dependence is demeaning. Indian folklore is filled with stories ridiculing greedy and pusillanimous Brahmans (Srinivas, 1976 : 1), and *pandas* at pilgrimage places are reputed to be especially greedy.

Anand Chaube admitted to me: "*hamara kam bhikh mangna hai*"—(our work is to beg). Another *panda* said to me as we were walking along on the 160-mile pilgrimage "*ham lenevala hai, denevala nahim*" (I'm a taker, not a giver). No clearer assertion of self-identity than that could be given; it sums up the significances, the moral identity, which Chaube *pandas* conceive themselves to have and a purpose (*dhyey*) for which they exist. As a taker, a *panda*'s entire livelihood and ancestral profession involves taking *daan* (religious donations) which *kulins* look down upon and *pandas* themselves fear because it carries with it inauspiciousness and even moral peril (see Parry, 1989 : 66-77; Raheja, 1988). According to Vishnu Chaube,

> **By giving me *daan* one gets *prayashchitt* (expiation) but it gives me your sins (*paap*). If I have power (*shakti*), then I can digest it (*hajam kar sakta*

> *hun*), it won't harm me. If I don't have power, then my mind (*buddhi*) will be destroyed because I have done bad things.

For that reason, whenever Chaubes intone for a pilgrim the *sankalp* (dedication) of an offering at a hallowed place, they end it with the incantation, "*Sri Krishna Arpan*," (an offering to Krishna) whereby the offering is handed over to Krishna who hopefully takes the responsibility for the money and its dangerous inauspiciousness, while the *panda* avoids the liability but keeps the money. Yet, one is never certain, for, as Vishnu Chaube also said, "*daan lena asaan hai, magar uska hajam karna kathin...cheej ek magar uska bhav alag*" (to take *daan* is easy, but to digest it is difficult... it [the money] looks like money, but it's really different).

Thus, in following their religiously ordained, patrilineally inherited, and socially sanctioned occupation, Chaubes, as *pandas*, paradoxically produce and reproduce their somewhat demeaned, but high status Brahman self-identity while perilously risking their very moral destiny. The contesting narratives of *panda* and *kulin* are about the significance of *daan* and go deeply into the very pith of the Chaube self, its moral value in society, and its ultimate destiny. Mahesh Chaturvedi, who identified himself as *kulin,* succinctly summarized the essence of those conflicting narratives of identity when he said to me "**none of us does *pandagiri* (the work of *panda*).... The main thing is that we do not take *daan*."

The situation of conflicting narrative identities is fraught with ambivalence for the *pandas* today. Not only have some emigrant *kulin* returned to Mathura where they operate shops and engage in other professions—thus, no longer keeping at bay, outside the city, an other self of the Mathura Chaubes—but also a goodly number of their own sons are increasingly turning to secular education and professions, particularly commerce and accounting. Thus, those sons bring the contesting identity *kulin* right into their own homes and bloodlines. *Panda* self-identity is in danger of becoming *kulin* other-identity.

The contrast between the two identities is vividly symbolized in the spatial separation of a father praying alongside other *pandas* at Vishram Ghat and a son bargaining alongside other merchants in a Chhata Bazaar store. It is also symbolized in the *Kams Mela* procession wherein old *panda* families sponsor Krishna and Baldev on the elephant, while the Chaturvedi Students Association and the Bombay Chaturvedi Progressive Association sponsor two colourfully decorated floats introduced in recent years. Many of the modern educated, some with Ph.D. and chartered accountancy degrees, are themselves migrants to Bombay, Delhi, Ahmedabad, and other cities of India. Marriages between members of new and old *kulin* families create for Mathura's Chaubes further confusion, tension and ambivalence about their identities.

In the past, patrons, particularly those of the Pushti Marg sect, for whom it was meritorious to give to Brahmans and to keep them well fed took generous care of their Chaube *pandas*. They gave Chaubes alms of gold, endowed them with religious guest houses (*dharmsalas)*, and even gifted them with dowries to marry-off their daughters. In return Chaubes provided patrons with ritual services, religious advice, visits during the year, and, in the case of Pushti Marg devotees, 40 days of guidance and assistance over unknown forest, field, and fen during the 160-mile annual pilgrimage (*Braj Chaurasi Kos Parikrama*).

In the present, however, the occupation is not as rewarding as it is reputed to have been in the past. Instead of visiting for a few days and staying at their *pandas'* own homes, some pilgrims stay at a hotel or guest house or leave by car within a day or so. Pious, generous pilgrims seem fewer and less generous, and the traditional cords tying priest to patron are wearing thin. Sukdev Chaube, an educated young man who frequented the religious guest house (*dharmsala*) where I lived said to me,

> "**In my grandfather's time things were different. People came for a pilgrimage, now they come just to tour around (*ghumne ke liye*)."

It is no wonder, then, that educated young Chaube men tend to evaluate the significance of *panda* identity, as would a *kulin*. Sukdev Chaube again said to me,

> "**I don't like this work of begging. Even now if there is a family register (*bahi*), on a man's death it is divided among sons and so on over the generations, until almost no patrons are left. Who can live from that?"

Another, Narendra Chaube, once confidentially said to me,

> **In the Arthashastra does it say there is any place for *sadhus* (holy men who live off the alms of others)? They can get food by begging, but there is need for more things than that, such as food and medicine. If you have money, then you will always have food.

Contested Identities

The Chaubes' contesting narratives of self-identity are matched by other narratives, some quite vicious, of contested self-identities told by non-Chaube enemies and detractors who go so far as to say that the Chaubes are really Muslims masquerading as Brahmans. Most significant among Chaubes' detractors are the Sanadhya Brahmans who themselves are the most numerous *pandas* controlling many of the sacred places throughout the Braj area except for Mathura city. (Entwistle, 1987 : 6).

Concerning Mathura's Chaubes, a Yadav said to me

> "**They were Lodhi Muslims. They were pushed out of their kingdom and came to Mathura. Their children began to show pilgrims around and slowly they took over that profession and became Hindus."

A non-Chaube Brahmani (female Brahman) spit out,

> "**The Chaubes are not real Brahmans. They came here with Akbar and were gravediggers. They were known as *pai mangna* [beggars for *pai*, an old copper coin of which there were about 4 in a paisa, Indian penny]. We don't have marriage relations with them."

Finally, another non-Chaube Brahman narrated to me the following, which in different versions others repeated:

> **The Chaubes are not real Brahmans. They came here from a city in Afghanistan called Chauba. Up until about 100 years ago they still had marriage relations with people there. They came from Afghanistan.... Babur brought them here to India, where they were slaves of Muslims. Even today there is a group among them known as *gulmate* [pl. of *gulmata*] that is the same as *gulamte* [*gulam*—slave]. There is a part of Chaubiya Para known as Taj Pura, which at first only Muslims occupied. They were the grave diggers for Muslims....During Akbar's time they moved to Chaubiya Para....Before this time, all was in control of other Brahmans. About 150 years ago there was a war over Vishram Ghat. The other Brahmans surrendered, and the Chaubes took over....After the battle for Vishram Ghat, Sanadhya Brahmans sold their *bahis* [register of pilgrims] to the Chaubes.

This narrative takes up the theme of Chaubes and the Muslims and strategically asserts not only that some of them were slaves and gravediggers for the Muslims, but worse that they *were* Muslims. That assertion implies that because one is a Brahman only by birth, then Chaubes still *are* Muslim by birth. It implicates, therefore, all Chaubes, not merely the *gulmata*, and strikes at the very heart of Chaube scriptural identities: Hindu, Mathur Brahman, *panda*, companion of Krishna, and slayer of Kans. If they are not Brahmans connected by birth to ancestral autochthones in Mathura, then the rituals they perform as *pandas* for pilgrims lack efficacy and are a travesty. Such narratives contest the vital, constitutive significance of Chaube narratives of identity framed in scriptural discourse. As well, they seek to invalidate Chaubes' claims to alms gathered at Vishram Ghat and elsewhere for performance of pilgrimage services.

Worth noting here, however, is that scriptural discourse, especially in modern times, has great capacity for meeting new and unexpected situations; although that is of little comfort to the Chaubes. Brooks (1989 : 106-141) has shown that in the pilgrimage town of Brindaban, six miles from Mathura, American Hare Krishnas have been accepted as real Brahmans. One reason pilgrims gave was that "if the deities accepted the foreigners, then so should they [the pilgrims]" (Brooks, 1989).

The narrative disclosure of Chaube origin in Afghanistan attempts to undermine every one of the narratives of self-identity dependent upon Chaubes' autochthonous origin in Mathura, the place of ultimate disclosure for their identities. Yet, Mathura Chaubes themselves, as well as some *kulin*, hint at relationships with Afghanistan up until the recent past that only muddle the issue. Mohan Chaube told me one such narrative:

> **In Moghul times two boys were forcefully taken away to Afghanistan. One died. The other was very beautiful and he fell into the favour of a woman there. She arranged to send him back and gave him two camels for his journey. He finally arrived back here, but no one would accept him as a Chaube. He had been outcasted. Finally [a].... headman (*sardar*) said that he would accept him back, and, after expiation (*prayashchitt*)..., publicly accepted him back into his family.

Moreover, the narrative of Chaubes as Muslims from Afghanistan is not unmotivated and tastes of sour grapes. The Sanadhya Brahmans in the past controlled more pilgrimage stations and temples in Mathura city than they do today. Chaubes, such as Binod Chaube, tell a counter-narrative of Chaube identity and of rights flowing from it.

> **When the Muslims came to Mathura, the Chaubes retreated to Tila Chaubiyana near Amresh Tila. They would come to Vishram Ghat only in the morning and evening. Thus, the Sanadhyas took over the Ghat for the rest of the time and began to monopolize it. This place where I live was inhabited by Muslims and was a burial ground (*kabristan*). The Sanadhyas live in Mandi Ram Das. When Muslim pressure died out in British times, quarrels began to arise between Sanadhyas and Chaubes about the Ghats and money given there. At that time all contributions were put in a common pot and 1/3 went to the Sanadhyas and 2/3 went to the Chaubes. The Sanadhyas wanted more and we wanted to cast them out. A court case arose that went all the way to Allahabad [location of the High Court], and the Chaubes won because they had papers and *Farmans* as proof.

Another narrative relates that the court's decision mentioned one of those *Farmans*, as the very one given by Akbar to Ujagar Chaube (Chaube, 1967). That case is part of the continuous record Chaubes have established for their own strategic assertions of identity, their use of legal discourse to do so, and their capturing the past as a scarce resource in constructing their identities.

In winning their case and the bitter enmity of the Sanadhyas the Chaubes not only gained complete control of Vishram Ghat, but also strengthened their claim to be pilgrimage priests as given by their control over Vishram Ghat with all its religiously constituted associations and their place in them.

In introducing this section, *Contested Self-Identities*, I explicitly inserted myself into my own narrative about the Chaubes when I said that some of their detractors' narratives are "quite vicious." In so doing, I revealed my own opinionated sentiments. Here I will deepen them by inserting an argument that Chaubes never explicitly made to me, but which is, I think, implicit in what they told me. Once again, actual historical events are not at issue; interpretation for strategic deployment in the present is. Some detractors of Chaubes say that Chaubes are not real Brahmans because they were not included in the categories of the Five Northern and Five Southern Brahman castes recognized by the great Hindu philosopher Shankaracharya (728-820 A.D.). According to Guru Sharma, "**Shankaracharya did not recognize them [Chaubes] as Brahmans because of mixed blood. He specifically excluded Brahmans of Mathura and Magadh from the Five Northern Brahmans (*panch gaur*)." That, however, contradicts the argument that the Chaubes came into India with the Muslims. It unwittingly asserts Chaubes' presence in Mathura long before the Muslim arrival and posits their Brahmanical status. In any case, Chaubes themselves retort that they were excluded only because they did not have to do penance due to taint of Buddhist influence; they always had remained pure and orthodox which other Brahman castes had not.[15] V.K. Chaturvedi put it well:

> " Two hundred preachers of the Buddhist Dharma lived here but no Mathur Brahman converted to that religion and none were caught up by political enticements. That is proven by Shankaracharya's not requiring the Brahmans of this place to do penance" (V.K. Chaturvedi n.d.:14).

Discussion and Conclusions

1. There is more than rings in the ear to the assertion that Chaubes originated in Afghanistan or elsewhere outside of Mathura. Space is never

neutral; it is always defined culturally as place. India itself is more than a politically defined, geographically bounded nation state; it is also a sacred place cosmologically constituted in Hindu belief. Almost all Mathur Chaturvedi Brahmans, resident in Mathura or not, agree that they are the Mathur Brahmans whose ultimate origin or place of disclosure is in Mathura. In that, they are like most other Indians who trace themselves back to some ancestral village or place, because ancestral place is a metaphor for self-identity, if not a metonym for it (see Daniel, 1984). Thus, when Chaubes assert their autochthonous origin in Mathura they simultaneously posit their self-identity not as man made, but as cosmologically given; they and Mathura are one. Mathura, as the place of fullest and most salient public disclosure of Chaube self-identity, grounds that identity in a primeval place of ontological significance. As a counter place of disclosure the narrative of Afghanistan seeks to totally deny to Chaubes their identity with all its constitutive importance for the significances of their social worth. The same can be said for the narratives of Karua who remain resident in Mathura and Mitha who now have an alternative place of disclosure outside of Mathura, as well as for the narratives of the *pandas* who locate themselves at Vishram Ghat and the *kulins* who locate themselves in the stores of Chhata Bazaar and Bombay.

Self, then, is culturally disclosed not by an interior place of conscious self-awareness, but by an external place of revelation. "What is relevant is not the capacity to have some inner sense of the human significances—this is a typically 'internalist' way of understanding it—but rather access to some force or to some region which lies outside of us" (Taylor, 1985a : 279). As self-defining agents, Chaubes narratively constitute both that place and its temporal location not through biological constants of development or so-called material forces, but rather through their involvement in the conversation or argument given through language.

2. My own narrative tends to conceal in its chronological ordering that Chaube self-identities are many, not one. Each narrative was told to me at different times, in different places, and by different Chaubes. Each was about a different identity in the *present*, for which the past was a politically strategic resource. For example, the *Kams Mela* asserts: I am a descendant of Kans's slayers, a warrior and a force to be reckoned with in Mathura, if not elsewhere. The food for Krishna narrative asserts: I am a *mast* Chaube who can even refuse Krishna while doing sacrifice, therefore, I am to be respected as a Brahman. The narrative of Ujagar and Vallabhacharya asserts: I am a descendant of Ujagar's people and therefore I am one of those who alone act as pilgrimage priests for the Pushti Marg sect. And

the narrative of the Karua Chaubes asserts: I am a defender of my Hindu religion and a speaker of the bitter truth.

Narratives of self-identity, then, concern two things of fundamental importance to the social order: identity and interests. In terms of identity they are concerned *about* significances, those strong evaluations that constitute the self's qualitative worth *vis-a-vis* others and ontologically locate it though language in some place of disclosure. That location is made culturally intelligible and salient through deployment of scriptural, legal, and performative discourses which as forms of knowledge are implicated in power. In terms of interests narratives are concerned *with* strategic assertions and claims. For the Mathura Chaubes, those interests involve claims to political dominance over others in Mathura and control over the *Kams Vadh Ka Mela*; claims of economic control over Vishram Ghat and the *Braj Chaurasi Kos Parikrama* (160 mile pilgrimage); and claims to social honour greater than that due to the Mitha or Kulin Chaturvedis or to the Sanadhyas.

3. From a narrative point of view *Karua, Mitha, panda, kulin,* and *gulmata* are not sub-groups of some larger group or caste; rather they are conceptually and strategically deployed names, not merely categories, asserting self-identities.[16] The "authentic" Chaube narrative self of scriptural discourse is not coherent, essential, and univocal. Rather, it is contingent, semiotically constituted and equivocal; it is historically and situationally refracted into the multiple, contesting narratives of *Karua* and *Mitha, panda* and *kulin*. As well, it is contested in the narratives of Chaubes as Muslims told by their enemies and detractors, just as it is reactively reproduced in Chaubes' own counter-narratives of heroes outwitting Muslim emperors and fearless warriors commandeering rights over Vishram Ghat. Authentic caste self-identity and status, then, has always been in flux, multiple and changing in ways other than that of Sanskritization (Srinivas, 1966) which importantly revealed change of *varna* categorization even as it concealed stasis of a bounded, essentialized caste-group (*jati*).

From such a perspective, a caste, like the eighteenth century Rajput state (Peabody, 1991), is not a rigid, bounded, essentialist group, but rather a fluctuating, fluid (Marriott, 1990; Shah, 1988a,b), unbounded collectivity of agents who deploy narratives of self-identities to deal with historical and situational contingencies. Today's *pandas* are tomorrow's *kulin*, and sometimes one is both. Orthodox Hindu and hegemonic academic theories conceal those fluctuating, contingent, and open boundaries as well as the multiple self-identities constituted through language. A narrative, processual and non-essentialist perspective, then, offers a revealing understanding of caste in India different from that of a totalizing, essentialist perspective.

4. Chaubes' detractors' narratives assert that Chaubes were Muslim. Yet, pilgrims today do not concern themselves with such narratives and defer instead to praxis, as in the case of the American Hare Krishnas in India who claim Brahmanical status (Brooks, 1989). Those, who achieve public recognition for their occupation, are who they claim to be. Important, too, is that it *is conceivable* among some Hindus that Chaubes were at one time Muslims but today are Brahmans.[17] Chaubes' detractors implicitly reveal such ironic possibilities whenever they tell their narratives. The line, therefore, between the dynamic semiotics of Hindu mythological thought, in which beings transform and transmigrate from one state into another, and a narrative semiotics of the dynamics of the social organization of castes is and was porous.[18] It is so in a way that remains merely the presence of an absence, a trace, in an essentialized and totalized theory. Even the concept of Sanskritization (Srinivas, 1966) did not suggest the possibility of non-Brahmans, let alone Muslims, moving into the Brahman category (*varna*).

5. Like sticks and stones, names in some cultures can hurt because they matter—they have moral value. Names—*Karua, Mitha, panda, kulin*—are important as summaries of the narrative self-identities that imply significances, strong evaluations constitutive of the self. Self-identities cannot, then, be reduced to material or political factors without depriving them of what is most humanly significant about them. Because self is constituted in and through public narratives, it is never totally known as a unique coherent thing; it can only be known and experienced by focusing on contingent identities through a space of disclosure in language. Thus, change in caste or other identities is neither changing an essential self nor putting on or off identities masking a more basic self.

NOTES

1. This essay is the result of fieldwork carried out in Mathura from September to December 1980, from August 1981 to August 1982, and from mid-June to mid-August 1985. The research from 1980 to 1982 was generously supported by a Senior Faculty Research Grant from the American Institute of Indian Studies. The essay has greatly profited from comments by Vijay Mishra, Sudhir Kakar, Mattison Mines, William Kelly and other participants in the August 1991 Conference on Self and Social Order held at the Center for Culture and Communication, in Honolulu, Hawaii. My thanks to Dr. Wimal Dissanayake for inviting me to the Conference and encouraging me to investigate this topic. I am grateful to Doranne Jacobson for her fine grained reading and incisive comments; to Joan Lehn for

her edits and penetrating questions; to Professors Arvind Shah, Jack Hawley and Alan Entwistle for sending me to sources I might otherwise have missed and for sharing with me their deep knowledge of Braj culture; to Diana Wells for her suggested improvements and comments; to Prof. Constance Sutton for her encouragement; and to Enid Lang for opening the way for me.

2. This figure is based upon a register book for a distribution of food called (*daini*) which is given to all male Chaubes in Chaubiya Para. The distribution was done in 1978 in celebration of a young man's sacred thread ceremony. The register lists 1,165 families with 5,574 male members. I have simply doubled that figure for a total of approximately 11,300. My reason for doubling the figure is that in the state of Uttar Pradesh the sex ratio is biased in favour of males. Chaubes say that in their community today females outnumber males, although in the past it was the opposite. Because I believe there is some truth to their assertion about the present, I have split the difference and evened the sex ratio. My figure is remarkably similar to that of Bhagvandatt Chaturvedi (1958 : 487) who says "The population of the Karuas today is 10 or 11 thousand and of these only about 600 live in different places in the country, while the rest live in Mathura city. The population of the Mitha Chaubes is many times that of the Karuas. The vast majority of Mathura's Chaubes live by alms for Brahmans."
3. A fourth reason for the theory's importance is its presentation of a strong argument for a non-reductionist understanding of human significances, whether they be vital, in terms of survival, or sentient, in terms of physiological processes. Such motives are in themselves not significant. They become so only by contextualization in terms of human significances, such that being a martyr to a cause can be judged either heroism or contemptible self-promotion. Thus, finding motivation in terms of so-called material economic gain, or drive to power, does not really explain without contextualization in culturally defined human significances. In this paper I am particularly concerned with human significances and their relationship to self-identity.
4. "The subject of radical choice is another avatar of that recurrent figure which our civilization aspires to realize, the disembodied ego, the subject who can objectify all being, including his own, and choose in radical freedom" (Taylor 1985b : 35).
5. One line of the inscription ends with the syllable, *ma*; the next line begins with the word *nacchondoga*. But, according to Luders (1961 : 126), "the meaning of *manacchandoga* has not yet been ascertained" and in footnote 4 of the same page he says "there seems to have been no more writing after *ma*." Chaubes are not so uncertain about the inscription's meaning and about a missing syllable after *ma* such that the word was Mathur. About this disagreement I heard nothing while in Mathura and, therefore, I have not discussed it as contested. I am very grateful to Alan Entwistle for directing me to Luders's work and to its possible implications for the Chaubes.
6. Narratives beginning with ** are from my notes and are my transcriptions of what I heard or remembered hearing on a particular day. Otherwise the narratives are verbatim.
7. Growse (1979 : 129) translates this line from the Varah Purana as "No God like Kesava, and no Brahman like a Mathuriya Chaube."

8. The mustache is a sign of virility, courage and honour. The mustache standing for the whole severed head is the defeated Kans castrated of his honour even in his death.
9. Alter's (1992) book on the discourses and practices of the gymnasium (*akhara*) and the body is an excellent example of how Indian wrestlers constitute their self-identity through the metonymically related places of disclosure: the wrestling floor and the body. The somatic self-identity of the wrestler has much to do with ethical and moral beliefs, or significances, in the world of *samsara*.
10. Information about Ujagar and especially his cousin Udhav, including their birth and death dates, is given by Bal Mukund Chaturvedi (n.d.).
11. I have written here [Ujagar] because I recorded Ujagar's name as that of his nephew, Udhav, with whom he is very closely associated and often paired. This was perhaps an error of memory during my first days of fieldwork with the Chaubes. The narrative itself was confirmed in other versions.
12. See endnote 3. for the number of Chaubes said to be living outside of Mathura in 1958. That number is probably much greater today. See also Mittal (1966 : 75) for a cultural historian's description of the impact of these events on the Chaubes.
13. For another version see Lynch (1990b : 97).
14. See Lynch (1990b) for the way in which Mathura's Chaubes categorize those seeking patrons in these two ways.
15. In 1980-81 Chaubes mentioned the need to regain the site of Krishna's birth which is supposed to be underneath a mosque now at that site. In 1987 when I visited them this topic was more in the air and I had the impression that the Chaubes saw themselves at the forefront of this movement, part of the long-term strategy of the Hindu nationalist movement propagated by the Vishva Hindu Parishad and the Bharatiya Janata Party. That movement in 1993 brought about the destruction of the Babri Masjid in Ayodhya and its violent aftermath. Chaube self-identification is anything but Muslim.
16. Although not taking a narrative perspective Shah (1988a, 1988b) has insightfully and with a wealth of rich data written about the multiple levels of identity in castes.
17. From an essentialist perspective one is a Hindu given by birth in, and ancestry from, a particular caste. Yet even within Hinduism there are competing perspectives on this question. In Arya Samaji teaching one is a Brahman by action not by birth. A group of south Indian untouchables who recently converted to Islam has now converted back into Hinduism. If that is possible, then most Indian Muslims who are descendants of Hindus could technically return to Hinduism and their former caste. There are untouchable and upper caste versions on whether Ravi Das was really a Brahman because of a previous birth or really an untouchable (Khare, 1984 : 40-50).
18. The space of disclosure, as public and social may paradoxically make change easier than when it is that of the interiorized, coherent and unified self. An externalized space of disclosure in a scripturally authenticated place opens up to Chaubes all the possibilities of India's vast corpus of myth that can be used to devise solutions for present day problems (Kakar, 1989), while the self of the interiorized place of disclosure is left to work it out from personal resources.

REFERENCES

Alter, Joseph (1992). *The Wrestler's Body: Identity and Ideology in North India*. Berkeley: University of California Press.

Appadurai, Arjun (1981). "The Past as a Scarce Resource". *Man* n.s. 16:201-219.

Barnett, Steve (1973). "Urban is as Urban Does: Two Incidents on One Street in Madras City, South India." *Urban Anthropology*, 2(2) : 129-160.

Barthes, Roland (1972). *Mythologies*. New York: Noonday Press.

Berreman, Gerald D. (1972). Social Categories and Social Interaction in Urban India. *American Anthropologist* 74:567-586.

Brooks, Charles (1989). *The Hare Krishnas in India*. Princeton: Princeton University Press.

Carrithers, Michael (1985). "An Alternative Social History of the Self". In *The Category of the Person*. Michael Carrithers, Steven Collins, and Steven Lukes, eds. pp. 234-256. Cambridge; Cambridge University Press.

Chaturvedi, Bal Mukund (1986). *Mathur Chaturvedi Brahmanom ka Itihas*. Mathura: Paliwal Press. n d. "*Brajbhasa ke Saisav-yug ke Mahamanoso Sriuddhav Ji Ujagar Ji*". In *Brij Bharati*. Radhesyam Josi, ed. pp. 27-34. Mathura.

Chaturvedi, Bhagvandatt (1958). "*Mathura ke Caube.*" In *Braj ka Itihas*. Sri Krishna Datt Vajpeyi, ed. pp. 487-489. Mathura: Akhil Bharatiya Braj Sahitya Mandal.

Chaturvedi, Jivanlal (1972). "*Braj ke Pramukh Mall*", *Mathura Patrika (Brajank)*. Mathura: Champa Agrawal Inter College.

Chaturvedi, Raghunath Prasad (1981). "*Ek Niscit Satya*" In *Mathur Pradeep* 2(7-8) : 6-16.

Chaturvedi, Vasudev Krishna n.d. *Mathura evam Mathur Chaturvedi Sankshipt Parichay*. Mathura: Sri Mathur Chaturvedi Sabha.

Chaturvedi, Yugal Kishore (1968). *Mathur Chaturvedi Brahman Parichay*. Jaipur: Agarwal Printing Press.

Chaube, Vijay Chand Bare (1967). *Mathur Kul Divakar, Dharm Murti, Vednidhi Tapasvi Sri Ujagar-ji Mathur Chaturved.*" In *Mathur Pradeep* 2(1-2) : 5-6.

Daniel, E. Valentine (1984). Fluid Signs: Being a Person in the Tamil Way. Berkeley: University of California Press.

Derrida, Jacques (1976). *Of Grammatology. Gayatri Chakravorty Spivak*, trans. Baltimore: John Hopkins University Press.

——(1973). "différance" In *Speech and Phenomena and Other Essays on Husserl's Theory of Signs*. David B. Allison, trans. pp. 129-160. Evanston, Ill: Northwestern University Press.

Duncan, James S. (1990). *The City as Text: The Politics of Landscape Interpretation in the Kandyan Kingdom*. Cambridge: Cambridge University Press.

Entwistle, A.W. (1987). *Braj Centre of Krishna Pilgrimage*. Groningen: Egbert Forsten.

Foucault, Michel (1972). *The Archaeology of Knowledge and the Discourse on Language*. New York: Pantheon.

Growse, F.S. (1979). *[1882] Mathura: A District Memoir*. New Delhi: Asian Educational Services.

Hardgrave, Robert L. (1969). *The Nadars of Tamilnad: The Political Culture of a Community in Change*. Berkeley: University of California Press.

Harirayji, Goswami (1904). "*Sri Govarddhannathji ke Prakatya ki Varta*. Pandit Mohanlal Visnulal Pandya, ed. Bombay: Sri Venkatesvar Yantralaya.

Kakar, Sudhir (1989). *Intimate Relations: Exploring Indian Sexuality*. Chicago: University of Chicago Press.

Kondo, Dorinne (1990). *Crafting Selves.* Chicago: University of Chicago Press.

Luders, Heinrich (1961). *Mathura Inscriptions;* Unpublished Papers. Klaus L. Janert, ed. Gottingen: Vandenhoeck and Ruprecht.

Lynch, Owen M. (1990a). "The Social Construction of Emotion in India." In *Divine Passions: The Social Construction of Emotion in India.* Owen M. Lynch, ed. pp. 3-34. Berkeley: University of California Press.

——(1990b). "The Mastram: Emotion and Person among Mathura's Chaubes." In *Divine Passions: The Social Construction of Emotion in India.* Owen M.

Lynch, ed. pp. 91-115. Berkeley: University of California Press.

——(1988). "Pilgrimage with Krishna, Sovereign of the Emotions." *Contributions to Indian Sociology* 22(2) : 171-195.

——(1969). *The Politics of Untouchability· Social Mobility and Social Change in a City of India.* New York: Columbia University Press.

Malinowski, Bronislaw (1948). *Magic, Science, and Religion and Other Essays.* Garden City: Doubleday and Co.

Marriott, McKim (1990). "Constructing an Indian Sociology". In *India Through Hindu Categories.* McKim Marriott, ed. pp. 1-40. New Delhi: Sage.

Mathur Mandli (1969). *[1901] Karravai Mathur Chaturvedi Mandli Mathura.* Mathura: Mathur Mandli.

Mauss, Marcel (1985). "A Category of the Human Mind: the Notion of Person; the Notion of Self." In *The Category of the Person.* Michael Carrithers, Steven Collins, and Steven Lukes, eds. W.D. Halls, trans. pp. 1-25. Cambridge: Cambridge University Press.

Mead, George Herbert (1934). *Mind, Self, and Society.* Chicago: University of Chicago Press.

Mittal, Prabhudayal (1966). *Braj ka Samskrtik Itihas.* Delhi: Rajkamal Prakasan.

Parry, Jonathan (1989). "On the Moral Perils of Exchange". In *Money and the Morality of Exchange.* Jonathan Parry and Maurice Bloch, eds. pp. 64-93. Cambridge: Cambridge University Press.

Peabody, Norbert (1991). "*Kota Mahajagat,* or the Great Universe of Kota: Sovereignty and Territory in 18th Century Rajasthan." *Contributions to Indian Sociology* n.s. 25(1) : 28-56.

Rao, M.S.A. (1979). *Social Movements and Social Transformation.* Delhi: The Macmillan Co.

Shah, A.M. (1988a). "Division and Hierarchy: An Overview of Caste in Gujarat." In *Division and Hierarchy: An Overview of Caste in Gujarat.* A.M. Shah and I.P. Desai ed. pp. 1-39. Delhi: Hindustan Publishing Co.

——(1988b). "A Response to the Critique on "Division and Hierarchy." In *Division and Hierarchy: An Overview of Caste in Gujarat.* A.M. Shah and I.P. Desai. pp. 92-133. Delhi: Hindustan Publishing Co.

Srinivas, M.N. (1976). *The Remembered Village.* Berkeley: University of California Press (1966) *Social Change in Modern India.* Berkeley: University of California Press.

Taylor, Charles (1985a). "The Person." In *The Category of the Person.* Michael Carrithers, Steven Collins, and Steven Lukes, eds. pp. 257-281. Cambridge: Cambridge University Press.

——(1985b). *Human Agency and Language: Philosophical Papers I.* Cambridge: Cambridge University Press.

27

Custom, Religion and Social Change Among the Meos of Mewat

ABHA CHAUHAN

The interface between custom and religion has acquired a new meaning in the changing context of those communities that are placed in the intermediary or fuzzy situation. The Meo of Mewat region in North India is one such community. The Meo consider themselves to be originated from Rajput caste and were converted to Islam at different periods of time in the last one century. Though then adopted Islam as religion but continued to follow non-Islamic customs and saw no contradiction between the two despite several upheavals that the community faced. In the recent years, as the gap between the two religious communities—the Hindus and the Muslims widened, the Meo became more conscious of their Islamic identity and consequently of leaving those customs that bring them closer to the 'other'.

This paper traces the relationship between the customary and religious laws and practices of the Meos and the dynamics of their interplay in the process of social change. The modem forces of change like formal education and new employments coalesce with customs and religion to produce new configurations in Meo society. The paper specifically deals with some of the customary kinship rules and practices of the Meos that have undergone changes in recent years and their implications.

The Meos of Mewat

The Meo is an agricultural community, with ninety-two percent people living in some 1200 villages of Mewat region. Mewat lies 70 kms. Southwest of Delhi and comprises districts of Haryana, Rajasthan and Uttar Pradesh. Mewat is known as the land of the Meos though a considerable number of them reside outside Mewat also. The Meo is a patrilineal and patrilocal community. In matters of name, descent, succession, inheritance, maintenance and adoption, the Meo follow their customary rules, though some people have begun to question and even started following the *Shariat* laws, which calls for the need to study the emerging dynamics.

There are certain matters however, in which the Meo follow Islamic rules quite strictly. *Nikah* is the Islamic element necessary for every Meo marriage. It is accompanied by *mehr,* an essential part of Muslim marriage. The circumcision and the burial rituals are essentially Islamic. Besides these features, during occasions like birth of a child, marriage, festival or any other ceremony the Meo follow various local customs and rituals like the gift of the ceremonial prestation or *bhat* by the maternal uncle, the ritual services of the paternal aunt and the payment of dowry or *dan.* Most of the rituals associated with these ceremonies have now been given up by the Meos. Their participation in the Hindu festivals and the visits to the *mela,* the mausoleums or *dargah,* even of their own saints have reduced considerably. The Meo women often talk about worshipping of the village well and local deity after marriage or the birth of the child, which they no longer follow. Change in several such practices now shows a clear shift. This paper however, does not deal with these kinds of changes in the beliefs and rituals of the people, which nevertheless are important, but more broadly about the rules of kinship and marriage.

The Meo enjoyed high social prestige as well as economic and political power in the past owing to their Rajput origin. They were the *jajmans* to the various Hindu and Muslim servicing castes, the *zamindars* of their own land and *chaudharis* of their territorial clans and lineages. The history of the region suggest their constant struggle and battle with the Mughals, the Britishers or other princely rulers which led to the formation of their image as rebels as well as their marginalization from a ruling group to much smaller peasants (Mayaram, 1997 : 27). They suffered the trauma of partition and the successive governments in Independent India could not attend to the problems of the Meos for the lack of the right type of leadership from among its own rank. This resulted in their neglect and alleged backwardness (Rathee, 1971 : 42).

Rather known for their ignorance about their religion in the days gone by, the Meos are becoming more aware of Islam (Powlett, 1878). From the mid 1930s, the Meos began to come under the influence of Tabliqi Jama'at (T.J.), which became active after 1947. Under its influence the Meos abandoned many of the Hindu rituals, ceremonies and festivals. The changes are most visible in the recent years with the increase in the number of *madarsa* and the number of children, particularly girls going to them. A large number of mosques have come up in the area as well. The people have become more religious in offering *namaz,* keeping *roza* and going for *haj.* A large number of people now participate in Jama'at after going through some training. The T.J adopt peaceful methods and preach the tenets of Islam and ask them not to follow non-Islamic customs. As Meos are rural and rustic people following several customary practices, the educated and more refined Meos ask them to leave the present social life *of Jahelat* and to become more religious.

However, though the Meos have adopted various Islamic features, they refuse to give up their caste and kinship system. The T.J. was keen that they give up these because the Meos trace their descent through the ancestors originated from Hindu Gods. The Meos kinship structure is an essential part of their social organization, which not only determines people's relationships and regulates their behaviour but functions towards continuity and their very survival. The Meos have rejected the attempts at the intra-clan marriages and those between the children of two brothers. The T J. has now given up such demands and the Meos have reconciled to their identity as 'better' Muslims, while retaining their caste and kinship systems.

There are mainly three reasons for Islamic revival in Mewat. Firstly after partitioned of India in 1947 state, antipathy between the Hindus and the Muslims was on peak. There was a large-scale violence and attempts were made to reconvert the Meos to the Hindu fold. For the Meos, this was an identity crises and threat to their existence. When the normal "situation returned, the Meos began to reassert their identity as Muslims—a construction readily embraced by the pan Islamic leadership.

The second reason has to do with the dominant caste status and the high social prestige as well as economic and political power associated with it. Though many previous British writers like Risley (1901) and Crooke (1907) claim that the Meo is a tribal group, some recent sociological studies (Aggarwal, 1971; Jamous, 1996) have shown that Meo is a caste category characterized by endogamy, hereditary membership and hierarchical position in relation to other castes. Since most of them are landowners, they are referred to as *zamindars.* They have been the *jajmans* or patrons to the several servicing and 'untouchable' castes of the region. (Jamous, 1996 : 182-183). The dominant position of the Meos in the social hierarchy makes them reluctant to give up their caste status. But now with the weakening of the caste system, decline *of jajmani* practice, changes in the occupational structure of the Meos and other castes, and commercialization of agriculture, the privileges of the Meos have been severely curtailed.

The third reason for the acceptance of Islam is that with the improvement of communication and other developments, the Meos feel that they could no longer remain isolated from the outside world. A step in this direction is to forge links with the Muslim community outsde Mewat [Weeks, (ed.) 1984 : 520]. Jamous (1996) notes that Meo still want to keep their local identity and local relationships though they are experiencing an increasing sense of solidarity with other Indian Muslims. They try to react to the new changes by mobilizing both the forms of their identity—as a Rajput caste and a Muslim community—even if these imply conflicting values (p.199). How long they will be able to sustain this conflict is to be seen as the drift between the two communities has widened. The situation 'changed even more since the mid-1980s, and after the incident at Ayodhya in 1992, the animosity between the Muslim community and some of the Hindu groups has grown dangerously' (*Ibid*: 194-195).

Caste Endogamy

The Meos by and large marry within their own caste. Though remarriage is allowed, both for women and men, the first marriage between the unmarried couple is the most preferred one. In case of second marriage, late marriage or in a situation of poverty, men marry non-Meo women from outside Mewat as well, though the opposite is not true. In this sense then, the rule of caste endogamy operate for women and not so rigidly for men, even though such marriages are not held in high esteem or follow the same rituals. They are not prohibited in Mewat but do not have the same status as they are held due to poverty and imply a notion of 'selling' or being 'paid for'. They are however, perfectly legal marriage the children born of such union adopt the name and clan of their Meo fathers, and their marriages are arranged as per the local customs. The rules of succession and ownership of property apply to their children in a similar manner as to the children born of a Meo woman. It is also seen that educated Meo men marry Muslim women of their own choice from outside Mewat and such marriages usually carry a better status because the girls in such cases are educated and from well-to-do families. As marriage between educated and employed people carries more prestige, it shows that these factors are considered to be important by the people.

It has been observed that the Meos have started marrying Muslim women from outside Mewat in the last 20 years or so when it became difficult for men to find girls for remarriage. The men and women ratio in Mewat has always been low and they were in great demand owing to the important role they play in the agrarian economy. According to the local informants, one could find nearly 15-20 widow every village some 30 years age as, the customary law of the Meos did not allow the marriage between a Meo man and a woman of the inferior caste. The rigidity of the kinship rules that do not allow cousin marriages or even exchange marriages further restricted their choice. The exigency of the situation fostered the possibility of inter Mewat links and Islam provided stimulus to such marriages by not opposing them. However, the widening of this choice was utilized by men alone in the Meo patrilineal society as women were in no way allowed to go in for exogamous marriages as that may lower down the status of their families and those of their children.

Clan Exogamy

The Meo is divided into a number of patrilineal clans and the mythical founding ancestor of each is considered to be descendant of Hindu divinity. This is evident from their oral tradition, visible during certain occasions like marriage. There are 13 main clans called *pals* which are also territorial units believed to have descended from the Rajput clans. There are also 52 or more clans called *nepaliya, i.e.* without pal territory. Each pal is divided into a number of villages as each clan or *gotra* is divided into lineages. The marriages between the *pal* and *nepaliya gotra* occur frequently and there is no status difference between the two categories. The heads of these pals are no longer important as they used to be, though their voice is still heard and considered in the formation of marriage alliance and disputes regarding them.

Earlier the Meos followed *four-gotra* rule, but now they have restricted to only one. The Meos are very particular about this rule and any attempt to change this has been vehemently opposed and meted with the severest of punishments. In the 60s, *maulvis* of three villages tried to arrange marriage between children of two brothers. The Meos not only boycotted the marriage but also butchered one of the *maulvis*. Going around the villages in Mewat one can hear a few stray incidents of *intra-gotra* marriage. Such marriages are usually not allowed or if done without information is later boycotted. In one case of village *Jaitaka* of Gurgaon district, a marriage was performed in the late 80s between the members of *Dhirwal gotra,* one of the 13 pal *gotras.* In this the boy with his very close relatives came along with the *Qazi. Nikah* was performed but the girl was taken away only later. There was no *barat,* no other ritual ceremony or feast to the entire village as is the usual custom. When people of village *Jaitaka* came to know of this marriage later, they showed their resentment and disapproved the marriage. It was after a considerable period of time that the relations of this family with other villagers became normal. Religion here was used to legitimize the decision and as this family was rich, educated and influential, it exercised its influence on the pretext of being more aware of Islamic injunctions. There are few families in Mewat that are more educated and also more religious. The number of these families, though slowly but steadily increasing. By their personal conduct, they are able to influence people in Mewat. The Meo panchayat, besides other things, has also started focusing on the non-Islamic practices of the people urging them to abandoned them and become true Muslims. In the Panchayat held of Meos from hundreds of villages in Firozepur Jhirka town in July 1998, the Meos decided among many things, to avoid pomp and show in marriage, to take very few people in the *barat* and not to give or take dowry. Ironically, though plight of young girls and women was discussed not a single woman was present which shows the domination of men in decision-making and the rigidity in gender-relations in Meo society. The few cases, which have come to light in Mewat in the recent years, are those where people do not take *barat*. After the brief ceremony of *nikah* the girl is later left at her in-laws house.

Though the justification for all such changes are given on religious ground, the main reason behind all these changes lie elsewhere. The Meos have been following Islam for centuries, but the changes have only started recently. The role of religious organizations like T.J. is also not new. The main reason for avoiding the pomp and show and taking the *barat* is usually to avoid the economic expenditure. In general people still value marriage with customary rituals and high dowry and take pride in it. Those who cannot afford this take recourse in religion except very few who are committed religious people. The thinking that let others know of your activities, especially the ones that command respect is in the psyche of the people and therefore despite concerted efforts people still take *barat*, give lavish feast, and also accept dowry.

Prohibition of Marriage between Cousins

It is not enough to say that *gotra* exogamy is the rule as marriage prohibitions extend beyond one's *gotra*. Besides one father's brother' children, a man is not allowed to marry his father's sister daughter, mother's brother daughter and mother's sister's daughter. The latter three forms of cousin marriages are outside the man's *gotra*, but nevertheless prohibited. It can therefore be said, that the rule among the Meos in marriage alliance is—no marriage between cousins-cross and parallel, even if they belong to different *gotras*.

According to the *Riwaz-i-Am,* a Meo man cannot marry any woman where relationship with him is close enough to be traceable, and also a woman whose relation is traced through consanguineal kin (Wilson, 1882). It was noticed in the mid-1970s that the Meos avoided both cross-cousin and parallel-cousin marriages. Though no definite rule has been there, any person with whom a cousin relationship can be traced cannot be considered for marriage (Aggarwal, 1976 : 278). As late as in the 1980, Jamous noticed that no one could marry any parallel-cousin or cross-cousin. (p. 189). A nice from her paternal aunt was considered to be a preferential marriage.

Since early 1990s, a significant change is witnessed in this rule, *i.e.* the Meos have accepted and also started practicing the multilateral cross-cousin marriage or the marriage between a man and his mother's brother daughter. In Mewat today, no one will oppose this kind of marriage and though still rare one can hear of instances where a woman is the bride's father's sister as well as her mother-in-law. The increasing demand of dowry, extravagant expenses and ill-treatment by mother-in-law are reasons for increase in such marriages. Moreover such marriages are allowed in Islam. Some people feel that this will strengthened the ties between the families of brother and sister.

Religion thus is an important source of change here, but its impact is circumscribed by that of customary rule. This is evident from the fact that even if Meo have started practicing one form of cross-cousin marriage, they strictly oppose the second form a marriage between a man and his father's sister daughter. The reason for this is explained in Islam in the wife-giver and wife-taker rule. However, the Meos agreed that the marriage between children of two sisters is possible provided other kinship rules are followed but they do not practice this form of marriage.

The other kinship rules prevalent in this area make such unions difficult to operate and Meos are still apprehensive of the fact that proximity breeds contempt and try to avoid marriage with close relatives. The patrilateral cross-cousin marriages in Mewat are loosing ground due to growing animosity between the mother and her daughter-in-law. The elder woman usually complains about her daughter-in-law, who is also her brothers' daughter saying *isne mera pihar chudwa diya* (She is responsible for making me leave my natal home). And it is well known how *pihar* (natal home) is important for a woman in rural India. In Mewat women visit their *pihar* regularly throughout their lives though this reduces with time and age.

Village Exogamy

Earlier it was the practice for the Meo man not to marry a woman of the village of his mother, but this rule has been changed now and there is no problem in arranging marriage alliance in the mother's village. In fact now a person can marry his own maternal uncle's daughter who not only comes from the same village as his mother but also from the same family. In Mewat, it is a customary practice of giving *bhat* by maternal uncle at the marriage of his sister's children. Since it is possible for maternal uncle to be the father-in-law of his own nephew, another maternal uncle who is not the father-in-law gives the *bhat*. He performs all other activities associated with the position and duty of the maternal uncle. In such cases the girl in her in-laws house do not observe *purdah* from her husband's elder brothers as is the usual practice, because they happen to be her cousin brothers.

With the change in the demographic structure of Mewat and shifting of population, it is difficult for people to avoid territorial units of *pal* and *thamba* but as social units the rule is adhered to. Though one village is usually a one-*gotra* village, it is possible that the members of other *gotra* with whom the marriage alliance is possible live in the same village. But no marriage will be arranged and performed once they are a part of the same village. Such a configuration is possible when for example, a son-in-law comes to his wife's village and settles there and the number of his family members grows in a few years time. If he has to find a groom for his daughter then he must move to some other village.

Though the *gotra* exogamy is usually village exogamy, the two need not be synonymous and are maintained exclusive of each other. There is a fictitious kinship among the inhabitants of a village and a woman will either be a daughter or a daughter-in-law of the village. All relations irrespective of caste and communities would be accordingly maintained even when people make visits to other villages. An incident of an inter-caste marriage between two members of village Firozepur Narnak in Nuh block flared-up and received media attention not so much because of the inter-caste relationship (both were Muslims and the man was of a higher caste) but because the two were from the same village. Intra-village marital and sexual relations are still considered to be incestuous by members of all communities.

The Meo also follow the rule that they do not take girls from the villages to which they give. Though this rule could be synonymous with the *gotra* rule of wife-givers and wife-takers (explained ahead), it is followed even if this synonymy does not occur. For example, if *gotra* A from village I give girls in marriage to *gotra* B from village II, it cannot take girls of *gotra* B (from any where). But if there are girls of other *gotra*, for *e.g.* C or D in village II from whom as a rule, *gotra* A can take girls, it will not do so in this case. The entire village II acquires a status of wife-givers (Sharma, 1969 : 183).

Till as late as in the 60s it was noticed (Aggarwal, 1971:188) that the father and the son do not marry in the same village. According to Sharma if a boy is permitted to marry in his mother's natal clan, the boy must not look for a mate from his mother's village' (*Ibid*). In a later study by Jamous, it was noticed that no man could repeat the father's marriage, but it was possible to repeat the paternal grandfather's marriage (1996 : 189).

Over the years, there has been a distinct and clear-cut change in this rule. The first change was, when the restriction of father and son marrying in the same village was lifted. Very few old people remember that such a rule existed though it is mentioned in the *Riwaz-i-am*. A consistent trend is observed where brides are taken from the same *gotras* over generations. The recent changes have shown that now it is not only possible to repeat one's father's marriage but one can take a girl from the same family.

This shows that though one form of cross-cousin marriage is allowed in Mewat today and restrictions to take brides from the same villages have reduced, the concept of village as a unit of consanguineal relations has not declined at all. The village is an extremely important place for the people in Mewat irrespective of their caste and communities. For women, the natal village remains as important as their affinal village through-out their lives and various opportunities and occasions are utilized to maintain this link.

Wife-givers are Different from Wife-takers

The principle though is *gotra* and sub-clan or lineage based, one corresponds largely, but not always to the territorial divisions. Therefore, women on marriage not only move from some particular villages to some other particular ones, but also from some specified *gotra* to some other equally specified ones. In this sense, the marital relationship amongst the Meos follow a pattern of marriage alliance and to use Dumont's terminology, has a diachronic dimension as marriages ties are repeated and transmitted from one generation to another, even if they do not follow positive marriage rules.

Thus, though, the rule of *gotra* exogamy prevails where a Meo can find his/her marriage partner in any other *gotra* than his/her, the choice is quite restricted. The rise of these inter-pal clusters is explicable with reference to the demographic fact of the distribution of pals and the social fact of contacts with the affinals of one's local friends and fellows. All the pals and *gotra* have their respective concentration areas and it is the consideration of adjacency that plays a vital role in effecting these inter-pal linkages. One's contacts with the affines of neighbours and friends further facilitate the development of this pattern of marriage links. (Sharma, 1969 : 183).

The rule, that wife-givers are not the wife-takers and they are altogether different groups of people does not end here. Every clan or *pal gotra* is sub-divided into a number of groups called *thamba*. At one glance it appears that the Meo give girls to and take from the same group, but a deeper analysis into the working of the *thamba* suggest that the rule exists that wife-givers and the wife-takers are altogether a different set of people. For instance if *pal gotra* I is divided into *thamba* a, b, c and d and *gotra* II into i, j and k, it is possible that a, b and c give daughter to i and j *thamba* of *gotra* II and take daughters from only *thamba* k. There are several such configurations possible amongst various *gotra* and *thamba* in Mewat and all people know these very well, at least those that involve their own *pal* and *thamba*. Thus here pal I and II may seem to take and give girls amongst themselves, the *thamba* divisions serve as the basic units for maintaining exogamy. The pals and *thamba* amongst whom no give and take relationship occur, there is *bhaichara* or even enmity, but with those they have *bhaichara* their members are considered to be related by blood and hence no marriage. In this sense, similar to the *'inter-pal* alliances' are formed *'inter-thamba* alliances'.

The change in this rule that wife-givers cannot be wife-takers can be seen in Mewat even today where approximately 4-5 per cent of all marriages do not observe this rule. One of the reasons for this change is the addition of new restrictions to the already existing ones and the desire of the people to marry in a better-placed group. Earlier the status of family, particularly in terms of name and property was an important consideration. Focusing on these aspects the marriage used to be arranged in the prescribed group. With the increase in education of both boys and girls and of the good employment of boys in particular, the choice of male were further restricted. This again enhanced with the increase in personal choice and the desire of the boy to see the girl.

One can give several instances where this rule has been broken, but it is necessary to emphasize that these marriages are still regarded as aberrations and are usually opposed, even though the intensity of opposition has reduced. An advocate in Nuh block married a graduate girl in the late 80s. Though the marriage was arranged by bride' father there was a lot of opposition to this alliance because the *gotra* to which the boy belonged, give girls to the *gotra* to which his wife belonged to and do not take girls from them. This was the reversal of alliance, which the Meos as a rule do not follow. The opposition however subsided in the course of time and relations became normal. The fact that both were highly educated by Meo standards served as a diluting factor and also that they resided in Nuh town.

Another case of a similar kind resulted in altogether a different situation in village Bisru of Punhana block in Gurgaon district. In this case also the boy was an Engineer and the girl was twelfth pass. The marriage between the two was cancelled after a lot of opposition as this union too amounted to the reversal of alliance. This shows that in the rural areas of Mewat the customary practices dominate and the religious ones have a lesser role to play. In most of the cases, religion is used to justify the act rather than operate as a cause of social change. Education however, and good employment are seen to be more important sources of social change.

However, the ideology that wife-givers are different and inferior than wife-takers and must always remain separate is still strong in this area. It is because of this reason that there is opposition to all attempts to alter this. One can see the strength of this element in their refusal to accept another form of cross-cousin marriage, *i.e.* marriage between a boy and his father's sister daughter. In Mewat one does not come across any example of this form of cross-cousin marriage. The reflection of this ideology is also seen in their adopting of dowry system in much bigger way and giving up the marriages through bride price. Such marriages are looked down upon and are equated with selling of women.

Conclusion

This analysis of the changes in the laws and practices of the Meos and of their kinship rules in particular, suggest a shift towards uniformity in terms of religion and diversity in relation to their customs. This diversity at the wider level becomes crystallized into religious identity, which during crises situations becomes further intensified. The pan-religious leadership on the one hand, and political interests on the other, exploit the situation. The issues relating to uniform civil code and personal laws are often taken up on religious ground with political ramifications. In between are the groups that talk of gender-justice and human rights, many times without contextual and situational understanding.

A study of a community like Meos shows that such conceptualizations are at best theoretical which fail to understand the ground reality. Though Meos proudly proclaim themselves to be the followers of Islam, they equally take pride in their Rajput origin. If following of Islamic practices are important for them, so is the singing in praise of their ancestors. It has already been shown that despite several concerted efforts, the Meos have not given up their caste and kinship features. Though Islam played a catalyst role, the other modem factors of change have been equally or more important which though, have been more responsible for bringing about change in the Meo kinship structure, have also facilitated the emergence of religious consciousness and identity which leads to the realignment of groups and situations of conflict.

The studies like this could highlight for further probing, some of the emerging issues like the question of social identity. This has been adequately raised in the studies of the communities, which tend to foster new identities under the pressures of change. The other related issues of debate and dialogue could be the interface between the customary law and the personal law and the dynamics between them and the statutory law, the codification of various laws and uniformity in terms of the civil laws. Among Meos, one finds prevalence of the customary practices regarding inheritance, maintenance and adoption and of the Muslim personal laws in situations of divorce and remarriage. In some cases, the Meos also approach court for settling matters related to marriage and divorce particularly dowry harassment and maintenance grant. The focus on gender-relation in all these will explain the impact and magnitude of social change in a different perspective. This paper calls for attention to wider issues for debate and settlement, drawn from the experiences of such people as the Meos of Mewat.

REFERENCES

Aggarwal, P.C. (1971). *Caste, Religion and Power,* New Delhi. Shri Ram Centre for Industrial Relations,

Aggarwal, P.C. 1990 '(1973). "Caste, Hierarchy in a Meo Village of Rajasthan"in Imtiaz Ahmed (ed.) *Social Stratification among Muslims in India,* Columbia, South Asia Books.

Aggarwal, P.C. (1976). 'Kinship and Marriage among the Meos of Rajasthan in Imtiaz Ahmed (ed.) *Family, Kinship and Marriage among Muslims in India,* Delhi, Manohar Book Service.

Aggarawala, O.P. (1989). *A Digest of Customary Law,* Allahabad, The University Book Agency.

Ali, Hashim Amir, (1970). *The Meos of Mewat: Old Neighbours of New Delhi,* New Delhi, Oxford.

Crooke, William (1975). *The Native Races of India,* Vol. III, Delhi, Cosmo Publications.

Chakravarty-Kaul, Minoti (1996). *Common Lands and Customary Law Institutional Change in North India over the Past-two centuries,* Delhi Oxford University Press, Delhi.

Diwan, Paras, (1978). *Customary Law of Punjab and Haryana,* Chandigarh.

Dube, Leela, (1969). *Matriliny and Islam, National, Religion and Society in the Laccadives,* Delhi, National Publishing House.

Dube, Leela (1997). *Women and Kinship*, UN University Press, New Delhi, Vistaar Publications.

Goody, J.R. and S.J. Tambiah, (1973). *Bridewealth and Dowry*, Cambridge University Press, London.

Haye, Ch. Abdul, *The Freedom Movement in Mewat and Dr. K.M. Ashraf (1903-1962)* Akademic-Verlaw-Berlin.

Jamous, Raymond, (1996). "The Meo as a Rajput Caste and a Muslim Community" in C.J. Fuller (ed.), *Caste Today*, Oxford University Press, New Delhi.

Mayaram, Shail, (1997). (a), *Resisting Regimes: Myth Memory and Shaping of a Muslim Identity*, Oxford University Press, Delhi.

Mayaram, Shail, (1997). (b), 'Meos of Mewat Synthesizing Hindu-Muslim Identities', *Manushi*, No. 103, Nov-Dec.

Powlett, P.W. (1878). *Gazetteer of Ulwar*, London.

Rathee, C.R. (1971). 'Meos of Mewat: An Economic Analysis', *Mainstream* Annual.

Rose, M.A. (1919). *Glossary of the Tribes and Castes of the Punjab and N.W.F. Province*, Vol.III (L-Z) Delhi, Amar Prakashan,1980.

Saddique Ahmed, 1997. *Mewat Ek Khoj*, (Hindi), Doha, Gurgaon, Doha Taleem Samiti.

Shams, Shamsuddin, 1983. *Meos of Mewat: Their Customs and Laws*, New Delhi, Deep and Deep Publications.

Sharma, S.L. (1969). 'Structural Continuity in the Face of Cultural Change', *Eastern Anthropologist*, Vol. XXII, No. 2, May-August.

Siddqui, M.H., (1986). 'History and Society in a Popular Rebellion: Mewat, 1920-1933', in *Comparative Studies in Society and History.*

Vohra, M.B.L., M. Kaur & R. Gulati. *A Report of a Baseline Survey to Examine the Socio-Economic, Status of People in Mewat*, HIPA, Gurgaon.

Weekes, Richard, V. (ed.), (1984). *Muslim Peoples: A World Ethnographic Survey* Aidwych Press, London, England.

Wilson, J. (1882). *Codes of Tribal Customs of Twenty-one Tribes*, Lahore.

28

Dalits in India: Past Identities and Present Scenario

JAGDISH KUMAR PUNDIR

Introduction

The term Dalit has been used in its contemporary usage, in several ways conveying several connotations, evoking different images and having divergent meanings. In a broad sense the term refers to all the oppressed, depressed and down trodden section of society; however in operational terms it has been referred to that segment of society which has been placed at the bottom of caste hierarchy in the Hindu social order. Dalits have also been referred to as Achhuts (untouchables), Avarnas, Panchamas, Atishudras, Antyajas or Namshudras (Srivastava, 1997: 415). Gandhiji during the freedom movement called them as" Harijans (children of god), though it is said that the term Harijan also has existed much earlier. Since the Britishers enlisted such castes in a list and later it was recognised in the Indian Constitution, they are named as scheduled castes. The people belonging to these groups (castes) found these names as pejorative (or derogative), therefore in the recent times they preferred the term Dalits (Shah, 1990 : 107). The term Dalit in their view designates their (Dalit's) perception of oppression, denotes their traditional socio-cultural disabilities, describes their under privileged status and documents their cumulative deprivation. Though the English term "depressed classes" was in vogue during 1920's and 1930's but the term Dalit became more common since 1973.

The term "scheduled castes" became prominent much later (of course introduced in 1920's and listed in 1930's). The Dalit Panthers voicing their proletarian consciousness used the term in their manifesto to refer to the have-nots of the society, namely the scheduled castes, scheduled tribes, other backward classes, neo-Buddhists, peasants, working class people, landless labourers and other minorities and thus the whole lot of socially, economically, politically and religiously exploited people. In their usage the term Dalit referred not only to caste constellation, but to the entire under privileged class. In that sense, Dalit denotes both caste and class of a certain social category. Notwithstanding this notion or concept of Panthers the term Dalit in a popular usage refers only to the scheduled castes, scheduled tribes and backward classes. However the radical Dalit literature defines the term as including those who have been broken and grounded down by those above them in a deliberate and active way (Zelliot, 1978 : 1-2). Viewed in these terms, Dalit is not a homogenous category, meaning only the Harijans or untouchables, but includes all caste groups who have been, for times immemorial, subjected to inhuman wrongs, injustice, discrimination, social disabilities and political and economic deprivations and disadvantages (Srivastava, 1997 : 416).

Some other writers have noted (*e.g.* Epp; 1992) that Dalit means downtrodden, or oppressed people. The term refers to (the present) scheduled castes (ex-untouchables), tribals and other social groups that largely make up the depressed classes in India. Viewing the term Dalit in a different perspective it refers to a class having a distinct social character owing a history of long suffering and low social status. It is a class which seeks total emancipation from the cumulative chains of domination and control. Given a new social consciousness, the more appropriate term is coined, 'Dalitism', which refers to ideological transformation of these oppressed castes. It "indicates their heightened protest against the upper castes' domination by way of rejection of upper caste cognitive paradigms and creation of their own cultural idioms, literature and ethnic harmony" (Sharma, 1997 : 39).

In the contemporary sociological writings on the traditionally deprived castes, the untouchables transformation into Dalits has been accepted as a universal social fact. Recent writings have shown terminological shift and adaptation and have been perceived as conscious and awakened communities competing forcefully in the process of development for their own progress. Dalit has been used in this sense as a political community, an emergence which puts them in a position to protest against the dominant castes as it is equipped with parallel aesthetics and philosophy (Tiwari, 1998).

All these various connotations attached with several attributes like new consciousness, awakening, emerging capacity to protest and participation in the developmental processes etc., along with new ideological moorings viewed from different perspectives may need a separate and detailed analysis in a full fledged exercise. For the present purpose, avoiding such an exercise, we need to arrive at or deduce 'a common denominator' for the term 'Dalit' and focus on the main issues of identities and emerging scenario. Considering, these various connotations and paradigms as they are, the commonality of divergent connotations, it may be indicated that the caste groups presently known as scheduled castes (though a constitutional category if not a sociological category) may be operationally considered as "Dalits", as a distinctive category indicating socio-cultural, economic and political dimensions of deprivation, new consciousness and awakening.

Dalits, thus recognised operationally as scheduled castes, constitute 16.2 percent of the population of India (Census of India, 1991) and are a decisive political force in the democracy of India at present. What has been their identity and how they have been known and recognised through the various periods in Indian society in terms of their social status and cultural traditions? In what way or ways they have been coming up, if at all? What have been the mechanisms of their transforming identity through various efforts of others, their own efforts and the efforts of the state? These are the main issues and concerns explored in the present paper. Their social position, cultural patterns, position in the economic and political structures are described over a period of time in order to highlight their past identities and to arrive an understanding of their position in the present and emerging scenario. The social and cultural status includes the position of the Dalits in the social hierarchy of Indian society, their participation in the economy and thereby their position in the economic structure, their say in the community affairs *i.e.* their participation in the polity or political system. In a way it means their participation in the culture as a whole and their placement and adjustment in the overall socio-cultural system of the Indian society. Thus the present paper explores their position, and identification in the Indian social cultural system over a period of time. Considering the wider social processes and important events of Indian social political history the time frame may be divided operationally into four periods—the pre-British, the British period upto 1930's, the period of 1930's and 1940's upto Independence and the post independence *i.e.* the last about 50 years.

Since the present Dalits or scheduled castes as they are known with different names, some even derogatory connotations like outcastes, untouchables etc., were neither recognised as a numerically significant force in the past, as is considered in the democracy now, nor any such efforts were made for uplifting their socio-cultural position. More or less their same conditions continued during the Moughal period. They were considered neither problematic, nor any concept of welfare of such groups was deliberately planned. Their lowest position was defined in the varna system of Hindu social order and it was accepted as such, leaving aside the period when some of the Hindu castes were converted to Islam. Therefore this period may be considered as the period of identifying their position as defined and existed as per the traditional moorings.

The British period may be taken as a separate period, more so upto 1930's on some identifiable grounds. The British period was marked not only for the East India Company's business and establishing the rule of the company and later that of the British crown in India, but some efforts were made by the missionaries during this period to open educational institution and also to provide medical aid to these people. Of course, these concerns also initiated the process of Baptizing largely the lower and poorer sections of society like the presently known scheduled castes and scheduled tribes, in various regions of India. The situation became more known in various others ways like the promulgation of various rules by the British crown especially after the mutiny of 1857. Upto 1930's the British period can be taken or dealt with separately as the efforts of the British rulers were further strengthened by initiating educational policy and accommodation of various groups. But by 1930's (mid 1930's) these groups of minorities, the untouchables (also clubbed with minorities) were identified for special concessions and privileges and were apparently brought closure to the British rule for support. In addition, Mahatma Gandhi and Dr. Ambedkar also appeared on the scene advocating different approaches for the integration and upliftment of these untouchables or Sudras and to strengthen a demand of self rule. But the British policy in India after the first world war focussed upon for providing a 'responsible government' in India instead of 'self government' as demanded. By 1930's this confrontation was also becoming clear.

The period of 1930's to the time of Independence (more so till the promulgation of the Constitution of India) is marked by the upheavals or period of transition from the policy of 'responsible government to self government' and in between the issues of the minorities, the scheduled castes (listed earlier) and tribes also appeared. The various kinds of adjustments were demanded in the future democratic polity' for these sections like separate electorate, welfare measures and so on under the leadership of Dr. Ambedkar. Therefore this period needed separate analysis and has been dealt with separately.

The period of Independence, particularly since the promulgation of Constitution of independent India wherein several provisions have been made like that of the removal of untouchability by law, reservation of posts in services and seats in all democratic bodies and special policy initiatives, plans and programmes for these weaker-sections, ex-untouchables etc. needs separate treatment and thereby treated separately. The policies and programmes initiated, changes brought in these programmes, their impact upon the position and condition of these ex-untouchables, their own participation are the additional factors for a separate treatement. Thereby this time period of Independence has been dealt with separately in the present endeavour.

The earlier studies, the works of British administrators, of social science researchers, writers, activists and other contemporary writings have been taken into account to depict the above formulated identity of the Dalits. These various writings and significant events also suggest the above operational division of time spans. Survey of literature on scheduled castes (Sachchidananda, 1974) also incorporated several processes and factors of change among the scheduled castes (Dalits) which clearly indicates that some socio-cultural changes have been taking place among the scheduled castes over a period of time in different phases. The individual and collective efforts of the Dalits themselves also brought changes at the individual level and at the community level. Thus the change in their identities is reflected in various periods of time and in different areas of life, as well as to some extent' in different regions differently with some commonality of course. The present effort is also aimed at incorporating these issues of differential changes in different walks of life and different areas. The paper, as proposed above, takes note of the socio-cultural dimensions of the status identifying attributes of the Dalits in terms of social position, cultural patterns and their position in the economic and political structures of the Indian society. The Paper hereafter is divided into five parts. The first part takes note of their identity during pre-British period. The second part includes their identity during the British period upto 1930's. The third part takes note of the period from 1930's till the time of Independence. Their emerging identity in post-Independent India is narrated in the next section. Summing up of changing socio-cultural identies and emerging scenario is undertaken in the last part, 'the outcome'.

I. Identity During-Pre British Period

Most of the accounts of the communities in India indicate that the Indian Society (largely Hindu Society) has been divided into four varnas. Some others indicate that some people were even away from this system of four fold division of society and were known as the out castes. According to them the Hindu Society is divided into five folds, namely Brahmins, Kshatriyas, Vaishyas, Shudras and lastly the untouchables. According to this formulation the present day scheduled castes were recognised as the outcastes or untouchables (Srinivas, 1978 : 265). But some of the sociologists and other writers do not agree with the five fold division and the outcastes are considered as the fourth varna as Sudra and the present scheduled castes have been recognized as included among the Sudras of the Hindu Society. Whether they were outcastes or Sudras, in either case their position was at the bottom of the hierarchy. They were engaged in unclean occupations like hide and skinning the dead animals and were known for eating beef and dead animals. Economically they were deprived of any ownership on the resources of production or property. Politically they were not given any power positions nor considered worth to share it. They constituted a separate culture of isolation in many ways, living in habitats, many places separated from the main locality of the village community. Thus they shared a culture of deprivation, indignity and meanslessness. They were not allowed to participate in religious rites and rituals and were kept away and out from the cultural patterns of the other three varnas. Even the services of Brahmin priests were not available to them. Thus economically deprived, socially outcastes, untouchables, unclean by following unclean traditional occupations and politically underdog were the attributes attached to them during the pre-British period. This isolated culture, socially, economically and politically deprived status marked the identity of the Dalits in this period. Since their identity was subjected to least change or no change at all their position is just briefly narrated in Indian society and culture.

II. Identity During the British Period (Upto 1930's)

Brief references of this period about the living conditions of the untouchables or scheduled castes are available in travel accounts and government records published from the beginning of the nineteenth century like Journals of Hamilton Buchana and more detailed references are available in W.W. Hunter's (1868) Statistical Annals of Bengal. Later references are found in the volumes of castes and tribes for different parts of India (Sachchidanda, 1974 : 276-77). These sources described the culture of their low socio-economic position, stigma of untouchability, menial and unclean occupations.

Some earlier and recent studies on Dalits have referred to changing socio-cultural position during this period as some reform movements got started especially for their upliftment. For example the Satnami sect was initiated in 18th century by one Jagjivan Das in Uttar Pradesh and later popularised by Ghasi Das who proclaimed equality of men. Ghasi Das enunciated seven principles which included abstinence from liquor, meat and certain red vegetables and abolition of idol worship. Worship of only one god was ordained and they worshiped sun as representing the supreme God. Satnami movement was essentially a social uprising of the Chamar Caste. The fundamental tenet of the doctrine was abolition of the caste and authority of the Brahamana. The Satnamis expected better treatment from high caste Hindus. With this feeling they incurred the antagonism of the high castes and displayed an astonishing courage in their fight for public recognition. Thus Satnami became practically a sub-caste of the Chamar. It provided a religious frame work and also a basis for the political power. This movement had illustrated how a social reform can transform a whole community in a region (Babb, 1970).

Briggs (1920) also acknowledges the impact of high caste Hindus on Chamars. He gave an account of the various reform movements among Chamars leading to the formation of certain sects such as the Shiv Narain, Satnami and Dadupanthi. So named after its founder 'Shiv Narain' is a unitarian sect which claims a large number of scheduled castes adherents such as Jaiswar, Chamar, Dhusadh and others joined the sect in large numbers. Truth, abstinence from liquor, honesty, mercy and charity etc. were considered as the cardinal virtues of the Shiv Narain sect. They believed in only one God. Emphasised elaborate ritual performances and had established a number of monasteries in Eastern Uttar Pradesh. For followers of Shiv Narain, polygamy was prohibited (even if some one could afford) and some of them also took to the title of Bhagat. The founder also observed that Christianity has offered to Chamar a satisfactory place in social order and a satisfactory religious life and that it was in Christianity that there was a hope of redemption for them.

In the nineteenth century Ghasidas led a reform movement (extension of the Satnami movement) in the Chattisgarh region (Fuchs, 1965). His teachings and preachings have been further noted in terms of fostering aspiration among the backward castes people for equality and breaking humiliating Hindu caste traditions and rise in the caste hierarchy. Other structural conditions of the region like scarcity of labour in particular areas in the last century also benefited the Chamars by enabling them to enter the cultivator class. Thus their economic conditions also appeared to have promoted the breaking up of the old caste traditions.

In Bengal, in this series of reform movements, Matua religion was innovated by 'Lord' Hari Chand Thakur of 'Orakandi' 'in the Gopal Ganj district of present day Bangladesh. Born in 1812 in Namshudra untouchable community, he became active at a time when untouchables of East Bengal were converting to Islam and Christanity on a large scale due to ill treatment by upper caste Hindus. Lord Hari Chand saved the untouchables from conversion by innovating Matua religion. Matua maintained continuities with conceptual language of Hinduism his followers knew, but reconstructed it to honour untouchables and advance their interests. His son, 'Guru Chand', further continued to preach the religion among Dalits and promoted their upward mobility by launching his famous educational movement in 1881. Due to this movement the Dalits became literate and politically conscious. Considered as another Avtar' (Shiva Avtar), Guru Chand integrated Namsudra community into one unit from its eight divisions and skillfully organised their on-going mass conversion to Matuaism in protest against Brahaminism. Hiariliamrita, the first scriptural work of Matua religion, is a multi volume poetical epic-style life history of Lord Harichand Thakur, the founder of Matua religion. This is considered as the core scripture of the Matua religion. Many folk versifiers (Lok Kabi), who almost all belong to the Dalit community, direct their songs to Hari Chand, Guru Chand and Matua religion. Matua religion sees the world as a creation of the supreme God (Hari-post Vedic Vishnu), repeating some motifs of high Sanskrit Hinduism and diverging from others (Walker: n.d.).

In early nineteenth century among the Madiga (an untouchable community) of Andhra pradesh appeared a prophet called Yogi Vira Brahma. He taught that 'God is one and has created all the things and prevades all things'. He called upon the people to turn from the wickedness and foster the spirit of truth and sincerity. He taught them to look forward to the coming incarnation of God. After his death in the middle of the nineteenth century, his disciple, Siddappa, directed his preachings mainly against caste and prophesied, in the name of his master, that God would reappear then caste would vanish and then all men would be equal. The movement was abandoned later on and most of the followers of the Guru became Christians (Sachchidananda, 1974). Another process of improving their social status was through sanskritization. In this process the lower castes were adopting the ways of life of higher castes in order to get a better position in society within the caste system. This process has been aimed at adopting rather than rejecting, the ways of life of the higher castes by leaving their own ways of life due to which these sections were considered lower. Such a social movement was also observed in Kerala. The Ezhavas, the traditional toddy tappers of Kerala, experienced a movement under the leadership of Narayana Guru, a teacher. Later he was initiated into Yoga and led the life of a mendicant. He believed in the existence of God, the unity of mankind and the natural goodness of men. He believed in the social and economic reform and organized his sect around Ezhava priests and Sanyasis. Although there was some resistence from the caste Hindus, but Narayana Guru ultimately overcame such difficulties. He received encouragement from many sections of society in his social work of reform (Sachchidananda, 1974).

There have been social reform movements in other parts of india in the nineteenth century and also continued later like Adi-Dharmi in Punjab (Sabbarwal,1976), Arya Samaj movement in North India, the famous and strong Dalit movement in Maharashtra and Adi-Dravida movement in South India. The above cited evidence is just illustrative and it is to indicate that the concerns of the Dalits were taken up and efforts from within and from outside for their upliftment started during the British period in different parts of India. All these efforts started crystallizing in the early part of the twentieth century. After the appearance of Mahatma Gandhi and Dr. Ambedkar on the national scene in 1930's the British also started showing concerns for these untouchables. The British were less willing to lend the civil power to uphold prerogatives claimed by higher castes in intercaste relations. In addition, secular ideas displayed and emerged in the general use of public facilities such as schools, wells, roads and of course the legal system that did not discriminate anyone on the basis of caste during the British rule (Galenter, 1984: 20-21). However the higher castes quickly grabbed the avenues of employment in government institutions since they were already enjoying the necessary skills of education and wealth. The new opportunities created further gulf between the higher and lower castes.

In this period, the Dalits became a part of the processes of social reforms initiated by several saints or saint like personalities, movements of self-respect, anti-Brahmin and anti-caste Hindus and also influenced by processes of slow uprising through purifying ways of life. They also became a part of the national movement as they were recognised and efforts for their integration were made by the then leadership. Their concerns became social and political during this period. At this point the new forces also emerged.

III. Identity During 1930's to 1947

This period has been taken separately because of the historical reasons as it is marked by the event of formation of the people's governments in the states on the democratic patterns though the central control of British

Crown continued. But these governments were short lived, The British rulers by this time had also started showing concerns for the upliftment of Dalits and minorities. It is during this period that a listing of such castes were started. Simultaneously the national movement for Independence had also come up in its full swing. The Indian National Congress had also showed its concerns for such groups, particularly Mahatama Gandhi , who gave them the name 'Harijans' (Children of God). Integration of all communities was necessary for freedom and Gandhi could realise this fact very well. Attacks on untouchability figured during this period from several corners. As stated earlier reform movements were also going on in North India as well as strong Adi-Dravida movement in South India. All these movements were anti-Brahmin, anti-caste Hindus and were aimed at self-respect and upliftment of these untouchables. The processes of following the cleaner ways of life which were also propagated by reform movements in the nineteenth century also had their effects by this time. The effects of the processes like westernization and revolutionization had also been observed. More than all these Dr. Ambedkar had emerged on the scene during this period as a crusador for the cause of these untouchable communities. A large number of civil rights which were a prerequisite for upward mobility of any kind were denied to them and any attempt at imitation of the ways of the higher castes by them was resented by the caste Hindus. This resulted in violence and out breaks of riots between the scheduled castes and the caste Hindus (Beteille, 1967; Hutton, 1951; Ambedkar, 1936).

An exploration of the Constituent Assembly Debates (Saxena, 1981) shows that the position of the scheduled castes and the scheduled tribes (nomenclature for these classes differed earlier) had historically become a part of a much larger problem of minorities. Overwhelming minority in India were Muslims. In the name of taking care of these minorities the Britishers introduced a system of representation (in other words reservations). It was shown as the sacred trust of the British Government to ensure that the minorities (including the scheduled castes) were "protected from oppression and exploitation at the hands of the majority. More and more minorities were identified for this purpose and the protection to them included separate representation in the legislatures, reserved quota in the public services and in various other ways. The Sikhs, the Anglo Indians, the depressed classes (scheduled castes and others), the backwards and the hill people were recognised and treated as minorities. The presently known Dalits thus *became a* part of the minorities during this period which deserved special treatment. Separate electorate was demanded for them by their leaders (especially Dr. Ambedkar, who had figured as the most important and influential leader of Dalits from within). Mahatama Gandhi opposed this issue of separate electorate for the depressed classes and minorities.

Integration of these people and the removal of their special social problems did not figure in the provisions relating to them in the Government of India Act, 1935 (Saxena, 1981: Xiii, Xiv). Broadly the approach was to keep the tribal areas under direct rule (of Britishers) and therefore keep them in isolation, while the scheduled castes were to be provided a bit of attention by way of facilities of education etc. The scheduled castes were brought under the perview of popular government under the 1935 Act subject to special powers of the governor. This resulted in the direct control of these groups by the governor and therefore no specific socio-economic programmes for their amelioration was required. Issue of roastering of vacancies in the public services for a number of minorities (including the scheduled castes) and even weightage for some came up but the concrete achievements were far away. This developed the feeling of insecurity among the scheduled castes and tribes and other minorites.

During this period the issue of scheduled castes got crystalised as a category, which was identified as a category of oppressed, exploited and down trodden who deserved some special treatment. The process was started by the Britishers but later on taken over by the national leaders (leaders of the freedom movement) in which Mahatam Gandhi and Dr. Ambedkar became the key figures. The scheduled castes (Dalits) became a political issue or category in addition to their identification as minorities who were deprived of some civil rights. This time period may be recognized as the period of the processes in which concerns of and provisions for the Dalits were crystalised side-by-side their integration with Independence movement. This crystalization of issues, concerns and provisions is to be looked into as the background of the concrete provisions and programmes which followed in India after Independence.

When India became free, issues of their socio-economic upliftment were discussed and incorporated by the constitution frammers and special provisions were in fact included.

IV. Identity During the Period of Independence

The position of scheduled castes has undergone some change in Independent India as a consequence of several processes some of which were initiated even before Independence. Changes though limited in absolute terms but are significant if we view those against the background of their traditional status. Social science scholars and others have noted these changes along three avenues: first avenue was provided by reform movements, second recorded by processes through which a caste group or a group of people could move up in the social hierarchy by adopting the style of life of upper castes and the third inspired by the process of westernization (Sachchidanand, 1974 : 278-79). Several studies have indicated such changes. In addition an important dimension has been added by Dr. Ambedkar who has done so much to raise the position of scheduled castes as their champion and gave a new identity to the scheduled castes. He claimed to the extent that the Shudras of the Indo-Aryan Society were Kshatriyas. He denied the racial origin of untouchability and produced the theory that untouchables were broken men who, in contrast to settled tribesmen, did not give up Buddhism when Brahminism triumphed in India. He announced his intention to leave the Hindu fold and converted to Buddhism before his death in 1956 alongwith his followers (Sachchidananda, 1974 : 284). Other factors of social change which also helped in consolidating the identity of the scheduled castes were the promulgation of law such as law against untouchability, reservation of seats in elected bodies and of posts in the public services.

The intervention of state in favour of Dalits has been highlighted in various ways. It included: (a) an array of constitutional and legal provisions, (b) positive discrimination in government employment and in elected bodies through reservations, (c) budgetary support through special component plan approach, (d) special programmes of health and education, (e) priority in all rural development programmes, slum improvement and anti-poverty programmes, and (f) technological changes for release of persons engaged in traditional occupations etc. (Srivastava, 1997 : 430) These provisions and programmes have been classified as social (*e.g.* removal of untouchability), Political and Economic such as reservation of seats and posts in democratic bodies and public services and special component for their economic development (*e.g.* rural development and self-employment programmes) (Pundir, 1998a). Whatever may be the categorisation of the provisions and programmes some changes have taken place in the status and conditions of the scheduled castes in Independent India (Sachchinand, 1974: 223) though the rate and quantum of change has not been to the extent it was ought to be (Pundir, 1997). Recent studies also indicates that the voluntary efforts of the scheduled castes themselves have added, wherever possible, to this changing scenario in a desired direction (Kumar, 1998; Pundir, 1998b),

The latest position of scheduled castes has been noted through an all India Survey of Communities under the *People of India Project* by the

Anthropological Survey of India in 1993. Excerpts of the findings are reproduced here to take note of their latest position on the indicators of their identity in terms of socio-cultural, economic and political life.

As per the study of Anthropological Survey of India, The People of India, there are 450 scheduled castes including 45 unlisted sub-groups. The total number of scheduled caste communities and their segments thus comes to 751. This includes also those scheduled castes who embraced Buddhism as most of them consist of communities which suffered from social stigma of untouchability, there are also a few communities among them which did not suffer the stigma of untouchability *e.g.* scheduled tribes which later notified as scheduled castes in Uttar Pradesh and in some other states of the north-east India. There are also some professional groups which have been notified as scheduled castes *e.g.* Nats, Turi, who are touchable and considered backward enough to be included among the scheduled castes. Some of them may be transistory but majority are permanent. In considering the scheduled castes here again the consideration has been guided by the notifications of the government of India from time-to-time and thus considered, as they were, as a constitutional category and less as a sociological category. Indeed plural identities of these people are largely due to the processes of fission and fusion that plagued the Indian caste system and the reform movements that have changed community names many times ever (Singh, 1993 : 2).

The size of scheduled communities is an important factor. Some of these consist of more than a million people, whereas others number fewer than 1000 persons. Larger communities are Chamar, including Chambhar, Adi-Dravida, Madiga, Mala, Dhoba/Dhobi, Dusad, Mahar etc. At present the scheduled castes constitute 16.2 per cent of the total population of India. As far as their habitat is concerned only 16 per cent live in cities and towns and 84 per cent of the scheduled caste people live in rural areas. The largest concentration of the scheduled castes is in Uttar Pradesh (22.39%), followed by West Bengal (11.48%) and the lowest is in Delhi (1.07%) and in terms of number the smallest number is in Mizoram. Only 105 communities perceive their distribution at national level rest consider themselves as local or regional communities. Majority (385) recall their migration to their present habitat from their original place which was some where else. This indicates migratory character of scheduled castes.

In terms of life styles and habits, the scheduled caste communities largely are non-vegetarian except few such sections who have been influenced by Bhakti movements. Like other communities scheduled castes also have various social divisions (87.10%). In adopting the names of *gotras* they have been influenced by Brahmins and other higher castes.

Differentiation among sub-groups are found at social (428), occupational (125) and religious (63) levels. Stratification has emerged with the rise of elites among them. Polarization and inequality have also emerged among various strata of the scheduled castes. These are evident for example from Panchama cluster of scheduled caste communities in Andhra Pradesh who consider themselves as the fifth varna. A number of them do not recognize or place themselves within the varna system, though substantial number (70.2%) recognise it and even place themselves in it. A majority (70.2%) recognized themselves as Sudra, as Kshatriyas (7.6%), as Vaishya (1.2%), and as Brahman (0.4%). This corresponds to their self perception.

Various constitutional measures have been initiated for providing them privileges in positions in the democratic institutions and thereby the scheduled castes are substantially represented in statutory panchayats, assemblies and the parliament. Political leadership has emerged at village level (39.40%), at regional level (18.5%), and at the national level (14.5%).

Economically majority of scheduled castes are still landless (69.6%) with little control over resources such as land, forest and water. However land reforms and distribution of land has led to an increase in the number of land holders (28.5%). Majority of them follow a vide variety of traditional occupations some of which are rapidly disappearing. Greater work participation (36.13%) is reported in comparison of the total population (33.45%).

Scheduled castes have their own class and family deities (6.71%) and wider pantheons (78.8%). Their involvement in the worship of village deities shows their integration with Hinduism in all its forms at the village level. (Some sociological studies show that in recent times in villages separate temples or places of worship have come up where idols of Lord Buddha are placed and also some times statue of Dr. Ambedkar is also placed in them.)

There have been laws against untouchability but persistence of untouchability has been reported particularly in rural areas, in relation to the exchange of water and food with communities considered higher in social hierarchy, even though commensal norms have generally weekend. On occasions of marriage and other feasts it has been observed that the scheduled castes are served along with other guests by high caste hosts indicating acceptance of commensality with them. On the other score education has made an impact and promoted mobility which is evident from the fact that a class of public servants, teachers, administrators, entrepreneurs/businessmen has emerged among them. Education, the adoption of modern occupations and emergent leadership among them has forged modern inter-community linkages across communities, scheduled castes or otherwise. All this has brought about a unity among the scheduled castes, to a certain extent, which did not exist earlier. This is reflected in economy, culture and politics.

The scheduled castes were considered as degraded people because of their lowely origin. But there has been a sea change in recent times in their perception about themselves with a new sense of self-respect. A new strand in the self perception of the scheduled castes are the Neo-Buddhists who stress their identity as members belonging to an order that stands outside the varna system. In fact theirs is a new found sense of dignity in their identity as members of the scheduled castes without associating themselves either with the sanskritization process or various protest and reformist movements. In fact a new sense of self-respect is in the air. Old myths which legitimized degradation are being discarded. There is new sense of dignity and self assertion symbolized by Dalit literature. The scheduled castes now not only question the varna system and the ideology underlying it but consider their movement as a larger struggle for equality. In this respect they have not only continued with Dr. Ambedkar's struggle for equality and self-respect but have taken it into new areas. The new leadership articulated a radical counter ideology, powerfully expressed in a burst of creative writings (Extracted from Singh, 1993 : 1-14).

V. The Out Come

In the present paper an effort has been made to trace the identity of Dalits over a period of time. The 'Dalits' have been referred to by various connotations, such as the Achhuts (untouchables) , the outcastes, Avarnas, Panchamas, Atishudras, Antyajas, Namshudras etc. Though differing in terminology their common substantive images they have carried althrough signifies their perception of oppression, sufferings from traditional socio-cultural disabilities, underprivilidged status, and cumulative deprivation. In the twentieth century they have come to be known and recognised as a constitutional category, "Scheduled Castes" and have been recognized as low class, landless and working class in the rural and urban social structures. The identity under the banner, of course a new name, 'Dalit' includes also the Neo-Buddhists, the Ad-Dharmis, the Dalit Christians and others in addition to Hindus.

The glimpses of the history of the socio-cultural conditions, and position of the scheduled castes indicate some changes in their overall conditions. On the basis of traditional unclean occupations, they were identified as untouchables. This caste defining status was perpetuated by inheritance over a period of time. It is this basis which has been attacked by various reformers and inturn this was an attack on the caste system as well. Among all those reformers the strongest protest came from Dr. Ambedker who followed the more secular and social path through education, organization and ensured to provide them special consideration in the Constitution. Thus, they retained not only a social cultural identity but became a political and constitutional identity in the recent time. Thus in Independent India a different identity of scheduled castes is emerging.

Though the instances of resistance were noted even earlier yet such resistance more manifestly continues even now but the scheduled castes appear to face these with more strength, political support and defence of law. The scheduled castes have acquired a different identity, but they have still to go a long way towards becoming a part of an egalitarian society.

REFERENCES

Ambedkar, B.R. (1936). *Annihilation of Caste*, Aligarh, Anand Sahitya Sadan (Reprint 1989).

Ambedkar, B.R. (1946). *Who are the Sudras*? Bombay, Thacker & Co.

Babb L.A. (1970) "The Political Involvement of a Religious Movement: The Satanamis" in *South Western Journal of Anthropology*, Vol. 26.

Beteille, Andre (1966). *Caste, Class and Power*, Bombay, O.U.P.

Beteille, Andre (1967). "The Future of Backward classes; competing Demands of Status and power" in Philip Mason (ed) *India and Ceylon: Unity and Diversity*, London, O.U.P.

Briggs, G.W. (1920). *The Chamars*, Calcutta, Association Press.

Cohen, B.S. (1955). "The Changing Status of a Depressed Caste" in Mckim Marriott (ed.) *Village India: Studies in the Little Community*, Chicago, University Press of Chicago.

Epp, Linda J. (1992). "Dalit Struggle, Nude Worship and the Chandragutti Incident" *Sociological Bulletin*, Vol. 41 Nos. 1 & 2, pp. 145-68.

Fuchs, S. (1965). *Rebellious Prophets*, Asia Publishing, Bombay.

Galenter, Marc (1984). *Competing Equalities*, New Delhi, Oxford University Press.

Hunter W.W. (1868). *Statistical Annals of Bengal*, London (Reprint 1883, quoted by Sachchidananda (1974 below).

Hutton, J.H. (1951). *Caste in India* (II Edition 1961), London O.U.P.

Isaac, Harold (1965). *India's Ex-Untouchables*, Bombay, Asia Publishing House.

Jogdand, P.G. (1991). *Dalit Movement in Maharashtra*, New Delhi, Kanak Publications.

Kumar, Anoop (1998). *Rural Development Programmes, Voluntary Efforts and Development of Scheduled Castes in Kishtwar (J&K)* Ph. D Thesis in Sociology, C.C.S. University, Meerut (Unpublished).

Lynch, O.M. (1968). "The Politics of Untouchability: A Case from Agra India" in M. Singer and B.S. Cohen (eds) *Structure and Change in Indian Society*, Chicago, Aldine.

Pundir, J.K. (1997). *Changing Patterns of Scheduled Castes*, Jaipur, Rawat.

Pundir, J.K. (1998a). "Rural Development Programmes During 50 years of Independence of India and The Scheduled Castes", paper presented in *European Conference on "Modern South Asian Studies"*, Prague, Sept. 7-12.

Pundir, J.K. (1998b). "State Voluntary Effort and Entrepreneurship Development by Scheduled Castes", paper presented in the *XIV World Congress of Sociology*, Montreal (Canada), July 26-Aug 2.

Rao, N. Sudhakar (1999). "State Agenda and Discursive Practices in Backward Classes Movements", paper presented in the *National Seminar on Indian Society at the Turn of the Century, Perspective from Below*, Dr. Ambedkar Chair, C.S.S.S. J.N.U., New Delhi, March 25-27.

Sabberwal, Satish (1976). *The Mobile Man*, Shimla I.I.A.S.

Sachchidananda (1974). Research on Scheduled Castes with Special Reference to "Change" in ICCSR's *A Survey of Research in Sociology and Social Anthropology*, Vol. I, Bombay, Popular.

Saxena, H.S. (1981). *Safeguards for Scheduled Castes and Tribes Founding Fathers' View*, New Delhi, Uppal.

Shah, Ghanshyam (1990). *Social Movements in India A Review of Literature*, Delhi, Sage Publications.

Sharma, K.L. (1997). "Caste and Class in the Emergence of Dalit Identity and Movement", *The Administrator*, Vol; XIII (Jan-Mar).

Singh, K.S. (1993): *Scheduled Castes (People of India* Vol. II), Delhi, OUP.

Srinivas, M.N. (1978). "The Caste System in India" in Andre Beteille (ed) *Social Inequality*, Penguin, pp. 265-72.

Srivastava S.P. (1997). "The Dynamics of Dalit Oppression" *The Eastern Anthropologist*, Vol. 50, Nos. 3-4, pp. 415-32.

Tiwari, Badri Narayan (1998). "Semiology of Dalit Consciousness. A North Indian Experience", *The Eastern Anthropologist* Vol. 51 No. pp. 169-84.

Zelliot, E. (1978). "Dalit in New Cultural Context for an Old Marathi World" in *Contribution to Asian and African Studies* Vol. I (quoted by S.P. Srivastava, 1997).

29

Proselytism and Status Enhancement: A Comparative study of Scheduled Castes and Christian Converts from Scheduled Castes

D. VENKATESWARLU AND REV.V. ANTONY RAJ

This paper proposes to evaluate the impact of proselytism on the social status and educational levels of the Christian converts from scheduled castes in comparison with those of scheduled caste Hindus.

Christianity is fairly old in India, having come to this land in the first century through St. Thomas and St. Bartholomew the immediate disciples of Jesus. It is believed that St. Thomas had preached the Gospel of Jesus in the southern parts of India, especially Kerala and St. Bartholomew in the Western parts of India, especially near present day Bombay (Hambye, 1952; Allepy and Moraes,1964). The first converts of St. Thomas were mainly from high caste Hindus who continued to maintained the caste hierarchy. They also continued the Hindu way of celebrating the ceremonies of birth, death and marriage (Brown, 1956). Then for about three-centuries, very little is known about the Christian community. The Roman Church came to India in 1498 through the Portuguese under Vasco de Gama. Attempts to Indianise Christianity started in India from 1605 through Robert de Nobile. Serious attempts at conversions may be said to have started in the early 18th century with the arrival of the protestant missionaries. From the 19th century onwards, the missionary activities spread rather fast.

Christianity came to Telugu-speaking region at the beginning of the 16th century on the arrival of Louis de Salvador, a Portuguese ambassador to Vijayanagar. Mass conversions are believed to have taken place among the Telugus in 17th/18th centuries (Solomon, 197?). By 1736, Telugu Christian spread out over a large area. The mass conversions gained further momentum in Andhra through the Mill Hill Missionaries (MHM) from 1876 onwards.

Christians formed 2.34 per cent of the Indian population in 1981, numbering 665,287,849 and 4 per cent in Cuddapah numbering 78236. The Christians in Cuddapah district where the study was undertaken in 1986-87 belonged to the following nine different churches.

1. The Roman Catholic Church
2. The Church of South India (C.S.I)
3. The Society for the Propagation of the Gospel (S.P.G)
4. The Bhakt Sing (Bershaba) Church
5. The Seventh Day Adventist
6. The Lutheran Church
7. The Brethren
8. The Pentecostal Mission
9. The Church of God

However, for the purpose of this study, only the first three denominations have been chosen as only their numerical strengths in Cuddapah district are significant.

The scheduled castes formed 12.98 per cent of the population in Cuddapah district in 1981. Mostly, they belonged to the castes of Mala and Madiga.

As stated at the outset, the objective of this paper is to evaluate whether proselytism of the scheduled castes to Christianity has had any impact in respect of their social status and educational levels by comparing them with the scheduled caste Hindus (in respect of the same variables). This study is a synchronic study and not a diachronic one as the data were not collected at the different periods of time which was beyond the scope of this paper but a single stretch of field work spread during 1986-87. This was done following a logical assumption that the converts from scheduled castes had a similar social and educational status as the SCs and would have continued to remain so keeping the pace of change or development on par with the latter but for conversion. Thus if the converts have achieved higher social status and educational levels, that can be attributed to conversion. Therefore, a synchronic study was undertaken.

Sample and Research Tools

A total sample of 200 heads of households was selected each from the Christian converts from scheduled castes and the scheduled caste Hindus to collect primary data to measure the social status enhancement and educational mobility among the former in comparison with that of the latter. These samples were distributed in different Taluks of the Cuddapah district. Interview scheduled and informal talks were employed to gather data.

Impact of Proselytism on Social Converts

A few studies already done on conversion have established the motives of conversion. For O'Mobery, conversion may be for the "development of a new conception of self in which ... the soul is reoriented around new values." Gough (1961) observed that conversion to Christianity had served as a means for the low caste Hindus to improve their social status. Alexander (1977) had a different opinion with regard to the status of the converts. He found that the lower caste converts in Kerala continued to be treated as Harijans by all sections of the society. In another study also, he observed that there was not much of social mobility among the converts from backward classes (Alexander, 1968).

However, it was with a strong resolve to improve their social status that most of the converts took to conversion. The years and years of stigmatized life, deprivation of educational, economic, cultural, political and religious equality frustrated the aspirations of low-caste Hindus to achieve respectable status. One option open to them was religious conversion and when the opportunity came to almost their doorstep through missionaries and Christian social workers, they grabbed it.

In the following pages a comparison is made between the converts and the scheduled castes to find out if the conversion has had any effect on the social status of the former after the conversion. An evaluation of their own status by the Christian converts (CCs) and the scheduled caste Hindus (SCs) has been undertaken here mainly through two parameters of nature of social treatment by the upper caste Hindus (UCHs) and perception of their own status in relation to the UCHs. The subjective reasoning that they have provided are also stated. An overall assessment of their status by the converts due to conversion is also discussed.

Nature of Treatment by the Upper Caste Hindus

A majority of the SCs feel that there is a perceptible change in the nature of their treatment by the UCHs. 35.50 per cent of them feel that the UCHs interact with them freely shedding their earlier attitude of maintaining discrimination even in social interaction. A quarter of them also say that the

UCHs maintain equal commensal relations with them. Although none of them says that there is intermarriage between the SCs and the UCHs, a few of them (7%) feel that they are treated as social equals by the UCHs. This is manifest in day-to-day interaction, the manner of addressing, taking into consideration their opinions on matters of collective concern, and so on (Table 1). A comparison with the SCs shows that none of the CCs said that they were treated in a subordinate manner by the UCHs. Whether it is in respect of force interaction, commensal relation or equal treatment, a higher percentage of them said that they enjoyed better treatment. Of course, none of them said that there was intermarriage between CCs and the UCHs.

Table 1: Nature of Treatment of SCs and CCs by Upper Caste Hindus

Nature of Treatment	*Scheduled castes % N=200*	*Christian converts % N=200*
Free interaction	33.50	45.00
Acceptance of food and water	25.00	35.00
Intermarriage	Nil	Nil
Equal treatment	7.00	20.00
Subordinate treatment	34.50	Nil
Total	100.00	100.00

When asked to evaluate their own status in relation to the UCHs, the SCs and CCs responded differently in their estimations. Eighty four per cent of the SCs felt that they were still inferior to the UCHs whereas just one CC respondent said so. While no SC thought that he was superior to the UCHs, 61.50 per cent of the CCs claimed that they were so. Although such a response may appear to be unrealistic, it has to be viewed in the context of their aspirations and defiance of the traditional status that is ascribed to them. However, 38 per cent of the CCs said that they felt equal to the UCHs and only 16 per cent of the SCs said so, a significant number for them (Table 2).

Table 2: Perception of Own Status by SCs and CCs in Relation to Upper Caste Hindus

Level of status	*% of SCs N=200*	*% of CCs N=200*
Inferior	84.00	0.50
Superior	Nil	61.50
Equal	16.00	38.00
Total	100.00	100.00

The SCs who admitted that they were inferior to the UCHs gave different reasons for their feelings. An overwhelming number of them gave such reasons as social stigma (20.24%), dependence for livelihood on their

UCHs landlords (27.98%) and general subordinate treatment by the caste Hindu society (25.60%). A significant number (19.05%) stated poor financial status as the reasons. Although, some SC respondents gave more than one reasons like social stigma and poor financial status, poor financial status and dependence for livelihood and others, their number was insignificant (Table 3).

Table 3: Perception of Reasons for Feelings of Inferiority among SCs

Reason	*% of SC N=168*
Social Stigma	20.24
Poor financial status	19.05
Dependence for livelihood	27.98
Subordinate treatment	25.60
Social Stigma and poor financial status	1.79
Social Stigma and dependence for livelihood	2.38
Poor financial status and dependence for livelihood	0.59
Poor financial status and subordinate treatment	0.59
Dependence for livelihood and subordinate treatment	1.78
Total	100.00

Similarly, those SCs and CCs who claimed that they were equal in status with the UCHs were asked pointed questions as to in what respect they were so. The differences were marked between the SCs and the CCs. Whereas 3.12 per cent of the SCs said that they had equal or better financial status, 19.74 per cent of the CCs said so, 46.05 per cent of the CCs claimed equal educational qualification while only 9.38 per cent of the SCs did so: significantly, 46.88 per cent of the SCs said that they had no belief in the caste system while only 26.32 per cent of the CCs expressed absence of belief in the caste system, and a higher number of SCs (37.50%) believed that there was no ontological difference between themselves and the UCHs while only 5.26 per cent of the CCs believed so. A few respondents on earlier side gave more than one aspect in answer (Table 4).

Table 4: Reasons for Feelings of Equality

Reasons	*% of SCs N=32*	*% of CCs N=76*
Equal/Better Financial Status	3.12	19.74
Equal Educational Qualification	9.38	46.05
No belief in caste system	46.88	26.32
No ontological difference	37.50	5.26
No belief in caste system and no ontological difference	3.12	Nil
Financial Status and Educational Status	Nil	2.63
Total	100.00	100.00

The converts were asked to give an overall assessment of their social status due to conversion. An overwhelming number of them (81.50%) expressed that their social status had improved, while only 7.50 per cent said that it had not. Others did not respond to the question at all.

Impact of Proselytism on Educational Levels of Converts

Data on literacy and educational levels of the converts was especially collected to see if the conversion had any effect in that respect, and as expected, the difference between the SCs and the CCs were glaring. Whereas literacy was to the extent of 73 per cent among the converts, it remained at 42 per cent among the SCs. Even in respect of achievement of higher educational levels, the converts were ahead of the SCs. Most of the educated SCs did not studied beyond secondary education and only a very few of them studied up to intermediate (3.50%) and graduation (2%). Among the CCs, the graduates (7.50%) were higher in number, there were also 3 per cent of the P.G.s, two had a polytechnic degree, and two more had a medical degree (Table 5).

Table 5: Educational Qualification

Educational Qualifications	*% of SCs N=200*	*% of CCs N=200*
Illiterate	58.00	27.00
Primary Education	21.00	22.50
Secondary Education	15.50	3.00
Intermediate	3.50	8.00
Graduation	2.00	7.50
Post-Graduation and above	Nil	3.00
Technical	Nil	1.00
Medical	Nil	1.00
Total	100.00	100.00

The illiterates in both the categories had different causes for their state. A majority of the SC illiterates (36.21%) said that they could not study as their parents did not realize the value of education followed by those (27.59%) who said that none in the family took interest in their education, and (26.72%) could not study due to financial difficulties. A very few of them (9.48%) did not study as no school was available nearby. Among the CCs, a majority (46.30%) could not study due to financial difficulties, followed by those (24.07%) who could not study as nobody had shown interest, and the parents of 22 per cent did not realize the value of education. Like among the SCs, among the CCs too, a very few (7.41%) could not go to school as none was available nearby (Table 6).

Table 6: Causes of Illiteracy

Cause	*% of SCs* N=146	*% of CCs* N=54
None took interest	27.59	24.07
Financial difficulties	26.72	46.30
Non-availability of Schools nearby	9.48	7.41
Parents' Ignorance of value of education	36.21	22.22
Total	100.00	100.00

The literacy of any individual is invariably influenced by his parents' educational background. Even in this, the differences between the SCs and the CCs are sharp. Ninety-three per cent of the SCs had illiterate father and among the CCs, such a number was 78 per cent. Whereas, no SC had any educated mother, 7.50 per cent of the CCs had an educated mother. With regard to the education of their other natal family members, the CCs had more of them educated. In their own nuclear families, the CCs had again more of them educated. For instance, in the case of wife, 36.92 per cent of the CCs had an educated wife while only 10.36 per cent of the SCs had one. The wide difference continues even in the case of son and daughter. Needless to stay, one's awareness of the value and benefits of education is a major factor in the education of one's own children. This is reflected in the figures for educated sons among both the SCs (80.54%) and the CCs (92.94%). These figures are certainly high and indicate a very high level of awareness among the SCs also and definitely so among the CCs (Table 7).

Table 7: Family's Literacy Levels

Relation	*Uneducated*		*Educated*	
	SCs	*CCs*	*SCs*	*CCs*
Father	93.00	78.00	7.00	22.00
Mother	100.00	92.50	0.00	7.50
Brother	70.04	45.73	29.96	54.27
Sister	91.93	66.49	8.07	33.51
Wife	89.64	53.08	10.36	36.92
Son	20.62	7.06	80.54	92.94
Daughter	40.43	21.40	59.57	78.60

Note—Percentages have been worked out separately for each individual relation.

The converts were asked as to who had sponsored their education as they might have been responsible for higher levels of education among them. It was assumed that the Church might have played a dominating role in their education. But surprisingly, it was the parents who had supported the education of 64.38 per cent of the CCs. The Church's role was confined to only 12.33 per cent of them, and the Church and other relations had supported 1.37 per cent of them, but the Church and the parents had supported 19.86 per cent of them. Thus, if taken directly the Church had contributed to the education of about one-third of the respondents (Table 8).

Table 8: Sponsors of Education among Educated Christian Converts

Sponsor	*% of CCs*
Parents	64.38
Church	12.33
Relations	2.06
Parents and Church	19.86
Church and Relations	1.37
Total	100.00

Conclusion

The objective of this paper had been set forth at the beginning to evaluate the impact of proselytism on the social status and educational levels of the Christian converts from the scheduled castes in comparison with those of the scheduled caste Hindus. This impact has been sought to be studied not through a diachronic method but through a synchronic method itself by comparing the Christian converts from scheduled castes with the scheduled caste Hindus. This followed the logical assumption that prior to conversion, the converts had social and educational status similar to that of SCs and whatever change or development has occurred subsequently among them leading to difference between the two was due to conversion. The impact has been different in respect of social status and educational levels of the converts.

One of the strong motives of the converts for taking to conversion was to lead a respectable life by gaining religious and social equality, if not superiority. To a certain extent, this seems to have been achieved as a significant number of the converts claimed that they were not meted subordinate treatment but equal treatment. This was also substantiated by higher favourable response in respect of free interaction and commensal relations with the UCHs. However, even among the SCs also a significant number claimed such a similar treatment. This should not be ignored. The difference between the SCs and the CCs continued in their perception of their own status and reasoning for feelings of equality or inferiority.

In respect of literacy and educational the different between the SCs and the CCs are wide and striking. Literacy was higher among the CCs and their educational achievement were also higher. Most of them were highly educated which benefited them to achieve better and higher employment levels. The church and the Christian schools have contributed very significantly towards the higher literacy and educational levels among the converts.

Thus it can be said in conclusion that conversion had helped the converts from scheduled castes to achieve respectable social status to a certain extent and higher literacy educational levels to an appreciable extent.

NOTE

1. As the study was conducted in 1986-87, only 1981 census figures are considered here.

REFERENCES

Alexander, K.C. (1968). *Social mobility in Kerala,* Poona, Deccan College.

Alexander, K.C. (1977). "The problems of caste in the Christian churches in Kerala" in Harjinder Singh (ed.) *Caste Among Non-Hindus in India,* New Delhi, National Publishing House.

Alleppy and Moraes, G.M. (1964). *A History of Christianity in India,* Bombay.

Brown, L.W. (1956). *Indian Christians of St. Thomas,* New Delhi, C.B.C.I. Centre.

Gough, Kathleen (1961). "Nayar of Central Kerala" in Schineider and Gough (eds). *Matrilineal Kinship,* Berkeley University of California Press.

Hambye, E.R. (1952). *St. Thomas and India*

O'Mobery, David (1962). *The Church as a Social Institution,* New Jersey, Prentice Hall

Solomon, T. (1977). *Structure of Church in Andhra Pradesh,* Secunderabad.

30

Implications of Socio-Economic Adversities of Farmers in Punjab: A Case Study

SUKHDEV SINGH AND MANDEEP KAUR

The exploitation and backwardness of farmers has been centuries old phenomenon. A look at the history of peasantry reveals that the peasants in India had been under troublesome conditions due to one reason or the other and remained increasingly under financial constraints leading to their backwardness of various types (Garg, 1999; Shergill, 1997). However, in the traditional subsistence economy the socio-economic disparities among the farmers were not much skewed and socio-economic relationships were also smooth. The arrival of capitalism has disturbed the old socio-economic fabric and inequalities among the farmers are increasing rapidly (Desai,1984; Bhandari, 1982). The recent phenomena of globalization has further given impetus to this process due to receding role of the State in agriculture and the forces of "market culture" have put the peasants, particularly the small and unskilled ones, in precarious situation.

The farmers of Punjab are known as enterprising, hardworking and adventurous; who have successfully translated the idea of green revolution into reality and consequently the food-deficit State of India is now food-surplus State (Jodhka, 2000; Sehgal & Arora, 2000; Parmar, 1985). High production of crops, largely due to the application of new technology has led the farmers to achieve better socio-economic status coupled with sweep changes in social relations (Parmar, 1985). For the last about one decade, the farmers of Punjab in general and of southern part in particular, are reported to be under severe strain leading to the various social, economic and psychological problems. Further, chronic domestic discord, drug abuse, alcoholism and heavy debt have goaded many farmers into the seductive arms of self-inflicted death *i.e.* committing suicides (Bobby, 1998; Shiva, 1998; Diwakar, 1998; Gill *et al*, 2000; Bhalla *et al*, 1998; Jodhka, 2000; Singh, 2000). To know the ground realities regarding the socio-economic adversities of Punjab farmers an effort has been made in this paper to answer the following questions:

1. Which are the factors that lead the farmers towards distress state?
2. What are the main implications of adverse socio-economic situation?
3. How to arrest this adverse situation?

Methodology

This study is based on data collected from the Muktsar district of Punjab. This district was deliberately selected as highest number of suicide cases were reported from this area of the State. Out of four blocks of the district, three blocks namely Malout, Lambi and Gidderbaha were chosen for the present investigation, which constitute almost all the rural area of the district. Five villages from each selected block were chosen randomly and in addition some cases of suicide victims were also identified from other four villages and thus the total number of villages included in the study comes to nineteen in all. From each selected block 50 respondents were contacted on the basis of availability of such type of respondents. In all, the total sample consisted of 150 respondents including the family member of those farmers who had committed suicide. Data was collected personally by the investigator with the help of semi-structured and pre-tested interview schedule.

Findings of the Study

A. Socio-Economic Characteristics of the Respondents

The socio-economic characteristics of the respondents under study are given in Table 1. It reveals that more than one-third (35.33%) of the respondents were in the age group of 30-40 years of age while a little less than one-third (29.33%) were in the age group of 40-50 years. This indicates that majority of the respondents were in between 30-50 years which means that most of them belonged to the middle-age group. Majority of the

Table 1: Socio-Economic Characteristics of the Respondents

Sl. No.	*Attribute*	*Category*	*Frequency*	*Percentage*
1.	Age (Years)	Upto 30	30	20.00
		30-40	53	35.33
		40-50	44	29.33
		50 and above	23	15.34
2.	Religion	Sikh	147	98.00
		Hindu	3	2.00
3.	Caste category	Higher caste	148	98.67
		Backward caste	2	1.33
4.	Marital	Married	134	89.33
		Un married	16	10.67
5.	Family type	Joint	52	34.67
		Nuclear	98	65.33
6.	Family size	Upto 4	35	23.33
		5-7	77	51.33
		8-10	28	18.67
		11 and above	10	6.67
7.	Education Level	Illiterate	57	38.00
		Primary	14	9.33
		Middle	19	12.67
		Matric/10+2	38	25.33
		Graduate and above	16	10.67
		Special training	6	4.00
8.	Housing type	Katcha	8	5.33
		Pucca	82	54.67
		Mixed	44	29.33
		Any other	16	10.67
9.	Subsidiary occupation	Dairy	28	18.67
		Poultry	4	2.67
		Bee-keeping	2	1.33
		Service	11	7.33
		Combine harvester	7	4.67
		None	98	65.33
10.	Land holdings (operational)	Upto 5 acres	43	28.67
		5-10	50	33.33
		10-15	29	19.33
		15-20	16	10.67
		20 and above	12	8.00
11.	Source of Irrigation	Tubewell	5	3.33
		Canal	9	6.00
		Tubewell + Canal	136	90.67
12.	Total annual income	Upto 50000	39	26.00
		50000-100000	48	32.00
		100000-150000	29	19.33
		150000-200000	22	14.67
		200000 and above	12	8.00

respondents (98.00%) hailed from the Sikh religion and belonged to the higher caste group (98.67%) and were married. As regards the family type the major proportion of respondents (65.33%) belonged to nuclear families while about one-third had been living in the joint families. Nearly half of the respondents, *i.e.* 51.33 per cent had the family size of 5 to 7 members and only a few (6.67%) had very large family, *i.e.*, exceeding 11 members. 38 per cent of the respondents were illiterate followed by 25.33 per cent who had studied upto matriculation and 10+2 level while only a few, *i.e.*, 4.00 per cent of the respondents had undergone some special training, in like poultry, electric works etc. Slightly more than fifty per cent (54.67%) of the respondents were residing in the *pucca* houses while one-third of them (29.33%) were having mixed type of houses. A few of the respondents (5.33%) were found to have *katcha* houses while remaining had some well-build bungalow type houses. About 35 per cent of the respondents were either engaged in some subsidiary occupations like dairy, poultry, bee-keeping and/or working as school teacher, bank employees, factory workers etc. The remaining 65 per cent were not engaged in any subsidiary occupations. Majority of the respondents had landholdings of less than 10 acres, *i.e.* 28.67 per cent of them had less than 5 acres and 33.33 per cent had 5 to 10 acres of land which is indicative that most of the respondents were in the category of small farmers. Majority of the respondents (90.67%) were having tubewell and canal both as sources of irrigation. The table shows that about one-third of the respondents, *i.e.* 32.00 per cent had their total annual income between Rs. 50000 to Rs. 100000 while 26.00 per cent of them had annual income upto Rs. 50000. So, almost 60 per cent of the respondents of the area had their total income below Rs. one lakh per annum, while the remaining respondent's income was in higher brackets.

B. Factors Leading the Farmers Towards Socio-Economic Adversities

One of the major objectives of this paper is to highlight the factors which are responsible for increasing the adversities of the farmers and in this section these factors have been discussed.

(i) Disproportionate Ownership of Farm Power Machinery and Durable Goods

An effort was made to asses as to whether the respondent-farmers possessed the material in proportion to their land holdings or income or not and the data in this regard is presented in Table 2A and 2B. One of the notable point is that besides draught animal and bullock cart, almost all (94.00%) of the respondents had tractor with trolley and other accessories and tubewell while a few of them had thresher and harvest combine also.

The fact is that lot of the respondents could not afford the tractor as it is costly and under-utilized, but farmers purchased such machinery not only as per their requirements but out of their ego and other social factors such as to maintain status in village, to show their wealth, due to social compulsion and to maintain pride of the ancestors etc.

Similarly lot of farmers having even less income prefer to have certain material possessions like scooter (88.67%), television set (84.67%), cooler (85.33%), refrigerator (83.33%) etc. (Table 2B). Almost one-third of the respondents also possessed other material items like cycle, car, mixer, washing machine etc. Some of the respondents even had telephone, which are highly under-utilized. There were significant differences as regards to ownership of material possessions by the respondents. It was found that receiving lot of gadgets in dowry was one of the reasons for having a considerable proportion of the above material and hence it seems that materialism is increasing considerably among ruralities.

Table 2A: Distribution of the Respondents on the Basis of Ownership of Farm Power and Machinery

Farm Power and Machinery Owned	*Block I (N=50)*	*Block II (N=50)*	*Block III (N=50)*	*Grand Total (N=150)*
1-2 Draught animals	32 (64.00)	36 (72.00)	30 (60.00)	98 (65.33)
Bullock cart	32 (64.00)	36 (72.00)	30 (60.00)	98 (65.33)
Tractor with trolley	43 (86.00)	50 (100.00)	48 (96.00)	141 (94.00)
Tubewell	46 (92.00)	48 (96.00)	47 (94.00)	141 (94.00)
Thresher	7 (14.00)	5 (10.00)	5 (10.00)	17 (11.33)
Harvest combine	2 (4.00)	2 (4.00)	3 (6.00)	7 (4.67)

$F_{5.10}$ = 255.27** *CD* (10 d.f.) = 3.87 **Singificant at 5 per cent level.

Table 2B: Distribution of the Respondents on the Ownership of Materiat Possessions

(Multiple response)

Item	*Block I (N=50)*	*Block II (N=50)*	*Block III (N=50)*	*Grand Total (N=150)*
Cycle	21 (42.00)	12 (24.00)	18 (36.00)	51 (34.00)
Scooter/Motorcycle	42 (84.00)	45 (90.00)	46 (92.00)	133 (88.67)
Car	12 (24.00)	13 (26.00)	19 (38.00)	44 (29.33)
Radio	12 (24.00)	8 (16.00)	8 (16.00)	28 (18.67)
Television set	45 (90.00)	46 (92.00)	36 (72.00)	127 (84.67)
Video Cassette recorder	3 (6.00)	4 (8.00)	2 (4.00)	9 (6.00)
Mixer	19 (38.00)	21 (42.00)	7 (14.00)	47 (31.33)
Cooler	44 (88.00)	40 (80.00)	44 (88.00)	128 (85.33)
Refrigerator	40 (80.00)	44 (88.00)	41 (82.00)	125 (83.33)
Washing Machine	15 (30.00)	14 (28.00)	19 (38.00)	48 (32.00)
Any other	3 (6.00)	7 (14.00)	9 (18.00)	19 (12.67)

$F_{10.20}$ = 49.91** *CD* (20 d.f.) ** Singieicant at 5 per cent level.

(ii) Low Crop Return

An effort was made to find out the per acre and per farm crop return of the respondent-farmers and result in this regards are given in Table 3 which reveals that the per farm as well as per acre net returns were much higher in case of *rabi* crop as compared to *kharif* crop in the selected blocks. In case of *kharif* crop the average net returns of all the blocks per farm were just Rs. 4279 and per acre were Rs. 484 as compared to the *rabi* crop where average net returns per farm were Rs. 26211 and per acre were Rs. 2968. The overall average net returns for both the crops in a year were Rs. 30490 per farm and Rs. 3452 per acre. The low returns are attributed largely to the reasons like water logging, salinity, attack of pests, untimely rainfall etc., leading to the overall damage to the *kharif* crop as the nature has been unfavourable to farmers in the area under study for the last many years. Low income may be one of the factors forcing farmers to take the steps like selling of land, jewellery and in few cases committing suicide. The studies of Gill *et al.* (2000) and Shiva, (1998) have also indicated almost similar results.

Table 3: Per Farm and per Acre Net Returns from Selected Blocks

Season	*Block I (Rs.)*	*Block II (Rs.)*	*Block III (Rs.)*	*Overall Average (Rs.)*
Kharif	4972 (546)	4006 (477)	3860 (429)	4279 (484)
Rabi	24920 (2738)	27240 (3227)	26472 (2941)	26211 (2968)
Yearly	29892 (3248)	31246 (3704)	30332 (3370)	30490 (3452)

Figures in parentheses indicate per acre returns.

(iii) Increasing Annual Family Consumption Expenditure (Rs.)

Table 4 gives the information regarding annual family consumption expenditure on food items, non-food items, socio-religious ceremonies and beverages and drugs. It was observed that majority of the respondents, *i.e.* 67.34 per cent had spent below Rs. 20000 on food items while 31.33 per cent had spent between Rs. 20000 to Rs. 40000 with a very few respondents spending above Rs. 40000. The first two categories of respondents were quite predominant as compared to the last category. More than half of the respondents, *i.e.* 54 per cent had spent between Rs. 20000 to Rs. 40000 on non-food items followed by 26.67 per cent of the respondents who spent below Rs. 20000. The amount spent on education and medicine was negligible as compared to money spent on clothing, housing, fuel etc. There was preponderance of the respondents who spent between Rs. 20000 to Rs. 40000 on non-food items. Most of the respondents *i.e.* 63.33 per cent spent upto Rs. 10000 on socio-religious ceremonies including expenditure on recreation, participation in marriage, rituals, puja towards ancestors etc. There were significant differences as regards the expenditure on socio-religious ceremonies by the respondents. The first two categories of respondents were more predominant as compared to the last category and they were also significantly different from each other. The data indicates that 40.00 per cent of the respondents spent upto Rs. 5000 on beverages and drugs while 34.00 per cent spent between Rs. 5000 to 10000 on these items indicating that the rural people spent quite large amount on beverages and drugs like liquor, *zarda*, tobacco, tablets etc, leading to their socio-economic adversities.

Table 4: Distribution of the Respondents on the Basis of Annual Family Consumption Expenditure

Annual Expenditure	*Block I*	*Block II*	*Block III*	*Grand Total*
FOOD ITEMS				
Upto 20000	31 (62.00)	40 (80.00)	30 (60.00)	101 (67.34)
20000-40000	18 (36.00)	10 (20.00)	19 (38.00)	47 (31.33)
40000 and above	1 (2.00)	–	1 (2.00)	2 (1.33)
Total	50 (100.00)	50 (100.00)	50 (100.00)	150 (100.00)

$F_{2.4}$ = 29.78** *CD* (4d.f.) = 11.88.

Annual Expenditure	*Block I*	*Block II*	*Block III*	*Grand Total*
NON FOOD ITEMS				
Upto 20000	13 (26.00)	15 (30.00)	12 (24.00)	40 (26.67)
20000-40000	28 (56.00)	23 (46.00)	30 (60.00)	81 (54.00)
40000 and above	9 (18.00)	12 (24.00)	8 (16.00)	29 (19.33)
Total	50 (100.00)	50 (100.00)	50 (100.00)	150 (100.00)

$F_{2.4}$ = 25.46** *CD* (4d.f.) = 7.11.

Annual Expenditure	*Block I*	*Block II*	*Block III*	*Grand Total*
SOCIO-RELIGIOUS EXPENDITURE				
Upto 20000	27 (54.00)	33 (66.00)	35 (70.00)	95 (63.33)
10000-20000	16 (32.00)	13 (26.00)	14 (28.00)	43 (28.69)
20000 and above	7 (14.00)	4 (8.00)	1 (2.00)	12 (8.00)
Total	50 (100.00)	50 (100.00)	50 (100.00)	150 (100.00)

$F_{2.4}$ = 40.91** *CD* (4d.f.) = 8.58.

Annual Expenditure	Block I	Block II	Block III	Grand Total
BEVERAGES AND DRUGS				
Upto 5000	7 (14.00)	10 (20.00)	6 (12.00)	23 (15.33)
5000-10000	23 (46.00)	21 (42.00)	16 (32.00)	60 (40.00)
10000 and above	7 (14.00)	5 (10.00)	4 (8.00)	16 (10.67)
Total	50 (100.00)	50 (100.00)	50 (100.00)	150 (100.00)

$F_{3.6} = 6.80$ ** CD (6d.f.) = 9.42.

**Significant at 5 percent level. Figures in parentheses indicate percentages.

(*iv*) *Amount of Credit, Its Sources and Purposes*

The credit position of the respondents are given in Table 5A which indicates that a major proportion of the respondents, *i.e.* 28.67 per cent had taken credit between one lakh and two lakh while 25.33 per cent of the respondents had taken credit between two lakh and three lakhs. Only 4 percent of the respondents had taken credit even above four lakhs ,whereas 8.67 per cent did not take any credit. There were significant differences as regards the amount of credit borrowed by the respondents. The categories that had borrowed between Rs. 100000 to 200000 and Rs. 200000 to 300000 were more predominant in comparison to other categories. The amount scenario indicates that borrowing by farmers was quite high for some beyond their capacity to repay, which may be a factor leading to their economic adversities.

Regarding the sources of loans, it was found that farmers do not hesitate to take loan from more than one source. They take loans from institutional as well as non-institutional sources (Table 5B). For example, if the cooperative society does not lend due to default, farmers explore other sources. The main sources of loans are commercial bank, cooperative societies, and private moneylenders and many farmers take loans from many sources at the same time. The notable point is that major sources of credit in rural areas are moneylenders (20.43%) and cooperative societies and moneylenders (34.31%).

Regarding the purpose of loans data show that 84.67 per cent took loans for the purchase of agricultural inputs followed by 44.52 per cent who took loans for the purchase of farm machinery, and 31.38 per cent borrowed to buy durable goods. Almost equal number of respondents *i.e.* 21.16 per cent, 19.70 per cent and 21.89 per cent took loans for purposes like purchase of livestock, construction work and repair and for medical treatment respectively. During the course of data collection it was found that majority of the respondents had outstanding credit amount ranging from Rs. 50000 to Rs. 200000, which may also be one of the factors for increasing adversities of the farmers.

Table 5A: Distribution of Respondents According to Amount of Credit Taken (1998-2001)

Amount Taken (Rs.)	*Block I*	*Block II*	*Block III*	*Grand Total*
Not taken	3 (6.00)	7 (14.00)	3 (6.00)	13 (8.67)
Upto 100000	4 (8.00)	8 (16.00)	10 (20.00)	22 (14.67)
100000-200000	16 (32.00)	15 (30.00)	12 (24.00)	43 (28.67)
200000-300000	15 (30.00)	9 (18.00)	14 (28.00)	38 (25.33)
300000-400000	9 (18.00)	9 (18.00)	10 (20.00)	28 (18.66)
400000 and above	3 (6.00)	2 (4.00)	1 (2.00)	6 (4.00)
Total	50 (100.00)	50 (100.00)	50 (100.00)	150 (100.00)

$F_{5.10} = 11.66^{***}$

Figures in parentheses indicate percentages.

Table 5B: Distribution of the Respondents According to the Sources of Credit/Loan

Sources of Credit/Loan	*Block I (N=47)*	*Block II (N=43)*	*Block III (N=47)*	*Grand Total (N=137)*
Commercial banks	4 (8.51)	2 (4.65)	4 (8.51)	10 (7.30)
Agriculture cooperative societies	7 (14.90)	8 (18.60)	10 (21.28)	25 (18.25)
Private lenders (arhtiyas)	8 (17.02)	11 (25.60)	9 (19.14)	28 (20.43)
Commercial banks and private money lenders	5 (10.63)	4 (9.30)	1 (2.12)	10 (7.30)
Cooperative societies and private money lenders	15 (31.91)	14 (32.55)	18 (38.30)	47 (34.31)
Cooperative societies and relatives	6 (12.77)	4 (9.30)	2 (4.26)	12 (8.76)
Any other	2 (4.26)	-	3 (6.39)	5 (3.65)

** Significant at 5 per cent level.

Figures in parentheses indicate percentages.

Table 5C: Distribution of Respondents According to the Purpose of Taking Credit (1998-2001)

(*Multiple response*)

Purpose of Taking Credit	*Block I (N=47)*	*Block II (N=43)*	*Block III (N=47)*	*Grand Total (N=137)*
Purchase of farm machinery	21 (44.68)	18 (41.86)	22 (46.80)	61 (44.52)
Purchase of agricultural inputs	40 (85.10)	35 (81.39)	41 (87.23)	116 (84.67)
Purchase of livestock	9 (19.14)	8 (18.60)	12 (25.53)	29 (21.16)
Construction work and repair	8 (17.02)	10 (23.25)	9 (19.14)	27 (19.70)
Medical purposes	9 (19.14)	11 (25.58)	10 (21.27)	30 (21.89)
To buy durable goods	15 (31.91)	12 (27.90)	16 (34.04)	43 (31.38)
For expenditure on socio-religious ceremonies	13 (27.65)	15 (34.88)	12 (25.53)	40 (29.19)
Any other	5 (10.63)	7 (16.27)	3 (6.38)	15 (10.94)

$F_{7.14} = 53.75^{**}$ *CD* (14 d.f.)=3.38

**Significant at 5 per cent level.

(v) Failure of Crops

The reasons of failure of crops, as given by the respondents, are presented in Table 6. The most important reasons given for the failure of their crops were the attack of pests and plant diseases particularly during *kharif* crop (cotton), (72.54 percent). 52.94 per cent held untimely rainfall responsible as the major reason for failure of their crops. The other reasons for failure of crops were small size of land holding (3.92%), excessive use of chemical fertilizers (19.61%), high cost of inputs (13.73%) and water logging (23.52%). There was considerable variability in relation to reasons for failure of crops, however, the attack of pest and plant diseases and untimely rainfall showed their preponderance over other categories.

Table 6: Distribution of Respondents on the Basis of Reasons for the Failure of Crops

(Multiple response)

Reasons for Crop Failure	*Block I (N=17)*	*Block II (N=15)*	*Block III (N=19)*	*Grand Total (N=51)*
Small size of land holding	2 (11.76)	–	–	2 (3.92)
Untimely rainfall	7 (41.17)	9 (60.00)	11 (57.89)	27 (52.94)
Inadequate irrigation facilities	1 (5.88)	–	2 (10.52)	3 (5.88)
Excessive use of chemical fertilizers	3 (17.64)	2 (13.33)	5 (26.31)	10 (19.61)
Attack of pests/plant diseases	10 (58.82)	12 (80.00)	15 (78.94)	37 (72.54)
High cost of inputs	4 (23.52)	2 (13.33)	1 (5.26)	7 (13.73)
Water logging	3 (17.64)	4 (26.67)	5 (26.31)	12 (23.52)

$F_{6.12}$ = 24.60** *CD* (12 d.f.) = 2.72 **Significant at 5 per cent level.
Figures in parentheses indicate percentages

(vi) Reasons for Expenditure on Socio-religious Ceremonies

Table 7 reveals that 62.67 per cent of the respondents spent on socio-religious ceremonies to maintain their status in village followed by 46.00 per cent of the respondents who spent due to social compulsion. The other reasons were to show their wealth (20.00%) and to maintain pride of ancestors (11.33%). Thirty per cent of the respondents spent either in imitating the well-to-do people or to keep daughter happy after marriage. There are significant variation as regards the reasons for spending on socio-religious ceremonies. Our data supported the finding of Kaur, (1982) and Gill *et al.* (2000).

C. Implications of Socio-economic Adversities of Farmers

The thrust of the present paper has been to highlight the implications of socio-economic adversities of farmers. In this section an effort has been made to present the effects of socio-economic adversities on farmer.

Table 7: Distribution of Respondents According to the Reasons for Expenditure on Socio-Religious Ceremonies

(Multiple response)

Reasons for Expenditure	*Block I (N=50)*	*Block II (N=50)*	*Block III (N=50)*	*Grand Total (N=150)*
To maintain status in village	31 (62.00)	34 (68.00)	29 (58.00)	94 (62.67)
Show their wealth	10 (20.00)	12 (24.00)	8 (16.00)	30 (20.00)
Due to social compulsion	27 (54.00)	22 (44.00)	20 (40.00)	69 (46.00)
To maintain pride of ancestors	8 (16.00)	5 (10.00)	4 (8.00)	17 (11.33)
Any other	12 (24.00)	15 (30.00)	18 (36.00)	45 (30.00)

$F_{4,8}$ = 48.34** *CD* (8 d.f.)= 4.81 **Significant at 5 per cent level.
Figures in parentheses indicate percentages.

(i) Distress Selling of Land or Valuables

As a result of economic adversities about one-fifth (19.33%) of the respondents sold their land and other possessions (Table 8). About 55 per cent of the respondents sold their land or valuables for repayment of loans while 45 per cent sold their possessions due to continuous losses and to meet the expenses on social ceremonies like marriages, deaths, etc. The other reasons were due to natural calamity, division in the family and uneconomical size of land holding.

Table 8: Distribution of the Respondents on the Basis of Distress Sale of Land or Valuables

Sold Land and Valuables	*Block I*	*Block II*	*Block III*	*Grand Total*
Yes	9 (18.00)	8 (16.00)	12 (24.00)	29 (19.33)
No	41 (82.00)	42 (84.00)	38 (76.00)	121 (80.67)
Total	50 (100.00)	50 (100.00)	50 (100.00)	150 (100.00)

Reasons for Selling	*Block I (N=9)*	*Block II (N=8)*	*Block III (N=12)*	*Grand Total (N=29)*
Subdivision of family	–	1 (12.5)	–	1 (3.44)
Due to uneconomical size of land holding	1 (11.11)	–	1 (8.33)	2 (6.89)
Due to constant losses	3 (33.33)	6 (75.00)	4 (33.33)	13 (44.82)
Repayment of loans	5 (55.55)	4 (50.00)	7 (58.33)	16 (55.17)
To meet expenses on social ceremonies	3 (33.33)	4 (50.00)	6 (50.00)	13 (44.82)
Due to natural calamity	2 (22.22)	1 (12.5)	2 (16.66)	5 (17.24)
Any other	2 (22.22)	–	2 (16.66)	4 (13.79)

$F_{6,12}$ = 9.77 *CD* = (12 d.f.) = 1.84.
** Significant at 5 per cent level.
Figures in parentheses indicate percentages.

(ii) Migration of Family Members

Table 9 shows that the family members of 15.33 per cent of the respondents had migrated due to economic adversities to nearby towns, cities and other countries. About 9 per cent of the respondents migrated to nearby towns followed by 39.13 per cent whose family members had migrated to cities while the family members of 52 per cent migrated to some other countries.

Table 9: Distribution of Respondents on the Basis of Migration of Family Members Due to Economic Adversities

Migrated	*Block I*	*Block II*	*Block III*	*Grand Total*
Yes	6 (12.00)	7 (14.00)	10 (20.00)	23 (15.33)
No	44 (88.00)	43 (86.00)	40 (80.00)	127 (84.67)
Total	50 (100.00)	50 (100.00)	50 (100.00)	150 (100.00)

Place of Migration	*Block I (N=6)*	*Block II (N=7)*	*Block III (N=10)*	*Grand Total (N=23)*
Nearby towns	1 (16.67)	-	1 (10.00)	2 (8.70)
Cities	2 (33.33)	4 (57.14)	3 (30.00)	9 (39.13)
Other countries	3 (50.00)	3 (42.86)	6 (60.00)	12 (52.17)

$F_{2.4}$ = 6.09ns.

Figures in parentheses indicate percentages.

Table 10: Distribution of the Respondents According to the Reasons for Non-Repayment of Credit in Time

Reasons for Non-Repayment	*Block I (N=31)*	*Block II (N=27)*	*Block III (N=34)*	*Grand Total (N=92)*
Crop failure	12 (38.70)	10 (37.03)	14 (41.17)	36 (39.13)
Insufficient income generation	16 (51.61)	11 (40.74)	13 (38.23)	40 (43.47)
High cost of production	21 (67.74)	18 (66.66)	23 (67.64)	62 (67.39)
Uneconomical size of land holding	4 (12.90)	6 (22.22)	4 (11.76)	14 (15.21)
Poor managerial ability	2 (6.45)	-	1 (2.94)	3 (3.26)
High rate of interest	10 (32.25)	12 (44.44)	15 (44.11)	37 (40.21)
Loans used for socio-religious purposes	5 (16.12)	3 (11.11)	4 (11.76)	12 (13.04)
Any other	8 (25.80)	8 (29.62)	6 (17.64)	22 (23.91)

$F_{7.14}$ = 37.93* *CD*(14 d.f.) = 3.13

** Significant at 5 per cent level.

Figures in parentheses indicate percentages.

(iii) Reason for Non-Repayment of Credit in Time

The information given in Table 10 shows that most important reasons for non-repayment of credit were high cost of production (67.39) and insufficient income (43.47%). Almost equal number of respondents, *i.e.* 39.13 per cent and 40.21 per cent held crop failure and high rate of interest of credit as the prime reasons for non-repayment of credit in time. The other reasons were uneconomical size of land holding, poor managerial ability, diversions of loans and loans used for socio-religious purposes. There was considerable variation as regards the reasons for non-repayment of credit in time with preponderance of categories not able to repay due to high cost of production, insufficient income and crop failure.

(*iv*) *Effect on Social Status*

Table 11 reveals that 20.00 per cent of the respondents said that their social status has gone down due to economic constraints. Sixty percent of the respondents whose social status had been affected gave economic instability as a reason for change in their social status, followed by 56.67 per cent of the respondents who felt that reduction in expenditure on luxuries has affected their social status. Half of the respondents consider their inability to spend heavily on socio-religious ceremonies as the reason for their status loss. Statistically there was significant variation as regards reasons for effect on social status and there was preponderance of the first three categories.

Table 11: Distribution of the Respondents According to Whether their Social Status has been Affected in the Village

Social Status Affected	*Block I*	*Block II*	*Block III*	*Grand Total*
Yes	13 (26.00)	9 (18.00)	8 (16.00)	30 (20.00)
No	37 (74.00)	41 (82.00)	42 (84.00)	120 (80.00)
Total	50 (100.00)	50 (100.00)	50 (100.00)	150 (100.00)

Reasons Due to Which Social Status Affected	*Block I (N=13)*	*Block II (N=9)*	*Block III (N=8)*	*Grand Total (N=30)*
Reduction in size of land holding	2 (15.38)	–	1 (12.50)	3 (10.00)
Economic instability	8 (61.53)	4 (44.44)	6 (75.00)	18 (60.00)
Decrease in expenditure on luxuries	7 (53.84)	5 (55.55)	5 (62.50)	17 (56.67)
Inability to maintain a rich lifestyle	4 (30.76)	2 (22.22)	–	6 (20.00)
Not able to spend heavily on socio-religious ceremonies	5 (38.46)	4 (44.44)	6 (75.00)	15 (50.00)

$F_{4,8}$ = 13.76** *CD* (8d.f.) = 1.99.

**Significant at 5 per cent level.

Figures in parentheses indicate percentages.

(v) Symptoms Showing Effect on Physical and Psychological Health

The data reveals that almost an equal number of respondents, *i.e.*, 39.25 per cent and 41.12 per cent experienced irritability and hypertension due to social and economic adversities (Table 12).The table further shows that 32.71 per cent experienced frustration while 30.84 per cent had frequent quarrel with their family members due to mental tension. Further, 25.23 per cent of the respondents experienced depression followed by 16.82 per cent who indulged in excessive drinking due to the economic adversities while small percentage of respondents became in drug addict and a few experienced frequent illnesses. The categories showing irritability and hypertension, as symptoms were significantly more as compared to other categories.

Table 12: Distribution of the Respondents on the Basis of Symptoms Which Show Effect on Physical and Psychological Health

Symptoms	*Block I (N=39)*	*Block II (N=33)*	*Block III (N=35)*	*Grand Total (N=107)*
Frustration	14 (35.89)	12 (36.36)	9 (25.71)	35 (32.71)
Depression	10 (25.64)	6 (18.18)	11 (31.42)	27 (25.23)
Irritability	13 (33.33)	15 (45.45)	14 (40.00)	42 (39.25)
Frequent quarelling with family members	14 (35.89)	9 (27.27)	10 (28.57)	33 (30.84)
Hypertension	12 (30.76)	14 (42.42)	18 (51.42)	44 (41.12)
Excessive drinking	6 (15.38)	7 (21.21)	5 (14.28)	18 (16.82)
Drug addiction	2 (5.12)	2 (6.06)	4 (11.42)	8 (7.47)
Frequent illness	5 (12.82)	4 (12.12)	2 (5.71)	11 (10.28)

$F_{7.14}$ =12.92** *CD* (14d.f.) = 3.85.

**Significant at 5 per cent level.

Figures in parentheses indicate percentages.

(vi) Reasons for Committing Suicide by Family Members

Table 13 shows that 4 per cent of the farmers had committed suicide. The reasons for committing suicide were domestic discard, inability to repay debts, repeated failure of crops, frustration due to chronic illness and unnecessary harassment by the private moneylenders. The data reveals that farmer commits suicide not only for economic reasons but other factors also force them to take such an extreme steps. Our finding are in accordance with the finding of Gill (2000) and Bhalla (1998).

Table 13: Distribution of the Respondents Whose Family Members had Committed Suicide

Committed Suicide	*Block I*	*Block II*	*Block III*	*Grand Total*
Yes	3 (6.00)	1 (2.00)	2 (4.00)	6 (4.00)
No	47 (94.00)	49 (98.00)	48 (96.00)	144 (96.00)
Total	50 (100.00)	50 (100.00)	50 (100.00)	150 (100.00)

Major Reason for Committing Suide	*Block I (N=3)*	*Block II (N=1)*	*Block III (N=2)*	*Grand Total (N=6)*
Inability to repay debts	_	1 (100.00)	_	1 (16.67)
Domestic discord	1 (33.33)	_	1 (50.00)	2 (33.32)
Repeated failure of crops	1 (33.33)	_	_	1 (16.67)
Frustration due to chronic illness	_	_	1 (50.00)	1 (16.67)
Unnecessary harassment at the hands of private money lenders	1 (33.33)	_	_	1 (16.67)

Figures in parentheses indicate percentages.

Conclusions

This study was aimed at to pinpoint the factors, which were responsible for increasing adversities of Punjabi farmers, particular of small ones, and to highlight the implications of such adversities. In all 150 respondents were selected including a few whose family members committed suicide. Results of investigation indicate that majority of the respondents belonged to the middle age-group, Sikh religion, higher caste having medium family size, holdings less than ten acres, with total income below one lakh per annum and possessing certain farm and material possessions.

Study indicates that almost all farmers possess farm power and machinery in disproportion to their landholdings and income levels. Baring a few all of them possess costly material items like scooter, car, refrigerator etc. These trends quite often lead the farmers to take loans from various sources. Data revealed that 93 per cent of the farmers were under debt, ranging from Rs. 10,000 to about four lakh, taken from institutional as well as non-institutional sources. Private moneylenders and cooperative societies were the most important sources for getting loans. It was found that the farmers did not restrict only to one source of getting loan, causing heavy amount of debt even beyond their capacity to repay. The major purpose of getting loans were, purchase of farm machinery and agricultural inputs, to buy durable goods and expenditure on socio-religious ceremonies etc. Due to high cost inputs, water logging, untimely rainfall, attack of pest, overdose of chemical fertilizer, adversely affected the production. The major areas of spending on social religious ceremonies were to maintain status in village, and due to social compulsion.

The major implications of the above situation resulted in selling of land and valuables, migration of the family members to other areas for better employment and some farmers took the extreme step of committing suicide. Due to crop failure and overspending on social heads, most farmers were not able to repay their loan in time. The social status of 20 per cent respondents has also been affected towards negative side. Physical and psychological problems such as frustration, depression, irritability, drug addiction and frequent illness were also reported by the respondents.

Adoption of high value crops, proper and judicious use of farm resources, adequate support to be provided by government, vocational training in agriculture and allied activities, streamlined and farmers friendly institutional credit system, special help for the farmers showing suicidal tendencies adequate compensation from government in case of crop failure, scientific support to cope problems in water logging etc. are some of the suggestions which may be helpful for arresting the adverse situation prevailing among the Punjab farmers.

Suggestions

Study leads to the idea that lot of factors are responsible for the precarious situation of farmers and it is a matter of concern for government as well as other concerned people.

As lot of rural people spent on heavy machinery, durable goods and socio-religious ceremonies in disproportion to their income, which quite often leads them towards socio-economic problems, therefore, counselling is required for the judicious use of their income which may save them from hardship. Community level organizations may be helpful to achieve this goal. Further, as the size of landholdings are going down, farmers must adopt some high value crops and other subsidiary occupations which may enhance their income level. Setting up of agro-based industries in the rural areas may employ many rural people from where a regular flow of income may be expected. Other suggestions are:

(*i*) Farmers should be educated towards the judicious use of fertilizers, pesticides and farm machinery.
(*ii*) Institutional credit structure should be made more active and farmer friendly.
(*iii*) In case of natural calamities and successive crop failure government should provide special assistance to the farmers.

(*iv*) The people showing the symptoms of depression should be treated properly as this may force then to commit suicide.

REFERENCES

Bhandari, D.K. (1982). *Social Tensions and Political Consciousness as a Result of Green Revolution*, M.SC Thesis, Punjab Agricultural University Ludhiana.

Bhalla, G.S., Wig N.N., Sharma S.L. and Mehta S. (1998). "Suicides by Punjab farmers not due to indebtedness ", *The Times of India*, Oct. 12.

Bobby, J.V (1998). 'Killing Fields ?", *The Hindustan Times*, No. 8.

Desai, A.R. (1984). *Rural Sociology in India* Popular Prakashan Bombay.

Diwakar, G. (1998). "Lingering Pain in Andhra Pradesh", *Frontline* 15:94.

Garg, B. (1999). "Debts a Millstone round farmers' Neck", *The Hindustan Time* Jan.13.

Gill, S.S. Bhardwaj, V.S, Singh, S, Ghuman. R.S Brar, J.S, Sohal, B.S, Uppal Cheema S.S and Singh S. (2000). *Punjab de Pendu Khetar vich Aattam Hatyaavaan.Ik Report*. Jamhoori Adhikar Sabha Punjab, Jila Ekai, Patiala.

Grewal, S.S, Sidhu, D.S and Sidhu, M.S (1990 far) *A study of farm incomes in Punjab*. Department of Economics and Sociology, Punjab Agricultural University Ludhaina.

Jodhka, S.S. (2000). "Green Nod to final exit", *The Tribune*, May 21.

Kaur, J. (1982). *Agricultural Development and Demographic Changes in RuralPunjab*. M.Sc Thesis, Punjab Agricultural University, Ludhiana.

Kohal, V. (2000). "Hypothecated Tractors Change Hands but their paper's don't", *Punjab Newsline*, July, 28.

Parmar, K. (1985). *Effect of increased agricultural production on the living conditions of rural farm families*. M.Sc Thesis, Punjab Agricultural University, Ludhiana.

Sehgal, V.K. and Arora M. (2000). "Post-harvest technologies in rural entrepreneurship through agro-industrial complexes", *Political Economy Journal of India* 9:22.

Shergill, H.S. (1997). *Rural credit and indebtedness in Punjab*. Institute of Development and Communication. Chandigarh.

Shiva, V., Jafri, A.H. (1998). *Seeds of suicide: The ecological and human costs of globalization of agriculture*. Research Foundation for Science, Technology and Ecology, New Delhi.

Singh, H. (2000). "Why farm sector income low in Punjab", *The Tribune*, Feb. 28.

31

Kitchen to Kitchen Via the Market: Poor Women becoming Self-Reliant*

NISHITHA SHARMA NÉE ATAL

In 1954, three desperate women approached the Mahila Mandal (Women's Centre), in Udaipur, Rajasthan, India, a women's educational institution, for work. The institutional didn't provide work, but it felt it should. It recognized that in a society where the family almost literally removed its protection from widows, and divorcees and from wives who fell out of favour with their in-laws, some means of survival and dignity had to be provide for them.

A project producing spices for the kitchen was developed. It involved grinding and pounding and mixing spices for everyday use, an activity performed by practically every Indian housewife. The project did not succeed in the nineteen fifties because the upper middle class housewife mixed her own spices, but the position changed in the nineteen seventies, and commercial enterprises such as Lizzat which made and exported papads, Bedekar and TRAS which made pickles, established that there was market out there for the things women churned out daily in their kitchens.

The nineteen seventies also marked the decades of women and the International Labour Organisation (ILO) launched an active programme to train women in various income-generating activities. The concepts of

---

* Originally published in *Poverty in the 1990: The responses of Urban Women* (ed. Fatima Meer); UNESCO and the International Social Science Council, Paris, 1994.

"self-help", and of making women "self-reliant" constituted important guiding principles in these programme of income-generating activities. The focus was on involving women in activities which could be carried out without dislocating them from their families, utilizing skills that they already possessed, or could easily learn, and to produce goods not for domestic consumption but for the market.

Inspired by these new signals, Udaipur's Mahila Mandal decided to revive the project that was aborted in 1955 and established Griha Udyog Pratishthan [Cottage Industry Cell (CIC)], with the following guiding principle:

> "It is our belief that the prestige of women should be enhanced in the family and society. This is possible only when they became self-reliant through gainful employment, and thus are enabled to make financial contributions to the family. This would lessen the injustice done to them, and atrocities committed against them, and they would be able to lead a life of self-respect."

The Mahila Mandal began the project in 1973 with three women, one of whom was Durga Devi, a thirty-six year old widow who eventually became the prime force behind the project, and a small capital grant of Rs. 10,000 (US $ 1,335) from the Khadi and Gramodyog Ayog (Khadi and Village Industries Commission). Durga Devi was promptly sent for training to the Lizzat factory in Bombay to understand the process of papad-making and the organizational structure and marketing procedures. Upon her return she took over the responsibility of managing the entire Cell, supervising the production process, marketing the products, keeping accounts and running the office. She recruited twenty workers through personal canvassing and placing advertisements in the papers and they began producing powered spices. Initially the "sisters" as the workers are called, canvassed sales by approaching consumers directly at home. Sales were made despite doubts about the quality of the product, because of the philanthropic appeal, but soon the consumers interest focussed on the product itself and the fact that they gained double value, a good product and simultaneously, an expression of their philanthropy, sales soared and the enterprise grew as is reflected in the growth of sales between 1975 and the current date.

The Committee diversified its activities and introduced papad rolling and making of wadi (dried dough balls of bean pastes, mainly of split Moong beans), and employment expanded. The cell set up it own godown for its processed raw material and its own chemical testing laboratory for quality testing. Between 1980-1990, the CIC sales went up nearly 15 times from Rs. 2,32,942 (US $ 23,290) to Rs. 34,04,455.00 in 1990.

The cell has two primary goals:

(*i*) to help needy and distressed women become economically self-dependent; and
(*ii*) to ensure production of better quality, unadulterated food items of taste for the consumers.

The success of the project is in no small measure due to the personality and devotion of Durga Devi. Her emphasis on "Service to the Society" rather than work for material gain, and her treatment of fellow workers with sympathy and affection has earned her respect and the women see her as a surrogate mother or sister.

Women Working at CIC

The project began with 20 women in 1975. There are nearly 160 women working in the plant today as food processors, supervisors and office staff. In addition, there are the women who take work home on commission, mostly from the lower middle class, eager to enhance family incomes. The work of rolling papads is commissioned out. The women come to collect the requisite dough balls and return the dried papads. A special centre has been opened for this purpose in a shanty colony on the slope of the famous Machhla-Magra hill for the convenience of the poorer women residing there. The centre is located in a room and run by Manju Singhvi, the wife of the District Secretary of the Communist Party of India (Marxist). She also serves as the "go-between", between the Mahila Mandal and the women doing commissioned work.

Manju, in her forties, first came in contact with the CIC when her husband served a nine-month jail sentence as a political prisoner in 1974. Left by herself, she had to find a source of income to support her family of three children. Political difference notwithstanding, Mahila Mandal gave her a job at the CIC which helped her financially. Upon the release of her husband, she gave up the job. When two years ago some of the women from the shanty colony came to her to seek ways to enhance their income, she opened the CIC outlet for commissioning papad rolling with the co-operation of CIC's Durga Devi. Manju devotes two hours a day to the outlet. Dough balls are delivered by an auto-rickshaw in the morning and collected and rolled out in the evening. Nearly 40 women from the neighbourhood collect these dough balls every day.

The Women Who Work in the Cell

The women who work in the cell fall into two categories, those driven to destitution by widowhood and cruelties of husbands and in-laws, and those who seek employment to improve their lower middle class lives.

Sovani Bai and Rukmani Bai are both widows from the village of Paneriyo-Ki-Madri, Udaipur. Sovani, semi-literate, was trained at CIC to work the machines and earns Rs. 600 (US $ 24) per month, Rukmani earns Rs. 500. Both 'sisters' work nine hours a day from 9 am to 7 pm. They consider their wages adequate for the lifestyle they are accustomed to. Their monthly household expenditure, including rent comes to Rs. 400 and therefore they are able to save for the proverbial "rainy day".

Sohani Bai, Mangi Bai, Leela Devi Maheshwari, Fatima, Manorama Mathur and Hansa Bai are all victims of family cruelties at the hands of husbands or in-laws, or both.

Mangi Bai was deserted by her husband and had become a burden on her father's meagre pension. She now helps her father with her wage of Rs. 400 per month. Sohani Bai's life became intolerable in her husband's home because of his drinking and her parents-in-law's constant nagging about their dependency on the family. She found employment as a janitor with the CIC, and having earned financial independence with an income of Rs. 450 pm, moved out with her three children and set up her own home. Leela Devi was left stranded with her in-laws and subjected to their taunts. Her husband worked away from the village and sent no money home. She went out in search of work, found it with CIC, and settled in the city. Her husband has now joined her and they share the family responsibilities.

Fatima's husband lost interest in her, took another wife and left her with his parents who treated her with unbearable cruelties. She eventually ran away from home and hid with a friend where her mother found her and took her to the Mahila Mandal where she works today earning Rs. 900 a month.

Teenaged Manorama's husband was retrenched from work and didn't contribute sufficiently to the extended family. Her in-laws sent her out to earn a few rupees a day at a restaurant, ill-treated her and gave her left-overs to eat and at times, nothing at all. She arrived at Mahila Mandal one day, hungry and crying. She has now been working at CIC for sixteen years and earns Rs. 900 a month.

Hansa Bai had worked at the CIC as a young woman. She left her employment on marriage and went to live with her parents-in-laws on their farm and promptly became their prime labourer. She would have tolerated this had she been shown some regard and affection, but indeed she was blamed for her husband's unemployment, and constantly taunted. One day, unable to bear the cruelty any longer, she stood up against her mother-in-law and was sent to her room without food. She heard movements in the dark, made out her father-in-law's form and saw that he had a scythe in hand and fearing that he intended to kill her, climbed into the attic and remained there till the morning when she left the house, traveled to Udaipur and returned to CIC as an employee. Her husband joined her there. She now earns Rs. 900 with overtime.

Narmada, Kanchan Nandana, Laxmi, Nani Bai and Rajkumari Jain work at the CIC to increase the family income, Rajkumari Jain has an MA and works at CIC at Rs. 800 per month because she likes it there. She could very probably earn more elsewhere.

Narmada's husband is a teacher, they have four children. She contributes Rs. 650 per month to the family which has three working members. Nani Bai's husband is a farmer; the Rs. 600 a month she brings in helps them to live in comfort. Twenty year old Laxmi's Rs. 700 per month is a great help to her large thirteen members family.

Summary and Conclusions

CIC is a success story of a non-governmental project carried out by a small team of dedicated workers. Not geared to profit-making this project is now providing employment directly to about 160 women, and indirectly to several others. The commodities produced are not seasonal and in continuous use as consumable items in the kitchen; demand for them is likely to increase rather than decrease.

The attitude of the housewives to time consuming traditional activities is changing. Those who go out to work do not have time for the traditional chores and the well to do use their time in other chores. This has opened up a market for ready-to-use commodities which are being prepared less and less in the home, and opening up opportunities for groups such as the CIC of Mahila Mandal. The market for these commodities was in the first instance established by profit-seeking small entrepreneurs, who farmed out work to the women in their homes and hired extra labour to produce formerly home made items for their shops. The shops provides the incentives for concerns such as the CIC.

The government stepped in with limited assistance in the early 1950s and 1960s as part of the strategy of economic development. Special co-operative banks were established to provide loans to co-operative societies, initially in the rural areas but later also in the urban areas. This was an attempt to encourage entrepreneurship and equal partnership, and to abolish the role of brokers who benefited through the exploitation of both the producers and the consumers.

Associated with the Co-operative movement was the campaign for the promotion of cottage industries running parallel with capitalized industry to protect artisan groups from crushing competition.

CIC is an example of combining economic activity with social reform. It is a concrete demonstration of how poor and distressed women could enter into public life and get relief from the distress caused by their affinal kin. It gives its women workers a sense of self-respect, and confidence.

Charismatic personalities are invaluable to community projects, but they don't live forever and for the project to continue, it has to be institutionalized. The expansion and growth of the project CIC, under the charisma of Durga Devi, has taken place on an *ad hoc* basis. There is now a need to systematize its organizational structure, to decentralize leadership, and to create an institutional data base.

It is important to note that despite seventeen years of existence, and a quantum jump, in sales which now totals nearly Rs. 3.5 million (approximately US $ 140000), CIC has been able to provide full-time gainful employment for only 160 women, which represents a minuscule of the abysmally large constituency of poor women in the region. The solution lies in either Mahila Mandal CIC expanding itself, or more CIC units emerging. The latter may be the solution as increasing the size of an organization such as the CIC, would mean transforming a cottage industry into a large scale enterprise. In large complex organizations, the human touch generally disappears. If that was to happen to CIC, it would lose its unique character and its social reform goal.

The *Griha Udyog Pratishthan* of Mahila Mandal is commendable the very first of its kind in Rajasthan. It provides a good reference model for others to emulate to develop self-help among women.

List of Publications of Dr. Yogesh Atal

BOOKS : English

1967 *Urban Reaction to Sino-Indian Conflict* (co-author: V..K. Sethi); Institute of Social Sciences, Agra .

1968 *The Changing Frontiers of Caste;* National Publishing House (Second Printing 1979), Delhi.

1971 *Local Communities and National Politics;* National Publishing House, Delhi.

1974 *Social Sciences in Asia* (edited); Abhinav Publications, New Delhi.

1976 *Social Sciences: The Indian Scene;* Abhinav Publications, New Delhi.

1981 *Building a Nation: Essays on India;* Abhinav Publications, New Delhi.

1982 *S.C. Dube on Crisis and Commitment in Social Sciences* (edited); Abhinav Publications, New Delhi.

1987 *Social Sciences and the Government* (co-edited with Iqbal Narain); Lancer International.

1989 *Daulat Darbar* : *The life story of a Retired Station Master;* National Publishing House, Delhi.

1990 *Culture Development Interface* (edited); Vikas Publications, New Delhi.

1992 *Understanding Indian Society* : A *festschrift in honour of Professor S.C.Dube (edited),* Har-Anand Publications, New Delhi.

1997 *Perspectives on Educating the Poor* (edited); Abhinav Publications, New Delhi.

2000 *MaNDAte for Political Transition: Re-emergence of Vajpayee;* Rawat Publications, Jaipur.

2002 *Poverty Question: Search for Solutions;* Rawat Publications, Jaipur.

2003 *Indian Sociology: From Where to Where;* Rawat Publications, Jaipur.

BOOKS edited for UNESCO

1976 *Asian Rethinking on Development;* Abhinav Publications, New Delhi.
1979 *The Social Sciences in the Man and the Biosphere Programme.*
1982 *Social Sciences in Agricultural Education—Eight status reports from Asia.*
1983 *Swidden Cultivation in Asia: Volume One: Content Analysis of the Existing Literature.*
1983 *Swidden Cultivation in Asia: Volume Two: Country Profiles*
1984 *Dynamics of Nation Building: Volume One—Country Profiles in Historical Perspective.*
1984 *Organization of Social Science Information and Documentation—Reports on 11 Asian Countries.*
1984 *Sociology and Social Anthropology in Asia and the Pacific;* New Delhi, Wiley Eastern Ltd.
1984 *Women in the Villages, Men in the Towns.*
1984 *Biogas: Social Response to a Technological Innovation.*
1985 *Swidden Cultivation in Asia: Volume Three—Empirical Studies in selected Swidden Communities.*
1985 *Teaching and Research in International Law in Asia and the Pacific.*
1985 *Economics in Asia.*
1985 *Dynamics of Nation Building: Volume Two—Communication in Crisis Situations.*
1986 *Middle East Interlude: Asian workers Abroad.*
1986 *Mass Media and the Minorities.*
1987 *Migration of Talent: Causes and Consequences of Brain Drain.*
1987 *Food Deficiency: Studies and Perspectives.*
1989 *Women in Asia: Beyond the Domestic Domain.*
1992 *The Changing Family in Asia.*
1993 *Violence Against Women.*
1993 *Women in Politics.*
1993 *The Futures of Asian Cultures.*
1996 *UNESCO and the World Summit for Social Development.*
1996 *Commemorating the 125th Birth Anniversary of Mahatma Gandhi.*
1996 *Participation of the Poor in Civil Society (edited with Else yen);* Abhinav Publications, New Delhi.

1999 *Poverty in Transition and Transition in Poverty* (edited); Berghahn Press, New York and Oxford.

BOOKS: Hindi

1965 *Adivasi Bharat*; Raj Kamal Prakasha, Delhi.
1989 *Daulat Darbar*; National Publishing House, Delhi.
1989 *Toot Ki Kavitayen*; National Publishing House, Delhi.
2003 *Anjaan Kshitij*; Rajesh Prakashan, Delhi.
2003 *Khamoshi ke Baad*; Rajesh Prakashan, Delhi.
2003 *Ped Ki Peeda, Peeda ke Ped*; Rajesh Prakashan, Delhi.
2003 *Bharatiya Samaj: Badalta Parivesh:* Rajesh Prakashan, Delhi.

Hindi Translation of English/Spanish Books

1969 *Samaj Shastra: Ek Vidhivat Vivechan* (Harry M. Johnson: Sociology—A Systematic Introduction); Kalyani Publishers, Ludhiana.
1975 *Ek Bharatiya Gram* (S.C. Dube: Indian Village); National Publishing House, Delhi (Second Edition in 1996 by Vani Prakashan).
1996 *Aur Nahin Ab* (Poems by Federico Mayor, titled *Patterns*); Vani Prakashan, Delhi.

ARTICLES in Professional Journals and Books

1961 "Rural Studies : Indian Village"; *The Eastern Anthropologist*, Vol. XIV, No. 3, pp. 249-57.
1961 "The Cult of Bheru in a Mewar Village and its Vicinage" in *Aspects of Religion in Indian Society* (ed. L.P. Vidyarthi); Meerut, Kedar Nath Ram Nath.
1962 "Short-lived Alliances as an Aspect of Factionalism in an Indian Village"; *The Journal of Social Sciences* (Agra), Volume 3, No. 1.
1963 "The Tribe-Caste Question"; *Bulletin of the Bihar Tribal Research Institute* (Ranchi), Vol. 1.
1963 "A Kulu Hill Village: Prefatory Notes"; *The Journal of Social Sciences*, (Agra), Vol. 2, No. 1.
1964 "Rural Sociology in India" in *Sociology in India* (ed. R.N. Saksena) Agra, Institute of Social Sciences.
1965 "Social Onomastics in Village India"; *The Journal of Social Sciences* (Agra), Vol. Four, No. 1.
1967 "Evolution of Content Analysis as a Research Technique: A

paragraph in the History of Content Analysis"; *Quarterly Journal of Indian Studies in Social Sciences*, Vol. 1, No. 1.

1967 "Voting: Expectation and Turnout"; *Political Science Review* (Jaipur), Special Number on Fourth General Elections.

1967 "Conceptual Framework for the Analysis of Caste"; *Sociological Bulletin*, Vol. 16.

1967 "The Case Study Approach in the Analysis of Short-range Social Change"; Seminar on Research Methodologyin the Study of Change, A.N. Sinha Institute of Social Studies, Patna. (Also published in *Social Change* (Ed. K.S. Mathur) Lucknow, 1973.

1968 "Anthropology in India : The Needs of the Day"; *Indian Social Scientist* (Rajpura), Vol. 1, No. 1.

1968 "Prerequisites and Requisites of a Democratic Polity : The Question of Elections"; *Interdiscipline* (Varanasi), Volume 5, No. 4.

1968 "Subordinate State system and the Nation Set : Tools for the Analysis of the External Milieu"; *South Asian Studies* (Jaipur), Volume Three, No. 2 pp. 40-53 (Also reprinted in *Foreign Policies of South Asia* ed. S.P. Varma and Iqbal Narain).

1969 "Citizen's Sense of Political Efficacy"; *Economic and Political Weekly*, Annual Number, Volume Four, No. 1, pp. 170-178.

1971 "Professionalization of Sociologists"; *Economic and Political Weekly*, Volume Four, No. 6, pp. 431-433 (Also published in *Indian Journal of Social Research* (Meerut) Vol. XXII.

1971 "Social Implications of Poverty: Role of Values and Institutions" in *Challenge of Poverty in India*(ed. A.J. Fonseca); Delhi, Vikas Publications,pp. 87-104 (Reprinted from *Social Action*).

1971 "Caste in Indian Politics"; *The Eastern Anthropologist*, Volume XXIV, No. 3, pp. 309-318.

1971 "Ideological Proximity Among Parties"; *The Hindustan Times* (March 26).

1971 "Caste and Change", Working Paper presented in Panel III of eleventh All-India Sociological conference, Ahmedabad; published in *Journal of Social and Economic Studies*, (Patna), Vol.1, No, 2 (September 1973), pp.191-215. Reprinted in Atal (1981) and Atal ed.(1993).

1972 "Project CLAPP : Studying Political behaviour in a Region" in *Beyond the Village : Sociological Explorations* (ed. Satish Saberwal); Transactions #15, Simla, Indian Institute of Advanced Study, pp. 21-54.

1972 "Rural Development for Weaker Sections: The Sociological

Dimension"; Seminar paper published later in the proceedings by Indian Society of Agricultural Economics.

1972 "Indian Social Sciences: In Response to Demand Structure"; Paper presented in the Seminar on Social Sciences and Social Reality (IIAS, Simla). Published in an elaborated version in the proceedings of the Seminar with the title: "Social Sciences in the Changing Environs".

1973 "Dynamics of Nation Building: Insulators and Apertures"; *Indian Horizons*, Volume XXII, No. 3-4, pp. 5-26.

1973 "Dinamica en la construccion de Una nacion: aislantes y aperturas"; *Papeles De la India*, Volume Two, No. 3-4, pp. 5-29.

1973 "La dynamique de l'edification d'une Nation: Isolateurs et Ouvertures"; *Rencontre Avec l'Inde*, Volume Two, No. 3-4, pp. 5-29.

1973 "The Role of elites in Economic Development"; *Indian Journal of Social Sciences* (Hyderabad), Volume Two, No. 1&2, pp. 27-53.

1973 Social Sciences in India" in *Social Sciences in Asia* (ed. Atal); New Delhi, Abhinav Publications.

1974 "Some Aspects of Employment and Unemployment" in *Population in India's Development, 1947-2000* (ed. Ashish Bose et al.); Delhi, Vikas Publishing House, pp. 232-44.

1976 "Sociology in the Indian Campus" in *Main Currents in Indian Sociology* edited by Giri Raj Gupta, New Delhi, Vikas Publishing House.

1976 "Administrators of Technical Institutions: Views on Social Sciences" in *Social Sciences in Professional Education* (ICSSR), New Delhi, Allied Publishers, pp. 189-208.

1976 "Social Scientists in Technical Institutions" in *Social Sciences in Professional Education* (ICSSR), New Delhi, Allied Publishers, pp. 209-46.

1977 "Communication" in *India since Independence: A Social Report — 1947-1972*, edited by S.C.Dube; New Delhi, Vikas Publishing House.

1977 "Communication and Nation Building in India" in *Dimensions of Social Change in India* edited by M.N. Srinivas; Bombay, Allied Publishers.

1978 "Continuity and Change in a Complex society: Caste Hierarchy in a Madhya Pradesh Village" in *The Eastern Anthropologist*, Volume XXXI. No. 1, pp. 41-63.

1978 "Observations on Research for Development Planning" in *Paradise Postponed* (essays on Research and Development in the

South Pacific), edited by Alexander Mamak and Grant McCall, New South Wales (Australia), Pergamon Press, pp. 252-55.

1978 "Going Beyond the Village" in *Field Studies on the People of India* (ed . Surajit Sinha), Calcutta, Indian Anthropological Society.

1980 "Can anthropology Help Solve Problems Beyond the `Past' and the 'Primitive'?", *The Diliman Review* (July-August 1980), pp. 49-52.

1981 "The Call for Indigenization" in *International Social Science Journal*, Volume XXXIII, No. l, pp. 189-197 (also printed in French & Spanish).

1981 "Rethinking Relevance" in *The Eastern Anthropologist,* Volume XXXIV, No. 2, pp. 87-94.

1983 "Social Sciences : The Tasks and Challenges for the 1980s in Asia" in *Social Sciences in Asia in the 1980s:Tasks and Challenges,* New Delhi, AASSREC.

1982 "Social Sciences in Agriculture : Intrusion or Invitation" in *Social Sciences in Agricultural Education,* UNESCO, Bangkok.

1983 "Using the Social Sciences for Policy Formulation" in *International Social Science Journal,* Volume XXXV, No. 2, pp. 367-77.

1983 "Introduction" in *Swidden Cultivation in Asia: Volume One*—Content Analysis of the Existing Literature: A Stocktaking Exercise, pp. 1-12, UNESCO, Bangkok.

1983 "Introduction" in *Swidden Cultivation in Asia: Volume Two*—Country Profiles, pp. 1-20, UNESCO, Bangkok.

1983 "Introduction" in *Dynamics of Nation-Building—Country Profiles in Historical Perspective,* pp. 1-7, UNESCO, Bangkok.

1983 "Introduction" in *Organization of Social Science Information and Documentation,* pp. 1-9, UNESCO, Bangkok.

1984 "Growth points in Asian and Pacific Sociology and Social Anthropology" in *Sociology and Social Anthropology in Asia and the Pacific,* New Delhi, Wiley Eastern Ltd.

1984 "Filth as fuel and Fertilizer : The Sociology of Biogas" in *Biogas: Social Response to a Technological Innovation,* UNESCO, Bangkok.

1984 "Swidden Cultivation in Asia : The Need for a New Approach" in *Nature and Resources,* Volume XX, No. 3. July-September 1984, Unesco, Paris (Also in French, Spanish, and Chinese).

1985 "Communication and Crisis: Framework and Findings" Introduction to the 2nd Volume on *Dynamics of Nation Building,* UNESCOnesco, Bangkok.

1985 "Entering the Global Village", *Media Asia* Volume 12, No.1.

pp. 3-6.

1986 "Asians in the Middle East : A New Dimension to International Migration". Introduction to *Middle East Interlude*, UNESCO, Bangkok.

1986 "Sociology and the Future", *International Social Science* Journal, Volume XXXVIII, No.2, pp. 303-10.

1987 "Theorizing Brain Drain: A Prefatorial" (Co-authored with Luca Dall'Oglio) in *Migration of Talent: Causes and Consequences of Brain Drain*, UNESCO, Bangkok.

1987 "Transferring Knowledge: Policy Relevant Issues";*Journal of Education and Social Change*, Pune, Volume I, No 1, pp. 100-12. also published in Education Report 40 of the *Deutsche Gesellschaft fur Technische Zusammenarbeit* (GTZ), Eschborn, Germany.

1987 "The Communication Revolution in Asia", in *Media* Asia, Vol. 14, No. 1, pp. 3-6.

1989 "Sociology-Anthropology Interface", *ICSSR Newsletter.*

1989 "Introduction" to the book, *Women in Asia: Beyond the Domestic Domain.* UNESCO, Bangkok.

1989 "Outsiders as Insiders : The phenomenon of Sandwich Culture—Prefatorial to a possible theory"; *Sociological Bulletin* 38 (1), pp. 23-41. Also published in the *Indian Ocean Newsletter.*

1991 "Indian Cinema in Thailand : Lost in Video's black hole" in the Daily *The Telegraph* (Calcutta).

1992 "Exordial" to *The Changing Family in* Asia; UNESCO, Bangkok.

1992 "*Samajik Sarokar ka Samajshastra*" (Hindi) for *Jansatta* (New Delhi).

1993 "Asian Cultures : What Destination?" an Introduction to *Futures of Asian Cultures*; UNESCO, Bangkok.

1994 "Man in the Middle : The New Paradigm of Development" in *Frontiers of Anthropology* edited by Ajit K. Danda, Amitabh Basu, and Arabinda Basu; Indian Anthropological Society, Calcutta.

1995 "Arrivals and Departures: The Case of Political Science in Asia" in *Regime and Discipline: Democracy and Development of Political Science* edited by David Easton, John G. Gunnell, and Michael B. Stein;The University of Michigan Press, Ann Arbor.

1996 "Asia" in *Encyclopedia of the Future*, Volume 1(pp.39-41) edited by George Thomas Kurian and Graham T.T. Molitor; Simon & Schuster Macmillan, New York.

1997 "One World, Multiple Cultures" in *Media and Politics in Transition: Cultural Identity in the Age of Globalization* edited by Jan Servaes and Rico Lie; Uitgeverij ACCO, Leuven, Belgium.

1997 "Tradition and Modernity : Revisiting the Paradigm" in *The*

Eastern Anthropologist (Special Golden Jubilee Number) Vol. 50:3-4, pp. 335-46.

1998 "Japan in India and India in Japan : Perspective of a Sociologist" in *IASSI Quarterly*, Vol. 17, No.2, pp. 1-20.

2000 "Indigenization : The Case of Indian Sociology" in *IASSI Quarterly*, Vol. 18, No.3. pp.28-44.

2001 "Managing Multiplicity : The Insider-Outsider Duality" in *Economic and Political Weekly*, Vol. XXXVI, No. 36, (September 8), pp. 3459-66.

2002 "Managing Diversity in a Multicultural Society" in *Media Asia* An Asian Mass Communication Quarterly, AMIC, Singapore), Vol. 29, No.2, pp.63-66.

Index